Learning Together with Young Children

Other Redleaf Press Books by Deb Curtis and Margie Carter

The Art of Awareness: How Observation Can Transform Your Teaching, second edition

Designs for Living and Learning: Transforming Early Childhood Environments, second edition

Reflecting Children's Lives: A Handbook for Planning Your Child-Centered Curriculum, second edition

Training Teachers: A Harvest of Theory and Practice

The Visionary Director: A Handbook for Dreaming, Organizing, and Improvising in Your Center, second edition

With Wendy C. M. Cividanes and Debbie Lebo

Reflecting in Communities of Practice: A Workbook for Early Childhood Educators

Learning Together with Young Children

A Curriculum Framework for Reflective Teachers *Second Edition*

DEB CURTIS AND MARGIE CARTER

Redleaf Press®
www.redleafpress.org
800-423-8309

Published by Redleaf Press
10 Yorkton Court
St. Paul, MN 55117
www.redleafpress.org

First edition 2008. Second edition 2017.
Cover design by Jim Handrigan, with Jeanne Hunt
Cover photograph by Deborah Reid, Highlander School teacher
Interior design by Erin Kirk New
Typeset in Adobe Minion
Printed in the United States of America

Image on page 241 excerpted from *GOLD® Objectives for Development &
Learning, Birth Through Third Grade.* © 2016 by Teaching Strategies, LLC. Used by
permission.

In Appendix B, curriculum and assessment statements are from Te Whāriki;
Kei Tua o te Pae by the New Zealand Ministry of Education (Wellington, New
Zealand: Learning Media, 2006). © 2006 by Crown. Reprinted with permission
from Learning Media Limited.

Library of Congress Cataloging-in-Publication Data
Names: Curtis, Deb, author. | Carter, Margie, 1942– author. | Curtis, Deb.
Title: Learning together with young children : a curriculum framework for
    reflective teachers / Deb Curtis and Margie Carter.
Description: Second edition. | St. Paul, MN : Redleaf Press, 2017. | Includes
    bibliographical references and index.
Identifiers: LCCN 2016056446 (print) | LCCN 2016057626 (ebook) | ISBN
    9781605545226 (paperback) | ISBN 9781605545233 (ebook)
Subjects: LCSH: Early childhood education—Curricula—United States. | Early
    childhood education—Activity programs—United States. | Reflective
    teaching—United States. | BISAC: EDUCATION / Teaching Methods &
Materials
    / General. | EDUCATION / Preschool & Kindergarten. | EDUCATION /
    Professional Development.
Classification: LCC LB1139.4 .C876 2017 (print) | LCC LB1139.4 (ebook) | DDC
    372.210973—dc23
LC record available at https://lccn.loc.gov/2016056446

Printed on acid-free paper   U19-11

About the cover

Rukia Monique Rogers was an early
childhood teacher when she appeared
on the cover of the first edition
of *Learning Together with Young
Children.* Now, almost ten years later,
she is a Harvest Resources Associate
and has opened her own center,
the Highlander School, in Atlanta,
Georgia, where she continues to teach
while being the director. Rukia is
featured with Malcolm Jean on the
cover of this second edition.

Jocelyn (Barbarin) Myres
1951–2001

Jocelyn's leadership in the early childhood field inspired us on many levels.

We first met her as a colleague doing community college field instruction in child care programs across the Seattle area. Wanting to be more closely involved with the lives of children, she took a job as a child care director, and a few years after that, returned to the classroom as a preschool teacher. Jocelyn's unusual career path inspired Deb to return to work directly with children herself.

Jocelyn led by example. Her classroom is prominently featured in our video, Children at the Center: Reflective Teachers at Work. Through this window into her thoughts and actions, Jocelyn has inspired early childhood educators across the United States and Canada. Her untimely death is a tremendous loss to the Seattle early childhood community. Her memory and contributions live on as a powerful reminder for what is possible in our work with children and families.

Contents

Acknowledgments

As always, our families, colleagues, and friends have been incredibly supportive of us during the writing of this book.

We have learned to be better writers, thanks to working with our editor, David Heath at Redleaf Press. For this second edition, we are deeply grateful that he stuck with us, even though the demands of his family and work responsibilities might have led him to pass this book on to another editor. He supported us through difficult cuts in a manuscript that was far too long and offered valuable feedback for the structure of the text.

The staff of Redleaf Press with whom we worked, particularly Kara Lomen, Alyssa Lochner, Sue Ostfield, Doug Schmitz, Jim Handrigan, and Ashley Robinson, had the challenging task of balancing our fierce advocacy for early childhood educators in the trenches with their publication guidelines, production standards, and marketing agendas.

Every book we write is a collaborative process, not only between the two of us, but also including a wide range of early childhood educators who generously welcome us into their lives, minds, family child care homes, classrooms, and program cultures. People contributed far more stories and photos than we were able to use in this book, but all their contributions have made their way into our thinking and will no doubt appear as examples in the workshops, presentations, and consultations that are central to our professional lives. We are enormously grateful for the engagement and generosity extended to us across North America, Australia, New Zealand, and Italy.

We want to specifically acknowledge the following individuals and organizations and apologize for any unintended omissions:

Evie Lieberman opened her home to us for our initial writing retreat to launch the first edition of this book.

Pauline Baker and the Tucson Children's Project hosted a wonderful gathering of colleagues and loaned us a copy of *The Power of Protocols: An Educator's Guide to Better Practice* by Joseph P. McDonald to stimulate our thinking. This recognition of the value of protocols for educators ultimately led us to advocating for protocols as a valuable tool for professional development.

During that gathering, Teresa Acevedo thrilled us with her courageous act of resistance against bureaucratic mandates that would undermine her Head Start program.

Our work over many years with Ann Pelo has been invaluable to our thinking and ability to understand how educators can translate philosophy and theory into concrete practices. Ann has contributed numerous stories to each of our books and been featured in a series of videos about teaching in early childhood programs. Analyzing how Ann worked with children and then as a mentor with teachers enabled us to co-construct the Thinking Lens® Protocol with her, which has become the heart of this book; one of Ann's own books, *The Language of Art* (2017); and most of the work our associates do with Harvest Resources.

During our year of writing the first edition, Tom Hunter sang and collaborated with us to come up with the concept of taking responsibility for living fully and teaching well. He inspired us to keep on singing, even in his absence, as we worked on this second edition.

Special thanks to some of our wonderful Harvest Resources Associates who let us interrupt their busy lives again and again with requests to track down a relevant resource, story, photo, or permission slip for this and many of our other books: Lorrie Baird, Wendy Cividanes, Ann Marie Coughlin, Eliana Elias, Sarah Felstiner, Nadia Jaboneta, Brian Silveria, Ijumaa Jordan, Debbie Lebo, Kristie Norwood, Kendra Pelo-Joaquin, Rukia Monique Rogers, and Kelly Mathews.

Children in all kinds of early childhood settings have welcomed us with open hearts and genuinely allowed us to learn alongside them.

We appreciate the following family providers, teachers, directors, and teacher educators who took time from their other commitments to answer questions and share experiences, observations, and a multitude of photographs for both editions of this book.

Australia: Jenny Dwyer, Fran Bastion, Nicole Tytherleigh, Diane Duvall, and Gillian McAuliffe, who have shown us beautiful examples of educators and children learning together.

Aotearoa/New Zealand: Over many years we, along with others in our study tour groups, have benefited enormously from seeing and learning firsthand what early childhood programs grounded in a competent image of children and teachers, along with restorative justice, looks like: Thanks to Chris Bayes, Lorraine Manuela, Karen Liley, Thelma Chapman, Huhana Winiata, Heather Durham, Julianne Exton, Bridgette Towle, Jenni Jones, Adrienne Thomson, Therese Visser, Sharmini Paddick, Bronwyn Glass, Adrienne Wilkens, Brenda Soutar, and the many other generous educators and leaders who have opened their hearts and doors to us.

Canada: Lorrie Baird, Sheila Olan-MacLean, Carol Anne Wien, Annette Coates, Bobbie Lynn Keating, Terry Bussey, Ron Blatz, and Bev Onysko, who have made contributions to this book.

United States: Donna King, Children First; Deborah Reid, the Highlander School; Annie White and Aunica DeFalco, CAL State University Channel Islands; Cathy Inamasu and Naomi Miura, Nihonmacki Little Friends; Marcia Rysztak, Aviva Dorfman, Renee Slaton, Lydia Salivar, and Julia Koumbassa, Michigan Inspirations; Abhirami Gunasingam, Allison Horne, and Dayle McLead, Early Learning Children's Community; Amy Piersol and Lynn Schintzer, Clifton School; Betsy Kempter and Sarah Cornette, Sunflower School; Kate Thegen, Quality Circle; Mona Jackson, Dawna Nifong, Brett Engisch, and Jenifer McKee, Coordinated Child Care in Pinellas County; Jacky Howell, Montgomery Child Care Association; Susan Stacy and Katie Lugg, New Hampshire Technical Institute; John Nimmo and Rebecca New, University of New Hampshire; Karen Opstad and Janelle Clemensen, St. Charles Community College Child Development Center; Brenda Sottler, Bobbie Jones, and Jill Baker, Northland Head Start; Billie Ognenoff, Heart and Home Family Child Care; Gabriela Kocian, Sophia, Miss B., Hattie White, Barry Swartwout, Shannon McClellan, and Marcela Clark, United Way Bright Beginnings; Cleta Booth, University of Wyoming Child Development Center; Marsie Habib and Marta Marin, Manzo PACE Program; Rosemary Hooper, Paradise Valley Community College Child Development Center; Judy Poggi and Linda Jimenez, East LA Community College Child Development Center; Kathryn Ingrum, Grossmont Community College Child Development Center; Gregory Uba, Kisha Williamson, and Alise Shafer, Evergreen School; Carline McGrue, Erika Flores, Neda Gilson, and Rhonda Iten, Cathedral Oaks School; Will Parnell and Ellie Justice, Helen Gordon Child Development Center; Nancy Gerber; Erin Robb, and Kathleen Tracy, Lakewood Co-op Preschool; Carol Wroth, Mother's Quality; Deadru Hilliard, Michael Koetje, and Christina Aubel, Martin Luther King Jr. Day Home Center; Vanessa Maanao, Wanda Billheimer, and Charling Chow, Puget Sound ESD; Deb Walrath, Every Voice; Janie Castiliano and Sheila Carrigg,

Sedro Woolley Head Start; and Hilda Magana and Martha Diaz, José Martí Child Development Center.

Other contributions have come from our colleagues Marilyn Chu, Jean Kasota, Joan Newcomb, John Nimmo, Miriam Zmiewski-Angelova, Elidia Sangerman, LaTisha Pearson, Elma Horton, Kim Nave, Michelle Grant, and Julie Garrett

Margie extends a special appreciation to colleagues at the Refugee and Immigrant and Family Center (RIFC) and Southwest Early Learning Center (SWEL) who generously welcomed her again and again into their programs, to visit in classrooms, attend staff meetings, interview them, and read their wonderful documentation. No matter how busy they were, Luz Casio, Karina Rojas, and Javier Casio Gomez made themselves available to us. And to colleagues at Hilltop Children's Center, past and present, we extend our gratitude. For this second edition, we especially thank Bria Bloom, Sandra Clark, Sarah Felstiner, Philip Kendall, Jacob Leavitt, Joel Metschke, Chelsea Myers, Cassie Tondreau, Myrna Canon, Emily Viehauser, Ilene Stark, and Liddy Wendell. Against the persistent barriers inherent in full-time, not-for-profit child care, their remarkable dedication to working with children and families in the manner described in *Learning Together with Young Children* is truly inspiring and reminds us all that another way is possible.

Margie also appreciates colleagues on the national level who steadily advocate for and diligently work to improve early childhood education in the United States. Several contributed resources to our appendices that ultimately couldn't be included. Thanks to Louise Stoney with the Opportunities Exchange and Shared Services Alliance; Marcy Whitebook at the Center for the Study of Child Care Employment/Institute for Research on Labor and Employment at University of California–Berkeley; Geralyn Bywater McLaughlin at Defending the Early Years (DEY); and Julian Weissglass, Kari Thierer, and Victor Carey with the School Reform Initiative (SRI). Tom Drummond generously offered some documents for our appendices as well.

Deb is especially grateful to her previous coworkers at the Burlington Little School: Cindy Hayertz, Carrie Waterworth, Kirsten Thompson, Cathy Bamba, Linda Henning, Rebekah Mills, Amber Crane, Kami Manley, Marlys Vollegraaf, Victoria Thulman, Ted Wellander, Lindsey Carlson, MaryAnn Nurkiewicz, and Sarah Bishop. And she thanks her current coworkers at Epiphany Early Learning Preschool who have contributed to this second edition: Sandra Floyd, Emily Claire Patton, Joyce Jackson, Megan Rupert, Veronica Reynoso, Nikki Frumkin, and Julie Bisson.

Deb also works around the country setting up communities of practice who have contributed careful study and stories to this second edition. Special thanks to teachers and mentors in the Early Learning Matters project with Southwest Human Development in Phoenix, Arizona; teachers and administrators at Compass Children's Services in Peterborough, Canada; teachers in the Pedagogical Leaders Project at Sound Child Care Solutions in Seattle, Washington: Monica Martinez, Luz Casio, and Javier Casio Gomez; teachers and administrators at Second Presbyterian and Highland Presbyterian Nursery and Weekday Schools in Louisville, Kentucky: Stephanie Schneidtmiller, Kristen Hayden, Cheryl Smith, Lisa Warner, Ann Lacy, and Amy Fitzgerald; and Brian Silvera, Nadia Jaboneta, Sabrina Scherer, and Riley Graham Muak at Pacific Primary in San Francisco, California. Also in California, Deb thanks Jesly Morales, Uwimana Middleton, Michael Burrell and Katja Davis.

In recent years, Deb's work with Jamie Solomon greatly enhanced her understanding of the connection between the brain and big body movement and provoked her research with teachers in this area.

This long list of acknowledgments confirms that the notion of "teacher as researcher" is being practiced on a daily basis by an ever-growing cadre of dedicated early childhood educators. Surely *Learning Together with Young Children* qualifies as a research-based curriculum!

Introduction

Education is an arena of hope and struggle—hope for a better life and struggle over how to understand and enact and achieve a better world. We come to believe that we can become makers of history, not merely the passive objects of the great human drama. —**Bill Ayers**

Never has there been a more important time for us to ask ourselves what we believe the purpose of education to be. The future of American democracy may well depend on it. Do schools and early childhood programs primarily exist to produce compliant workers for economic function? Or is the goal to help children grow into their full potential as informed, engaged citizens, eager to make contributions to their communities? Do educational goals narrowed to test scores prepare children to be successful in an increasingly complex world? Should early education focus solely on children's futures or does providing enriched childhood experiences give them a better future?

The answers to these questions determine the approach to curriculum in early childhood education programs. Should teachers design curriculum to meet children's current needs and correct their deficits, or should they focus on children's inherent competencies, ideas, and questions? Can stronger policies and curriculum mandates really improve learning outcomes? Or should the emphasis be on improved working conditions, salaries, and teacher education to support the role of teachers in children's learning? What are your views on these questions?

Education always represents a philosophical and political point of view and serves a particular agenda.

The task for educators is to know our history, probe deeper, ask critical questions, and find the ground we want to stand on. Engaging in this critical thinking process has brought us to stand with the voices for progressive education. We first came to the teaching profession in the 1970s, a time of great upheaval but also great promise. Ordinary people, such as ourselves, our friends, our coworkers, and our neighbors, were having lively debates about where we wanted to take our country. We saw ourselves as makers of history, not passive citizens giving up on America's failure to live up to our democratic ideals. It was an exhilarating time—a time of rage, joy, determination, dancing, and singing—a time of great hope. A fierce sense of possibility first brought us to work with young children and here we are, many years later, clamoring again at the gates of hope.

Perhaps you, like us, came to work in the early childhood field because you wanted to secure the future for young children and because you wanted to be reminded of the joy and passion for living that young children offer nearly every minute. But in the United States today, childhood, early childhood education, and the teaching profession are under siege, with so much conspiring to diminish our dreams. Educational policies are taking us away from the joy we once felt. Educational authorities want us to believe education should be about teacher-proof, mandated curriculums; high-stakes testing; and conformity. The energies of teachers and administrators are pulled toward an avalanche of regulations and accountability systems. We say, "*¡Basta!*" We can do better than this for our children and ourselves.

1

Questioning Current Thinking and Approaches

We know this problem is complex, and simple solutions do not exist. When we wrote the first edition of this book, we identified a number of factors contributing to problems in current approaches to curriculum for young children. Over a decade later things have become still more complicated with no large-scale improvement in innovative curriculum for children or in supporting teachers with better salaries, working conditions, and pedagogical guidance. Of particular concern is the growing inequity in the opportunities for meaningful learning provided for more privileged white children compared to those offered to their counterparts in publicly funded programs that primarily serve lower-income families of color. Sadly, despite models of outstanding early childhood systems in other countries and the hard work of countless educators and advocates across our own country, this second edition of *Learning Together with Young Children* still has a list of what we see as wrong-track thinking with the way early childhood education is being conceptualized in the United States:

- Definitions of quality are inadequate.
- Factories serve as a model for education.
- Teachers lack philosophical foundations.
- Adults view children as needing to be "readied" and fixed.
- Teachers are viewed as deficient, with their professional abilities diminished.
- Play is not considered an acceptable source of curriculum.

- Child-directed and teacher-directed approaches are presented as opposed and incompatible.
- School readiness takes precedence over brain development.
- There is no program infrastructure to support teachers' reflective practice.
- Teachers and programs are required to adopt quantifiable "research-based" curricula.
- Despite public funding, the gap between rich and poor children in the United States has widened, not narrowed. There is unconscionable evidence of a "preschool-to-prison pipeline" for young children of color.

As we finish edits to this second edition of *Learning Together with Young Children,* even further challenges have been unleashed for our democratic ideals in the United States. Our 2016 elections revealed the suffering, frustration, fear, and anger that millions have been living with across our nation. This unrest represents a great economic and racial divide that has been fueled by violence and growing bigotry. In this disturbing context, our opening sentences to this introduction seem all the more relevant. "Never has there been a more important time for us to ask ourselves what we believe the purpose of education to be. The future of American democracy may well depend on it." To this we must add, "Never has it been more important for early childhood educators to re-anchor ourselves in our profession's anti-bias goals," which are a valuable resource from Louise Derman-Sparks and Julie Olsen Edwards (2010). Our country, with all its flawed history and contradictions, was founded on "liberty and justice for all" and we must never forsake those ideals.

Problem: Definitions of Quality Are Inadequate

In the United States, decade upon decade of research, professional efforts, and advocacy have attempted to demonstrate and put into place the components of good experiences for young children. Other countries have advanced far more impressive early childhood frameworks to guide educational practices with children, based on seeing them as eager, capable learners. Despite the substantial body of research demonstrating that quality early childhood experiences are directly related to healthy brain development and to social, emotional, and cognitive maturity, the status of early care and education in the United States is a national crisis, full of inequities, and should be a national shame.

If our profession is to take charge of the direction of early care and education, we must begin to ask, "What is quality?" and the more important question, "Who gets to decide?" What assumptions, values, and agendas do you want to guide efforts to revamp early care and education in the United States? Each community and early care and education organization must undertake an open discussion of its purpose and the values, philosophy, and theoretical frameworks it wants to guide everyday program practices.

Children First

Stone Soup

Family provider Donna says she considers "layers of value" when choosing what curriculum ideas to pursue. "We are so ambitious for the children and for ourselves! Because we have a relatively small amount of time with the kids and want that time to be meaningful, I strive for what I call at least 'three layers of value' in everything we choose to take up. By this I mean, when our goals for children are self, community, nature, skills, and dispositions about work and play (such as risk taking, persistence, passion, curiosity, and joy), then anything we plan must relate to at least three of these areas. For instance, we once made stone soup with the children and invited their families to the feast. Reflecting back on the activity, we decided it had so many layers of value that we wanted to keep it as a tradition. The process and tradition of making stone soup includes working with food in its raw, natural form; the connection between story and the lives we actually live; developing skill with paring knives for work that would be appreciated by the people we love the most in the world; integrating food that came from each person's home into one big pot of soup we all eat together; and even singing, math, writing, and drawing. It was rich: Worth our time, and worth the children's time. The curriculum we pursue and traditions we adopt help define our program culture. They have to resonate with our values at a high level of detail."

As we've traveled across our own country, Canada, Europe, Australia, and New Zealand, we've been enormously inspired to see dedicated early childhood professionals who remind us that something else is possible. In many places, we have seen what deep respect for children can look like, what securing the future for our children can look like, what an educational system based on wonder, curiosity, joy in learning, focusing on relationships, and engaged investigation looks like. Sadly, most of these innovative models of teaching are not visible to the everyday early childhood practitioner, or the models are dismissed because they have privileged resources and are viewed as elitist. We are particularly impressed with the strong government support for progressive-minded early childhood education some nations offer. New Zealand, in particular, shows us how a country can face a history of injustice by seriously refocusing its resources toward a bilingual, bicultural early childhood education system.

Problem: Factories Serve as a Model for Education

Despite the lip service to individualized learning (and in some cases the genuine efforts of programs to be child-centered), most child care and Head Start settings in the United States resemble a factory model with a culture of compliance, schedules, and required curriculum components. Monitors focus on paperwork and crunch numbers to ensure accountability. Teachers move children through the day as if they are cars on an assembly line. Neither the teachers nor the children are allowed time to ponder, wonder, and make meaning out of the day's activities. Increasingly, teachers are given scripts or teacher-proof curriculums to follow. Some early childhood commercial curricula even market themselves like one-minute managers, proclaiming, "This lesson will only take five minutes of your day." You should question why that might be a good thing. If it's worth learning and adding to your program, doesn't it deserve more time? What about the learning that comes from really slowing down and paying attention to what you are undertaking?

Perhaps there is no greater influence in the teaching and learning process than how time is viewed and used (Phillips and Bredekamp 1998). We live in an era shaped not by the rising and setting of the sun and moon, as in eons ago, but in one where technology and a sense of urgency speed up everything we do. This cultural reality slips into early care and education programs with policies and mandates that fragment our time into little boxes on a schedule. Carol Anne Wien (2004) suggests that because we are so removed from the rhythms of the natural world, we approach time with a linear, not cyclical, mind-set. Examining how you use time and allocating it closer to your values and human development knowledge is one of the most important undertakings for early childhood educators.

An unhurried pace fosters a sense of security and possibilities, while a rushed one creates stress, fragmentation, and a sense of discouragement and resignation. When you slow down, you see more; you allow more time for relationships to grow and thinking to deepen. Research has shown that children need at least thirty minutes of uninterrupted play and exploration to engage fully and reap the benefits (Johnson, Christie, and Yawkey 1999). If teachers want children to be learning social skills in group times; acquiring language and nutritional knowledge during eating times; developing coordination, strength, and neurological connections while outside; and expanding their knowledge of materials, others, and themselves in their play activities, why are they continually rushing children on to something else? It isn't mere exposure to these things that heightens the possibilities for development and learning. Rather, children need time to really immerse themselves in these areas for meaningful learning outcomes to occur.

Problem: Teachers Lack Philosophical Foundations

In the United States, most teacher education efforts within the early childhood realm happen in the in-service, instead of pre-service, arena. Directors feel fortunate if they can hire a teacher with an associate's degree. In-service training for teachers is typically focused on how-to skills, at best attached to some understanding of child development. Seldom do these teacher education efforts raise philosophical concerns, challenge teachers to question the purpose of education, or reflect on their teaching practices.

We believe that teaching strategies should flow from a consciously defined belief system, not a set of regulations, a series of activity books, or a bag of tricks. Your curriculum and teaching behaviors reflect a set of assumptions about how you view children and your role as a teacher, whether or not you have examined these underpinnings. Taking the time to understand and clarify your own values and understanding of education, and those of your coworkers, will help you become a more thoughtful, effective teacher. When you are clear about the ideas and values you want to guide your work, you will be less likely to drift down a side stream or jump on a runaway train headed somewhere you don't really want to go. With this clarity, you will find more intellectual vitality and heart energy in your work.

The philosophy behind *Learning Together with Young Children* comes from the tradition of prog-

ressive educators such as Jerome Bruner, Carol Brunson Day, John Dewey, Maxine Greene, Asa Hilliard, Jonathan Kozol, and a host of other important voices. We believe, as they do, that the purpose of education is to live into a true democracy, to flourish in our humanity, and—as the educators of Reggio Emilia remind us—to find depth, meaning, and joy in the teaching and learning process. The pedagogy we champion is strongly influenced by our study of Jacqueline Grennon Brooks, Lisa Delpit, Eleanor Duckworth, Erik Erikson, Paulo Freire, Friedrich Froebel, Howard Gardner, bell hooks, Elizabeth Jones, Zaretta Hammond, Ann Pelo, Loris Malaguzzi, Maria Montessori, Jean Piaget, Carlina Rinaldi, and Lev Vygotsky. We mention these names to acknowledge some of those who have inspired and taught us, but there are many others, too numerous to mention. We suggest you take it upon yourself to learn more about these pioneers and the related approaches to education with names like "social constructivism," "empowering or participatory education," "critical pedagogy," "multiple intelligences," and "inquiry-based learning." Grounding yourself philosophically is essential to developing a pedagogy and curriculum approach that reflects your beliefs and goals for living and learning with children. (See the appendices for tools that will help you with this process.)

Problem: Adults View Children as Needing to Be "Readied" and Fixed

The concept of school readiness is full of complexity. On one hand, whatever their circumstances, children are born eager to learn. However, failing to recognize this, adults immediately impose their wills, perspectives, and agendas on children, in some cases

neglecting or abusing them. Traditional approaches to education have viewed children as empty vessels to be filled instead of recognizing the existing knowledge they bring to learning opportunities. When children fail to thrive in our educational settings, educators think children need remediation or, even worse, punishment. In most cases, it is the curriculum or pedagogy that needs fixing, not the children.

Fortunately, a number of teachers embrace a strength-based approach to education. Educators from Reggio Emilia in Italy, among others, challenge us to see the competency of each child, to believe in children, and to commit ourselves to helping them reach their potential.

Problem: Teachers Are Viewed as Deficient, with their Professional Agency Diminished

As policy makers begin to recognize the links between early education and academic success, they have marginalized our professional knowledge and decision-making power, and directed quality reform efforts toward measurable outcomes and high-stakes testing. And, as is the custom in US culture, commercial interests then swoop in with quick-fix, easy solutions—so-called teacher-proof curricula, time-saving literacy strategies, tools that take the guesswork out of assessment. "No need to worry or trouble yourself with thinking too hard about all this" is an appealing message for distraught educators. It is also a big source of our problems.

Problem: Play Is Not Considered an Acceptable Source of Curriculum

In today's world, play-based curriculum approaches are increasingly viewed with skepticism. In part, this is because children's play is often not what it used to be. Consequently, there are good reasons not to trust it as the natural basis of learning for a range of domains—dispositional learning, language and literacy, math and science, and so on. Unfortunately, television, electronic media, and commercial toys have invaded young children's play, often overtaking it with commercial scripts and agendas. Children have limited time to acquire play skills because their lives are scheduled from the time they wake until they go to bed, and they have very little freedom or time outdoors (Louv 2005). No wonder so many children don't learn how to independently investigate, invent, or problem solve with any complexity.

Teachers, too, have contributed to a mistrust of children's play as a vital source of learning. When children engage in self-initiated play, teachers don't always recognize the learning possibilities unfolding or know how to facilitate play for deeper learning. They lack confidence in articulating learning outcomes embedded in children's play. Furthermore, their own education hasn't prepared teachers to recognize cultural differences in how children learn through play (Neugebauer 1999).

However, the early childhood profession has long recognized that play is important for children's growth and development. In "Chopsticks and Counting Chips," Elena Bodrova and Deborah J. Leong (2004, 3) cite a body of research on the value of play, concluding, "Studies show the links between play and many foundational skills and complex cognitive activities such as memory, self-regulation, distancing and decontextualization, oral language abilities, symbolic generalization, successful school adjustment, and better social skills." In particular, they detail the study of Daniel Elkonin (1977), who identified four principal ways play influences child development and lays the foundation for learning in school.

1. Play affects children's motivation, enabling them to develop a more complex hierarchical system of immediate and long-term goals.
2. Play facilitates cognitive decentering as children take on roles in their play and negotiate different perspectives.
3. Play advances the development of mental representations as children begin to separate the meaning of objects from their physical form.
4. Play fosters the development of deliberate behaviors—physical and mental voluntary actions—as children learn to sequence actions, follow rules, and focus their attention.

Elizabeth Jones (2004) has written extensively about the ways teachers support children's play as a source of learning. "Teachers support play by providing a variety of things to do, observing what unfolds, and staying nearby to help as needed and to acknowledge children's actions and words. . . . We teach young children to play by providing them with space, time, and materials; offering them support in problem solving; presenting new problems for them to solve; paying attention to their spontaneous interests; and valuing their eagerness to learn about the world in which we all live together" (24–25). Contrary to the prevailing wind, then, we believe young children's play is both an essential learning tool and deeply affected by the quality of teacher interactions and the teaching environment in which it takes place. Increasingly, play is becoming an equity issue, with privately funded programs that primarily serve more privileged white families using play-based curriculums, and publicly funded programs that primarily serve low-income families of color denied play-based learning in favor of prescribed "drill and skill" curriculum (Gramling 2015; Jordan 2016). It's worth finding the resources to help teachers learn to do the deep work of preparing for, encouraging, supporting, and building curriculum from children's play.

Problem: Child-Directed and Teacher-Directed Approaches Are Presented as Opposed and Incompatible

For too long, early childhood educators have used either/or thinking, juxtaposing child-initiated play against teacher-directed curriculum. Supporters of emergent curriculum have adopted a hands-off approach, mistakenly believing that an emergent approach requires teachers to wait for children to initiate a curriculum idea. Conversely, advocates of the direct-instruction approach have overlooked the learning that can emerge in children's play, believing children can't learn unless they are taught by adults. With the passage of the federal No Child Left Behind Act, many teachers have brought worksheets and drill-and-practice teaching back into early childhood classrooms, believing this is the way to ensure school readiness.

The tension between these two approaches has been heightened by the dynamics of racism, poverty, and privilege. White, middle-income children are raised with the expectation that they will self-initiate and tend to do well with this curriculum approach. This is less true for children of color and low-income families who often grow up with a cultural expectation that they will learn what to do from their teachers (Delpit 2006).

We've come to understand that the divide between child-directed and teacher-directed curriculum approaches is an oversimplification of the complex process of teaching and learning. Sue Bredekamp and Teresa Rosegrant (1995) describe these as a continuum of teaching behaviors, acknowledging that a curriculum responsive to children, as well as to desired learning goals, requires a teacher to move across this spectrum. To determine helpful teacher behavior at any given point, teachers need relationships with the children and their families, and attention to the details of what is unfolding in the classroom. We propose that teachers master a repertoire of possible actions that can be used as a protocol for guiding children's learning, including skills in supporting and extending child-initiated activities, and expertise in teacher-directed curriculum. When they are guided to learn this repertoire and supported by a program culture that invests in and trusts them, teachers become effective facilitators of learning.

Problem: School Readiness Takes Precedence over Brain Development

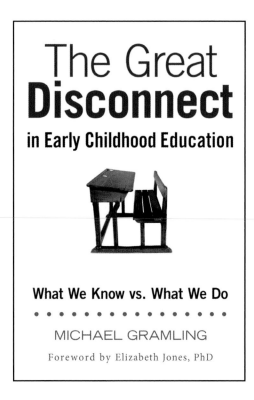

To be sure, there is quite a lot of talk about the importance of early childhood and brain development, but walking this talk has become confused with school readiness mandates. Michael Gramling (2015, x) reminds us, "What is most fundamental during early childhood, we have learned, is not the alphabet—it is healthy brain development. The brain goes through an intense period of activity that will never be repeated in later years, and the extent and effectiveness of that activity is to a large degree a product of the experiences and conversations to which the child is exposed during the early years." His important book has much to say about where the school readiness standards have gone wrong, how they confuse and conflate ideas. He suggests that current early childhood education (ECE) trends

- equate instruction with assessment
- confuse child development with early learning
- substitute early information for early experience

Brain development, and child development in general, involves complex processes that can't be translated into performance objectives or a set of subjects that young children can be taught in incremental steps. Children need experiences that engage them to develop critical brain pathways for executive functioning, self-regulation, and empathy. This second edition of *Learning Together with Young Children* offers a new chapter specifically focused on the active body/brain connection.

Problem: There Is No Program Infrastructure to Support Teachers' Reflective Practice

The culture of most early childhood programs reflects an insidious mentality of compliance and scarcity. Teachers are viewed as technicians accountable to an ever-growing body of standards and curriculum content. Simultaneously, budgets for teaching staff are carefully limited to meeting ratios with children and adhering to labor laws. Most accredited programs give teachers paid time for weekly planning and annual professional development opportunities. While this is a step in the right direction, it is hardly adequate for teachers to do their job well. Our earlier book *The Visionary Director* offers numerous ideas for creating a program that goes beyond meeting requirements or delivering curriculum to children.

In today's education world, with increasing emphasis on standards and outcomes, a bigger vision can seem like pie in the sky. Sometimes, the force of one person or small team can push a vision forward, but without an infrastructure to support the actual work of living into a vision, sustainability is difficult. Teachers and administrators burn out, become cynical, or give up. Moving a program toward the curriculum approach proposed in this book requires a close examination of your organizational culture and suggests a new approach to your professional development. It isn't appropriate to just require teachers to start adopting some new practices. To support teacher efforts and ongoing professional growth, organizational systems, policies, and distribution of resources will likely need some realignment. Administrative roles and coaching offered through quality rating and improvement systems (QRIS) or public funding systems should be designed to offer not only technical assistance but pedagogical guidance with protocols to engage teachers in reflection.

Problem: Teachers and Programs Are Required to Adopt Quantifiable "Research-Based" Curricula

Teachers have a range of curriculum models to choose from, many of which address current educational thrusts and policies aimed at measurable learning outcomes. Increasingly, programs find mandates requiring them to adopt a quantifiable, scientific, "research-based" curriculum. These mandates should prompt us to ask questions such as these: Who are the researchers? What is their cultural framework? What research methodology and measurement tools were used? Is there any one research methodology that is reliable for all children (NAEYC 2007)?

Thanks to the work of the educators of Reggio Emilia, many early childhood teachers in the United States are being encouraged to see themselves as researchers (Meier and Henderson 2007; Gallas 1994). In light of this possibility, why would anyone adopt a curriculum that gives a script for teachers to follow? In contrast, Daniel Meier and Barbara Henderson (2007) suggest that teacher education involving teacher research holds great promise for improving reflective practices. The National Association for the Education of Young Children (NAEYC) now includes a focus on teacher research on the Voices of Practitioners menu of their website.

We find value in curriculum models that are environmentally based, see children as active learners, offer children choices, encourage teachers to build curriculum from children's interests, and use ongoing observations with a focus on strengths for assessments. We believe curriculum should strengthen children's identities as thinkers and responsible citizens as well as creators of a life-sustaining culture. Curriculum should be developed in conjunction with children's families and communities and be respectful of their cultures and home languages. Over the years, we have gained insights from the curriculum approaches promoted by the British Infant Schools, Bank Street College in New York, and Pacific Oaks College in Pasadena, and our colleagues at the HighScope Foundation, Teaching Strategies, California Tomorrow, Reggio Emilia, and Aotearoa/New Zealand. The early *Alerta* curriculum (Williams and De Gaetano 1985) and the more recent bilingual, bicultural curriculum approach offered by Sharon Cronin and Carmen Masso (2003) have offered us important insights into culturally relevant programming for young children.

While we understand why a scope-and-sequence curriculum model might appeal to those required to adopt a formal curriculum, we encourage you to consider whose interests are served by doing so. We have seen far too many programs pay more attention to scripts for outcomes than to what is most significant from the children's and teachers' points of view. It is also worrisome to see training focused on how to deliver a curriculum instead of how to think through the complexities of the teaching and learning process. Again, who benefits and who loses with the promotion of a teacher-proof curriculum? Teachers who only focus on carrying out the curriculum and completing their paperwork ultimately lose heart and question whether they want to stay in the field. Defining your work around issues of compliance will leave you feeling like a victim and deaden your spirit. And such a misguided focus could ultimately lessen your ability to create a vibrant learning community in your early childhood program. There are other, more rewarding choices you could make.

You might have a different story. You could be saddled with a curriculum model that has already been adopted for your program, all or some of which seems counter to the approach you would like to take. Perhaps you are a family provider or a teacher

A Learning Organization

Consider this story of a Head Start director who told us of the hours and hours she spent researching a curriculum to adopt for her program.

Teresa narrowed the curriculum choices down to three, carefully studied all the materials, and met extensively with each of the companies' representatives. Though all of the curriculum packages under consideration were comprehensive in their scope-and-sequence approach, she found pieces in each that were problematic for the approach to curriculum and assessments that she wanted to unfold in her program. Teresa was devoting this part of her early childhood education career to creating what Peter Senge (2012) calls a "learning organization," a Head Start agency that nurtures the thinking abilities of parents, staff, and children. She believed any lock-step, sequenced, teacher-proof curriculum would undermine this goal. Teresa agonized over how in good conscience she could justify spending close to a hundred thousand precious taxpayer dollars to adopt this kind of curriculum for her large agency with multiple sites, many human-resource needs, and a series of budget cuts coming down the pike. Finally, though anxious about potential misinterpretations and findings by her upcoming federal review, Teresa made the brave choice not to adopt any commercial curriculum. Her decision was guided by her vision for her program and the values she couldn't compromise. And, in the end, her federal review team agreed with her approach.

in a program with no clear philosophy or curriculum approach guiding your work, independently sorting out how to structure your time with children. Have you been inspired by the stories of the in-depth curriculum work from the schools of Reggio Emilia but can't imagine how to implement such an approach in your setting? As a family child care provider or an infant and toddler caregiver, you might be struggling to understand how to keep your homelike focus while still embracing this notion of curriculum and ensuring that children are learning during their time

with you. You could be a preschool teacher working hard to integrate the new content-driven curriculum resources that address standards for math, science, language, and literacy and losing heart trying to juggle it all. Whoever you are, we want to address your concerns, inspire you, and strengthen your ability to live fully and teach well. In this second edition, you'll find a number of stories from innovative educators, administrators, and coaches who are crosswalking mandated standards with a more expansive view of what is possible for the teaching and learning process.

Problem: Despite Public Funding, the Gap between Rich and Poor Children in the United States Has Widened, Not Narrowed

While we want to celebrate the infusion of public dollars coming into the early childhood field, those dollars come with some serious problems. Not only do bureaucratic requirements begin to burden teachers and administrators with endless accountability tasks, but many of the mandates and assessment tools aren't supportive of diverse cultures. In some fundamental ways, the right to play becomes an equity issue. Early childhood consultant Ijumaa Jordan (2016) describes it this way:

> In an early education environment where more assessments and regulations are administered, the unintentional consequence has been the lack of play and more teacher-directed activities to "teach" children the skills that will make them "school ready" and "close the achievement gap." Teachers are pressured to raise assessment scores, so they "teach to the assessment." These educational reforms applied to low-income children, children of color, and native children are restricting their access to self-initiated, complex play. It's time we discuss and analyze how systematic classism

and racism privileges play for some children, while devaluing it for others. With the goal of moving play back to the center of childhood experiences for all.

Michael Gramling notes that "current federal and state school readiness standards have been written for and applied almost exclusively to children from low-income homes. Evidently, children served by these programs are not capable of processing rich discourse. We have been taking this approach for nearly two decades, and if it represented best practices in the field, one would assume there would have been a narrowing achievement gap, not . . . growing disparity" (2015, 161). It is our contention that what has come to be called the achievement gap is actually an opportunity gap. The children are not the problem; poverty and an unequal distribution of resources is the problem. Low-income children in early childhood programs that offer them engaged, meaningful, and culturally relevant learning opportunities don't have an achievement gap.

Holding Ourselves Accountable

Luz, the director of a publicly funded dual-language preschool, says, "We have outcomes for children and teachers that we want to hold ourselves accountable for.
   Outcomes for children include the following:

- growing in trust and confidence from being in a culturally safe, joyful place
- being curious and loving to learn
- developing a strong identity as a learner and as a member of a culture and community
- going to kindergarten with a photo book about their strengths and 'funds of knowledge' so they are seen and known right away by their new teachers

Outcomes for teachers include the following:

- seeing children's strengths and competencies rather than deficits
- having a new sense of curiosity and purpose in their role as teacher
- gaining confidence in using observations and writing meaningful learning stories

Refugee and Immigrant Family Center, a chapter of Sound Child Care Solutions

- finding their own voice and leadership style
- enjoying their work and imagining a career in early childhood education
- becoming an advocate

   Along with our own desired outcomes, I should mention that our children's scores on assessment tools demonstrate we have no achievement gap for the children of low-income families that we serve. We have room to grow, but I know we are on the right track."

A New Way

Our aim with this book is to put a spotlight on curriculum practices that are meaningful for children as well as their teachers. We offer you a curriculum framework with a repertoire of possibilities to stimulate deeper learning. Our goal is to demystify some big theoretical concepts and offer a way to think about the teaching and learning process that is emotionally and intellectually engaging for teachers and children. During a recent seminar, a provider asked us, "Are you talking about a way of teaching or a way

of living your life?" We could only smile and answer, "Yes."

   With all the demands and ups and downs of working in the early childhood field, how does one approach the job with a lively mind and spirit? What will fuel your passion and your determination not to be held back by a narrow understanding of who children are and what they deserve from us? How can you rise above constraining requirements, limited time, and limited resources to develop more significant experiences for the children and yourself? How can children's curiosity and risk taking and their eagerness for relationships and learning further empower you? What will help you listen more deeply, reach out beyond your comfort zone, be brave, and work for a world that is just and joyful? Whether you are an early childhood education student, family child care provider, center-based teacher, administrator, coach, or teacher educator, this book attempts to help you find your own answers to these questions and to strengthen your ability to think through the complex issues of the teaching and learning process.

We want you to see yourself as an inventor who can demonstrate a better way to meet desired learning outcomes and, in the process, nourish the heart of your teaching and the vision of what early childhood education could be. Whatever your setting, you can use these ideas to deepen your intellectual and emotional engagement in your work. You and the children will find living and learning together a more joyful experience. You will contribute to a revitalized democracy where people have the desire, skills, and opportunity to make contributions, think critically, negotiate conflicts, and invent equitable solutions that respect our planet and all its inhabitants. *Learning Together with Young Children* invites you to take back the joy and meaning of the teaching and learning process. Consider it a call to action.

1 A Curriculum Framework for Reflective Teaching

To enter into a style of teaching which is based on questioning what we're doing and why, on listening to children, on thinking about how theory is translated into practice and how practice informs theory, is to enter into a way of working where professional development takes place day after day in the classroom. —**Sonya Shoptaugh**

When teachers go about their daily work with curious and questioning minds and see themselves not as disciplinarians or mere transmitters of information but as researchers learning alongside children, then new knowledge is always under construction. As Sonya Shoptaugh suggests, this way of working leads to ongoing professional development for teachers and creates meaningful outcomes for children. This new edition of *Learning Together with Young Children* is a curriculum framework intended to bridge the gap between credible educational theories and research, and the everyday practices of early childhood teachers. While it is important to pay attention to learning domains and standards when planning curriculum, the process involves far more than that. We recommend that teachers take a comprehensive approach to curriculum development that keeps brain development in mind and not focus solely on school readiness. More than just learning how to plan activities or lessons, teachers who follow the tenets of this book will understand how they can draw on their philosophy and values, along with pedagogical theories, to create a vibrant classroom culture focused on relationships and inquiry. They will design the physical and social-emotional environment with great care. This initial and ongoing work is the foundation or core of our curriculum framework.

From this hub, a wide-ranging repertoire of teacher actions spirals outward, ensuring important learning will take place in daily moments as well as in long-term investigations and projects. As children explore relationships, materials, and activities in a thoughtfully planned environment, both indoors and on the play yard, teachers move through a continual observation/reflection/action cycle, what Paulo Freire (1970) calls *praxis*. Teachers observe and collect descriptive details, photographs, and samples of the knowledge children have been expressing and investigating. They spend time talking with the children, help them see what others are doing, and describe how the activity is related to other experiences, domain knowledge, and academic standards. They offer additional materials, model dialog and conversation to extend vocabulary, coach children to acquire useful skills, and continually challenge children to go deeper with their learning. At each juncture, teachers ask themselves the following questions (and others) to critically reflect on what they are seeing and the documentation they are collecting. The process of self-inquiry becomes a thinking lens for uncovering possibilities for action and decision making.

- What details stand out that I can make visible for further consideration?
- What in my background and values is influencing my response to this situation and why?
- How might issues of culture, family background, institutionalized bias, or popular media be influencing this situation?
- Where do I see examples of children's strength and competency?

- How do I understand the children's point of view in this situation?
- How are the environment and materials affecting what's unfolding and what changes could be made?
- How are my actions affecting this situation?
- What learning domains am I addressing here, and what other learning domains could I address?
- What theoretical perspectives, child development principles, and brain research could I draw on to inform my understanding and action?
- What values, philosophy, and goals do I want to influence my response?

Because we believe teachers are creative, competent, and eager to help children learn, our curriculum approach offers a wide berth for their autonomy. Of course, teachers, like children, need others to believe in them, support them, and mentor them into their full potential. For their creativity to flourish and for their continued professional development, teachers deserve collegial work environments with the time, tools, and technology to support reflective practice.

We know teachers work in a variety of settings, each with its own complex web of concerns that should be taken into account in the curriculum-planning process. If your early childhood program has a centralized, top-down set of mandates, standards, and assessment tools, our curriculum framework will guide your thinking as you translate these requirements into specific and meaningful experiences for the children.

On the other hand, if your program offers you little in the way of philosophical or pedagogical guidance, our framework will help you clarify your values and beliefs about the teaching and learning process, and will offer a structure for responding to children and planning a curriculum that reflects your values and learning goals, and the children's interests. Our goal is to engage your mind in the dynamic process of teaching and learning, which, in turn, will strengthen your skills and confidence as a reflective teacher. Curriculum for children can't reach its potential for deeper meaning and learning without teachers engaged in their own learning process.

Learning Together with Young Children: The Curriculum Framework

Our curriculum framework comprises six critical core practices, which are discussed in detail in chapters 2 through 7. Each chapter provides specific principles to guide you in adapting that core practice for your setting:

Chapter 2–Create a Nourishing Classroom Culture
Chapter 3–Enhance the Curriculum with Materials
Chapter 4–Expand Opportunities for Children to Use Their Active Bodies
Chapter 5–Bring Yourself to the Teaching and Learning Process
Chapter 6–Coach Children to Learn about Learning
Chapter 7–Dig Deeper to Learn with Children

Two of our earlier books, *Designs for Living and Learning* and *The Art of Awareness,* are focused respectively on designing physical environments and mastering observation and documentation skills. These core practices are referenced as part of the *Learning Together with Young Children* curriculum framework but not given their own chapters as curriculum core practices here. Neither is the topic of assessment. Tools for assessing children are prolific throughout the early education field, and we don't intend to introduce yet another. The assessment approaches compatible with our curriculum fall under the rubric of authentic (Meisels et al. 1994) and are based on documentation data from children's everyday work (Horm-Wingerd 2002). In this regard, we value formative assessment (low stakes, providing ongoing feedback) over summative assessment (a high-stakes evaluation against benchmarks). We particularly favor the approach to assessment used in New Zealand with the tool referred to as "learning stories" (Carr 2001; Carr and Lee 2012) and hope it will become more widely used in the United States. In New Zealand, assessments are viewed as another way we help children construct an identity, a goal and process very compatible with the core practices explored in this book. Throughout *Learning Together with Young Children,* you will find examples of an observation and documentation process that can easily feed into existing assessment tools and address educational standards.

Planning curriculum that is responsive to children's lives and learning styles requires far more of teachers than simply choosing a set of lessons or activities to offer. By the same token, it is far more rewarding. Rather than mandating a step-by-step protocol to follow, *Learning Together with Young Children* offers a framework for thinking. When you continually cycle through the questions we offer for reflecting on your observations and actions, this reflective thinking process will become second nature to you, just as protocols for diapering and handwashing do. We've come to describe this protocol for reflection as the Thinking Lens.®

As you internalize the principles in each of the core practices of our curriculum, we believe you will become excited about making them your own. While teacher-proof curricula overlook teachers as the most important element in children's learning, our curriculum framework recognizes your critical role and asks you to bring yourself fully into the planning and implementation process.

Chapter 2 Core Practice:
Create a Nourishing Classroom Culture
If you are clear about the ideas and values you want to guide your teaching, the next step is to make sure

these values are reflected in the learning environment you create. Our earlier book *Designs for Living and Learning* offers many examples of how programs have gone about this task. If you aren't familiar with this resource, consider reading it as you begin using the ideas about curriculum we offer here. In some ways, *Learning Together with Young Children* is a sequel to *Designs for Living and Learning.*

Once you have created an environment that reflects your philosophy and values for children and families, then what? Your next step is to use those same values in creating a classroom culture—a set of expectations, routines, and ways of being together. This often requires rethinking some of the usual ways teachers organize time for children; how you spend your time as a teacher; the language and systems you use for communications; and the ways you come together, see each other, and negotiate your ideas, desires, and different points of view.

Chapter 2 will introduce you to a set of principles to guide your work in creating a classroom culture that demonstrates respect for children as capable learners and members of families and communities. You'll also find guiding principles for forming respectful partnerships with children's families, from first encounters through ongoing communications and gatherings. This chapter includes ideas for bringing democratic ideals, culturally responsive teaching, and anti-bias goals into your classroom routines, and for fostering relationships and a sense of belonging and responsibility. And all of this is brought to life with specific examples from actual teachers across North America, Australia, and New Zealand.

You will find inspiring examples of classroom cultures that help children see themselves as learners and resources to one another. And, finally, there are ideas for creating memory-making rituals and celebrations that go beyond birthday parties and graduation ceremonies. Creating a classroom culture involves continually thinking about your values, being willing to experiment and take risks, and constantly paying attention to relationships and the learning environment. This is the core practice of our curriculum framework—all other teacher actions flow from this foundation.

Chapter 3 Core Practice:
Enhance the Curriculum with Materials

Having an environmentally based curriculum means you pay attention to the environment on both the macro level (the room or outdoor design and setup) and the micro level (the materials that are available and how they are presented to children). Again, your values and images of children and the teaching and learning process influence which materials you offer. Our curriculum approach suggests you reconsider many of the typical learning materials. Of critical

importance is thinking about which materials and equipment you can offer to encourage children's brains to develop through large-motor physical activity, not only outdoors but within your classroom as well.

We encourage you to see yourself as an inventor of new combinations of materials. You'll find it engaging for yourself as well as the children to draw on your philosophical foundation, your observations of what children enjoy doing, and your knowledge of brain research, child development, and schema theory to put together interesting groupings of materials for children to explore. Your choices will also be influenced by the dispositions, relationships, and learning outcomes you have in mind for children and the pervasive or subtle biases you want children to overcome.

Chapter 3 offers numerous principles for selecting and offering materials to children. With the kinds of

Earlwood Children's Centre

play (Piaget 2001), schema theory (Piaget and Inhelder [1969] 2000; Van Wijk 2008), and the developmental themes (Curtis and Carter 2011) reflected in children's ongoing play in mind, you can begin to offer combinations of materials that allow for these open-ended approaches. Learning some basic principles for combining and presenting materials as "invitations for learning" will help you encourage children's exploration and enhance their ability to focus. With the children actively engaged, rather than dependent on your instructions for investigation, you will be able to stand back, observe, and make deliberate choices about your next actions. When you design open-ended invitations with particular schema or learning domains in mind, you create more possibilities for gathering documentation to reflect the learning, help in planning next steps, and add to your assessment process.

Chapter 4 Core Practice: Expand Opportunities for Children to Use Their Active Bodies

Children are sensory/motor beings. They bring their bodies to every experience. The newest brain research suggests that children are not getting enough opportunities for active play in their neighborhoods, early childhood programs, or schools, and because of this, they are developing a host of challenges.

At home, many children spend hours every day in front of a screen and enjoy very limited time outdoors—a place that provides the freedom of movement and physical adventures that children crave. Teachers, increasingly focused on academic skills for young children, are creating small spaces for sitting quietly to learn. Many of the current assessment tools and curriculum approaches require specific areas in a classroom to focus on each academic domain, from math to science. As teachers use these approaches, they are dividing their often very tiny classrooms into smaller and smaller spaces, filled with tables, chairs, and shelves. The resulting lack of space not only limits children's opportunity to be active in their bodies; it also makes it difficult for them to pursue big ideas. Indeed, if you have only a 2' x 3' space for block building, you are restricting children's bodies as well as their ability to think big.

Consider the following quote on how unrestricted outdoor play makes for strong, competent, capable children from a 2015 *Washington Post* article by Angela Hanscom (who later wrote a book, *Balanced and Barefoot*, on this topic):

> If children are not given enough natural movement play experiences, they are more likely to be clumsy, have difficulty paying attention, have trouble controlling their emotions, utilize poor problem-solving

Burlington Little School

methods, and demonstrate difficulties with social interactions. We are consistently seeing sensory motor and cognitive issues pop up in later years because of inadequate opportunities to play and move in the early years.

Chapter 4 discusses the warnings from this research and helps you examine your own current practices that may limit children's active playtime. The chapter offers information about children's sensory/motor systems and the vital importance they play in the brain development that leads to self-regulation and focus. You will be invited to study children as they seek out these sensory/motor experiences and be offered examples of teacher documentation highlighting the skill and competence children have when moving their bodies.

You will also learn how your own reactions to children's risk taking and physical challenges can affect the opportunities children have to develop these essential skills.

Chapter 5 Core Practice: Bring Yourself to the Teaching and Learning Process

A good deal of pre-service teacher education and ongoing professional development is focused on what and how to teach, leaving out of the equation

who is doing the teaching. In *The Courage to Teach*, Parker Palmer (2007, 4) reminds us that this constitutes a fundamental deficiency for teachers.

The question we most commonly ask is the "what?" question—what subjects shall we teach?

When the conversation goes a bit deeper, we ask the "how?" question—what methods and techniques are required to teach well?

Occasionally, when it goes deeper still, we ask the "why?" question—for what purposes and to what ends do we teach?

But seldom, if ever, do we ask the "who?" question—who is the self that teaches? How does the quality of my selfhood form—or deform—the way I relate to my students, my subject, my colleagues, my world?

Chapter 5 describes a core way that our curriculum framework addresses this dilemma for teachers. If you don't know yourself well, if you feel powerless in your job, how can you be an effective teacher? Bringing yourself, not just your teaching goals and techniques, to your days with children requires that you recognize how you instinctively react to things that unfold with children. You can begin to develop this insight by asking yourself these questions:

What past experiences influence who you are as a teacher?

What do you value and want to pursue with the children you teach?

What do you bring from your cultural or family background that influences your work with children and families?

What anti-bias practices do you want to strengthen in yourself?

When you reflect on your observations, what do you see as significant and why?

Your answers to these questions can help you define the opportunities you can offer children. Even if you are required to use a certain curriculum—or perhaps we should say, *especially* when you have such a mandate—you can claim your power to make your days meaningful and joyful. Remembering that curriculum is everything that happens in your time with children, your keen eyes and ears must tune in to how to support what is significant to them. In addition to principles for self-awareness, we offer ideas for cultivating a mind-set of receptivity and an ability to notice details. In this book, you will find principles to help you think through possible actions to take. These include staying alert to personal or institutional assumptions that might reflect undesirable biases, seeking the children's point of view, extending conversations, and bringing awareness to how you are becoming a group of responsible, competent learners.

Chapter 6 Core Practice: Coach Children to Learn about Learning

Begin by creating a classroom culture that fosters respectful relationships and an eagerness to explore the provocative materials you make available. Next, develop a repertoire of possible teacher actions that will increase your ability to co-create a curriculum that goes beyond the superficial into the exciting process of constructing knowledge. Co-creation is the operative idea here. Until recently, the early childhood education field juxtaposed two possible approaches to curriculum: teacher-directed and child-initiated. Proponents of one view tend to think negatively about the other. Though our profession's definition of *developmentally appropriate practice* (Bredekamp and

Copple 2009) rejects a drill-and-recitation approach, that was never intended to mean that teachers should play a passive role. While teachers may not be directing children's recitations, they are continually playing the role of stage and prop manager, coach, model, and improvisational artist helping children learn as they play (Jones and Reynolds 2011).

There are many things children can learn only with instruction and support from more experienced people. Studying Vygotsky's theories of scaffolding and the zone of proximal development will help you see the vitally important role adults can play in enhancing children's learning (Berk and Winsler 1995). When young children demonstrate an excitement about the learning process, how do teachers use their skills and knowledge to support them without taking over? The challenge is to foster eager learning dispositions in children, helping them gain skills and resources in order to understand and take more responsibility for their own learning. Chapter 6 offers specific principles to help you and the children see that learning is a process with specific strategies you both can use. Teachers become aware of cognitive learning styles, often culturally influenced, and try to match these in a culturally appropriate way (Hammond 2015). They provide direct coaching when particular skills, tools, or know-how would be useful to the children. With careful observation and listening, you can formulate questions that help children uncover their curiosities, theories, and own questions. You show them how to turn to

Martin Luther King Jr. Day Home Center

their friends, reference materials, and stories to take charge of their own learning. You continually reinforce a self-identity in children that they are competent learners who are able to research, think through challenges, and solve problems.

Chapter 7 Core Practice: Dig Deeper to Learn with Children

A popular sentiment in the United States is that "more is better" and, in early childhood education, this often translates into superficially exposing children to a wide range of curriculum topics. Brain research suggests that children are drawn to new things, so they will easily go from activity to activity (Gopnik 2009). Yet they also like repetition and immersing themselves in their current passions. Teachers can provide experiences with different approaches to the same idea along with appropriate materials to help children go deeper in their pursuits rather than looking for the next entertaining activity.

When trying to use an observation-based, emergent approach to curriculum, teachers often think they should wait until the children express an interest in something and then plan a unit around the topic. For example, if children's play is repeatedly centered on dinosaurs, then teachers plan a series of lessons related to dinosaurs. How does jumping in with this emergent curriculum "theme" differ significantly from a preplanned version of a dinosaur curriculum project? What might your teaching goals be with such a project? If the curriculum is primarily teacher driven and remains superficially focused on the names and habits of different dinosaurs, the children may acquire some more information, but deeper investigation or significance is limited.

A more engaged approach to co-creating curriculum with children's emerging pursuits involves careful observation, analysis, and meaning making. You are guided by an awareness of your values and curiosities. You work with intention but aren't constrained by predetermined outcomes. You put your heads together with those of the children, their

families, and your coworkers to study the outcomes your documentation reveals and the possibilities that could deepen learning. At times you stand back, while on other occasions you take action, allowing time for joy and meaning to unfold and build. You invent ways of demonstrating how your curriculum meets educational standards, revealing courage and a willingness to be different.

Young children have many modes of learning, which Howard Gardner (1999) describes as "multiple intelligences" and the educators of Reggio Emilia (Edwards, Gandini, and Forman 2012) refer to as "the hundred languages." By offering a wide range of materials for children to use in thinking through and expressing their feelings and ideas, teachers can counter the prevailing educational trend to focus only on verbal linguistic modes. This fuller, more complex view of teaching and learning is a reciprocal process where adults learn as much as the children. Reggio educators liken this to a dance or a game of catch. Everyone has an active role in the teaching and learning process. Children are learning about the world, their own competence, how to work with others, and the contributions they can make. If we are open to it, they teach us to see the world with fresh eyes. By challenging children to go further with their learning, you learn more about the dynamics of teaching as you support children in expressing their thoughts, feelings, questions, and discoveries.

As soon as teachers and children become fully engaged in learning, they don't want their time chopped up into little curriculum boxes. Teachers come to recognize that children deserve time for fuller investigations, and teachers deserve time to reflect on how to support that inquiry. With this understanding, you work to identify particular studies to take up with the children in a more focused and extended way. The question shifts from "What can I think of to do tomorrow?" to "What focus should I choose from the many possibilities unfolding?" Your choices are guided by your values, your program context, and your desire to integrate meaningful experiences with learning domains and assessment standards.

Chapter 7 focuses on this core practice of our curriculum framework—going deeper into the possibilities for learning. Principles here guide you in using the wide range of children's natural learning inclinations as a springboard for multiple intelligences to come alive. This includes music, drama, drawing, stories, and big-body activities. Central to this process is an understanding that whenever you invite children to express the ideas they are pursuing in a variety of ways, they are challenged to consider new perspectives and clarify their thinking. Using your

documentation directly with children provides a mirror for further reflection and illumination.

Chapter 8 Core Practice: Adapt the Curriculum Framework for Different Settings

As your teaching begins to incorporate the principles for the core practices of the *Learning Together with Young Children* curriculum framework, you will find ways to adapt the curriculum for different settings.

Most early childhood programs lack the resources and working conditions necessary for the reflective teaching and professional development Sonya Shoptaugh describes in the opening of this chapter. Administrators haven't understood the remarkable advancements their teachers could make if they would reconceptualize their in-service training systems and allocate their dollars accordingly. Carol Brunson Day (2006) describes how this revamping could affect curriculum practices:

> The economics of paying teachers for five hours of planning time each week seems daunting for Americans, but rather than rejecting this strategy as too costly, it would be instructive to determine what is

spent by school systems and Head Start on other forms of in-service training that do not as directly affect classroom practice and do not transform performance. Head Start actually has an ideal staff structure for easily transforming their programs. Education coordinators could become what Reggio educators call *pedagogisti*. Instead of bureaucrats, they could be teacher educators-in-residence. The rich practice we see in Reggio grows out of the continuous exchanges within and among the teaching teams, the analysis and re-analysis of the daily classroom experiences with input from people who have various levels of experience and expertise. The yield is the power to create a personalized, culturally responsive curriculum at the center level. (personal communication)

Whatever the constraints or strengths of your early childhood setting, you can take the curriculum core practices we offer and make them your own. To guide you in translating our framework into your program, we offer numerous examples, each with a principle to inspire your own adaptations. In chapter 8 you will read how teachers in part-time programs with different groups of children and teachers with the challenges of sharing a space use their documentation to create connections among the children. Teachers describe how they are inventing new ways to meet requirements and expand possibilities for using prescribed curriculum. There are principles for documenting experiences that meet standards and make assessments relevant and meaningful. Maybe you are lucky enough to be working in a program that includes paid time for planning or collaborative reflection on your documentation. If so, our principles for using children's ideas to pursue extended investigations, working with different perspectives, and learning from conflicting ideas will help you make the most of the support your program offers you.

Each time a provider or teacher discovers a way to put one of our principles into practice, they expand the possibilities for our profession. With our curriculum framework, outcomes for teachers involve lively daily interactions with children. Outcomes for children include the satisfaction of generating their own learning, rather than being the target of someone else's lessons. Unlike the experience of working with many prescribed curriculums, education with these outcomes offers an experience of living fully now, not only preparing for the future. There are also outcomes for the future, to be sure, because teachers and children become hungry learners and knowledge-seekers, eager to invest their time in further education.

Chapter 9 Core Practice: Claim Your Responsibility to Live Fully and Teach Well

As you conscientiously practice the different possibilities for teacher actions outlined in our chapters, you will find a natural rhythm and intuition about which to use when. This curriculum approach uses the Thinking Lens® Protocol and a methodology for growing yourself as a teacher, along with in-depth curriculum experiences for children. It is important, however, that you not do this work in isolation. Working alone will ultimately leave you frustrated, discouraged, and headed for burnout. Here's a story about Margie's grandson, Coe, when he was six years old. Coe's beloved first-grade teacher, Grant, had a car accident and was unable to return to work. Coe and his classmates endured a revolving door of substitute teachers, which caused an increasing amount of unrest among the children and their families.

By February, Coe's ideas about teachers sounded like this: "These teachers don't know what they are doing and should be fired. They are just too mean to help us really learn." When April arrived, he had some additional ideas: "We need to kill these teachers' techniques by just being nice ourselves so they'll calm down and let us do some fun things." As the school year was coming to a close, Coe's insights deepened: "Teachers need to find someone to talk to. It's really lonely being a teacher."

Finding colleagues to discuss ideas with, cultivating

a can-do attitude, finding ways to get past barriers, and satisfying mandates are essential elements of developing yourself as a reflective teacher. The final chapter of this book offers examples of early childhood educators stepping outside the doors of their minds, classrooms, and programs to engage with others in creating new possibilities for themselves, their students, and their students' families. The principles offered in chapter 9 remind you to see children's competence, find collaborators, take risks, visit inspiring programs, and continually explore "why?" in order to challenge your thinking. You will find examples of how to strengthen yourself as a growing leader and change maker.

The appendices in this book and available online include a range of materials to help you implement the ideas in this book. For instance, you'll find sample self-assessment forms, experiments with curriculum documentation to meet requirements, more resources on using the Thinking Lens®, learning stories, and anti-bias practices. We've also included examples of organizational structures that support administrators and teachers to be reflective and responsive to children and families, including ways programs have used this book for professional learning for their staff. Finally, we include resources on important advocacy efforts that hold promise for expanding possibilities for early childhood education.

Understanding the Structure of This Book

Learning Together with Young Children is a curriculum guide but not an ordinary one. We have not written this book as a prescriptive, scope-and-sequence curriculum. Our curriculum approach is based on a wide, eclectic body of research, particularly from those working to bridge the gap between theory and practice. It draws on neuroscience and academic as well as action research. Most curriculum books are about what you do to and for children. They do not present the teaching and learning process as a dynamic, collaborative experience where the teacher is learning about teaching and learning while also facilitating children's learning. Curriculum books rarely discuss how a teacher's values, ideas, reflections, decisions, and ongoing learning are central to her ability to guide children's learning. In this curriculum book, you "hear" the children's voices and the thinking that influences the teacher's actions. *Learning Together with Young Children* not only promotes a philosophy of praxis—observation, reflection, action—it also brings forth the voices of family providers, Head Start, pre-K, and child care teachers, administrators, coaches, and teacher educators

engaged in this actual practice. Here is the opportunity to learn right along with them and the children. You will find components of other curriculum books here—materials to use, activities to try, questions to consider—but rather than presenting the core practices in lists and directions, they are revealed in principles with stories, photographs, and challenges to make them your own. Each chapter begins with a quote, often from outside the early childhood field, but with pertinent wisdom for the curriculum core practice at hand. We recommend you read each quote several times and consider what it means to you before you read further. When you come to the end of each chapter, you might revisit the quote again to see if it provokes more reflections for you.

After the opening quote is an overview of that chapter's core practice of the curriculum framework, followed by a list of principles to guide your thinking and practice. The stories within each principle offer you a description of how it could look. Teacher stories are a powerful professional development tool (Patterson, Fleet, and Duffie 1995). Most of the time our stories are followed by a section called

"Listen to (name)," which will contain a quote from the provider or teacher that offers a window into his or her thinking. Each story concludes with a section entitled "Reflect," which provides more guidance for uncovering the possible learning within the story. Sprinkled throughout each chapter are spotlight vignettes, which highlight more examples of how providers and teachers have translated our principles into action.

Throughout the book we have included two ways to practice the reflective process. We call them Your Turn and Use the Thinking Lens® Protocol. In each chapter you'll find specific assignments under the heading Your Turn that will help you practice an aspect of the curriculum framework. Unless you are reading this book as part of a class, it might be tempting to just read these activities and skip over the actual task. We strongly recommend you make time to accept our invitation to construct further understandings for yourself. Ideally, you would do these activities with your colleagues.

The second opportunity we regularly offer for you to practice the cycle of observation/reflection/action will appear in the Use the Thinking Lens® Protocol sections. Here you will find questions on one or more of the areas for reflection to consider before taking action. The more you practice cycling through this Thinking Lens® Protocol, the more instinctive and natural this reflective process will become in your teaching.

My Eyes Have Changed

Family provider Kelly describes her professional development as she's begun using our curriculum framework:

"I am not the same teacher I was when I started this work. The way I think about what I do has changed. I am more comfortable challenging myself to take on different roles with the kids. I have doubled my efforts to strengthen my relationships with my kids so they have that foundation to take risks and to fail and to rebound together. I have made a point of trying new things in front of my kids, so they can see me fumble—authentically fumble and fail—and we can rebound together.

"My eyes have changed. What I pay attention to has changed. I look for multiplicity now. How many different ways can I understand what I am seeing? I am not so timid about voicing what I see my kids doing. I am getting better at uncovering what they are thinking about as they work. I view multiplicity

as a gateway to complexity, whether it is being able to use a craft stick in twelve different ways or revisiting the 'same' idea and uncovering a new way to understand that concept.

"What I love, though, hasn't changed. The children show up every day expectant of the wonderful things we will create together. It is what drives me to do this work with such thoughtfulness and intention."

Use the Thinking Lens® Protocol

Kelly's story "My Eyes Have Changed" offers a model of being a reflective practitioner. She tells us what it looks like to be self-aware and open to new perspectives. She describes new practices she is learning: taking on different roles with children, valuing the complexity of different perspectives, and being authentic while fumbling and failing at things. Use Kelly's story as an opportunity to practice your own reflections with our Thinking Lens® Protocol. For each area for reflection in the Thinking Lens®, we offer you some sample questions to consider. As you become more familiar with this protocol, you will find it natural to come up with additional questions.

Area for Reflection: Know yourself
- Do you appreciate complexity or prefer to keep things simple?
- How comfortable are you fumbling or making mistakes in front of children?

Area for Reflection: Find the details of the children's competencies that engage your heart and mind
- How often do you see things in children that delight you or spark your curiosity?
- What do you specifically pay attention to as you seek to uncover children's thinking and skills?

Area for Reflection: Examine the physical/social/emotional environment
- How do you plan your environment to foster relationships?
- What do you do to deepen your relationship with each child?

Area for Reflection: Seek the child's perspective
- How natural or challenging is it for you to accept that children have perspectives different from yours?
- What strategies do you use to seek children's perspectives?

Area for Reflection: Consider other perspectives
- What child development principles do you draw on when planning for or responding to children's learning?
- How might cultural or family background issues influence the roles you want to play in guiding children's learning?

Area for Reflection: Consider opportunities and possibilities for action
- What values, philosophy, and goals do you want to influence your work with children?
- What learning goals do you have for yourself at this time?

With this snapshot of what is to come, you are now ready to move through the chapters of *Learning Together with Young Children*. Each chapter builds on the next and, depending on where you are in your teaching journey, you will likely spend more time with some chapters than others. Returning again to the words of Sonya Shoptaugh, you are embarking on a way of working where professional development takes place day after day in your classroom.

2 Create a Nourishing Classroom Culture

School schedules and teaching strategies need to fit children's natural rhythms rather than trying (and failing) to force them into an artificially adult world which mimics our fast-paced, hard-driving business culture. . . . We need to stop hurrying children. Our school days require time. Time to wonder, time to pause, time to look closely, time to share, time to pay attention to what is most important. —**Chip Wood**

Every classroom has a culture—a set of expectations, language, routines, and ways of being together that shape the group's identity. The culture you develop sets the tone, reflects who you are, and expresses how you want to live and learn with children. If you strive for joyful days and see yourself as a learner right alongside the children and their families, you'll work with a set of values, not just regulations.

Close your eyes and visualize the qualities you want in your time with children and their families. When you consider the ideal rhythm for your day, would it be a song most like a march or a lullaby, or would it be soul, country, or hip-hop? Your policies, the words you use, the pace, the sound, and the feel of your everyday actions and routines shape an identity for the children. Pay attention to how your classroom's culture influences the children's dispositions (and yours!) toward learning and caring for those around them. Teachers and providers typically establish classroom rules, space, and schedules with an eye to classroom management and teacher convenience. It's easy to think of these logistics as just the framework that allows you to teach and not the teaching itself. But what opportunities for learning

do the rules and routines offer? What are children learning from the space itself? These logistics actually have a huge impact on classroom culture and in many ways determine what teaching and learning are possible.

As you consider the classroom culture you would like to foster, use quality research to guide your thinking, policies, and practices. In particular, consider neuroscience research that offers increasing insights into how the brain develops in young children, including the roles of culture, physical activity, nutrition, and strong relationships. For instance, Rima Shore describes neuroscientific discoveries of how the brain responds constantly and swiftly to ongoing conditions that promote or inhibit learning. Shore states, "The impact of the environment is dramatic and specific, not merely influencing the general direction of development, but actually affecting how the intricate circuitry of the brain is wired" (1997, 15). You can have extensive curriculum goals, but if children don't develop strong relationships and feel comfortable enough to make choices, take risks, or try new things, then the learning outcomes are likely to be limited to behavior compliance and recitation, not the intellectual curiosity and emotional security that sustains lifelong learning and altruistic endeavors.

Zaretta Hammond's research (2015) on the relationship between equity, instruction, and brain science has tremendous implications for our work, particularly in our efforts to overcome the opportunity and achievement gaps between children of color and their European American counterparts.

Hammond challenges us to recognize that while all children are wired for expansive learning, we need to carefully examine what is going wrong for children of color. They are typically viewed as needing more drill-and-skill instruction, which fails to develop higher-level thinking skills. Rather than characterizing these children as unready or unable to succeed, we need to apply more culturally responsive teaching practices that promote their higher order thinking, problem-solving skills, and independent learning.

Taking research findings seriously may mean challenging some traditional routines and policies. For example, numerous studies show that positive relationships among teachers, children, and families are essential to learning (Shonkoff et al. 2000). Yet many programs still move children from room to room based on ratios, birthdays, or enrollment openings, disrupting the bonds and friendships that have been forming among the children, teachers, and families. Ask yourself, "What are we doing to honor existing relationships and keep them strong?"

If you value the research about relationships, consider ways of keeping the children, teachers, and families together for a two- or three-year period. One possibility is looping, or continuity of care, where a group of children stays with the same teachers as they grow older. The term *looping* refers to teachers working with the same group of children as they grow older, typically for two to four or even five years. When the children graduate or transition to a new program, the teachers loop back to the beginning to work with the youngest children again. An advantage of looping is that children do not have to start over each year and adjust to a new classroom culture.

Think carefully about each aspect of your policies and practices, in your daily life with children as well as during special rituals and celebrations. The following principles can help you create a classroom culture that welcomes diverse children and families and supports desirable dispositions and outcomes. These will ensure that you have vibrant days of living and learning with children.

Principles

- Involve children in welcoming families.
- Honor each family's uniqueness.
- Invest in learning each family's culture and funds of knowledge.
- Keep children connected to their families.
- Gather families for explorations.
- Focus on relationships, not rules.
- Arrange your space and routines to promote community.
- Give children ownership of routines and schedules.
- Use children's ideas to pursue investigations.
- Help children see themselves as learners.
- Coach children to develop negotiation and collaboration skills.
- Incorporate the four anti-bias goals into your classroom culture.
- Develop rituals that create memories.
- Celebrate real accomplishments.

PRINCIPLE Involve Children in Welcoming Families

Developing your classroom culture involves thinking through your values and philosophy so your room setup, use of language, and daily routines create the rhythm for the "dance" you are all undertaking. Your most important dance partners are, of course, the children's families, who can keep you in step with culturally appropriate and meaningful experiences for their children. To make this partnership

Nancy Gerber Family Child Care

Sign-in table

work, you need to hear each other's beats and find a common rhythm. This process of tuning in to one another begins with first encounters. It is supported by ongoing communications, systems, and policies that provide multiple opportunities for collaboration in shaping the life of your classroom.

When families enroll their children in programs, they are usually handed a stack of forms to complete. The provider or director goes over policies, business details, and perhaps a typical menu, curriculum plan, or assessment tool. Teachers may or may not be part of this process. In some programs, teachers do home visits, often with a questionnaire or more paperwork in hand. But if you think of enrollment as the beginning of relationships and participation in a program culture, you might want to rethink these initial encounters. Rather than treating first meetings as service arrangements or business transactions, conduct them as if you were welcoming someone into your home.

There are many stepping stones to think about: how to give a tour to a family, the sense of support and collaboration you seek to create during the orientation process, the child's transition into the program, and initial family group meetings. Making sure each of these occasions provides listening ears, sensitive communications, and opportunities for making connections will go far in helping children and their

families feel at home with you. Start with the simple things that are in easy reach to make families feel comfortable and invited into a relationship with you.

- Create meaningful documents that relate to fond memories, not just required information.
- Use photographs to help associate names and faces.
- Host family gatherings that go beyond presentations and help people develop a sense of camaraderie.

Through the Children's Eyes

Beyond a formal parent handbook, homemade welcome books for each new family offer a concrete way to introduce your program culture. By including the children's ideas on what other students need to know to become part of the group, you are clearly demonstrating that this is a place where children's ideas are valued. Family provider Donna and center-based teacher Ann guide children in making pages for the welcoming book with questions and suggestions like these:

- *How can new children and families learn what we do here?*
- *Can you make a map of our space with ideas about what you can do in the different areas?*
- *How can other kids learn how we share and take turns here?*
- *What can you tell new kids about the kinds of things you might learn when you're in the program?*
- *Can you give ideas on how to be responsible and contribute to the group?*
- *What should kids do if they have a problem?*
- *What special activities can new families look forward to?*

The following pages are extracted from a welcome book at Donna's program, Children First.

(sample page from Children First welcoming book)

Helping

Kids have many important jobs at Children First, jobs that help keep our school tidy and make it a comfortable place to work and play.

Clean-Up Time

Every day before meeting, kids work together to clean up the classroom and playground. Cleaning up is hard work, but when you tackle a big job and get it done, you will feel very proud of yourself!

Gigi drew "the mess in the blocks" and "the clean up," counting carefully to make sure every block in "the mess" was put on the shelf in the cleaned up picture. Gigi said,"This is Emi if she cleans up the blocks, she's got two blocks. These are the shelves, you clean the blocks to put on the shelves."

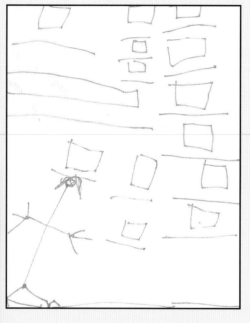

Aimee, Zora and Gigi clean up the big blocks outside.

Audrey: You can't stop clean up-ping you have to clean up until it's clean. And the people who are helping you with the job have to stay until you're done.

Gigi: They can clean up the blocks or the kaplas if someone needs help, someone can help somebody. Like a kid or a teacher can help someone.

(sample page from Children First welcoming book)

Taking Care of Messes

When kids are working and playing, sometimes they spill or make messes by accident. Making mistakes is always OK. What's important is doing what you can to fix your mistakes—like sweeping up rice that spills out of the rice table, or mopping up water you spill. Sometimes you can help with messes you don't make, too—like the way Gigi is helping the teachers sweep leaves off the deck. And sometimes you tidy up just because it's fun—Annabelle is sorting the rice table toys by color.

(sample page from Children First welcoming book)

Helping Your Friends

There are many important ways kids help each other, like Gigi is helping Ian with opening his lunch, and Lee is helping Susanna steady her pile of climbing-up pillows, and Ayla is helping Audrey with her shoes. Friends help each other with their work and with their play and especially with their feelings.

Here's what the Children Firsters want you to know about helping other children:

Emi: Kids help each other when one kid like gets hurt then the other kids says, "I'll go get a teacher."

Gigi: That they can help any people, any people can help the other people to know how to write or draw if they don't know how to write "Annabelle" or "Zora" or "Ayla" or "Lee" or "Micah" or "Joseph" or "Susanna"—that's the lot of kids.

Ayla: Well, once Lee couldn't reach the calendar so I helped her.

Micah: You have to help them if you want to. You hold your hand and pick them up with your hand.

First Encounters

Providers and teachers that keep relationships at the center of their thinking create an embracing social-emotional climate where people are seen, heard, and acknowledged for who they are. Miss Dee Dee, a lead teacher in a child care program, often gives tours to prospective families. How would you describe the tone she sets during these first encounters? Do you see her efforts to immediately immerse visitors into the culture of her program? How is this similar to or different from what happens in your program?

Martin Luther King Jr. Day Home Center

When families call to inquire about openings in this center, they are asked to first bring their child for a visit. Miss Dee Dee wants all visitors to her classroom to be warmly greeted by the children and the environment, and she explains this to the children before new faces arrive. She asks them to remember what they felt like when they first started child care and to think of ways to welcome new children. To make adults feel welcome in her room, Miss Dee Dee has used a portion of her precious supply money to purchase a small couch and adult-sized chairs. She hopes this will ease families into this place that is as different from home as it is from a traditional school classroom.

As a prospective new family arrives, Miss Dee Dee invites them to sit in the classroom with her briefly and encourages the other children to introduce themselves and invite the visiting child into their play.

The visiting child can then stay in the room or join the adults as they tour the rest of the center. There are relaxed introductions as they move around the center, with children in a room sometimes sharing a story or offering an invitation to join them in play or a snack. She makes a point of introducing the on-site staff, including the cook, janitor, and volunteer helpers. The family typically extends their visit in the child's potential classroom, and then before they leave, Miss Dee Dee escorts them to the office for further conversation with the director. During this time, the family receives additional information about the program, answers to any questions, and a registration packet that includes a general center handbook and a welcome letter from the child's prospective teachers.

Reflect

Because most of the connections a family will have in a center are with those in their child's classroom, Miss Dee Dee's program launches first encounters there. Hoping the family will feel embraced by the essence of the room, she invites family members to talk about their child, their ideas about becoming part of a child care center, and their hopes for a partnership with a child care program. Miss Dee Dee strives to get a sense of what's important to the family, exploring whether her center will be a good fit for them. She is eager for the family to get a sense of the program culture through encounters with the physical environment, the children, and the other staff members. Paperwork, policies, and business matters are the last thing taken up during this first visit because they have the least relevancy to making connections as human beings.

PRINCIPLE Honor Each Family's Uniqueness

Every family faces emotional and logistical challenges when they put their children in someone else's care, and often financial challenges as well. Schedules must be followed, mornings are often rushed, traffic can be a problem, and underneath it all, families may have a nagging worry about leaving their kids outside their kinship group. "Will these people really know who my child is? Will our family life be respected? Will I be judged if my child misbehaves?" Reassuring words from teachers can help, but remember the idiom "Actions speak louder than words." Find ways to help families see the things they have in common with others in your program. And use concrete objects and symbols to honor each family's uniqueness.

Symbolic Connections

Family home provider Donna plans a series of gradual steps to bring new families into her program. As you read her story, notice how she simultaneously pays attention to getting families connected to one another while seeking out ways to make the uniqueness of each child visible.

Donna and her coworker create thoughtful beginnings with symbols for new families coming to their program. During a spring orientation, she asks some of the current families to be on hand to welcome the new ones. This is the first of several low-key gatherings alternating between her home and those of the new families', during which Donna seeks insights into the essence of each child. She takes photographs of the child and family members, and gives each family a folder of "homework" to complete over the summer. Each new family is assigned a buddy family who stays in touch with them during this time. During their last visit before the fall program begins, Donna offers each child a set of possible graphic symbols to choose from, which will be used as a visual element to accompany the child's written name. She creates these symbols from her conversations with the family during home visits, infusing deeper meaning into the HighScope idea of giving children symbols as an initial literacy device to learn to recognize their own and one another's names.

Reflect

Donna makes an enormous investment in developing a personal relationship with each new family that enrolls in her program, believing this is what they deserve when they entrust their children to her. For Donna, the challenge to design a set of potentially meaningful symbols for each child pushes her to connect intimately with something important about that child and family. She believes that making this visible will make them feel more at home in her early childhood setting. Entry into her program stretches over a few months, so by the time the families come for the first official day in the program, they already have some connections and memories formed with Donna and other families. And they have a clear idea of some specific things to look forward to.

P R I N C I P L E   **Invest in Learning about Each Family's Culture and Funds of Knowledge**
Whether they are coming to a family home program, preschool, child care environment, or Head Start classroom, each day families have a significant transition to make as they entrust their children into a care and educational setting outside their control. This transition can be eased when providers and teachers create conditions that invite a mutually respectful and trusting relationship. Take time to learn the

Children First

particular strengths of the children's families, their cultures, and their community. This helps you see each culture as more than a set of artifacts, recognizing such things as strongly held values, communication patterns, and protocols for relationships so you can be more culturally responsive in welcoming families into your program. In their book *Funds of Knowledge: Theorizing Practices in Households, Communities, and Classrooms* (2005), Norma González, Luis Moll, and Cathy Amanti describe how teachers can enhance children's learning and strengthen relationships with their families by exploring the extensive knowledge and skills embedded in their experience, history, and web of community connections. The research explored how home visits can uncover extensive know-how in areas of agriculture, mechanics, engineering, carpentry, economics, transportation, health care, and household management—all of which affect the child's ongoing learning and identity development.

Relationships are two-way streets. How can you extend yourself so the children and their families get to know you personally? What gestures will encourage them to share their lives with you? How can you use community connections or technology to include a wider circle of each child's family?

Denise Louie Head Start

bus pulls into the parking lot of her building. Children spill out and rush to her with hugs and exuberance. Other children arrive by car with family members and Kristin stays on the playground to meet them as well. She exchanges greetings with the families, often lingering for informal conversation, stories, and updates on happenings in their lives.

Crossing the Threshold

When Kristin, a Head Start teacher, first visits the home of an incoming family, she uses the time to play with the child and share information about herself— her family, her favorite activities, and her approach to teaching. Often working with an interpreter, she asks the family members what they would like her to know about them and how she can support them as they send their child to her classroom. She listens for insights into what they value, how they spend their time, and what is important to them in their community. She explores ways the family can become involved in the classroom activities. Then, during the school year, Kristin waits at the gate as the Head Start

Reflect

Kristin is thoughtful about how she starts and maintains her relationships with children and families, initially in home visits and then each day of the week. She recognizes that learning doesn't just occur during her planned activities for the children, but happens at home as well. The foundation of her curriculum depends on having solid relationships with the children's families, demonstrating cultural sensitivity and attention to the dynamics of power and privilege. While families certainly need to fill out forms, that isn't Kristin's main focus in these relationships. To develop trust with families, she knows she can't appear to be an interrogator or home inspector, but rather someone who is respectful and forthcoming. In asking about them and sharing stories about herself, she invites a relationship with the family's stories. Then, throughout the year, whatever the weather, Kristin starts the day outside. She's noticed that her immigrant and English-language learning families are more willing to stick around for a while when they enter through the playground area, rather than immediately crossing the threshold of the classroom door. Kristin's strategy of beginning the day on the playground with the children stems from her child development knowledge as well. She recognizes that when children arrive at the program, they have been sitting on a bus or in a car for a while and they need some big-body time.

PRINCIPLE Keep Children Connected to Their Families

Early childhood lore suggests our goal is to help children separate from their families when they come to our programs. This contradicts the substantial body of research and literature emphasizing the importance of attachment between a child and his mother or primary caregiver and the experience of loss when they are separated. Attachment theory has been applied to parenting approaches and explored more scientifically with contributions from neuroscience (Schore 2000). Yes, we want children to feel at home and form strong relationships in our programs, but we must simultaneously do all we can to keep children connected to their families when they are with us. Likewise, teachers should be empathetic when children miss their families but also aware of which routines make them feel powerful, not like victims of circumstances. Do your routines encourage children to see themselves as emotionally strong and capable of problem solving? Do you notice how children are a resource to one another, offering comfort and encouragement?

Carrying My Mama Around

In a classroom culture that honors and encourages strong connections, even very young children will demonstrate their abilities to empathize and negotiate relationships. For instance, when Deb began working with toddlers, she created routines to smooth the transition between home and child care. The children began to draw on these routines to comfort one another. Does the following story challenge you to rethink any prevailing theories about children's egocentrism?

Throughout Deb's toddler room, images of the children's families add to the homelike atmosphere. Large framed photos of the children and their family members hang on the cupboard doors. The photos are accompanied by a short description of their family life. On any given day you will find children excitedly pointing to these pictures, acknowledging who they recognize in their own family or those of their

playmates. Sometimes they kiss the image behind the glass or use a sponge to wipe their mommy or daddy's face. The children often carry around other smaller frames of family photos, at times putting them in the doll bed or on a table where they are playing. After morning drop-off and separation, Deb prompts children to find their family's photo. The children become accustomed to this routine and, during the day, might take a framed photo to a child who is in need of com-fort. They do this as well with the homemade books featuring photo stories of the children reuniting with a parent. Each of these gestures offers reassurance and supports the children's connections with their families and one another.

A Family Altar

When Mia and her family went to China to adopt their second child, Mia's teacher Myrna suggested they bring back something to represent their trip and expanded family. Myrna wanted to acknowledge this big change in Mia's life and provide ways for her to play out any of her feelings, be they excitement, pride, fear, or insecurity. Mia returned with a little tea set for the classroom, and Myrna used it as a way to invite Mia to share her story with her classmates.

Hilltop Children's Center

Reflect

Deb's story highlights how concrete objects can make values and early childhood research come alive in the classroom. Deb has created an environment where familiar family faces provide comfort and ease feelings of loss during the long hours children are away from their families. Noticing how happy both the children and their families are when they reunite at the end of each day, she photographs these moments and creates little homemade storybooks to help the children remember that this joyful time will come again at the end of each day. When you watch them closely, you see how observant children are to everything around them. We wonder how Piaget (2001) overlooked some easy-to-see empathetic gestures and concluded that toddlers are egocentric!

Your Turn

To assess how your environment acknowledges understandings of attachment theories and the importance of sustaining children's connections with their families, sketch the floor plan of your room. Then go through each of the following possibilities, coding your floor plan with the numeral indicated.

- Put a 1 in all the places where children's family life and culture are reflected and nourished.
- Put a 2 in all the places where children can find comfort when they miss their families.
- Put a 3 in all the places that remind children that they will be reunited with their families.
- Put a 4 in all the places where the children's family members can feel at home, relaxed, and respected in the room.
- Put a 5 in all the places where the children and their families can get to know more about and bond with you.

How do these ideas support children's need to have secure bonds with their families and caregivers?

If your current environment doesn't include clear examples of the above items, think about how you can add any missing elements. Then move on to assessing how your daily routines and policies support connections. Are there any changes you want to make? For each idea you have, make an action plan with a timeline for yourself.

Hilltop Children's Center

PRINCIPLE Gather Families for Explorations

Most programs hold some kind of a fall meeting for families, sometimes including the children and in other cases, just adults. When you plan these initial and then ongoing family gatherings, consider how they can reflect your values and goals for mutual relationships. Such meetings will have a very different feel than ones where the teacher or director is on a one-way street—giving out, but not receiving, information, expectations, or expertise. To support the classroom culture you are trying to develop, think in terms of family gatherings as opposed to business or information meetings. Food and music are always helpful components, as are easy ways for people to mingle, converse, and get a sense of one another and your program. When you do take up business or devote time to communications about your philosophy, routines, and pedagogy, do so in a way that parallels what you do with the children. Providing experiences, not just information, builds solid partnerships and reframes the notion of parent education.

Exchanging Ideas and Gifts

Ann and her coworkers have developed key elements for their family gatherings that involve different explorations from year to year. As you read this story, ask yourself how sharing the children's ideas might inform the collective understandings of their families. What's the purpose of their gift exchanges?

In planning their fall gathering, Ann and the other teachers choose a big question or idea to explore first with the children in the classroom and then with the families during their meeting. For instance, one year Ann chose the question "What's the same or different between home and school?" and another year she and her team focused on "How do very young children understand friendship, and how is that the same or different from how adults understand friendship?"

As the families discuss their ideas, teachers offer documentation of the children's thinking on the questions, which typically provokes a deeper discussion about the topic and the ways in which children can inform our understandings. Teachers also offer parallel hands-on experiences for the children and parents, asking them to leave surprise gifts for one another. Examples of these gifts include painted dishes, personalized nap pillows, or treasure boxes. One year, Kendra and Brad, Ann's after-school teaching colleagues, created an activity around the idea of bedtime rituals. The children created a representation of their bedtime rituals, leaving their names off their pages so their families had to guess which page belonged to which child. This was not only a sweet gift for the families, but it also provided a way for them to explore the similarities and differences among their families as they read and looked at the children's work. As their return gift, the children's family members each created a page about their childhood bedtime rituals, which were then bound together into a book with the children's pages.

Reflect

Rather than repeating the same activity during each fall family gathering, the teachers in the story draw on the same elements and pedagogy but pose a different set of questions. This keeps both the teachers and families looking forward to the tradition and the resulting creativity. Exploring the same question with the children and the families broadens perspectives and deepens insights. When the families hear the collective voices of their children, they move beyond a concern about whether their individual child "measures up" and marvel together at how children's thinking can enhance their own. Making surprise gifts brings excitement and shared anticipation. These experiences illustrate the value of making memories rather than buying things. They provide opportunities for each group (families and children) to think about the others' perspectives and what might bring collective joy to people they love.

Expressing Wishes

Working in a large child care service in Canada, Bev uses her September meeting as a two-way street, not only answering the parents' questions but asking them to consider hers. She provides paper and drawing tools and asks, "What kind of adult would you wish your child to be? Please write or draw your thoughts." Though some parents are hesitant to participate in this activity at first, Bev offers encouragement, humor, and thoughtful questions to get their creative juices flowing. As the evening comes to a close, a lively discussion and heartfelt, original creations emerge. These pages with parent wishes are posted for a few weeks in the hallway and then preserved in a book, which is kept in the classroom.

Discovery Children's Centre

As parents, you are your child's most important teacher and we value your insight. We asked that every parent create a page that answers the following question:

"What kind of adult would you wish your child to be?"

Your Turn

Practice planning a welcoming routine or family gathering that reflects the values you want to incorporate into your classroom culture. Use these questions to guide your planning process:

- What elements do you want to include as you welcome new families into your classroom?
- How can these be translated into specific practices?
- For an initial classroom family gathering, what could you focus on to create an activity that offers the families an enjoyable way to connect to one another while also making connections with experiences or ideas their children are exploring?

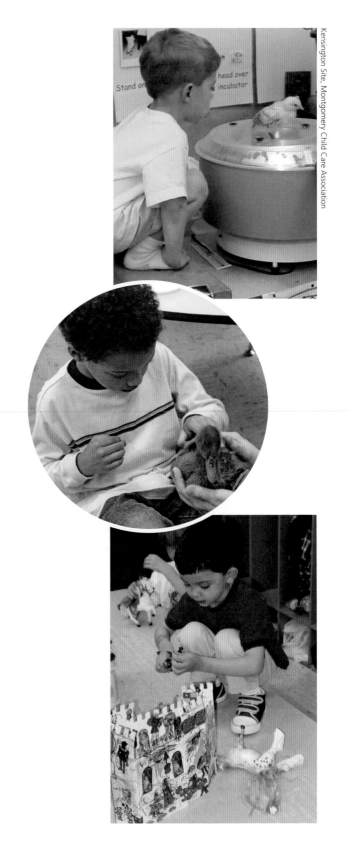

PRINCIPLE   **Focus on Relationships, Not Rules**

Every group needs a set of norms to work with. In most early childhood programs, this typically consists of a list of classroom rules on the wall and the teacher's voice continually reminding the children of how to behave. However, a classroom culture focused on relationships and shared excitement in learning sets an entirely different tone for behavior management. Teachers plan for and respond to children's curiosities with shared inquisitiveness. They encourage children to learn about one another and the world around them, and the teachers recognize that this will reflect what Howard Gardner (2011) calls "multiple intelligences," instead of conformity to a standard way of acquiring knowledge. Classrooms focused on relationships are lively, not quiet and orderly. They are living laboratories for learning to negotiate individual desires while participating as citizens in a democracy and caring for our planet.

Talking Chicks

As you read the following description of Jacky's classroom and look at the photos, ask yourself, "What could she be thinking?"

Located in an old elementary school building, Jacky's room has many of the features found in a typical early childhood environment, including limitations such as built-in counters and inadequate storage space. Around the room are learning centers with child-sized furniture and a variety of materials at children's eye level. The room includes a number of plants, and Jacky brings in unusual animal visitors, like the chicks and duckling in the photos, and helps the children care for them. Noticing the children's repeated efforts to be close to the chicks, she puts one of the chicks on top of the incubator to suggest the idea that the chick, too, might desire a "talking" relationship with the eggs still hatching. She approaches an intrigued child who has dragged a chair to boost himself up on the counter. "What do you think the little chick is trying to tell the eggs inside?" she asks. Children move about the room in a relaxed, easy way, enjoying the materials and one another's company. When Jacky spots a child who has climbed on a table for a better look at his castle drama, she joins him with an invitation to converse about his idea. As she gathers the children together on the rug for group times, Jacky invites them to choose a seat, join in the singing, sharing, and story time, or just be an observer.

Reflect

Creating a community of active, joyful learners is central to Jacky's thinking. She wants children to feel connected to and care for one another and the natural world, so she brings the natural world into her classroom. Jacky believes children are capable of making responsible choices, so she respects where they want to sit and the ways they choose to participate during group times. Jacky's classroom culture focuses on caring, curiosity, and inventiveness, not children's compliance with rules. Rather than scolding or invoking a keep-your-feet-on-the-floor rule, Jacky recognizes and supports children's interests and their unusual solutions to the barriers they encounter.

PRINCIPLE **Arrange Your Space and Routines to Promote Community**

As you set up your room environment and create routines, think in terms of community more than classroom. Young children feel more relaxed in a homelike environment than in an institutional school setting. Jim Greenman (2006) suggests early childhood programs set aside the term *classroom* in favor of *home bases* when assigning children to rooms. Our earlier book *Designs for Living and Learning* offers numerous examples for arranging your space to create a welcoming, cozy environment. The process of creating and maintaining such a setting requires ongoing reflection of your values and a willingness to continually adapt the environment to meet the needs of your specific group of children.

Likewise, as you develop routines for the children and their families, focus on nurturing a sense of belonging to a community.

Worms and Hot Wheels

Notice in the following story how Myrna and John have designed their space and routines for their group of three-year-olds in their full-day child care program. Look closely at how they spend time at the start and end of each day. What is the role of their tabletop invitations in their routines to welcome children and families?

To begin each day, Myrna puts a few things on tables, including breakfast food and interesting materials to pique the interest of those entering the room. As they arrive, the children hang up their coats and immediately go exploring, sometimes with a parent in hand. Myrna moves between greeting new arrivals, replenishing food at one table, and sitting with the children at another, conversing about what they are discovering. Today she has put out a tray of dirt with worms and magnifying glasses. She takes a few minutes to jot down observations and take pictures. When most of the children have arrived, Myrna gives a reminder

Hilltop Children's Center

about breakfast and how much time remains before they will gather for circle time. She collects some tools for cleanup and eases children into the transition to their group time with requests and comments such as, "Who would like to learn how to use this dustpan? There are sponges and a bucket for our table cleaners."

Hilltop Children's Center

John works a later shift in this same room, and he ends the day in a way that mirrors how Myrna starts it. He puts out snacks and some interesting materials on a table with an eye on welcoming families to relax a bit after their busy day. He offers items from his own childhood, such as his Hot Wheels car collection, inviting parents to linger and reminisce before rushing home.

Reflect

Myrna and John believe children and families need time to transition between home and child care. They use routines that feel more like home than school, with relaxed eating and conversations. Their rhythms and pace allow them to make connections with individual families and accommodate different preferences and schedules. Both of these teachers create invitations related to their own passions; Myrna is an avid gardener, and John is a Hot Wheels collector. Instead of flashing lights or ringing bells for transitions, John and Myrna use their relationships with the children to engage them in cleanup. They know the children love to use adult tools and see themselves as able to make a contribution to the smooth functioning of the room. Routines in this room create a welcoming, relaxed atmosphere, giving both children and parents a sense of belonging.

Don't Get Stumped

Shaping your environment with your philosophy and values isn't a onetime endeavor. As children use the space, continually consider whether it is working to support your goals. The following story describes a teacher engaged in this ongoing reflective process. As you read, notice how Deb uses her observations of the children to make adjustments and include their families in the classroom culture.

Deb holds group meetings with the children in the large block area of her small, cottage-like classroom. For a while, an exceptionally large wooden stump served as a focal point in the area, reminiscent of a space where people could gather around a campfire to sing and tell stories. During their playtime, children often used the stump as a setting for little dramas. Ultimately, the stump proved too small for displaying the variety of objects children brought to group meetings. As a result, Deb invited the children's parents to a party to construct a new platform to replace the stump in the center of the block area. The work party itself had the feel of the children's building and construction activities, with lively stories, laughter, and different ideas about the best design for the new platform. The children now use the resulting platform for some of their building and construction. When they gather together for meetings, they put samples of their work or objects from home on the platform. Sometimes Deb spotlights a new material in the center of the platform, discussing possible ideas for its use.

Reflect

Growing relationships is central to how Deb thinks about growing curriculum. She wants the children to experience themselves as part of a community, and she sees group gatherings as an important expression of that. However, Deb recognizes that her personality doesn't lend itself to easy group management, and she doesn't want to become the preschool police. She wants group meetings to have the enthusiasm of gathering around a campfire or dining room table, instead of the aggravation of constant reminders to sit quietly on a designated space or carpet square. The tree stump offered this spirit, so when it proved too small, Deb sought to replace it with something that created the same sense of a gathering place. Instead of simply finding or building something herself, she invited parents to work together to build the platform for their children, hoping to create the same lively community experience she provides the children.

Go Out Singing

Taking a step beyond individual classroom singing, Ted and his colleagues have developed a Friday afternoon community singing ritual to end their week together. Ted moves from room to room with his guitar, inviting all the children to gather. Teachers, office staff, and often the children's family members attend the sing-along as well, sometimes bringing a new tune to share. Over time, the children have learned a wide repertoire of songs, which have been put into songbooks that travel between the children's homes and school.

Burlington Little School

Burlington Little School

PRINCIPLE   **Give Children Ownership of Routines and Schedules**

Most teachers follow a set of established routines and techniques for managing children's time. On paper, these get formatted into a daily schedule, which moves children through little blocks of time to cover their curriculum. Here's a sample daily schedule:

- large group experiences, typically referred to as circle time
- small-group time, usually led by the teacher with a particular lesson in mind
- snacktime
- free choice or learning center time
- outdoor time

But if you want your classroom to feel more like a nurturing learning community, you'll shape the structure of the day around the natural rhythms of breathing in and breathing out (cycles of robust activity, eating, resting). If you follow the ideas of Lev Vygotsky (1978) and social constructivism, your goal will be to set up routines and rules that encourage children to actively contribute to one another's knowledge, instead of emphasizing individual achievements. You will be looking for ways to have the environment and routines, as well as your interactions with children, scaffold the children's ability to focus and collaborate.

Putting the Children in Charge

When Kristin first began working as a teacher in Head Start, she inherited all the familiar routines of a typical early childhood classroom. But the more she began to consider her philosophy and values, the more dissatisfied she became with these standard practices. She steadily began making changes and her classroom now has a very different feel. As you read her story, how would you describe Kristin's image of children? Is this similar to or different from how you view children and your goals for their time with you?

At the beginning of her third year of teaching, Kristin's room no longer has a job chart posted on the wall. Instead, you see children moving around the room with tremendous confidence that they know what has to be done each afternoon they are together. To give children ownership of the room, Kristin uses small-group times during the first weeks of school to demonstrate how to tidy up different parts of the room, organize snacktime, welcome visitors, and even tend to one another's bumps and scratches. Now when Kristin approaches what in the

past would have been a rigid cleanup time on the schedule, she goes around to small groups of children at play, asking what they are working on and if they need more time or if they are ready to have snack or go outside. If the children have different ideas about this, they negotiate about when and how to move on to the next activity. Having taught one another how to count to ten in their home languages, they vote on which language to use for a countdown, and they begin restoring the room for their play the next day. Kristin rarely makes general announcements to the whole group unless it's about something exciting she wants them all to pay attention to at that moment.

Denise Louie Head Start

Reflect

As we see in Kristin's story, creating classroom norms can look and sound very different when you are consciously working with a set of values that go beyond group management goals. Kristin has set up an environment with materials placed at the children's level, and ownership of the schedule and routines is in their hands. Her classroom culture is very child-centered, where the teacher is a facilitator, not a director; a demonstrator, not a disciplinarian. Kristin decided that standard fixtures such as job charts didn't fit with her goal of creating a community where all the children care for one another and the room. She doesn't want to dictate or limit who will be a helper each day, but instead supports and nurtures the children's natural sense of empathy for one another and their desire to be helpful. Cross-cultural appreciation is woven into the fabric of living together as they learn words in one another's home languages and negotiate different paces and senses of time.

Your Turn

Aligning your daily routines with your philosophy and values is an ongoing process. To assess where you are in this work, spend some time analyzing your daily schedule. Jot down the daily schedule you imagine working best for you and the children, from the beginning to the end of their time with you, and indicate approximate time frames. Then assign one of three colors for each of the following categories and use them to color code your schedule:

1st color: Teacher chooses and directs what happens.

2nd color: Children and teachers negotiate the focus of what happens.

3rd color: Children choose and participate in self-directed activities.

Now, look at your color-coded schedule and add up the number of minutes devoted to each color and the kind of time planned for the children.

- Is the schedule balanced, or is it dominated by one kind of time?
- Count up the amount of time children spend in planned transitions on your schedule. What portion of the whole schedule do transition times consume?
- What chores and tasks in your room could children be invited to take more ownership over?
- What ideas do you have for new routines that help make your daily life with children compatible with your values?

PRINCIPLE   **Use Children's Ideas
to Pursue Investigations**

As teachers begin to work with the curriculum framework outlined in this book, they find many new, exciting ideas for extending children's learning. Your choice of the many possibilities to pursue will be guided by your values, your program setting, and your desire to incorporate meaningful experiences with anti-bias goals, learning domains, and standards. Consider how experiences common to children might hold potential for deeper learning and empower them to take some action based on their investigation. For instance, if the children seem fascinated by the arrival of the garbage truck each week, this could become the focus of study to undertake. The challenge with this kind of project work is to keep uncovering the children's interests and questions, rather than rushing in to teach them a bunch of information about garbage workers. Commit yourself to developing curriculum that uncovers more and more about the children's ideas, rather than shaping it around your own current knowledge and ideas. This not only demonstrates respect, but also helps children see themselves as thinkers, inventors, and theory makers.

We Have Stumps

As you read teacher Lynn's story, notice how her work to involve children in designing their new playground gives them ownership and a sense that their ideas are important and are taken seriously.

Lynn works in a large full-day child care program with a new Reggio-inspired building. As funds became available for new playground construction, the teachers began seeking a way to involve the children in its design. The initial formation of a work team or project group sprang from Lynn's reflections on a parent's passing comment about her child: "Rachel has some ideas about materials for the room." Lynn knew that Rachel had sophisticated conversation skills yet was hesitant to become involved in group endeavors. Would challenging Rachel to also think about materials for the playground strengthen her confidence to be actively vocal in group work? The next day, Lynn informally asked Rachel to find a few friends on the playground to come up with some ideas for the new design. Rachel approached two nearby girls and sure enough, her conversation and facilitation skills were evident. Here is Lynn's documentation:

Clifton School

   Rachel: "Do you have ideas for the new playground?"

   Natalia: "Stairs?"

   Rachel: "Stairs to go up? You have ideas for the climber. What do you want, Sarah?"

   Sarah: "Stumps."

   Rachel: "We have stumps."

   Natalia: "Other stumps."

   Rachel: "To go up the climber? What else? We're talking about the new playground. What do you want to add to the new playground?"

   As the children came inside, Rachel announced she wanted to tell Amy, the director, about the group's ideas, and after hearing her confident report, Lynn and Amy agreed that it was time to launch a formal project group to uncover the children's playground ideas.

Clifton School

Over a period of months, Lynn met with the project group, documented their ideas, and had the group report to the whole class. She met regularly with Amy as well, seeking threads of meaning and finding questions to guide her next steps. Lynn provided opportunities for the children to draw and represent their ideas. She introduced them to the blueprints the landscape architect had developed. She and Amy decided that the children needed to understand that a bike track was already a feature of the architect's design. As the children's drawings of their playground ideas proliferated, Lynn and Amy carefully studied them. They noticed that ideas were randomly drawn on their papers. To coach the children to better grasp the spatial relations involved, Lynn gave them each a piece of paper with a circle on it, representing the bike track, and told them the climbing structure they wanted would have to be built with the path in mind. The next time they met, she challenged them to move from individual drawings to one group drawing so they would have to make some compromises together.

Lynn projected an enlarged copy of the blueprints on the wall, asking the children to first trace the bike track. Those who had previous experience in tracing projected images taught the others how to do the drawing process.

Rachel: "You have to stand on the side so the shadow doesn't cover it."

Ellie: "We want to see what it looks like, not the people's shadows."

They traced a few other features of the architect's ideas and then put the paper on the floor to determine where to place the climbing structures they had in mind. Lynn decided it was time to go outside and walk the actual space.

Ellie: "I don't think there's enough room for all of our plans."

Rachel (walking around): "We can use that tunnel for the castle. It's going to be too small, but over there should be fine."

Many times the children would hold their arms apart when Lynn asked how big something would be. She asked them to think about where and how children would enter and exit the climber. With their ideas continuing to expand, Lynn told them they needed to choose some priorities. They decided that along with the castle, one stump cluster should go between the bike track and the classroom wall. The program gave the architect the children's ideas to include in the final design.

With a tight construction schedule looming, Amy and Lynn wondered whether it was time to bring the classroom project to a close. Would the children take up the challenge to now think about how their ideas could be built? Could they speculate about what John, their carpenter, would need to do to bring this design to life? Would this question launch a new phase of the project, uncover possible theories

Clifton School

about the construction process, and begin a potential investigation of the tools and equipment that would be needed? They would have to come up with a new provocation to test out these possibilities.

Listen to Lynn

"Each decision I made was guided by the goal of having some of the children's ideas come to fruition. I wanted them to realize that whatever structures they wanted would have to be either inside the bike track or have to go over it. Once I recognized they didn't have a clear sense of the spatial relations, I invented the circles for them to work with. Then I wondered, 'Would they be able to work with a formal blueprint? How might this challenge their ideas?' After we moved from individual to group drawings, I thought they needed to actually start putting their bodies in the space itself. They were extremely supportive of one another's ideas, but only Ellie seemed to realize not everything would fit. I'm afraid I introduced the idea of prioritizing what they wanted most, instead of gradually letting them reach that conclusion or coming up with another solution

on their own—a good lesson in slowing down and also seeking out more conversation with Amy or my coworkers. It's challenging to stay with the children's pacing of things."

Reflect

Lynn's ability to see Rachel's strengths and challenges was significant in forming the project group. At each step of the way, she reminded herself to take the children's ideas seriously, not dismiss them because the children didn't understand the spatial relationships between the bike path, their desire for a climber, and stumps that resembled a castle. Lynn actively used her documentation, not just for display but to collaboratively uncover the children's ideas with her director. Lynn realized she needed another set of eyes, ears, and perspectives on what ideas were worth pursuing. Lynn's introduction of the papers with circles, her challenge to create a group drawing, the projection of the blueprints on the wall, and the opportunity for the children to explore the space with their bodies were all strategies for scaffolding the children's learning—attempts to boost their grasp of the spatial

---

Use the Thinking Lens® Protocol

Area for Reflection: Know yourself

Lynn's reflections on her role in the children's learning leads her to some new thinking about herself as a teacher.
- What new insights have you gained from reflecting on the role you play in children's experiences and the impact you have on their learning?

Area for Reflection: Find the details of the children's competence that engage your heart and mind

Review Lynn's story and identify the competencies that are reflected in the descriptions of the children's ideas and actions.

- What delights, surprises, and challenges you about what you discover?

Area for Reflection: Seek the child's perspective

The children in Lynn's group have some flaws in their thinking about the changes they want to make to the playground.
- What is your response when you recognize that children's ideas may not prove successful?
- How does Lynn's approach deepen your thinking?

relation of the design and the social relations in their group. Finally, because she took time to reflect on her own actions, Lynn identified some fine lessons for herself.

This story illuminates some important "layers of value" for teachers questioning what projects to pursue:

- Will the work empower the children?
- How will we demonstrate that we respect their ideas?
- What are the possibilities here for our learning as teachers?

PRINCIPLE **Help Children
See Themselves as Learners**

Which of your routines shape children's dispositions to see themselves as members of a vibrant learning community? Which of your routines primarily serve your convenience and might undermine the children's eagerness to investigate and experiment? Lilian Katz (1993) suggests that dispositions, or habits of mind, are critical goals for children's learning. What changes are needed in your classroom practices if you value dispositional learning alongside the acquisition of knowledge and skills? For instance, if you want children to have what Katz calls a "robust disposition to be curious, to investigate, hypothesize, experiment, [and] conjecture," (19) you will need to make your own such dispositions visible to the children. You must let the children know that you see their desirable dispositions. Katz believes one of our primary educational goals should be to develop in children the disposition to go on learning. She says, "Any educational approach that undermines that disposition is miseducation" (20).

Engineers and Architects

As a preschool teacher, Adrienne uses daily routines that focus the children on what they are doing and learning together. After reading her story, ask yourself, "What are the goals this teacher has for the children's identity development?" Notice how she infuses her values and goals into the daily routine prescribed by the curriculum model her program uses.

A look around Adrienne's preschool setting reveals evidence of the classroom culture—little books with stories and photos of what the children do, say, and think in each area of the room. These homemade books grow out of her ongoing observations and conversations throughout the day. For instance, if you were to move in closely, you would hear a comment such as this from Adrienne as she approaches the block area where four boys are having a heated debate about the structure they are trying to build: "Oh, I see you guys are doing just what architects do, challenging one another's ideas about how to keep that building from falling. You might need to think like an engineer too. Engineers and architects work together to make sure that building structures are safe and won't fall down in earthquakes. They need to figure out how much weight the bottom supports can handle and how to balance the weight so things don't tip over. Architects try to find interesting shapes for their buildings so they look beautiful from the inside and from the outside. What engineering or architectural ideas are you trying to figure out?"

Throughout the day, Adrienne calls attention to what different children are doing: "Oh, look everyone, Marcella created this amazing shade of purple

on her painting." When she calls an end-of-the-day meeting, the children bring something they have been working on or thinking about to share with one another. A smile of recognition crosses the children's faces as they hear a familiar tune with new lyrics: "Good-bye all you painters, good-bye scientists too, good-bye you architects, we hate to see you go."

Reflect

Drawing on the HighScope Foundation's research of how children learn through play (Epstein and Hohmann 2012), Adrienne takes the HighScope notion of "plan/do/review" to a new level with her daily routines that include continually acknowledging, revisiting, storytelling, and singing about what the group members have been doing. Her goals go beyond just giving recognition to individuals. Adrienne wants her teacher talk and stories to help the children see themselves as thinkers, collaborators, inventors, friends, responsible community citizens, and contributors. As she integrates her values into the way she addresses learning domains, Adrienne uses vocabulary with the children that strengthens their understandings of possible academic pursuits for themselves. She creates documentation displays and homemade books to grow their sense of history and identity as learners. These classroom documents include examples from previous years so children recognize they are part of a larger group of investigators and inventors learning in her preschool program.

PRINCIPLE   **Coach Children to Develop Negotiation and Collaboration Skills**

Many teachers strive for conflict-free classrooms with rules about how many children can play in an area and a timer to enforce sharing of toys. But when your goals for children include developing skills for living in community and as citizens in a democracy (Johnston 2006), you will provide opportunities for negotiating conflicts, working with different perspectives, and taking responsibility for group decisions.

Teachers can find any number of resources on behavior management, but do these offer children ongoing ways to see themselves as problem solvers and competent negotiators? Children benefit greatly from routines that support them in working through conflicts in ways that reinforce values of mutual respect, empathy, and generosity. What routines give children experiences to nurture these dispositions and acquire problem-solving skills?

Spicy Work

Teachers at Hilltop Children's Center have built into their classroom culture a small-group routine they call "Spicy Work," adapted from the book *Tribes: A New Way of Learning and Being Together* (Gibbs 2000). Spicy Work takes its name from the notion of getting the right chemistry together, just as happens when you are cooking with an ingredient that alone could be an irritant but in combination with other ingredients creates something new and inviting. Notice how the teachers demonstrate that they trust the children while scaffolding their negotiation skills.

During the fall months of each school year, Ann, Sandra, and Megan talk with one another about how the children's relationships are developing and when the children might benefit from introducing their Spicy Work routine. Spicy Work groups give children a structured opportunity to learn and practice skills in communication, collaboration, and negotiated decision making. When they feel the time is right, the teachers call their whole group together to introduce the

Spicy Work idea as a new game to learn. The teachers group the children into teams of three and give them the task of making a plan together for how to spend their time. Ann, Megan, and Sandra craft Spicy Work teams with an eye on sparking new friendships. Sometimes they group three strong leaders together, hoping they'll challenge one another in useful ways; or they put together three children who are typically quiet and tend to cede their voice and power so they can experience the safety needed to take risks; or they may bring kids together across a broad age range to spark understandings across differences.

There are three rules to the Spicy Work game. The first rule is that you stick with your team; you might want to play on your own, but during Spicy Work, you stay with your group the whole time. The second rule is that all members of the team make a plan together for what to do. You have to keep taking turns telling ideas until you make a plan everyone agrees to. The third rule is that the whole team decides together when they're done.

Teachers demonstrate possible ways to move forward when the team can't agree on a plan. You can change your idea: "Let's build a spaceship instead of a house or a boat." You can put your ideas together: "Let's build a house that's also a boat." You can take turns with your ideas: "Let's build a house first; then we'll build a boat second." During the first stages of

learning Spicy Work, teachers initially coach children in how to take turns stating their ideas until they come to consensus. After each Spicy Work game, teachers bring all the children together to go over what happened and how they got through any disagreements around conflicting ideas. Using the Spicy Work routine every week or two through the winter and spring deepens relationships and enhances the children's social and communication skills.

Use the Thinking Lens® Protocol

Area for Reflection: Know yourself
- What is your reaction to conflict when it happens with your group of children?
- How does the Spicy Work routine resonate with or challenge your current thinking about conflict?

Area for Reflection: Seek the child's perspective
- How do you think your group of children currently views conflict in your classroom?
- What might their response be if you suggested they engage in the Spicy Work routine?

Area for Reflection: Consider opportunities and possibilities for action
- What changes in your values, thinking, and approaches would you need consider in order to take up the Spicy Work routine?

Reflect

The Spicy Work routine is a challenge for the children and teachers alike. Teachers have to trust in the process just as they trust children's efforts to learn to walk, speak, or ride a tricycle. This doesn't mean teachers abandon children and leave the process to chance. Instead, they carefully scaffold this learning with demonstrations and the language of negotiations. The language and structure of the Spicy Work routine gives each child the power to veto or to agree, to introduce or modify an idea. Teachers must remember that their job is to model how to negotiate when things get "real spicy" between the children, rather than jump in with a solution. A demonstration, as opposed to a rescue or adult takeover, gives children respect and an example to use in the future. Teachers can also share their own personal stories of learning to do something hard, the benefits of practice, and the rewards of making new friends.

Ann, Sandra, and Megan believe in children's abilities to work through difficulties. They honor their passionate negotiations, acknowledge the children's careful thinking, and celebrate the affectionate, warm relationships children develop as a result of using this routine. Once the children learn the Spicy Work negotiating routines, they readily bring these skills to other play experiences throughout the day.

PRINCIPLE   Incorporate the Four Anti-bias Goals into Your Classroom Culture

Children have a strong sense of fairness, and there is a great deal of unfairness in the world, both in acts of individual bias and in systemic structures that grant privilege to certain people over others. Young children instinctively seek human connections, sort and classify, and try to make sense of their place in the world. Early childhood is a prime time of life for children to develop a positive social identity and ease with human diversity, and it's never too early for parents and educators to take charge of this process. Louise Derman-Sparks and Julie Olsen Edwards (2010, 4–5) have identified four goals for anti-bias education, and teachers can develop their classroom culture, environment, and curriculum explorations with these in mind.

Goal 1: "Each child will demonstrate self-awareness, confidence, family pride, and positive social identities."

Goal 2: "Each child will express comfort and joy with human diversity; accurate language for human difference; and deep, caring human connections."

Goal 3: "Each child will increasingly recognize unfairness, have a language to describe unfairness, and understand that unfairness hurts."

Goal 4: "Each child will demonstrate empowerment and skills to act, with others or alone, against prejudice and/or discriminatory actions."

Brown Skin Twins

Bell and Luba, nearly four years old, have continued a strong friendship that began as toddlers. This school year brings some new faces and new skin colors to the playground. Bell is one of the first children to vocalize what she notices about the children's differences. She brings Luba over to one of the new children, and their teacher Sandra documents this conversation:

Bell: See, Luba, you and Mia have the same skin and hair! Is she your sister? Why did God make you have brown skin?

Luba: Because God made everyone different. Why? Do you want brown skin too?

Bell: Yeah, 'cause I like you.

Luba: And you want to be twins with me?

Bell: Yes.

Luba: Maybe when you grow up a little bit, you can change your skin and be brown like me!

(They both laugh, hug, and dance around. Later, in the bathroom, a boy with dark skin is washing his hands in front of the girls.)

Bell: Hey, Luba, look, he has brown skin, just like you.

Luba: Yeah.

Bell: I still want to be twins with you.

Epiphany Early Learning Preschool, a Chapter of Sound Child Care Solutions

Reflect

Committed to anti-bias practices, Sandra has created a classroom culture where children develop strong friendships and easily talk about what they notice. When they start comparing skin colors, she doesn't try to stop them but rather listens carefully to try to learn what understandings and theories they are working with. As Sandra witnesses their delight in wanting to be alike, lacking any indication of racial bias, she knows that most children their age begin to be curious about which parts of themselves are permanent and which will change. She is pleased that they feel safe enough to have these conversations and seeks out their families and her coworkers for any additional perspectives they may have to offer.

Use the Thinking Lens® Protocol

Area for Reflection: Know yourself
- What is your response to the children's conversation?
- What is your experience and comfort level with talking with children about any topics they might bring up, including skin color, race, and religion?
- As an early childhood professional, what values and beliefs do you have about your role in helping children understand these complex issues and guiding their development to value diversity?

Area for Reflection: Find details of children's competence
- What examples of the children's strengths and competencies do you hear in their conversation?

- What is valuable about the way the children talked about their different skin colors?

Area for Reflection: Seek children's points of view
- What was each child's perspective on their different skin colors?
- What understandings and misunderstandings do they have about these differences?
- Did you hear any unintentional bias related to skin color?
- How might the curiosity and ease with which the children talk about differences inspire your work as you navigate the best way to support their development?
- How do you think the children's desire for a relationship influences their conversation?

Dirty and Dangerous

Children gain information from the world around them through many different avenues. They see and hear stories from the news, their parents, their teachers, and other children. When given the opportunity, children reflect about issues they hear, many times coming up with solutions they believe will solve the problem.

Listen to Miss Allison

In our program, we value children's voices and their thinking. This is exemplified in our work on the Flint water crisis. This story reflects how young children advocate for strangers and their understanding of the injustice facing those families and children in Flint, Michigan. Our Flint water discussion started during rest time when I noticed Rowan writing a letter in his journal. When asked to share his writing, he said the people of Flint couldn't drink the water because it was dirty and dangerous for them and this made him angry. He symbolized his anger by writing a lot of W's in a note addressed to the governor.

Rowan's knowledge of this issue was both surprising to me and powerful; he had so much concern and passion for the unfairness surrounding this topic. I was interested to hear not only Rowan's ideas but other children's thoughts and feelings. Did they know what caused this unsafe drinking water? Did they have ideas of advocacy for the people in Flint, and if so, what were they? Michelle, my coteacher, and I felt this concern was very important to follow up on and began asking children questions at the snack table that same day.

Ms. Allison: "What happened to the water?"

Rowan: "Well, water got into the tubes and something mixed together and it got out of the tubes and people drinked it."

Ms. Allison: "Wow, something mixed together and people drank it?"

Rowan: "Yeah!"

Eleanor: "How do you know the dirty stuff mixed together?"

Rowan: "Well, um . . . it's kinda clear, like water, but it's dangerous!"

Brandon: "Dangerous?"

Rowan: "Children are drinking it and moms and dads and them get sick!"

Eleanor: "Oh . . . the water maked them sick?"

Rowan: "Yeah, like they could died!"

Farrah: "Like dead? The water makes them dead?"

Rowan: "Well, I don't know. They get sick cause the water goes through the pipes and stuff gets mixed in and it's bad!"

Farrah: "Oh!" [makes a sad face]

Ms. Allison: "Wow, that sounds serious! How do you feel?"

Rowan: "I'm mad! Cause, well, I'm mad at the governor, he's not helping them!"

Ms. Allison: "He's not helping them? Can we do something to help?"

Rowan: "Well, maybe write a letter to the governor, maybe he doesn't know all those people are drinking the bad water!"

Ms. Allison: "Yeah, maybe he doesn't know, you should write a letter to tell him!"

Rowan: "Yeah, cause if he knew about the bad water, he would call the police and the police would help those people and they would be safe, 'cause that's what police do, they keep people safe!"

I was deeply touched to hear and see the concern children had for people they had never met. This interaction made me more excited to explore their understanding of the crisis. How much did the children know? What were some of their deeper questions? Did they think a person put the lead in the water? Was it an accident or was it on purpose? How did they sort through the fact that people knew about this but didn't do anything about it? And how does this impact the children and families of our classroom? I wanted to know what the children's responses were to help solve this problem, so I continued to pose questions and encouraged the children to write letters. We continued discussions at morning messages and at our large-group time. We offered ways to express their understanding of why it was "bad

water." Some children created a representation of Flint's water by drawing the water, followed by the development of a list of materials needed to make the water. After creating their Flint water model, Rowan and Farrah shared their representations during a "serious meeting." This led to more children becoming involved in creating solutions to this problem.

One of the solutions Rowan offered was to send clean water to the preschools in Flint along with letters of sympathy. The letters included ways to make children feel better, such as stickers and drawings, along with their solutions of how to avoid using the bad water. Another solution proposed digging up and replacing old pipelines, drawn out using maps of Michigan. After some time, a member of our staff gave one of our state representatives a copy of the documentation we created. Our class was able to visit the state capitol and the children discovered their work on Flint's water crisis featured alongside our representative's other "treasures."

Rowan: "We did that, that's our Flint water!" Then he shouted, "Max! Come here, look!"

Maxwell: "What? In the Capitol's office? How did that get here? [grins and pauses] Some people need to see our Flint water because they haven't been in our classroom that much!"

Farrah: "Wait, so everybody can see it? And most of all . . . wow! [grins] I think they should leave it there for people to see!"

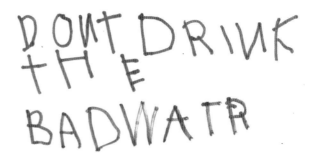

Gretchen's House Early Learning Children's Community

Rowan: "Yeah. It's a kind of bad thing, but now people will know, all the people in the capitol, 'cause they think it's all fine but it's not! I feel a little bad now, cause the people may be sick and dying! But kinda great because this is so special! [looks down and takes a deep breath] I don't know." [shakes head, continues to look down and takes another deep breath]

Throughout this experience, I was reminded that children are capable and competent and their ideas are valuable. They understand bad things occur in the world, and they are able to process through these bad things to find solutions to overcome the unfairness. Children are able to care for others outside of their own community and intimate space. This experience has given me a new understanding of how children are viewed by me and others throughout the community. I was surprised to find that others were as passionate as we were about this topic and interested in what children had to say about the issue. I realized how powerful it is to show children proof of their competency and ability to be impactful when we really listen to what they say. I continue to think of how to make the unheard voices heard.

Reflect

Allison and her team have created a classroom culture of deep respect for children, letting them know through listening, returning to conversations, and making their ideas visible in documentation that everyone's feelings and ideas are important and worth understanding. This is a foundation for incorporating the four anti-bias goals into your classroom culture.

In this story we see goals 3 and 4 in action, with children clearly able to recognize unfairness, describe how serious and hurtful it is, and search for solutions. Seeing that their ideas have been brought to the state capital building for everyone to view fills them with pride, even as their concern for those affected continues. As Rowan expresses the complexity of his mixed emotions, we see the value of creating this kind of classroom culture.

PRINCIPLE   **Develop Rituals**
That Create Memories

Planning for children's learning is no easy task. It is a complex process that requires careful attention to the many details of translating your values, philosophy, and research-based child development knowledge into a concrete pedagogy. Nonetheless, we recommend you take on this serious work with the spirit of planning a party to celebrate the lives of your favorite friends. After all, working in early child care and education, you have the opportunity to form relationships with our most precious citizens and their families. They bring you their hopes and dreams, sometimes undefined, nestled deep in their hearts. You have the opportunity to meet up with their longings, to be known, to learn, and to live fully in the world. Planning a party suggests a lively way of being together, rather than maintaining an institution with a culture of compliance. Parties are by nature very social. Sometimes they include a celebration of a special accomplishment, life transition, or event, and at other times they are designed just to bring people together to enjoy one another's company.

The human family thrives on rituals and celebrations. Rituals are different from habitual routines. Rituals may be simple or elaborate and, consciously

or not, they are created with a desire to honor or create a memory, often using symbolic gestures or objects. Children quickly come to understand the notion of a party, but the symbolic importance of a ritual may not be uncovered until they explore this memory later in their lives.

Dabs of Flour

In her family child care program, Billie doesn't use the formal "plan/do/review" process of the HighScope curriculum, but she does have a reflection time at the close of each day. As you read her story, ask yourself what children who leave your program might say many years later when they remember their time with you. What special memories are you trying to offer?

A big sign posted on Billie's refrigerator says "You Never Know When You're Making a Memory." You can see Billie's instinctive understanding of this motto in her daily routines. At the end of each day, before the children begin to leave her home, Billie gathers the group together and asks, "What do you remember about this day?" Their answers often include not just big events, but little details that reveal the importance of their relationships. For instance, one child described "watermelon juice dripping down Baby Keagan's chin and how his face looked when it hit his bare tummy." Another child remembered her friend

helping with an ice pack when she fell and scraped her knee. Sometimes the children mention something particular about Billie, such as "You put flour on our noses." And gleeful laughter tumbles from everyone when a child recalls, "You looked funny doing the chicken dance!" As parents arrive for pickup, some of these memories are shared again, offering a chance for questions and more smiles.

Billie gained a more powerful understanding of the important memories she created for the children she cares for when she went to the college graduation of Claire. She was the very first child Billie cared for in her home twenty years earlier. Billie asked Claire what she remembered most about the time spent in Billie's family child care home, and without hesitation Claire said, "You putting a dab of flour on our noses to make the recipe turn out whenever we baked cookies together." Billie was surprised because she had never thought of this as a big deal, and it certainly never appeared on any of her curriculum plans.

Reflect

Billie's story illuminates why it is important to view everyday moments as the foundation of your curriculum as well as the value of simple rituals for providing fond memories of childhood. It's tempting to view planned activities as your curriculum for children's learning. However, if you think about memory making, you can see that everything that happens is part of the curriculum and has the potential to symbolize a ritual—every interaction, song, phrase, ice pack, or dab on the nose. Grown-up Claire's words have helped Billie pay attention to how rituals become part of who we are. When they are baking, Billie still gently dabs a smidge of flour on the noses of the children she cares for in her home. It is a ritual of love that the children remind her to do if she forgets, so she knows it is important to them.

Planting Seeds

For fifteen years, the kindergarten children in Bev's class have been planting seeds from their lunchtime apples and oranges. Jeffrey, a kindergarten student, took great care in planting and tending his orange seed and sure enough, it grew quite well and became a significant feature in the classroom where it remained, even after Jeffrey moved on. Each time the plant was repotted, the story of Jeffrey's endeavor was told. Two of his younger sisters and his brother moved through the room, and they gave special attention to keeping this legacy growing. Jeffrey is nineteen now and occasionally returns to Bev's room to see how the tree is growing, liking that this part of himself has remained to help shape the room's identity.

Discovery Children's Centre

A Goodbye Book

For our friend

Natalie

From the kids and teachers

In the Garden Group

Hilltop Children's Center
April 2002

Raven: "I'll miss you, and I hope that this book that we're making you will help you remember us. I like the way you smile."

Liam: "I miss you. I like how you draw."

Drew: "Natalie, goodbye. I will miss you. Could you come visit our school sometime? I wish you have a happy time at your new school and your parents have a happy time at their work and that you have happy stay-home days. I don't like it when you go. I like being at Hilltop with you. And I love you. I hope you have happy days with your dad and mom. I like playing with you."

Marc: "Bye, Natalie."

Hilltop Children's Center

PRINCIPLE Celebrate Real Accomplishments

As you work to create long stretches of open time for children to play, negotiate relationships, and engage deeply with one another, supplement these daily experiences with specific activities and rituals that foster a group identity and sense of history for the children and their families. Remember to stop from time to time and acknowledge and celebrate the joys of living and learning together in ways that connect children to one another, their families, their culture, and their wider community. Most early childhood programs dedicate some time to recognizing birthdays, first steps, lost teeth, and special events such as an addition to or loss in the family, a trip, or a holiday celebration. This gives recognition to individual children, acknowledging that their community cares and honors important events in their lives. Once again, clarify the values you want to influence your choice of special rituals and celebrations. Plan events that will support your classroom group culture as well as appropriately acknowledge individuals.

Using Books to Mark Occasions

Ann, along with numerous other teachers, uses homemade books to mark important occasions in her classroom. What social, academic, and classroom culture goals does this activity meet?

Ann routinely has the children in her class, as well as the children's family members, create pages for homemade books, which are then used in the classroom or sometimes sent home as gifts for families. These books have words and images from the children as well as photographs, drawings, or symbolic collages, and they sometimes include the same components from families. A book might be focused on birthdays, how families celebrate winter holidays, Día de los Muertos (Day of the Dead), or heroes such as Rosa Parks, Martin Luther King Jr., and Cesar Chavez who inspire children to stand up for fairness. When a child leaves her group, Ann and her colleagues work with the other children to make a good-bye book (like the pages reproduced here from Natalie's good-bye book) with drawings, photos, and reflections on their friendships and memories. They unveil the book by inviting the departing child's family to a special good-bye celebration, usually with a snack at the end of the day.

Reflect

Rather than following the cultural trend to commercialize all occasions, Ann creates personalized ways to acknowledge significant experiences in the children's lives or their community. She also invites the children to commemorate people who are important to them. These homemade creations make the children's ideas visible and they serve as memory books for future years. They demonstrate to children how ideas can be written down and read back and explored more fully through drawings, photographs, and collages. This is an important literacy outcome for young children.

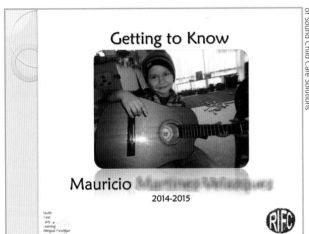

Sending Getting to Know This Child Books to Kindergarten

Homemade books can be used to introduce a child who leaves your program for another program or who goes off to kindergarten. Luz describes this process at her center in the following way.

We are committed to getting to know each child fully and when they leave us, we want to give their new teachers a snapshot of this. Our goal is to help the child's new teacher see who this child is, her special qualities, family strengths, learning process, and acquired school readiness skills. We see this as a gift to both the child and the teacher and as a tool for the child's family to use as her advocate. We try to high-light key aspects of who this child is to help draw the teacher to this child and offer a foundation to support her learning. We ask our teachers to address these questions in their Getting to Know this child books:

- *Who is this child as a member of a family/culture/community?*
- *What curiosities, interests, enjoyments does this child have?*
- *How does this child try to become a friend, and what friendships are emerging for this child?*
- *How does this child approach learning something new? Attempt to solve problems?*
- *Why are you delighted to have this child in your group?*

—Luz

Reflect

With many children to get to know, teachers can easily overlook, misjudge, or miss out on the strengths of children who arrive in their rooms. This can particularly be a problem when the teacher and child are from different cultures, when the family is still learning English, or when children are expressing their feelings or needs in ways that disrupt a classroom. As a director, Luz works hard to help her teachers form a strong relationship with each child and family, and after experiencing the value of this, the teachers want to offer what they've learned to the child's next teacher.

Crossing the Bridge

Graduation ceremonies are educational traditions, but are they developmentally appropriate for young children? Notice how Deb creates for the children a meaningful understanding of leaving preschool.

Burlington Little School

Deb has created a ritual to symbolize the transition from preschool to kindergarten by escorting each child across a garden bridge purchased from a landscaping store. During the weeks leading up to the ritual, she and her coworkers talk with the children about the meaning of this change in their lives and how it touches the hearts of their teachers and their families. The teachers describe how the bridge symbolizes this impending change. Some children are excited about becoming "big kids," while others are hesitant about leaving what is familiar. Each of these emotions is explored in conversation and with props. The children's collective sentiments are incorporated into the ritual, creating a unique celebration. For instance, one year, the children wanted to cross the bridge alone. The ritual was changed so that instead of the teachers holding the children's hands while they walked over the entire bridge, the teachers held the children's hands only until they reached the center of the bridge. At that point, the teachers dramatically threw their hands in the air with a celebratory cheer and the children finished crossing the bridge alone.

Reflect

Deb and her colleagues recognize that the end of a child's preschool years is significant for both the adults and the child. Some families are filled with pride and a sense of collective accomplishment because this is the first graduation for their children. Others are reluctant to see their babies grow up. Teachers, too, have these same emotions. They have invested themselves fully in these relationships and now the children will be leaving. When teachers are sensitive to the range of everyone's feelings and perspectives, they can translate the most common sentiments into a ceremony with authenticity instead of a meaningless school tradition.

Making Diplomas

During the weeks leading up to the last day of preschool, family provider Donna and parent co-op teacher Erin use the children's playtime to unobtrusively move around the room and ask the children what they have noticed each of the other children learning during the year. Family members are invited to add their ideas as well. The observations are recorded for each child on chart paper, rolled up as large diplomas, and read at the graduation ceremony with family members, friends, and classmates standing to cheer.

Creating a classroom culture with routines, rituals, and celebrations that communicate your values and intent for your time with children is like choreographing a dance to be performed over and over again, each rendition a bit different because of the ever-changing cast and the particulars of that time and place. When you invest the time to help everyone learn the dance and find their parts, you set the stage for great things to unfold.

Your Turn

Practice planning a ritual or celebration for a meaningful season or event with children and families in your program. As you plan, ask yourself these questions:

- What values should guide this experience?
- How can we make this ritual/celebration as inclusive as possible?
- What symbols can we include to represent the meaning of this event?
- How can we acknowledge our relationships in this ritual/celebration?

3 Enhance the Curriculum with Materials

The materials have their own inner life and their own story to tell. Yet they can be transformed only through their encounter with people. When we leave room in construction with materials, leave silence or pause or breathing room, that helps the materials themselves to express what they can express.

—Elena Giacopini

Materials in early childhood programs are the bones of the curriculum and the foundation of the teaching and learning process. They support what the program values and frame the possibilities and actions for living and learning with children. Collections, offerings, and arrangements of materials reflect your values, what you believe children deserve and are capable of, and how you see your role. As you take up the challenge of providing engaging materials for children's learning, begin by reflecting on the following questions:

- What guides your current thinking about materials and how children use them?
- Do you look forward to discovering interesting treasures to give to children?
- Do you eagerly anticipate what children might do with the materials you give to them?

If you compare collecting materials for children to the pleasure of finding a gift for a dear friend, you will likely transform the way you view your teaching job (Brosterman 2014).

When you want to give a gift to someone, you happily search for something you think she will love. You carefully select the gift and present it in a beautiful way, with colorful wrappings, ribbons, and fond words. You eagerly anticipate the surprise and delight your gift will inspire. You trust she will love it, because it came from your close relationship. In child care or teaching, the gift of materials comes from your relationship with the children. The materials represent a bit of you and who you are, as well as the tender way in which you know the children. The children accept these gifts with appreciation, bringing their own ideas and passions to them, which in turn is a gift to you from them.

To help children use the materials in ways that lead to more complex learning, you must challenge yourself to become mindful and deliberate with what materials you provide and how you provide them. In this chapter, we offer a set of principles to help you examine the elements and possibilities inherent in the materials you collect. These principles will enable you to see the "inner life" that materials can express during encounters with people, as Reggio educator Elena Giacopini suggests at the beginning of this chapter. The last half of the chapter presents an additional set of principles describing guidelines for how to organize and set up materials as invitations for focus and intention. If you carefully study the photos, examples, and stories in this chapter and take the time to try the activities mentioned here, you are certain to grow your skills, knowledge, and understandings, and experience the enhanced joy and richness materials can bring to your daily work with children.

Principles

Principles for Examining the Elements and Possibilities in Materials

- Select materials using an enhanced view of children.
- Invent new possibilities for familiar materials.
- Draw on the aesthetic qualities of materials.
- Choose materials that can be transformed.
- Offer materials that invite children to explore schemas.
- Provide real tools and quality materials.
- Supply materials to extend children's interests.
- Layer materials to offer complexity.

Principles for Arranging Materials as Invitations for Focus and Intention

- Create orderly, beautiful arrangements.
- Provide a background for the materials.
- Store diverse items in matching containers.
- Group together similar materials with different features.
- Give attention to size, scale, and levels.
- Arrange materials to suggest how they might be used.
- Reposition materials to spark a new interest.
- Display books and other visual representations with the materials.
- Offer collections of materials to highlight a learning domain.

Examining the Elements and Possibilities in Materials

Children constantly use materials to learn about the world, explore their questions, and represent their thinking. Their first job is to examine the properties and functions of materials. As children manipulate materials and learn their properties, they begin to notice something in the material that reminds them of something they already know. After making this connection to something familiar, they begin to use the materials to symbolically stand for that idea or experience. As children become more familiar with how objects can represent ideas and concepts, they begin to use materials for this purpose. Our colleague Joan Newcomb calls this "thinking in things." You can plan for and enhance this process by reflecting on your own ideas and experiences with materials. And you can work to know as much as you can about the materials you offer. The following principles and examples can serve as a useful lens for examining and selecting materials to heighten your curriculum.

PRINCIPLE   Select Materials Using an Enhanced View of Children

The educators from the schools of Reggio Emilia have advanced the professional conversation about how teachers' image of children dramatically affects the kinds of materials they offer and how they expect children to use them. In other words, your image of children limits or enhances their experiences and abilities. Consider the typical materials available for infants and toddlers. Most of them are made with bright, primary-colored, hard plastic surfaces and commercial cartoonlike figures designed to capture

Earlwood Children's Centre

Sandbox Gifts

Examine the collection of materials offered in the sandbox in the photo. The staff of this program took the time to collect and present materials in this way because they believe children deserve experiences that invite their fascination and sense of adventure. They also believe the children in their group will be capable of learning to use the materials with skill and care. As a result of these beliefs, the teachers make a commitment to find multifaceted materials, carefully arrange them, and then guide the children in their explorations.

children's attention. They usually have a cause and effect component for the child to stumble upon or be shown—a button or knob that rings a bell, whistles, beeps, or lights up when you push it. Once the child figures out the simple ways for using the toy, there is little else to engage with.

What do these materials say about the image of these young children? Inherent in these toys is the view that babies have limited capabilities or inner resources, so they require attention-grabbing, over-stimulating external experiences in order to stay interested in something. These materials have a narrow focus on health and safety, and a mistaken view that these children can't do much. Such materials do little to engage a child's lively mind or extraordinary ability for sensory exploration of textures, temperatures, motion, and sound. They don't tap into children's deep desire to learn and hone their skills and aptitudes, nor do they capture their attention for making long-term explorations.

If you were to examine what children are offered across different cultures, you'd learn that children acquire whatever the adults value and believe the children are capable of, need to know, and deserve (Small 1999). This is a powerful reminder as you consider your own view of children when providing and using materials with them. Reflect on your own attitudes and approaches as you study the following examples of teachers who offer materials based on their enhanced view of children.

Martin Luther King Jr. Day Home Center

The children in this room regularly climb on the chairs, tables, and anything else they can find to get up higher. The program budget is on hold, and the teacher has been told she'll need to wait to buy a piece of equipment for indoor large-motor play. In the meantime, she wants to offer the children a challenging but safe opportunity for climbing. She used some sturdy block shelves as the base for this mirror bridge. Sitting close to the children as they climb, she sees the determination and feeling of competence they gain as they make their way across the bridge. The teacher looks forward to helping the children negotiate the new challenge that emerges as they head toward each other in the middle of the bridge.

Burlington Little School

The variety of glass containers these boys are using offers them rich experiences for their sensory investigation, including exploring volume through the height, width, and transparency of the containers. The fact that the containers are glass instills a greater sense of responsibility as they play.

Your Turn

What is your reaction to the two photos on the left? How do your values and your view of children contribute to your response?

Now, consider how your view of children is influencing the materials you offer. Make a list of five materials that you regularly provide to children. What values and images of children do these materials suggest?

PRINCIPLE   Invent New Possibilities for Familiar Materials

Do you see yourself as an inventor and explorer side by side with the children as you plan and interact with them around materials? If not, you might start by looking at the typical materials associated with good early childhood programs—blocks, sensory tables, puzzles, painting easels, and clothes and accessories used for dramatic play.

Early childhood educators are indebted to the pioneering work of researchers and practitioners such as Friedrich Froebel, Rudolf Steiner, Maria Montessori, Caroline Pratt, and the educators from the schools of Reggio Emilia. Based on their deep interest in and observations of children and their fascination with theories about children's development and learning, they invented learning materials that today are often taken for granted and used without much thought. When you take the time to examine more closely why these materials are used throughout early childhood programs, you discover the obvious: young children are drawn to these materials because they offer multiple possibilities for pursuing different learning domains in an active, open-ended way.

Recent brain research reinforces the notion that open-ended materials with many ways to explore them are just right for the flexible, innate scientific brains of young children (Gopnik 2009). As you reconsider these familiar materials and study the vigorous thinking of the above-named inventors and researchers, you might discover for yourself the deeper fascination and insight that informed their work. As you look more closely at the possibilities, you will be able to highlight the attributes of familiar materials by offering them in different combinations or within a special setting. You can closely observe the children's use of these materials and work to expand the potential they hold for deeper meaning, joy, and complexity. Study the following examples for using typical materials in new ways.

These popular building toys are placed on a mirror in front of a sunny window, taking advantage of the translucent blocks. The addition of books related to color and other objects for investigating colors extends possibilities for further study and deeper understandings.

A thoughtful teacher carefully chooses puzzles with more than one way to use them. This particular puzzle can be put together in its frame or used to create a design using the elements of color and shape. How might further learning occur as a result of using the puzzle with the mirrors on the shelf and wall?

Observe the out-of-ordinary materials offered in this dramatic play area. Along with some traditional materials for dress-up and tea parties, there are also keys, stones, and various other loose parts. What guesses do you have about how children will use these props in their dramatic play?

Evergreen Community School

Block building in this room has many layers of complexity and, literally, multiple levels for investigation. Notice the different surfaces, heights, and sizes of the platforms for building. The clothesline, pulley system, and spotlights invite creative endeavors in engineering and design. How have these typical building blocks been enhanced by the teacher's invention?

Clifton School

The infants in this program will be surrounded by sounds, textures, and softness as they make their way into this unique structure designed for their exploration and learning. How did the inventor of this musical landscape take into account the children's abilities and interests in order to expand their exploration of sound?

Your Turn

- Choose a typical material in your room and observe how the children use it. Make a list of the many different ways the children use the material.
- Drawing on the children's current use of the material, brainstorm other ways this material might be used or added to.
- Try something from your list, observing what happens with the children as a result.

Martin Luther King Jr. Day Home Center

Wondrous Water

This water fountain is in the entry area of a child care program where children and families wash their hands upon arrival. The glimmering golden basin is irresistible to the children, as it is just their height and they can easily turn the water on and off all by themselves. If you look closely at the water on the child's hand and on the basin, you can see the beauty and wonder of this magical substance called "water" as it drips, splashes, and reflects the light and color around it. The expression on the child's face signifying his passion for this experience is infectious.

PRINCIPLE   Draw on the Aesthetic Qualities of Materials

All of us collect fortunes when we are children—a fortune of colors, of light and darkness, of movements, of tensions. Some of us have the fantastic chance to go back to our fortune when we grow up. Most of us don't have that chance—that is the tragedy. —**Ingmar Bergman**

Human beings, and children in particular, are drawn to the sensory and aesthetic properties of materials. Ingmar Bergman, the Swedish film director known for rich and unusual visual imagery in his films, reminds us in the quotation above that aesthetic elements are fortunes that heighten our pleasure and interest in the world. Young children continually notice these elements and offer you the "fantastic chance" to revisit them in your daily work lives.

Aesthetic is from the Greek word meaning "a perceiver" or "sensitive" and is a branch of philosophy dealing with the nature of beauty. The word *aesthetic* can be used as a noun meaning "that which appeals to the senses." The early childhood profession has a long history of providing sand, water, fingerpaint, and other materials that attract children because they excite and soothe the senses. Yet the notion of aesthetics can go far beyond these typical approaches. Cultivating an aesthetic sense enhances the ability to see, explore, appreciate, and find joy in the beauty of the world. Aesthetic beauty can be found in the shapes, forms, lines, patterns, textures, light, colors, shadows, and reflective aspects of the things around you. It is part of the natural world and also visible in most human endeavors, including art, architecture, many areas of design, and even cooking. Experiences within the aesthetic realm can evoke feelings of wonder, curiosity, surprise, humor, awe, inspiration, and a sense of peace and tranquility.

Rather than just relying on naturally occurring aesthetic experiences, imagine how you could boost children's instinctive tendency to notice aesthetic elements by paying more attention to them in your program. You can add liveliness, calm, complexity, and beauty to your curriculum by planning for these materials as an basic aspect of your days together. You can respond to children's innate awareness of this aspect of the world by carefully selecting and arranging materials to highlight the rich aesthetic elements surrounding you. Study the following examples of teachers bringing beauty and wonder to children's learning with attention to aesthetics.

Earlwood Children's Centre

The caregiver in this infant program has planned this offering of materials with attention to many aesthetic elements. Notice the variety of textures in the fabrics, feathers, pillows, and playthings. The sheer fabric hung above the area takes advantage of the outdoors, creating dappled light and shadows. Study how the use of color invites attention as well as unites the room and creates a soothing feeling. The children are drawn to the objects, which are hung within their reach, as they shimmer and move in response to the breeze as well as the children's actions. What else do you think will attract the babies as they spend time in this space with these materials? How would you feel as a caregiver in this environment?

Martin Luther King Jr. Day Home Center

Burlington Little School

The rich color, smooth textures, and interesting shapes of the wooden fruit trays collected from a thrift store make an aesthetically pleasing invitation for the children in this program. They are drawn to the way the items look and feel, and love holding them, banging them together, carrying them around, and placing objects in the divided sections of the trays. Contrast the aesthetic elements of these materials with the primary-colored plastic toys that are usually offered to toddlers.

The teachers in this room have added materials beyond those typically used for sensory play in order to enhance the children's aesthetic development. The shiny metal tubs that range in size from small to large and the matching metal containers and scoops invite children to notice additional aesthetic details beyond their sensory investigation. The sparkly sand pellets (found in the cat litter section of stores) and the plastic swans and snowflakes evoke treasure hunts, dramas, and a sense of wonder.

Evergreen Community School

Burlington Little School

Alhambra Head Start

Sunshine School

Look closely at each of these photos and note their sensory and aesthetic qualities. What do you notice about the textures, shapes, patterns, lines, light, and colors? What feelings do these collections of materials evoke?

Your Turn

Gather your own collection of materials that draw you to their aesthetic qualities. Explore these materials side by side with a small group of children. Observe closely what you see the children notice and also what *you* notice about the textures, colors, and shapes of the materials. Afterward, make a list of the words and phrases that describe the aesthetic elements you experienced, both the concrete aspects and the feelings. Keep this list as a reference for planning and for future conversations with the children.

PRINCIPLE   Choose Materials
That Can Be Transformed

Materials that are open-ended and can be transformed have the power to call on children's internal resources, experiences, and imagination in multiple ways for multiple purposes. Children have very flexible brains, which allows them to take in more information than adults. Compared with adults, they actually see more, hear more, and experience things more deeply. Children also have an innate drive to investigate materials for their properties and possibilities. They continually use cause and effect and problem solving to keep trying new ideas and actions (Gopnik 2009). This is why children have great energy and enthusiasm for open-ended materials with interesting properties that can be used for design or construction, or made into props for a drama or pieces for a game.

Recycled materials, special collections of unusual items or unknown treasures, and items from nature all encourage creative thinking as children use them for meaningful learning. These objects also promote recycling and reusing, rather than consuming and discarding. Materials with familiar shapes or forms can be gathered to suggest some possibilities for their use. Children are likely to incorporate these into a variety of play activities. They may be used in combination with other materials for inventions or representations of ideas they are exploring.

Study this collection of open-ended materials that adults gathered for children to discover. The following photos show the different ways toddlers, preschoolers, and school-age children used these materials.

This invitation includes stuffed and toy animals, a collection of animal-patterned fabric pieces and furs, baskets of napkin rings, bones, and brushes.

◄ The toddlers immerse themselves in the piles of fur, drawn to the sensory and aesthetic qualities of the materials, including the soft yet very different textures, and the interesting colors, shapes, and patterns. Notice how the children are examining specific aspects of the materials, looking closely at their attributes and then trying out ideas. The children discover that the basket can be a hat. Looking through the basket, they can see a different view of the world and they can also use the basket for holding other materials. Can you see how you might think of their behavior as asking and answering questions, or a way to try out their theories? "What does this look like, feel like, move like?" "How is this like something I already know?" "What can this be?" "What can I do with this?"

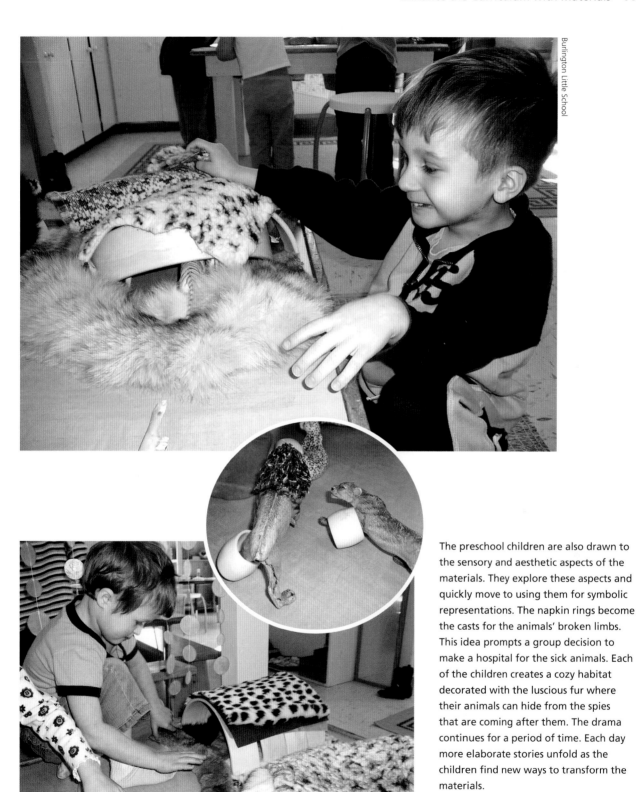

The preschool children are also drawn to the sensory and aesthetic aspects of the materials. They explore these aspects and quickly move to using them for symbolic representations. The napkin rings become the casts for the animals' broken limbs. This idea prompts a group decision to make a hospital for the sick animals. Each of the children creates a cozy habitat decorated with the luscious fur where their animals can hide from the spies that are coming after them. The drama continues for a period of time. Each day more elaborate stories unfold as the children find new ways to transform the materials.

Burlington Little School

◄ The abundant fur pieces evoke tenderness in these school-age children as they wrap the animals in the softness, creating comforting, cozy beds. Their designs and constructions grow, and the materials become a vacation resort, complete with swimming pools and a roller coaster. The architecture of the roller coaster is a serious endeavor, as the children work to connect the fur pieces together, keeping at it until they are successful at getting the basket of bears to zoom down and around the fur track.

Lining up the carpet squares

Building with spools and cove molding

Stacking hat boxes

Designing with triangle quilt rulers

Use the Thinking Lens® Protocol

Area for Reflection: Find the details of the children's competence that engage your heart and mind.

- Study the photos and descriptions of the ways that children of the different ages used the materials. What skills, competencies, and understandings do you see reflected in their work? What intrigues you about the differences and similarities?

Area for Reflection: Examine the physical/social emotional environment

- What do you notice about the properties and combinations of materials? What about the materials invite sensory investigation, building and construction, and drama? How do you think the nature of the materials affected the way the children played with them?

Your Turn

Now gather your own collection of open-ended materials and interact with them yourself, using these questions to guide your exploration:

- What do the materials look, feel, sound, and smell like?
- How do they move?
- What do they remind you of?
- How could you use them to build or construct something?
- How could they become a prop in a drama?
- How could you use them to play a game?

Next, offer these same materials to a group of children and observe closely how they use them. Notice how the children use the materials in similar and different ways than you did.

PRINCIPLE Offer Materials That Invite Children to Explore Schemas

When you observe the details of children's investigations with open-ended materials, you will see evidence of their active brains at work exploring schemas. A schema, as identified by child psychologist Jean Piaget, is a line of thought that is demonstrated by repeated actions and patterns in children's play. These repeated actions suggest that this play is a reflection of children's growing understandings of abstract ideas, patterns, and concepts (Van Wijk 2008). Here are some of the schemas Piaget identified (1969):

- **Transporting**: Picks things up, move things, puts down, or dumps
- **Transforming**: Uses materials to explore changes in shape, color, consistency, and so on
- **Trajectory**: Explores the horizontal, vertical, and diagonal movement of things and oneself; makes objects fly through the air, moves own body in these ways
- **Rotation and circulation**: Experiments with items that turn, such as wheels and balls; explores curved lines and circles
- **Enclosing and enveloping**: Surrounds objects with other things; uses self to get inside a defined area like blocks or boxes; hides, covers, or wraps self and other things
- **Connecting**: Joins things together and ties things up
- **Disconnecting**: Takes things apart and scatters pieces and parts (Van Wijk 2008)

When you watch children's play with schema theory in mind, you begin to see these patterns in almost everything children do. You realize their actions, which adults often find annoying and immediately stop, have significance that you didn't realize. For example, because you understand that throwing things to make them move and fly is the trajectory schema, you can find ways to support the children's work with the concept, rather than stop them. It also becomes less frustrating when you understand that dumping things out of containers or off the shelves over and over again is a schema children are using to grow new brain connections and understandings.

When children use their ever-growing brains to explore, they are learning unlimited possibilities for how the world can be. They consider and act on countless unconventional ideas that can alarm or delight us. This is the gift young children bring to the world and to us. The following photos of materials reflect opportunities for exploring schemas. Most of the collections have several possibilities for different kinds of schema play. Study the photos and identify the schema play available in each invitation.

Peterborough Centre

Epiphany Early Learning Preschool, a chapter of Sound Child Care Solutions

Your Turn

Observe how children play with the typical materials you have throughout your classroom. Where do you notice them using schema play? What particular areas and materials invite the most schema play? What can you add to your environment to encourage more schema play?

PRINCIPLE   Provide Real Tools and Quality Materials

Many of us were lucky enough to have relationships during our childhood with people who had passions and skills they were willing to share with us. Perhaps it was an aunt who taught us to use her sewing machine or the next-door neighbor who was an ace car mechanic, willing to coach us in using the shiny tools hanging in the garage. We likely have fond memories of these experiences because someone respected our capabilities and believed we could learn to use real objects from the grown-up world. When children are provided opportunities to use real tools and materials of high quality, they feel respected and taken seriously. When they are trusted and shown how to use and care for these tools and materials, children live up to the responsibility of using them and, as a result, bring more focus and intention to their work. Additionally, using real tools and high-quality materials helps children to produce more meaningful and beautiful work. The following examples show how powerful these materials can be for children's self-esteem and learning.

In these photos, four-year-old Priya is offered a collection of professional artists' tools, including a variety of brushes, ink pens, colored ink, and high-quality art paper. Notice her attention to detail and the purpose she brings to her work. As she explores the tools and the ways she can use them to achieve different effects, the result is a series of gorgeous paintings. Contrast this to the typical painting materials usually offered to preschool children—thick paints, thick brushes, and paper that causes the paint to run or drip—materials that don't lend themselves to the careful work Priya is engaged in here.

Children in this group earnestly took up the challenge of learning to use hot glue guns for their recycled sculpture projects. The teacher took advantage of the children's strong desire to use the real, somewhat risky tool by inviting them to think through their work more carefully. She began the project by instructing the children to use the tool safely to avoid burning themselves. She suggested they look through the materials and think about how they might use them in their sculptures. When they had gathered the materials, she challenged the children to draw a picture of what they wanted to build and then use the drawing as their plan for building the sculpture. The children eagerly took up her suggestions and increased their skills and competence with these challenging tasks.

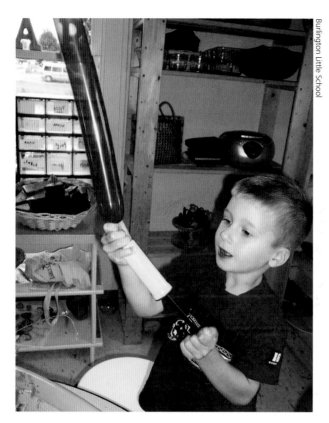

The children approached the work involved with using these air pumps seriously because these tools required skills and knowledge to get them to work successfully. They shared strategies they discovered for using the air pumps to fill the balloons with as much air as possible.

Tinkering Team

Teacher Joyce has been working with a group of children engaged in a long-term investigation of using real tools to take apart appliances and electronics. As you read Joyce's story, notice how seriously the children approach this work and the attention to safety they show when learning to use the tools.

This morning's team meeting started with a safety talk from four-year-old Ira. Ira wanted the other kids to know that since the phone was a new thing to work on, there was something they needed to know first. He explained to the kids that they may come across some sharp parts in this phone and if they do, they should be very careful not to get poked or hurt themselves. The kids had noticed two new things on the table and were very anxious to get started tinkering.

I, too, was ready to get started but first things first . . . we got new goggles today! After we put them on, Alex says, "Joyce, take our picture," so that's what I did. Once the goggles were on, the work began. This part is always exciting for me to see, as the kids immediately start to grab tools and then choose which thing they're going to work on.

Today we have a clock and a phone that the kids are anxious to get their hands on. Alex is very interested in the clock, and Ira expresses his interest in the phone. After a minute or so of choosing items to work on, the kids get busy and silence takes over the room. All I can hear is the cling-clang sounds of the tools and little excited sighs and oohs!

After a few minutes . . .

Ira: "I found it! It's the electric cable chamber! This is where they hold all the electric stuff. Look, look. Static electricity! It's sticking." (He's holding the screwdriver up with a tiny nail sticking to the end of it.)

Michael: "Ira, it's static electricity. Okay."

ZuZu: "I did three already! Now seven!"

Michael: "I think I found an opening in here; now I can pop this part out."

Alex: "This part is so hard to get off."

I walk over and show her a way she could try and pop the cover off the clock. She tries it a couple times and then has success. Yay Alex!

Alex: "It's off! Look."

ZuZu: "What about these parts? Maybe tweezers or wire cutters."

The kids are working so well side by side, and I notice how this week the calls for help are minimal. I like what I see here today. I am seeing a more confident group of kids who have learned their way around using certain tools that were unfamiliar to them a few weeks ago. They have also learned to use tools in multiple ways. They use the hammer and flat-head screwdriver to pry things apart and the wire cutters to loosen bolts. This is a creative bunch of kids, always thinking of new ways to use tools and also ways to use the parts that they've dismantled. As I listen to the talk today, I hear a few kids talk about certain cool pieces that they'd like to save to make a robot. I let the kids know that I hear them talking and I offer to find a special box to keep all the parts that they'd like to save for the robot making. The children all show so much independence, doing their own problem solving and helping each other out when needed. —Joyce

Use the Thinking Lens® Protocol

Area for Reflection: Know yourself

Recall a person in your life who trusted and mentored you to do real work using real tools. How did your experiences with this person affect you? What is you comfort level in offering children real tools that may be somewhat challenging or risky for them to use?

Area for Reflection: Find the details of the children's competence that engage your heart and mind

Think about times when you have been surprised by children's ability to accomplish something you didn't think they could do. What did you notice about their skills and competency? What role did you play to help them succeed? How did they feel about their accomplishments?

Your Turn

Reflect on the tools and materials that you offer children, including art, drawing, and writing materials; paints, paintbrushes, pens, pencils, and paper; and tools for cleanup and maintenance.

- How many of these tools and materials are made specifically for children?
- How many are real tools made of high-quality materials?
- What changes can you make to offer children tools and materials that will enhance their work?

PRINCIPLE   Supply Materials to Extend Children's Interests

Your observations of children's interests, developmental themes, family life, and cultures can guide your selection of materials. When seeking new, interesting materials for children, try to remember what you know about individual children in your group as well as their collective interests and developmental themes. As adults, we may become so familiar with common materials that we limit the possibilities we see in them. Young children, on the other hand, are new to this world and still see its magic and wonder everywhere around them. They approach experiences with an open mind, unencumbered by frameworks and labels. Because they are in the

Burlington Little School

Helena and Amelie have been playing side by side pretending to care for the baby dolls in the drama area. These three-year-old girls have a shared experience of new baby brothers in their families. To honor and respond to this life change and to help them see the connection they share, their teacher asked their families to bring photos of the girls with their baby brothers. The teacher then framed the photos and put them in the drama area. She also made sure to have plenty of baby care props in the drama area that invited the girls to play together around this new experience. The teacher's invitation is accepted, as the girls spend every day together learning to be caring big sisters and deepening their relationship as they play.

process of exploring and constructing an understanding of their world, they notice the details and experiment with everything they encounter. If you take on their point of view while looking for collections to offer, your planning and the children's exploration and learning will be more joyful. Study the following examples for ideas on how to offer materials to extend children's interests.

Burlington Little School

The children in this program enthusiastically explore the vibrant colors, varying weights, and different sizes of the pumpkins and other small gourds they see growing all around the farm valley where they live. They cart the pumpkins around and use them in their dramatic play. Then they cut them open to explore the gushy insides, roast and eat the seeds, and use the meat for cooking and baking projects. With the remaining pumpkins, the teacher gives the children opportunities for developing skills with hammers and nails, preparing them for later woodworking projects. The cycle is complete as they save some seeds and put the remaining pumpkin parts into the compost bin. Months of work with the pumpkins offers multiple opportunities for the children to feel connected with their farming community.

Martin Luther King Jr. Day Home Center

Noticing that her toddlers love to take the lids off of their food containers at snacktime, dump out the food, and then spend a long time putting the lids back on, this teacher made a trip to the thrift store and found a number of coaster sets of different shapes and sizes in matching boxes with lids. She arranged them as an invitation to challenge the children to match the coasters to their boxes and fit the lids on top. The variety of beautiful textures, colors, and shapes added to their investigation and enjoyment.

Your Turn

Observe a child or group of children using materials in your room. As you notice the details of what they say and do, can you see connections to what you know about them, their family life, and their stage of development? Decide what other materials you might offer them to extend an interest. Observe what they do with the items you offer.

Fairy Dramas

Sage came to school with a book about fairies that included illustrations of the fairies' beautiful homes in the natural world. Her teacher, observing that many children gathered with Sage during the week to look at the book, decided to offer some materials to extend their interest. The children eagerly took up the invitation to work with the appealing materials, using the craft sticks, beads, and artificial flowers to design and create their own fairy people, and a reference book to inspire their work. When the children completed the characters and their habitat, their work expanded as they began a drama using their inventions as props in the story. At the end of the afternoon, when they seemed to be done with their building and drama, their teacher encouraged the children to draw pictures and make a book about their fairy story so they could remember it when they came back the next day.

PRINCIPLE   Layer Materials
to Offer Complexity

To build on children's learning with materials, offer combinations of materials that lend themselves to many uses and extended investigation. When children are interested in an idea or concept, providing different materials helps them make further connections and build on their ideas. They use the materials not only to represent their current thinking but also to increase their skills and go deeper in exploring new ideas.

Jean Piaget named the different kinds of play he observed children use as a part of their learning (Mooney 2013). Drawing on his observations, you can offer combinations of materials for sensory exploration, functional play, construction, drama, and games. Providing a sensory base such as sand or playdough and then gradually adding materials related to the different kinds of play increases the length of time and complexity of children's play. Sensory materials keep children reinvesting in the invitation—seeing more possibilities for the other objects, such as building or designing something, creating a drama, or making up a game. Below is a series of examples of how family providers and teachers created an initial invitation using playdough as a sensory base and then added layers of possibilities over time. What ideas does this give you for using materials to expand the children's complexity of work with playdough and other favorite materials?

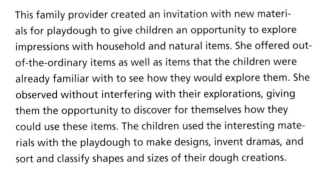

This family provider created an invitation with new materials for playdough to give children an opportunity to explore impressions with household and natural items. She offered out-of-the-ordinary items as well as items that the children were already familiar with to see how they would explore them. She observed without interfering with their explorations, giving them the opportunity to discover for themselves how they could use these items. The children used the interesting materials with the playdough to make designs, invent dramas, and sort and classify shapes and sizes of their dough creations.

Mother's Quality Family Child Care

▶ Four-year-old Beia eagerly accepted teacher Kelly's invitation to use new and interesting materials with the playdough. She started out with shells, pressing them into the playdough to make indentations and then creating a gorgeous shells sculpture. When she noticed the screws, she had a new plan. "I am making your birthday cake," she told Kelly. There weren't quite enough screws on the tray for Beia to finish going around the cake, so Kelly asked her how many more screws she thought she would need. Carefully, Beia touched several points around the remaining dough, counting.

"Five," she estimated.

So Kelly found some more screws, and to their surprise, five wasn't enough.

"Three more," was Beia's next guess, after eyeing the remaining space. Three did the job! After a moment or two, Beia removed the candles and put them back on the tray. Then she carefully covered up the holes that the screws had made.

A Place for You Family Child Care

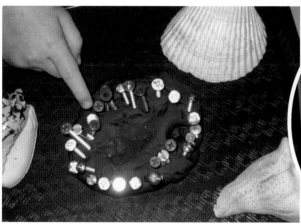

◀ This teacher has a science area located near the playdough table, and she noticed the children often brought the small plastic snakes and lizards from the science area to incorporate into their playdough work. The animals always sparked some very interesting dramatic play. The children built habitats and set up playdough communities for the creatures to live in. Since observing this play, the teacher now sets out thoughtful combinations of materials for building and designing as well as a variety of animals and people to extend the children's dramas with playdough.

Burlington Little School

"I'm Getting This Ready"

Teacher Janelle strives to artfully and creatively arrange and present materials, with the hope of inspiring further creativity from the children. Seeing materials arranged purposefully encourages the children to care for them in a more respectful manner. Emily, one of the oldest children in this mixed-age class, was inspired to start organizing invitations of her own. One morning, she spread a large scarf on the small table in the dramatic play area and arranged an assortment of crayons and markers in a beautiful basket. She then laid out a piece of paper by each chair at the table. When Janelle asked Emily what she was working on, she responded, "I'm getting this ready for the other children to use."

Arranging Materials as Invitations for Focus and Intention

If our goal is to invite children to pursue and grow their exuberant interests in the world and express their unique ideas, then just like thoughtful gift giving, we must pay careful attention to not only *what* materials we offer, but *how* we offer them. What's the curricular equivalent of beautifully wrapping a present for a friend? Children are very observant and alert to the way in which materials are made available to them. They look for cues from the adults and the environment to guide their actions in how to use things and how to care for them. If materials are carefully chosen and beautifully presented, children are more likely to respond by using them thoughtfully and caring for them. Children's ideas can grow if they are given enough materials and the space and time to use them.

The collections of materials you put together suggest possibilities. Where you place materials and how you arrange them communicates in a powerful way the values and intentions you have in mind. For example, offering materials with broken and missing pieces on crowded, cluttered shelves doesn't show respect for children's abilities nor does it invite them to focus on the potential for exploration and learning. This type of presentation also speaks loudly to children about the lack of care and attention to the things in the room. In contrast, thoughtfully collecting materials for their possibilities for investigation and action, and beautifully arranging them to draw attention to their attributes and relationships invites children to focus on what is available and to dive into engaging work. Drawing on ideas of other thinkers (see Mooney 2013 for examples), here are some principles and examples to consider when collecting, arranging, and offering materials.

PRINCIPLE   Create Orderly, Beautiful Arrangements

Picture a farmer's market or grocery store produce section with a stunning arrangement of fruits and vegetables. The produce is probably organized by variety, texture, and color. The grocer or farmer has purposefully fashioned different heights and levels for each of the items to create a sense of balance, order, and beauty so you are drawn to and can clearly see what is available.

These same elements of presentation can enhance children's attention to and use of materials. Like adults, children are drawn to orderly, beautiful arrangements of materials. Paying careful attention to the way you arrange materials communicates respect for the children and the importance of the activities you offer. When items are thoughtfully arranged, children can see more clearly the characteristics of the materials and the possibilities for their use. They also take extra care as they play, believing these must be special offerings because of the striking way they have been displayed. Study the following examples to inspire your own arrangements of materials.

This gorgeous presentation of materials beckons children with the magic and wonder it holds. The calming shades of blue and careful arrangement of the larger items on a larger mirror and the smaller stones on the smaller mirrors draws the children in, helping them to focus and inspiring their exploration and creativity.

This invitation uses natural colored mats and wooden bowls to contrast with the beauty of the greenery that the children are using for this work. The lovely wooden bowls highlight the color and shape of the materials, encouraging closer investigation. The orderly display of the materials also encourages children's attention to the task at hand.

PRINCIPLE   Provide a Background for the Materials

Including a background of a tray, cloth, or frame provides a figure-ground focus and a clear palette for children's use of materials. A background both draws your eye to focus on what materials are available and creates a container for the exploration process.

This collection of materials is an invitation to explore herbs and spices. Look closely at how each tray, plate, and basket defines the work area and highlights the work to be done. This presentation sends a message to the children that the herbs and spices share common elements and also have individual aspects to notice and ways to be explored.

The individual black mixing trays communicate that each child has a space for working alone to mix the colored water and cornstarch. The large white tray defines the space for the messy work of the whole group working together. Do you see how each background offers a clean but different focus for the task at hand?

PRINCIPLE   Store Diverse Items in Matching Containers

When you want to have a wide array of materials available for children, you are faced with the challenge of avoiding clutter and helping the children focus on what's available. Offering diverse materials in matching containers or baskets is one way to ensure that the children can clearly see the individual items and their unique attributes. Compare this to a jumble of items in one basket or to many different kinds of containers holding with many different items. Beyond the orderly, attractive appearance, an arrangement of diverse materials in similar containers allows the children to see what is available for their use and communicates respect for the materials used in the room.

Burlington Little School

With diverse items in each of these baskets, the shelf does not look cluttered because the baskets are the same color and size. The matching baskets create a context for each item and a clear view of the contents. Think of how differently this display would look if the materials were stored in containers made of different materials, colors, and sizes.

Tots Corner

Although this wooden planter box holds a number of different materials, each collection is easy to identify. The container itself, as well as the photos labeling the contents, creates a framework for seeing what's inside.

PRINCIPLE   Group Together
Similar Materials with Different Features

Offering a collection of materials with similar aspects (such as their color or what they are made of) but also different attributes (such as their size or texture) helps children notice and explore the differences more thoroughly than if they are offered a jumble of materials with nothing in common. Study the examples in the photos to see this in action.

Martin Luther King Jr. Day Home Center

▶ This observant teacher knows the babies in her room are drawn to objects that feel substantial to touch and have varying elements to explore with their eyes, ears, hands, and bodies. When she discovered a collection of wooden massage tools at a thrift store, she knew she had found treasures for her babies. These materials all have common elements, such as the lovely natural wood color and texture to explore. But they each have different shapes, sizes, bumps, and grooves. The babies find this collection intriguing to look at, touch, and manipulate in the process of comparing how the objects are the same and different. They find them interesting to hold, carry, drop, and make sounds with. The wheels and other moving parts fascinate the children as they turn and spin them.

Burlington Little School

◀ This collection of similarly colored containers in the sensory table is inviting and offers a deeper learning experience because all of the items have a similar transparent blue color and a common function as containers for dumping and filling the lavender-scented rice. But the materials also allow children to explore their different sizes, shapes, and textures. Compare this to the more typical disarray and overstimulation of a sensory table overflowing with an untidy heap of mismatched containers and other objects hiding the substance inside.

PRINCIPLE   Give Attention to Size, Scale, and Levels

When you change the scale of similar materials and offer them on different surfaces with different levels, children have more opportunities to use the materials in new ways. Providing materials that range in size from small to large, or offering them on a platform, the floor, or the top of a shelf, gives children new perspectives where they are confronted with different challenges. Notice the possibilities in the following examples.

These children spent a week exploring color mixing and pouring water with measuring cups and scoops. The teacher wanted to extend their investigations by offering a larger scale for mixing, dumping, and filling, so she provided these larger tubs. The children can draw on their previous experiences with the small materials and take their exploration to another level.

The teachers in this room offer multiple opportunities for building and construction on different platforms and various levels. The children can work directly on the floor, on the raised platform, or on the large trunk. Do you see how working on these different surfaces and heights might change and expand their play?

PRINCIPLE   Arrange Materials to Suggest How They Might Be Used

When you carefully select materials, you have ideas about how the children might engage with them. To help children notice the possibilities you see in the materials, create a suggestion as a part of the setup. This helps children create initial ideas about how to get started with the materials and may also encourage them to do something they might not have considered on their own. It's gratifying when children do what you imagined with materials. At the same time, be sure to stay open to the surprises they come up with that you never dreamed of.

Look closely at the collection of materials in this photo. The combination of materials and the way they are arranged suggest several different ways to explore them. The children are invited to look closely with the magnifying glass or to pick up the grapes with the tweezers and transfer them into the small bowls. What other guesses do you have about what children might do with this activity? What other suggestions could you offer by arranging the materials in different ways?

In the first photo, the teacher has assembled a beginning construction on the tray to attract the children's focus and attention. In the second photo, the teacher has hinted at a way to use the pattern blocks. These small suggestions spark the children's thinking and communicate that it's okay to dive in and get started.

▶ These items have been thoughtfully placed in the sandbox; their placement suggests the exciting possibilities for their use, a suggestion that will inspire the children's play. Examine this photo from a child's point of view. What does the setup suggest the children do?

PRINCIPLE   **Reposition Materials to Spark a New Interest**

Moving materials to a different location in the room or even outdoors can stimulate a new interest and a new way to use them. Materials that have been on a shelf for a long time may gain a new appeal when moved to a tray, a table, or the floor. Putting materials next to items they have never been used with helps children combine them in different ways. The following examples show this at work.

This teacher knew that magnets would stick to the metal pipes of the classroom loft, so she put a basket of magnetic tubes and balls up there for the children to discover. As you can see in the photo, the children soon found many new and interesting ways to explore these materials.

Moving materials outdoors invites children to consider different uses and extends outdoor learning. The teachers from this program use the outdoor learning spaces in the same way they use the indoor space, planning for small- and large-group areas and manipulative and dramatic play. What difference do you think this will make in how the children use these materials?

PRINCIPLE Display Books and Other Visual Representations with the Materials

Adding visual and symbolic representations to an arrangement of materials gives children another resource for investigation and learning as they make connections between the real objects and the photos, drawings, or stories about them.

Burlington Little School

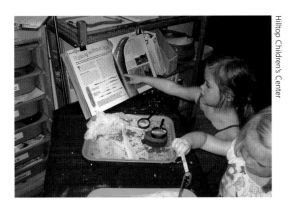

Hilltop Children's Center

This teacher was inspired by the work of artist Andy Goldsworthy, so she provided rocks and ice and an art book with his photos. Notice how the children used the book as a resource to create their own ice and rock sculpture.

◄ Along with magnifying glasses and real worms in petri dishes, this teacher provided books about worms. As you can see in the photo, the images in the book were pertinent to the children's exploration.

PRINCIPLE Offer Collections of Materials to Highlight a Learning Domain

Although learning is embedded in all the collections of materials described here, when you want to highlight a particular learning domain or concept, you can create invitations with that focus. As with materials provided for open-ended exploration, children often discover features, principles, and concepts or practice skills that are part of your desired learning outcomes.

Earlwood Children's Centre

Earlwood Children's Centre

The teachers in this program put forward special invitations throughout the environment for the children to explore academic concepts through self-directed lessons. The photo shows one they provided around letter recognition and use. Can you think of other ideas for using self-directed materials to increase academic skills?

These teachers wanted to provide more science learning for the children in their group and believed that children would be intrigued by studying frogs. They designed and offered this invitation and then got out their pens and clipboards to record what the children did with the materials and said about frogs. This gave them insight into where to go next with their explorations around science.

Your Turn

Each of the photos on this page reflects one or more of the principles for creating invitations for focus and intention. Review the principles below and study the photos to see if you can see the principles at work.

- Provide a background for the materials.
- Store diverse items in matching containers.
- Group together similar materials with different features.
- Give attention to size, scale, and levels.
- Arrange materials to suggest how they might be used.
- Reposition materials to spark a new interest.
- Display books and other visual representations with the materials.
- Offer collections of materials to highlight a learning domain.

Once you have studied these principles, practice offering invitations with playdough and props to four or five children. Provide a good quantity of freshly made playdough. The playdough should be white or a deep color. Supply an attractive, solid color mat or tray for each child to work on. Display a small collection of materials from each of the following lists, in attractive baskets, trays, or bowls.

Earlwood Children's Centre

Burlington Little School

Burlington Little School

St. Charles Child Development Center

Earlwood Children's Centre

Tools for Making Imprints

shells with textures

massage tools that move

other interesting objects with designs for imprinting using different sizes, shapes, or textures

Materials for Designing

shells of different sizes, similar and different kinds

small stones and rocks of different sizes, similar and different kinds

small tiles of different and similar colors and shapes (free samples are often available at tile departments of home improvement stores or specialty home decorating stores)

small beads and beach glass

incense sticks and herbs to add fragrance (such as lavender, rosemary, or mint)

Materials for Construction

craft sticks

sample paint chips (free samples are available at paint departments of home improvement stores or paint stores)

cubes (from early childhood catalogs)

sushi mats cut into smaller pieces

Props for Drama

small plastic animals

herbs and flowers, real and artificial

small tea sets and dishes

small wheeled vehicles

Set up the invitation on a table in an attractive way, arranging the trays or mats in front of each chair, with a large piece of playdough at each place. Put the baskets or trays with the tools and other props in the center of the table where everyone can reach them.

Offer the invitation each day, for a least a few weeks, adding props over time that respond to the children's interests.

Document what the children do with the materials by taking photos and writing down descriptions. Put these observations in a binder and add this to the table alongside the invitation. Use the following questions to reflect on what you are observing:

- What did you see? Be as specific as you can.
- What do the children seem drawn to or curious about?
- What is their interest in the materials?
- How did the way you displayed the materials inspire their play?
- What are you curious about? Are the children doing what you expected, or is something else happening? Why might their actions be the same or different from what you expected?
- Are there any assumptions, themes, or theories the children seem to be centering their exploration around?

As you reflect on your experiences with this activity, consider how it might affect your ongoing offering of materials to children, not only with playdough, but other invitations that might incorporate the principles discussed in this chapter. Materials that are layered with multiple possibilities allow you to stand back, observe, and have more to bring to your conversations with the children's families and your coworkers, as well as more insight into what next steps you might want to plan. As you build your curriculum around engaging materials, you will then be ready to explore other ways to expand your teaching repertoire, which is the focus of the remaining chapters.

4 Expand Opportunities for Children to Use Their Active Bodies

If children are not given enough natural movement play experiences, they are more likely to be clumsy, have difficulty paying attention and trouble controlling their emotions, utilize poor problem-solving methods, and demonstrate difficulties with social interactions. We are consistently seeing sensory motor and cognitive issues pop up in later years because of inadequate opportunities to play and move in the early years.
—Angela J. Hanscom

The early childhood profession has always understood the importance of active play experiences—that children need regular opportunities to move their bodies through both indoor and outdoor play. Many of us would say we know a lot about active play and believe that we provide for it. Yet this familiarity may have led to complacency as we deal with the pressure from more program requirements that are limiting children's active play throughout the day.

A number of factors have reduced the opportunities for children to be physically active in early childhood programs, including the following:

- school readiness agendas that emphasize sitting and listening to learn
- environmental rating scales that focus on requiring specific areas and materials for math, science, and literacy
- a heightened attention to safety and risk avoidance

Indoor environments are overcrowded with shelving, tables, and chairs; children have limited room to move or try out any big ideas. Teachers often work to prevent and stop children from indoor active play rather than planning for it. The average amount of time children in child care spend outdoors is often less than thirty minutes a day (Hanscom 2016), and when children are outside, playgrounds are often void of anything challenging to do. Familiar active play staples like swings and slides are being removed on behalf of safety. The statistics about children at home are no more hopeful, as they spend on average four hours a day in front of screens rather than running, jumping, and playing outdoors (Head Start Body Start National Center for Physical Development and Outdoor Play 2010).

When children actively move their bodies, more is going on than just staying healthy and getting their wiggles out. New information about the importance of active physical play for young children's development is showing up everywhere. There is growing alarm about how the lack of active play is affecting children, as the quote at the beginning of the chapter from Angela Hanscom reflects. Active play, which is a critical part of sensory motor development, actually builds neural pathways necessary for children to focus their eyes and attention, regulate their emotions, and develop the ability to plan and carry out a task. It seems that in slowing children down on behalf of helping them stay safe and learn, we are actually harming their capacity for learning now and in the future.

More Than Five Senses

The sensory motor system is the mechanism through which children take in and process information, which helps build essential neural connections in the brain. Processing sensory information is the foundation of all learning and vitally important in children's lives. Most people are familiar with five senses of the sensory motor system, yet there are actually seven. There is much to consider about how we provide critical sensory experiences throughout our environments, and you can read more about ideas for all of the senses in other chapters of this book as well as in our books *Designs for Living and Learning* and *The Art of Awareness*. In this chapter, we will focus on the movement part of the sensory motor system: the proprioceptive and vestibular senses.

Sensory Motor System

1. visual (sight)
2. auditory (hearing)
3. tactile (touch)
4. gustatory (taste)
5. olfactory (smell)
6. proprioceptive (body position)
7. vestibular (balance)

The *proprioceptive system* refers to the sensory input and feedback that tells children how their bodies are moving and where they are in space. There are tiny sensors in each of the muscles, joints, ligaments, tendons, and connective tissues. These sensors send messages to the brain that help children notice when they move, stimulating nerves and enhancing their ability to organize information. If the proprioceptive sense is not receiving or interpreting input within these muscles, joints, or other body parts, kids may become clumsy or uncoordinated and have difficulty

performing basic tasks and activities. Proprioceptive input helps children feel and see their bodies, which in turn helps them feel calm and focused (Ayres 2005).

The *vestibular sense* is a complex system located in the inner ear. It helps children negotiate gravity when running or swinging as well as during spinning movements. The vestibular system directs children to keep their balance and helps them to be safe in the environment. This system also plays a very important role in organizing which input from the other senses is and is not important, an activity that allows children to have optimal levels of focus and attention. Children who have underdeveloped vestibular systems have many problems including being clumsy, constantly tripping over things, falling, and running into walls. They generally have more physical injuries, are overly emotional, and seem unintentionally aggressive. In addition, they have difficulty sitting still and focusing (Hanscom 2016). It's clear that as early childhood educators, we have a crucial role to play in countering the problems resulting from children's lack of active play.

Informal Research

The good news is that children continually seek the movement experiences they need for building their brain pathways for learning, whether you plan for them or not. Deb gained a much deeper understanding of the importance of sensory motor play when she was working to help teachers transform their environments to invite focus, engagement, and complex play. In many classrooms, teachers were overwhelmed by the loud, big, active play happening in their small rooms that were primarily designed with learning areas to meet rating scale standards. There are no indicators on the rating scales that call for indoor active play areas, yet the children were finding many ways to meet their needs for this kind of play that proved problematic for the functioning of the classroom. Deb suggested opening up the space by removing furniture and shelving, which would allow the children to spread out and pursue big ideas and projects together. Even without creating designated spaces for active play, when the normal classroom areas were enlarged, the children's behavior changed. They were calmer and more focused, experienced less conflict, and stayed engaged for longer periods of time.

Understanding more about the proprioceptive and vestibular senses helps explain why room to spread out and move has such an impact on children. Deb studied this new information with other teachers and occupational therapists to learn more about the specific details and importance of children's sensory motor systems. They launched informal research projects, involving several groups of teachers in a variety of settings across North America. Their goal was to learn how children seek and benefit from active play. These small groups of teachers observed and documented children's activities in one another's classrooms and outdoor spaces. They focused on how, when, and where children use active play and how these experiences affect their engagement and interactions.

Most of the groups met regularly over several months to gather observations and photos. After each observation period, they spent several hours reviewing their documentation and the current body of research about active play to better understand what they saw. In all the groups, this work provided a powerful learning experience that helped the teachers connect their practices to the theory and led them to identify principles for enhancing their work with children. The principles identified here aren't necessarily direct actions for you to take, but instead offer guidance to help teachers see the importance and value of sensory motor experiences and, as a result, find more ways to allow and plan for them.

Principles

- Recognize that children continually seek proprioceptive and vestibular movement and how this affects all aspects of their daily experiences.
- Observe children involved in active play, to better understand and support them.
- Designate a space in your indoor environment to invite children to spread out and move.
- Notice children's competence as they take on physical challenges and risks, to allow and support their efforts.
- Create guidelines with children to help them take on challenge and risk.

- Encourage children to move their bodies before and during focused activities to help them stay engaged.
- Understand how children are more able to negotiate cooperative play when it involves movement.
- Provide loose parts and open-ended play equipment so children can find new ways to challenge themselves.

The following stories are just a few of the many examples of documentation teachers collected during the informal research that led to the principles.

PRINCIPLE   Recognize That Children Continually Seek Proprioceptive and Vestibular Movement and How This Affects All Aspects of Their Daily Experiences

One of the biggest outcomes of the teacher research was simply seeing how often children sought proprioceptive and vestibular input and the various forms this took. Although children's energetic play is very familiar to teachers, having a deeper understanding of why this kind of movement is important for children's brain development gave teachers a new perspective. When teachers recognized the deeper significance of children's active play, they were encouraged to pause and respond in more supportive ways, rather than seeing such activity as something to prevent, control, or stop.

Most of the teachers weren't surprised about the active play they saw outdoors. But they were astonished by the variety of ways children found to move indoors to help them focus. Teachers began to understand why children spend a lot of time stretching out on the floor, scooting, and crawling, and why they rarely sit in a chair if given the choice between standing or sitting. Teachers saw how moving during circle time actually helped children stay engaged.

They watched children move and drag their feet on the ground as they were seated, receiving useful proprioceptive input. The children stood, swayed, and stretched their legs to engage in vestibular experiences. When sitting on chairs, the children tried to get as much input as possible by sitting on their legs and feet, and leaning over to touch the surface of a table with their upper bodies.

One child, who usually had difficulty focusing, was observed remaining engaged at a paper-and-pencil task for almost an hour. He stood and laid across the top of the table with his upper body. He stretched his arm across the table to reach the paper and, gripping a marker tightly in his fisted hand,

Highland Presbyterian Nursery School

Pinehurst Child Care, a chapter of Sound Child Care Solutions

Pinehurst Child Care, a chapter of Sound Child Care Solutions

Southwest Early Learning Preschool, a chapter of Sound Child Care Solutions

used forceful movements to draw. As he worked, his jaw was clenched and moving the entire time. The teachers' new understandings helped them see that his movements—the pressure on his body from the table and floor, the way he moved with full strength as he stretched, and the clenching of his jaw—were giving his brain the proprioceptive and vestibular input that helped him concentrate and stay with the task. The most remarkable observation was that this was intrinsic behavior the child used to help himself engage during the experience.

In another group, the teachers watched a child try to negotiate climbing though several small, square openings on a wooden climbing structure. He wrestled with this challenge for quite a while and was only successful when he put a small stuffed animal in

his mouth and clamped down tightly. The proprioceptive input from his jaw enabled him to climb, balance, and get himself through the squares.

Another group of teachers observed several toddlers driving wheel toys in a very small indoor space, and not one of them ever ran into one another. And still another group was awed by how several active preschoolers worked together to move heavy tires. According to their teachers, these were children who usually had trouble playing together.

Heavy proprioceptive work and vestibular movement offer organizing and calming input for the brain. As teacher Jamie Solomon explains, "When children are calm, they are able to access parts of their brains that are not available when they are stressed. Children are often their best selves when engaged in these kinds of activities. Vigorous play seems to have an effect similar to meditation: allowing children to focus, concentrate, reach a sense of peace, go deeper and, in effect, realize their potential" (personal communication)

These observations as well as many others have transformed the way the teachers see children's active bodies and energetic play. Identifying and having a specific name and purpose for the movement they see has helped them value these experiences more. Teachers have become more relaxed about the behaviors that once left them anxious. They are more willing to allow boisterous play both indoors and outdoors because they now understand the deeper significance and see the children's competence in the ways they seek these experiences necessary for their development.

PRINCIPLE   Observe Children Involved in Active Play to Better Understand and Support Them

Observation is an essential tool for being a reflective teacher. Observing individual children helps teachers learn so much about who the children are and how to support them. The teachers in this project discovered how much you can learn about children when you observe how they approach and engage in active play. The ways children use their bodies tell so much about their dispositions and skills. By watching how children tackle physical challenges, you can determine whether they are cautious or bold, methodical or carefree, and expert or novice, and whether they flourish alone or with others.

After observing Evelyn, a child in her program, teacher Luz wrote a learning story to her, reflecting the lovely things she was learning about Evelyn. Her story demonstrates the power of observation in these moments to deeply learn about children, respect who they are, and support what they deserve.

Learning about Evelyn

Dear Evelyn,

Since you are a new child in our school, I would like to know more about you, and I was wondering what you are curious about and your interests beyond the classroom. While on the playground, I noticed you were observing Daniela and how she jumped in the puddle. This reminded me of how observant you are and how you quietly play with the doll house most of the time. You are often by yourself scanning the room as you continue with solo play.

Southwest Early Learning Center, a chapter of Sound Child Care Solutions

Evelyn, I observed how you walk around the playground stepping on the tree stumps several times, trying to go in different ways, even jumping with both feet at once. I am curious what this means to you and what you were thinking while seeking to step on the rocks, stones, gravel, grass, woodchips, the long log, and the tire. You took a few minutes looking at your feet and what you were standing on and then you would go to the next object! You walked around this same playground circuit several times.

You observed the tire for quite some time while pressing the woodchips with your feet, and then you walked into the tire, stayed for a few seconds and passed your foot over it, taking a moment to rub your foot before you got out. I wonder what crossed your mind or what you were feeling as you rubbed your feet on the tire.

Evelyn, it seems that you were examining the different playground surfaces and searching to understand your body in space by testing your boundaries and your proximity to others. You were finding balance and testing theories about the surface of the ground with your feet.

I could see you working on your vestibular sense and developing brain connections for a sense of balance. You were reaching higher and trying to balance yourself at the same time. I have learned that these actions are important for developing neural pathways, which helps you develop your communication skills.

I challenged myself not to ask you about what you were doing, but to just observe and not interrupt your focus. I expected to see physical activity, and you surprised me with how intent you were in your research of walking around and around the playground. This taught me that developing our physical skills can look differently if we put our attention to it as you showed me.

I'm wondering if you were getting comfortable in your new school by using your body to explore every aspect of the yard. Perhaps you were making your own connection to the space and seeing yourself as a part of it, and using your body in this way helped you feel calm and safe in this new setting. I want to keep watching you and perhaps offer more equipment for active play indoors. I also want to learn more from your family about how they see you. —Luz

Use the Thinking Lens® Protocol

Area for Reflection: Know yourself
- What is your reaction to Luz's story and why?
- What about Evelyn's journey was most interesting to you? What are you curious about? What delights you?
- What helps you get to know new or quiet children in your group?

Area for Reflection: Find the details of the children's competencies that engage your heart and mind.
- What skills and competencies did Luz observe in how Evelyn explored the playground?

- What other skills and competencies might you have noticed if you were the teacher observing Evelyn?

Area for Reflection: Take the child's perspective
- What do you think Evelyn is thinking and feeling as she makes her journey around the playground?
- What brings you to that conclusion?

Area for Reflection: Seek multiple perspectives
- What insights do you have about the impact of proprioceptive and vestibular experiences from Luz's documentation of Evelyn's journey?

Reflect

Getting to know children like Evelyn who are new to your program or who may be quiet or shy can be difficult during your busy days unless you stop to observe them carefully. Luz was able to see the deep focus and keen observation skills that Evelyn brought to her learning as she watched her move around and study every aspect of the playground. She noticed the physical skills and openness to challenges that Evelyn revealed during her explorations. Luz also gained insight into the power of active play for helping children feel comfortable, connected, and safe.

In the following story, Emily shows that observing children during vigorous physical activities can give teachers great insights in children's competence and challenges and how to support them.

Challenge and Perseverance

When we start hiking downhill, out of the sun and into the shade, a unique sense of excitement builds in the children. A city park just feet away from our classroom takes us down into a shaded ravine. Two children decide to hop down the trail instead of walk, another stops to pick up a hollowed-out branch as tall as her body, and still another chatters away about the times his family has gone hiking in the past. Down, down, down we hike, with our feet slipping on the dusty, rocky path and our bodies scooting away from the drop-off points. When we hit the lowest point of the trail and turn around to come back up, that's when the real challenge begins.

Hiking uphill goes a bit more slowly. The course feels steep to the young and old alike, so we take our time trudging upward. The children have navigated this path before, so they know how to balance carefully across the slippery, wet rocks and move over toward the wall of vegetation when runners and dog walkers speed past us. Step by step, we move up the hills, over the bridges, and around the sloping bends in the trail that got us down into the ravine. Children

clutch their partners' hands for balance, and some lean on their newfound walking sticks. Some say to one another, "This isn't too hard!" to demonstrate their determination. I notice that a couple of the children are actually wincing as we hike and I watch them carefully to make sure they're feeling all right. After a few more minutes of walking, I sense that one child might need a hand to hold. "Would you like to walk with me?" I ask. She nods and moves closer, taking my hand. I continue to monitor her as we slowly climb up the hill. A hand was all she needed, it seems, as she is now joining in games of I Spy and taking joy in the challenge of the hill. A sense of resolve replaces our fear, and we march up the muddy stairs that lead out into the sunshine. All the way up, up, up until our feet are back on concrete and we stand on level ground. The sunlight is a welcome reassurance: we did it!
—Emily

Epiphany Early Learning Preschool, Interlaken campus, a chapter of Sound Child Care Solutions

Epiphany Early Learning Preschool, Interlaken campus, a chapter of Sound Child Care Solutions

and pull down a thick vine and walk backward up the hill? This is a place where it's safe to test our bodies' limits and, in doing so, marvel at what we can do. When I see children overcoming a physical obstacle, I take a quick moment to celebrate—with the children, yes, but also in myself. The daily work of building resilience and persistence in young children is no small task. Seeing them put those temperaments into action is worthy of reflection. We develop a deeper sense of confidence and capability when we emerge, victorious and exhausted."

Reflect

Observing children using their bodies in all kinds of ways helps teachers see the wealth of skills and competencies children already possess and are capable of further developing. When we know children well, we plan for them and respond in ways that meet up with their interests, skills, and brave pursuits. The exuberant child deserves to feel joyful in the power of her body as she pushes her boundaries. And the cautious child deserves to move at his own pace and take up challenges he feels comfortable with to build his confidence to keep doing more. Studying the way children approach these experiences helps us know them better and brings us joy as we share in their exuberance and celebrate their accomplishments.

Your Turn

Choose a few children in your group to observe as they are engaged in physical activities. Study how each of them approaches these experiences.

- What do you notice about the challenges they take on?
- How do they negotiate risky situations?
- How do they respond to success and failure in their pursuits?
- How does their approach to physical experiences mirror how they tackle other activities?
- What insights do you have about each child from observing their physical activity?

Listen to Emily

"I love hiking in the woods because there are so few 'nos.' When we, as teachers, can expand our understanding of what is 'allowed,' we can focus on what the children *can* do. In the expansiveness of a ravine, larger-scale movements are not only allowed; they're necessary! I find myself thinking, 'Why not?' in response to many internal questions of arbitrary rules. Why not leap over the puddle? Why not tiptoe through a trickling stream? Why not kick a rock

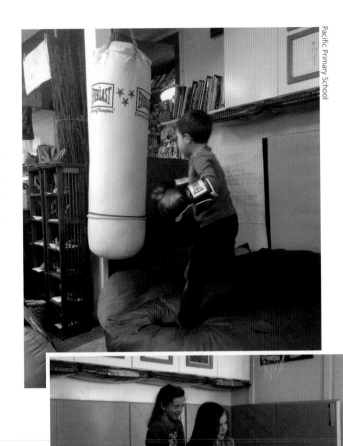

Pacific Primary School

PRINCIPLE   Designate a Space in Your Indoor Environment to Invite Children to Spread Out and Move

As a result of studying children's active play needs, many teachers have changed their indoor environments to include a designated space and materials for large body play. Nadia's story shows a brave teacher adapting not only her space but her attitude on behalf of children's right to move and feel powerful in their bodies both indoors and outdoors. The results have been positive for all.

Our Sensory Motor Area, Three Years Later

We added a sensory motor area to our classroom about three years ago. When we began thinking about the new area, we were responding to the constant need for big body play the children showed us daily. We worked with an occupational therapist to help us understand how important these experiences are for children's focus and learning. This area has become a very important space in our environment and is special to both the children and the teachers. Originally, the space was an inviting and unique dramatic play area that the children enjoyed using. Over the years, our teaching team had spent countless hours collecting and arranging real furniture and unusual props from garage sales along with lots of open-ended materials to explore. Changing that particular space was a big decision that took time, reflection, support, and collaboration. It was a hard choice to make, but it was well worth it!

The sensory area started with materials that were borrowed and donated (pillows, crib mat, punching bag, yoga mat, old nap mats). We have made many additions to the sensory area over these three years using our classroom budget as well as family donations. We now have safety mats, a giant crash pillow, a sturdy basketball hoop, ropes for climbing, a trapeze, and a variety of different textured balls.

The sensory motor area is a place where children can be active and use their bodies in big ways. It is a place where children can experience "yes" rather than "no." It is a place where children can feel both powerful and safe. The sensory area is open daily, and children eagerly sign up to have a turn. Children use the space in a variety of ways. Throwing balls and pillows, jumping, rolling, spinning, and climbing are just some examples. Recently, the children have used the space to create games. For example, the Bubble Gum Machine has been an ongoing game. Children line up a variety of soft balls on the ledge of a mat that is against the wall and then let the balls roll off

Pacific Primary School

Reflect

Nadia's indoor environment isn't very big and, as you read in her story, she values having an abundance of interesting and beautiful spaces and materials for her children. Yet she was willing to forgo some of that on behalf of sensory motor experiences. How do you respond to active play indoors in your classroom? What changes are you willing to make to provide for these important active play experiences?

Nadia's new coteacher, Riley, has come to see the beauty as well as the value of having this space in their room. As the learning story below reflects, Riley spends time observing the children in the area and sees the deep meaning of a child's actions, which brings pleasure to both the children and herself.

Flying High on the Trapeze

Dear Kaia,

We had the trapeze out in the sensory motor area one day in the Coyote Room. You were excited when it was your turn and sat and watched as your friends were on the trapeze. I wonder what you were thinking when you were watching. Were you planning how you would use the trapeze? When it was your turn, you approached the trapeze with intense focus. You spent the whole five minutes of your turn (and your subsequent turns) in your own world. You swung, spun, and flipped as hard and as fast as you could

onto their bodies. I can only imagine the sensation and input that the children get from feeling these balls land on them. Stuffy Basketball has been another game the children have invented. They use their stuffed animals from home to throw into the basket. Often, the animals get stuck in the net. Figuring out how to get the animals out seems to be the best part of the game.

Thanks to our families' auction donations this year, we are ordering more safety mats that will offer the children more opportunities to use their bodies in big ways. —Nadia

Pacific Primary School

go. You had complete control of your body and the trapeze.

Did you know that there are many ways in which the trapeze helps you grow? You learn about your body—its limits, strength, and ability. The risks you take give you the confidence to try new things. The ways that your body moves in the trapeze—upside down, back and forth, spinning—help you write and draw and will help you when you learn to read.

It was exciting for me to watch you on the trapeze. I know all the ways in which the trapeze helps your development, but what was most important for me was to feel the joy and passion you exuded as you swung.

Love, Riley

Pacific Primary School

You don't need to take on the task of creating such an elaborate area for big body play as Nadia and Riley did. You can create more focused, cooperative energy in your classroom by just providing a larger open space where children can move and including substantial materials such as large hollow blocks. Open space invites children to lay down, stretch out, crawl, and scoot, which provides opportunities for children to receive proprioceptive input. Blocks to stand and walk on offer indoor opportunities for balance and vestibular experiences. The following story from teacher Javier's classroom shows this principle at work.

More Space and Bigger Materials

Teacher Javier already had an adequate-size block area that was very popular with many of the children in his group. However, during one of the research observations, his coworkers decided to enlarge the space just a few more feet and add some big hollow blocks and long flooring planks. The children immediately began to do big, cooperative work using the materials in many ways. They built long ramps for racing cars, working together to carry the planks back and forth, adding them to one end, and then thinking of more ways to rearrange materials. They also constructed several different structures for walking and climbing. At one end of the area, a large group of children was doing this big work together, while at the other end a smaller group of children was quietly creating buildings using the many design materials to carefully embellish their work.

Reflect

The teachers who observed this experience were surprised at how well the children worked together. They saw lots of action and many changes to the structures as the children's work unfolded. No conflicts emerged and the children were intensely interested in building on each other's ideas. The children were alert and engaged for over an hour, and they would

have kept going, if not for lunch arriving. Cleanup was just as appealing and cooperative, as the children relished lifting and carrying the planks and blocks to put them away. The children had many opportunities for receiving proprioceptive and vestibular input as they used their strength to maneuver and move the planks and blocks, as well as engaging physically to climb and balance on the structures. The teachers were excited to see how the larger space allowed for the big, active play while still accommodating more careful work. They were most impressed with the children's level of cooperation and lack of conflict during this big play.

Your Turn

Spend time observing how children use active body play indoors in your classroom, even if you don't have a space designated for this. Where and how do children move? Try rearranging your room to open up more space for children to spread out and be active. What impact does this have on the climate of the classroom and the children's behavior? How can you provide more opportunity for active experiences indoors?

Southwest Early Learning Center, a chapter of Sound Child Care Solutions

PRINCIPLE   Notice Children's Competence as They Take on Physical Challenges and Risks to Allow and Support Their Efforts

Another significant insight for teachers comes when they begin noticing their own responses to children's big body play. They become aware of how they often underestimated children's abilities and jump in too quickly to stop physical challenges children pursue. Individual teachers can intentionally take on the role of observer, leaving supervision up to other teachers. Standing back and observing without a role allows teacher-observers time to watch something unfold with the children and notice their own thoughts and instincts. Teacher Stephanie's experience is a powerful example of this.

Balancing Balls

Teacher Stephanie chose to focus her active body observations on one piece of equipment—the large ball. As she watched, many different children used the ball in a variety of ways. Several children tried to get on top of the ball to sit. The ball was almost as tall as they were and difficult for the children to climb up and balance on. Stephanie observed a variety of clever ways the children figured out how to meet the challenge of getting up on the ball. Most of the children pushed the ball against the wall to help them balance. They held on to the marker tray attached to the white board for support as they climbed. One child balanced herself carefully with one leg while holding on to

the tray and then hoisted herself up. Another child wedged the ball into the corner for stability and used her arms on the walls to climb up and steady herself.

Listen to Stephanie

"As I watched the first child come to use the ball, it was all I could do to keep myself from jumping in to stop her. I was certain she would hurt herself on the marker tray as she used it to maneuver herself up onto the ball. The ball moved under her, and it was difficult for her to get her balance. She worked at it for quite a while, and to my surprise, she was able to right herself several times until she successfully made it safely to the top. This same thing happened over and over again. Each child struggled to get on the ball, and with each one I worried. Nevertheless, the children ultimately found a way to meet the challenge and not one of them got hurt. This was such a great learning experience for me. It made me realize how much I intervene in children's play without waiting to see what they can handle. Today, the children showed me how able they are to keep themselves safe in situations I might think of as too risky. I realize I need to pause just for a minute to see what is possible instead of jumping in when I'm not really needed."

Judging Jumps

Teacher Brian has been observing children's ability to keep themselves safe for a while. He intentionally designs challenging experiences that children of differing abilities and dispositions toward risk can use in ways they feel most comfortable. The following story is an example.

Brian created a place for children to climb and jump. As he built a staircase to the top of the platform, he kept the different dispositions and abilities of the children in mind. The hollow blocks were fairly easy for all of the children to climb, and when they got to the top, there were several possibilities for jumping. The children took up different kinds of challenges. One child stepped carefully down from the platform onto the tire and then gleefully jumped several times through the open space to get to the bigger landing pad. Another child bounced onto the tire, which launched her across the space onto the landing pad. And still another child expertly jumped all the way from the platform across to the landing pad.

Listen to Brian

"As I watched the children on the structure I set up for jumping, I was reminded of how well children know their own limits and only take up physical risks that are comfortable for them. I want to keep children safe and I also want to offer opportunities where they can see possibilities and challenges for themselves no matter what level they are. They watched and supported each other and only moved on to something more challenging when they felt ready. Observing the children's competence and thoughtful negotiation toward jumping deepened my trust in them and, as important, the trust they have in themselves."

Reflect

We all have different reactions to challenging situations and what we perceive as too risky. It is important for you to examine your views of these situations and make distinctions between your personal feelings and experiences, your coworkers' points of view, and children's strong desire for independence and competence. As the stories you've just read show, children don't often take risks they don't think they can manage. There is also a difference between a risk and a hazard. A *risk* is something that is possible to negotiate and may be appropriate for particular situations and children. A *hazard* is something that is inherently dangerous and needs to be remedied, such as a climbing structure with sharp edges or loose boards that could seriously injure children if they play on it. There isn't one right answer in situations involving risk. It takes observing children with an eye to their competence and acknowledging your own disposition to ensure children are safe as well as able to engage in appropriate challenges. Challenges are so vital for children's brain development and their confidence.

PRINCIPLE   Create Guidelines with Children to Help Them Take On Challenges and Risks

When concern for safety leads teachers to avoid, stop, or eliminate anything that might be a challenge for children, the role of the teacher is diminished. This is often referred to as "teacher-proofing" the curriculum. It doesn't matter who the teacher is or what the teacher does, because there is a rule or prescribed way to do everything. This approach leads teachers to take a less active role in thinking through safety issues as well as supporting children's learning. When children are involved in a situation that appears too risky or dangerous, rather than just stopping them, you can offer alternatives that keep children safe while preserving opportunities for them to manage the challenges themselves. The following are stories of teachers doing just that.

Building a Culture of Wrestling

Wrestling kept coming up in teacher Bria's classroom. The children clearly wanted to wrestle, and the teachers wanted to give them the chance. However, before jumping in, they decided to talk with the children about how to be safe and what agreements they should have about wrestling. Bria gathered the children together and they came up with the following rules:

"We can grab bodies."

"We can't pull hair."

"If a kid says 'stop,' we should stop."

"We should ask before wrestling with a kid."

Once the agreements were set, the children started wrestling.

Anna grabbed Aisha's feet and gently pulled her around. They were both laughing and wrestling hap-

Hilltop Children's Center

Listen to Bria

"As I watched the wrestling unfold, I wondered if having the children ask before engaging was changing the way they approached wrestling. Was too much time spent asking? Did it diffuse the situation in a positive way or a negative way? How could this be accomplished without having to constantly check in with each other and ask, 'Can I wrestle with you?' over and over again?

"When they began wrestling, the children were skeptical. After all that talk about agreements and what they could and could not do, they had a hard time launching themselves into wrestling. This made me think, Is wrestling something that comes up on impulse? Is it something that is only fun when it isn't set up? How did they feel about laying out ground rules for wrestling? Did that affect the purpose and draw of wrestling?

"Sure enough, after about five minutes of the constant check-ins, the children naturally began to wrestle without asking each other as often. It was clear that this agreement had inhibited their play, and it gave way to a more intuitive approach. They still paid close attention to when a child asked them to stop or said they didn't want to do something."

pily. After a few minutes, Aisha said, "That's enough, that's enough," and Anna immediately let go of her. Teacher Bria commented on how well the children were following the agreements.

"Anna, you heard her message about being done, and you let go right away. Good job taking care of your friend."

For the first few minutes, there was a chorus of "Can I wrestle with you?" Followed by either "Yes!" or "No." The children were very good at recognizing one another's feelings and needs, and checking in before they wrestled.

Hilltop Children's Center

Reflect

Young children are drawn to wrestling, tumbling, jumping, running, and many other forms of physical play. Some of this play can seem risky or tricky to manage, and parents or early childhood educators may wish to suppress it. However, there are many benefits children gain from this type of play, such as developing empathy, confidence, and self-regulation skills. By working with children to spell out simple ground rules, you can add a layer of learning to wrestling that includes an understanding of risk and the practice of empathy, in keeping each other safe and adjusting to each other's needs.

Getting a Monkey Bar License

Read teacher Donna's thorough and thoughtful approach to negotiating risk and challenge with children.

At Children First, like many programs that aspire to offer children a rich array of learning opportunities, we face the constraints of a small indoor space. In the 12' x 14' area we have set aside for big blocks, pretending, and music, we take advantage of vertical space and create a variety of play places and physical challenges using big wooden boxes with various child-size openings and a loft with two ways to go up and down. In January each year, we add to that arrangement a simple set of hand-over-hand monkey bars with a futon and pillows underneath.

At Children First, we value risk taking. We value the intellectual risk taking that happens when kids make guesses or venture opinions or try new materials. We value the social risks kids take when they play new games with new playmates or share their feelings honestly. And, of course, we value physical risk taking, as long as kids are the ones who choose the risks they want to take. Young children's sense of themselves resides very much in their sense of their bodies. When they pluck up their courage and ask their bodies to try something new and a little scary, they grow their sense of self-competence in a powerful way.

Safe Fun Monkey Bars
Three people on the monkey bars.

Only three people can use the monkey bars at one time. If it gets too crowded, people can get hurt. If you want a turn, let the kids using the monkey bars know they should come get you when they are done.

Safe Fun Monkey Bars
give a warning if you're going to drop!

If somebody is under you and you're going to drop, say, "Here I come! Make a space!"

I understand the agreements for safe fun monkey bars, and I will be careful to keep the monkey bars safe and fun for everybody at school. ALex

And, of course, we also value safety. The monkey bars offer a great example of "risky play" that grows children's judgment and self-awareness precisely because it requires attention to be safe. Around the monkey bars, we strive to create a set of agreements and a general environment—a system—that acknowledges the certainty of falls and accidents, but prevents unnecessary injury and conflict. When Monkey Bar Day finally arrives each January, children meet with me in pairs to read through the safety agreements that we've developed together over many years; to illustrate one of those agreements for the current edition of our book called Safe Fun Monkey Bars; and to sign a contract that stipulates, "I understand the agreements for safe, fun monkey bars, and I will be careful to keep the monkey bars safe and fun for everybody at school."

Of all the events on the annual Children First calendar, the reappearance of the monkey bars is one of the most anticipated. Continuing kids have a whole store of memories from the year before, and even first-year kids often remember the monkey bars from their winter admissions visits. When Reyna asks, "When do the monkey bars go up?" we invite her to "check the kid calendar." She and Lauren rush to the office to take a look. They find two different days marked with a drawing of monkey bars—the Friday home day that will be a teacher workday for rearranging the loft room and the following Monday, when the children will get their monkey bar licenses.

Reyna says, "Just one, two more sleeps and then the monkey bars! Then we get to hang upside down!"

The girls head back into the Loft Room to stand in the space they're thinking about and to act out some of the moves they're so looking forward to practicing.

Lauren says, "Remember how you could climb up here and then reach around to get out on the monkey bars? Remember this way?"

Reyna answers, "Yeah. And I could go up, up here and reeeeach over to hold on." The conversation continues in a spirit of mutual anticipation and delight.
—Donna

Your Turn

Stand back and observe children involved in vigorous, physical play without the role of supervisor.

- What do you notice about your disposition toward risk and challenge? When do you want to jump in and why?
- What happens when you don't jump in?
- How do children use their own judgment and caution to negotiate a physical challenge?
- How might you invite the children to think with you about how to keep a challenging activity safe?
- What benefits do think children gain when they can negotiate their own rules for safety and risk?

Reflect

A vital part of your work is to keep children safe. But it is equally important to support children in their pursuits to learn and grow. Physical experiences are essential for brain development, and a lack of these experiences harms children. This work requires that teachers pay attention to the children's perspectives, use their power thoughtfully, and act responsibly. Teachers can ensure that children have a childhood where they feel exhilaration while still being protected and supported by adults and their friends. You can support them as they learn that determination pays off, and they can become competent decision makers, able to assess risks, contribute to the well-being of others, and reap the rewards of their efforts.

PRINCIPLE   Encourage Children to Move Their Bodies Before and During Activities to Help Them Stay Focused and Engaged

Although it seems almost counterintuitive, active play and movement actually help children calm down and participate more fully. Teachers have come to see that sitting still, crisscross-applesauce, makes it more difficult for preschool children to pay attention at circle time. Teachers are now allowing children to spread out, lay down, and rock back and forth to help

them stay engaged. Teachers realize that standing at the table, rather than sitting for long periods of time, helps keep children focused on their work longer. Teacher Monica describes an observation in the next story that deepened her understanding of what helps children stay engaged.

Focused on the Mat

In our Montessori preschool class, children are provided with materials made to keep them focused and engaged. They are free to choose their own materials and to work with them for as long as they wish. This helps children because they are able to freely choose an activity that builds confidence, concentration, and discipline.

When a child is ready to get a work (a Montessori term for children choosing a material they are interested in exploring), they also need to get a Montessori Work Mat to use as a base. We use mats that are about 24" x 36". These mats are to define their work space, help them with their sense of order, and maintain one of the Montessori principles of "freedom within limits." The child is able to sit next to their mat, lay on their stomach, lay on their side, sit on their knees, etc.—any way they choose to do their work, including a little bit of stretching or different positioning of their bodies, to help them release any stress and keep them safely in control of their moving bodies.

Magic Lantern Montessori, a chapter of Sound Child Care Solutions

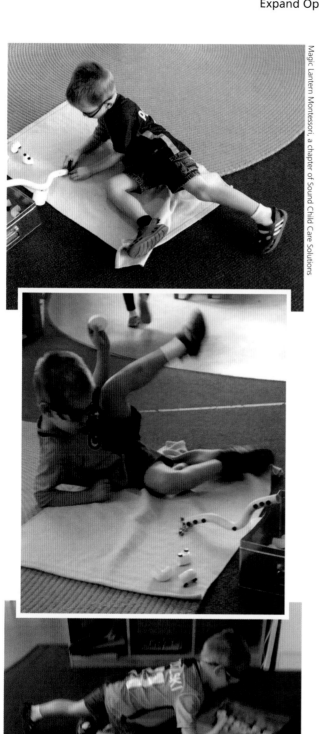

Avery, a child in our class, is demonstrating how he is using his proprioceptive and vestibular senses to help him stay focused. In these photos you can see how he is moving his legs around the mat, choosing different sides of the mat to see different visual aspects of his work. He is also laying on his stomach and pressing down on his tummy, which helps sends signals to his brain so he can successfully complete his task. He was fully engaged for about an hour before we wrapped up our Montessori-focused time to go outside and enjoy some sunshine.

A few days later, I tried a different approach with Avery. In the first part of the Montessori focused time, I asked him to sit crisscross and not move around the mat as before. He lost interest right away and did not complete his work. This mini experiment helped me see that by allowing Avery to move, he found his own way of controlling his body and movement.

Unfortunately, in life children are taught to be very quiet, stay still, sit crisscross, sit straight in a chair, but we don't realize that they really need to take advantage of as much movement as they can so they can focus. Just this simple task of stretching or moving their feet while sitting helps children stay engaged and release any tension they may have while completing a task. —Monica

Waiting is often difficult for young children. In the next story, teacher Megan observes the many strategies Jonah used to move his body to help him stay engaged while waiting to go outside. She wrote a learning story to him as a tribute to his patience and competence as well as her deep respect for him and his abilities to take care of himself.

Jonah and His Body

Dear Jonah,

When I started observing you this morning, you seemed really ready to go outside and move. The hard part was that no one else was ready to go with you! You wanted to move your body in big ways, and as I watched, I noticed you found many ways to meet your need for active play all around the classroom.

You had been in the classroom for a long time, and although you were engaged in the block area earlier in the morning—balancing and moving your feet on different surfaces and at different angles—you seemed done with that particular game. You zoomed around the room and came upon your friends in the drama area who were playing a game. You sat, curled up, in the middle of the group but not joining the conversation. Slowly, you stretched your whole body out, covering the rug. You sank your chin down into the carpet and then rolled on your back like a giant sea star. You rubbed your skin on the shag rug and stretched your muscles wide.

Next, you and Benny moved to the other side of the room, where you held hands and spun around. You twirled him around as if he were a toy plane attached to a string. I felt a little worried that he might actually fly away! You two have had a lot of practice playing big games together, and it showed, because even though you were moving fast, you kept each other safe.

You asked teacher Joyce if you could go outside, and she said you could after you helped clean up the block area. You didn't complain, even though you had already been so patient. You went straight for the big blocks, balancing the weight of blocks the same size on your arms. Instead of going around the blocks on the floor, you walked up and over each obstacle. Were you trying to reach new heights, always aiming for the highest place to stand?

At this point, you noticed I was watching you, and you wanted to try out something new. You started banging two large triangular blocks against each other, making a loud sound. You seemed curious about what I would say, but when I didn't respond, you stopped quickly. Perhaps because you were so eager to get the job done and get outside.

Then it was time to wait at the door for the group to gather. Instead of standing, you sat on your bottom, leaned back, and lifted your feet in the air. It was a wobbly position, and you were using different muscles in your core and legs while at the same time entertaining your friends who were also waiting. When you were in the hall, you were one of the quickest to get your coat and shoes on!

The waiting was getting pretty tricky, and you were very excited. Some of your friends were practicing tying their shoes, and it was so hard to be patient when the moment to go outside was so close. Finally, after I had been watching you wait for forty-five minutes, Will opened the door and you zoomed out! —Megan

Listen to Megan

"I was impressed by how Jonah figured out so many ways to use his body during this long period of waiting. Instead of asking his teachers over and over about going outside, he was creative in seeking out new experiences to keep his body engaged in a way that was safe for his environment and the friends around him.

"Research suggests that young children's brains are better able to build neural connections when their bodies are physically engaged. Now that I've observed Jonah, I wonder if the proprioceptive inputs he sought out during this time also supported his executive functions—his ability to wait, to plan ahead—and his cognitive flexibility.

"Jonah is very competent in his body. Keeping in mind the importance of movement for brain development, it is clear that as he practices using his body in different positions and on different surfaces, he is getting his brain ready to learn many important skills, from dancing and driving to reading and writing.

"He is also a competent friend and leader. Jonah

Epiphany Early Learning Preschool, a chapter of Sound Child Care Solutions

knows how to lead his friends in teamwork and how to safely play active body games with others. He is a risk taker, but because he is familiar with movement and pays attention to his environment, he can play big and fast games while keeping himself and his friends safe.

"As a result of my new understanding of the importance of vestibular and proprioceptive inputs for brain development, my reaction to big body play and movement has changed. When I see children squirming at circle time, I no longer ask them to sit still and crisscross. I understand that their movement may be helping them concentrate on the conversation or story.

"Another way I've changed my practice is by creating provocations that invite movement as well as encouraging focused play. For example, I might set up different types of seating around a sensory provocation. Or, if we are painting, I might hang paper that is tall and skinny, so that children may crouch down low and stretch up high to cover the page.

"I will continue to seek out new materials for Jonah and the other children to interact with and different spaces for them to move their bodies. I am excited to see how this new attitude toward movement affects the children's play and learning in the long term!"

Your Turn

Observe children engaged in activities that require focus, such as circle time, waiting in line, or working on a task at a table.

- What do you notice about how they move their bodies while engaged in these experiences?
- How does their movement affect their attentiveness and involvement?
- What new thinking do these observations leave you with?

PRINCIPLE   Understand How Children Are More Able to Negotiate Cooperative Play When It Involves Movement

The idea that children cooperate more fully when they move together seems counterintuitive to how teachers usually think about these situations. When children are crowded around a climber, all vying to get on, teachers often intervene with rules and reminders. When children are running together as a group, teachers may worry that someone will surely get knocked down and hurt. The following stories from teachers Matthew and Sabine reflect how able children are to negotiate these situations.

Duck, Duck, Goose

Teacher Matthew decided to teach the game Duck, Duck, Goose to his group of toddlers. He was surprised and a little worried when all of the children spontaneously got up and ran up the ramp to the small platform at the same time when the word goose *was announced. This became the unspoken rule of the game that the children joyfully played again and again. And amazingly not once did children run into each other, knock someone down, or get hurt.*

Listen to Matthew

"My first reaction to the children's idea to all run up the ramp at the same time was to be worried, and I wanted to stop them. But they moved so quickly I didn't have time to respond. As I watched, I was amazed how the children were able to negotiate their actions, even with eight or nine little bodies all moving in the same small space. When this happened safely several times, I decided to relax. I considered why the children were able to move together so successfully. It reminded me of birds flying in flocks, never bumping into each other, or herds of animals able to run together with no problem. Maybe all animals, including children, have an instinctive ability to see and manage personal space in a crowd.

"As I continue to reflect on this experience, I realized how much pleasure the children shared in the exciting moment of 'Goose' and I value their natural desire to share ideas and experiences. I think I will teach this as the new rule for this old-time game."

Hot Lava Game

Read teacher Sabine's story of new understandings and new roles she played to support the children's cooperative play during exuberant physical activity.

One afternoon I returned from my lunch break to find every single wiggle pad in the classroom strewn about on the rug, each one topped with a balancing, giggling child. Quick glances were exchanged by the seven boys; then one or two of them would jump across the rug to an empty wiggle pad—sometimes landing on both feet and frantically windmilling their arms to regain balance, or other times landing lopsided and sliding into the wiggle pad as if they were trying to steal second base. The children called out to each other intermittently. "Hot lava!" "I'm out!" "I'm not touching hot lava!" The game progressed for another fifteen minutes—crashing, slipping, falling, and laughing.

The wiggle pads so essential to this lively game of Hot Lava are normally used for children to sit on

during morning meeting. So my initial thought was to tell the children to stop, that these wiggle pads are tools, and jumping on them with such gusto might break them. Luckily, the giant smiles on the children's faces distracted me long enough to pause and reconsider the situation.

The energy was high, gross motor in its biggest form as child after child leapt through the air toward their next target. Yet this game also required focus—knowing when another child was jumping, an unspoken agreement every second, and constantly heightened spatial awareness. The children were seeking out a challenge and fascinated by balancing on non-static surfaces.

I asked myself, "If I tell them to stop this game, how can I provide them with a positive alternative?" We don't have any surface like those wiggle pads, outside or in. And clearly they were seeking it, thrilled by it, and needing to repeat the experience over and over again. They were being safe—if they fell, it was on carpet, on their bottoms, and often intentionally. And so the game continued, and I watched.

The next day as I set up the yard, I was inspired by the children's game and their exploration of balance. I made a makeshift seesaw out of building planks and a large halved PVC pipe, then duct taped gym mats to the top of the planks. I hoped that this would give the children what they were asking me for—a moving, squishy surface to challenge them to balance and give them the opportunity to jump and crash.

My "sensory seesaws" were a smash hit not just for our five-year-olds, but for all of the children at the school—two-year-olds just figuring out how to jump with two feet, children who do not usually gravitate toward big gross-motor obstacle courses, and even the oldest children in my own class who probably could have held their own on a much more challenging seesaw.

Billy hopped onto the seesaw. He walked from the end on the ground toward the end in the air. When he crossed the tipping point, the seesaw below him hit the ground with a muffled thud. His look of

surprise quickly morphed into a grin and he started walking back and forth, back and forth.

Neko and Lilly climbed onto the seesaw together. They stood in the middle of the seesaw and leaned one way, then the other, making the seesaw tip rapidly from side to side. They giggled, "Let's go faster!"

Chloe and Jacqui figured out a different way to use the seesaw. Jacqui lay down on the seesaw, while Chloe jumped from one side to the other, each time rocketing Jacqui's body an inch in the air.

All of these children were exploring the effects of gravity and motion on their bodies—the technical term is vestibular stimulation. *Vestibular stimulation can be calming, like rocking gently back and forth, or rousing, like being spun on a merry-go-round or jerked about on a roller coaster. As children develop and grow, they need both—and they will find ways to meet their needs. Like making up the Hot Lava game.*
—Sabine

Your Turn

Observe groups of children engaged in physical games and challenges together. What do you notice about their ability to see each other and cooperate during this kind of play? How do they regulate their own actions and negotiate the space as they play with others?

PRINCIPLE   Provide Loose Parts and Open-Ended Play Equipment So Children Can Find New Ways to Challenge Themselves

To their active body play, children bring their remarkable flexible thinking, problem solving, and eagerness to grow and learn. Teachers are often astonished as they observe the many ways children bravely devise more and more difficult physical challenges for themselves. Settings with open-ended play equipment and loose parts invite children to continually invent new ways to up the ante of physical challenges as they play. The stories that close this chapter show children using this innate ability and drive.

Sliding Sensations

Charlie discovered a variety of ways to use her body on the wooden half round. First she sat on her bottom, gripped the sides, and, using all the strength in her arms, pulled herself, scooting all the way down to the end of the round. Next she stretched out on her belly and used her hands and legs to snake across the surface. Then she turned over on her back, grabbed the top of the round, and used her arms and legs to again slide to the end of the round. Finally, Charlie found a half round that had been turned over to make a tunnel. She got down on her tummy and crawled into the tight space. With each of her actions, all parts of her body were touching the smooth wooden surface and she was using the muscles in her arms and legs to pull or push herself along.

Listen to Kristen

"Focusing on just Charlie as she interacted with the equipment was so eye-opening for me. I saw how she focused on using her body in different but similar ways. As she moved across the half round, she seemed to like the sensation of the smooth, hard wooden surface against her body and wanted to get that input to her chest, back, arms, legs, bottom, and tummy. She also showed me how strong she is for such a small child, as she was able to pull and push herself along to meet the challenges she had set for herself."

Moving Inventions

Over the course of several weeks, Deb offered a collection of active play equipment to her group of toddlers. These photos of two-year-old Emily illustrate how the children found many ways to explore their physical skills by rearranging the materials to create new challenges for themselves. Emily used each material on its own, finding all of the ways to balance, rock, jump, crawl over, press into, throw, roll, and carry. She combined the materials, using them to invent obstacles for walking, climbing, crawling, and jumping on and over. She studied the different sensations that each of the materials provided her feet and body, seeking pressure and practicing balance. She stuck with each new challenge, trying things over and over again until she had accomplished the tasks she set for herself.

Listen to Deb

"I've been astonished by the boldness and persistence of the children as I watch them take on the tasks of developing strength and control of their bodies. It's hard to believe only a year ago they were just learning to walk. I'm fascinated by the way the children use materials with their entire beings, not just moving with them, but seeking and immersing themselves in the sensations of movement and touching the surface of the materials with their feet, hands, face, and bodies.

"Many of the challenges they invent for themselves are risky, so I stay close to keep them safe while still honoring their fierce, unstoppable energy. Emily spent day after day figuring out how to balance on the rocking board and once she was able to do that, she took up the challenge of learning to rock back and forth. She was so proud when she finally succeeded! I was shocked when she used one of the rocking boards to create a bridge to climb onto the half round. It was a steep climb and the board kept falling off. Still, she never hesitated to get up and do it again. I offered pieces of no-slip fabric, and it did the

trick to keep the board stable. Up she went and then skillfully walked right back down.

"Not only do the children bring remarkable physical skills to this work; they also have countless ways to combine and use the materials. I have such great respect for their natural abilities to think and move. I'm even more impressed with their creativity, enthusiasm, and determination for this important work."

Reflect

The more you observe children, the more you can see the innate gifts they were born with that drive their development and learning. Deb's story reflects children's active brains at work—using flexible thinking and problem solving as well as seeking physical experiences that shape brain pathways. In this story, you read about Emily engaged in motor planning as she works day after day, building from one idea to the next, using her brain and her body together to grow new skills and understandings. These are vital, optimal experiences for Emily and the open-ended, flexible materials she was offered provide a rich environment for her to use her natural gifts.

Your Turn

Gather a collection of open-ended materials and equipment that children can use for active play (cardboard boxes, planks, logs, stumps, fabric, hoops, sticks, and so on). Then observe the children exploring these materials.

- How do they use the materials to seek proprioceptive and vestibular input (lift, carry, balance, jump, spin, roll)?
- How many different ways do you see the children using the same materials?
- Based on these observations, what insights do you have about the kinds of materials that invite children to engage in rich physical play?

5 Bring Yourself to the Teaching and Learning Process

If we are not fully ourselves, truly in the present moment, we miss everything. When a child presents himself to you with his smile, if you are not really there—thinking about the future or the past, or preoccupied with other problems—then the child is not really there for you. The technique of being alive is to go back to yourself in order for the child to appear like a marvelous reality. Then you can see him smile and you can embrace him in your arms. —**Thich Nhat Hanh**

When early childhood educators like you design learning environments with values in mind and offer engaging materials to explore, you set the stage for meaningful experiences to unfold. You have ongoing roles to play to deepen children's interests and knowledge, and to further your own passion for teaching. Your teacher behaviors must go beyond herding children through typical activities and outcomes associated with early childhood curriculum.

Then, as Thich Nhat Hanh suggests, you can let go of preoccupations and go back to yourself to really see children and the deep joy of this work.

But how can you do this when every year you face more guidelines to follow, more curriculum content to include, and more standards to meet? If you look honestly, it's not the curriculum or requirements, but your behavior and responses to children that most strongly influence what occurs in your room. When you heighten your awareness, you realize the power and possibilities you have to enhance experiences for both the children and yourself. As you take up the challenge and responsibility for this dynamic process of teaching and learning, careful observation is required, along with ongoing self-reflection and the courage to think and act outside the boxes on your curriculum form. The following principles will help you take charge of your role to build relationships and lively learning experiences with children.

Principles

- Claim your power.
- Think through your actions.
  Know your teacher scripts.
  Know your professional influences.
  Know your theoretical influences.
- Cultivate a mind-set of receptivity.
- Seek the child's point of view.
- Notice the details to discover more possibilities.
- Share conversations following the children's lead.
- Support children's connections with each other.
- Take action on behalf of children's strengths.

PRINCIPLE   **Claim Your Power**

You use power daily in your work with children, often inadvertently, without paying attention to your purpose and without examining the effects of your actions. Yet if you fail to think in terms of purpose and effect, you might easily ignore, stifle, or overwhelm children's innate desire to learn. In today's educational climate, you might feel obliged to use your power on behalf of curriculum mandates or outcomes. Yet policy makers, curriculum designers, educators from Reggio Emilia, or even your immediate supervisors are not often in the room with you when you are with the children. You may bring their influence and feel the pressure for accountability to outcomes, but you are the one who has the power in the moment-to-moment decisions and responses you make to children. You decide what to pay attention to, what to stop, what to emphasize, and what to help grow. When you stay mindful and act according to your values and goals, you become a powerful mediator of children's learning. Rather than abandoning your ideals or philosophy on behalf of mandated standards, you can take charge of the role you play in creating meaningful experiences for children.

Denise Louis Head Start

Kristin Sees the Light

As you read the following story about Kristin and the children in her Head Start class, notice how she is claiming her power to provide a meaningful approach to meeting outcomes.

Weeks of constant rain have kept Kristin and her group indoors where she has been busy observing and filling out required paperwork for the children's individual assessments. Late one afternoon, at the end of week three, the rain finally stops and a small sliver of blue sky and sunlight appears through the clouds. The children alert Kristin to the light peeking through the windows and she agrees it is time they all head outside. The children eagerly put their materials away and joyously spill onto the playground they haven't seen in days. Kristin takes her clipboard and camera

with her and begins to document the numerous play themes that spread out over the yard.

One group of girls is making sand birthday cakes with woodchip candles. Proudly counting their work, they declare, "We have eight cakes!" They invent an elaborate, collaborative system of sending buckets down the slide where one girl fills the bucket with sand to make a cake, then hands it off to another child to deliver to those waiting at the top of the slide. There the cake receives a candle and is placed on the birthday display. On the other side of the yard more counting is the focus as children are collecting worms. "Six worms!" a boy with limited English exclaims excitedly. One child mentions she has recently seen a snake, and a lively discussion ensues about snakes. "They stick their tongues out." "No, they go 'sssssssssss.'" "No, they wiggle back and forth!" The children teach each other English, Chinese, and Span-

ish as they share the words for snake *and* worm *from their home languages. By the doorway to the building, in a trench dug to ease the flooding, more children are digging out water with shovels and pouring it into bowls. One of the children names the muddy water* chocolate. *Now the game takes a different turn as the children scoop up chocolate ice cream. The play grows again as bowls of ice cream are offered for sale to friends in other parts of the playground. Much imaginary money changes hands as the eager children form a line to buy the pretend ice cream.*

Listen to Kristin

"These past few weeks of constant rain and our agency's emphasis on performance standards and paperwork have really dampened my enthusiasm for this work. But something happened for me today when we were finally able to go outside to play. At first I couldn't stop my worries about all the standards, the learning domains, the checklists, the assessments, the curriculum forms, and the administration looking at me with stern eyebrows wanting an explanation of how I will accomplish all of this. Right in front of my eyes, as I watched the children, I could see every area of learning represented on that playground today.

"It reminded me of my faith and beliefs that say these children are a precious gift. I am not here for the administration, for the government, or for the politicians. I am here to experience the joy of these children and to provide a place where they are allowed to be who they are. These are wonderful people who couldn't care less about muddy pants or raindrops on their noses, who aren't for one second thinking about 'school readiness.' They are simply being, and I am reminded I need to stop at times to simply *be*. Sure, I will take pictures and share them with the children. We will pore over them and decipher ways to build upon their interests and learning. But today I reminded myself that these experiences are valuable for what they are: spontaneous moments of wonder, discovery, and delight. They are an opportunity for me to really see."

Reflect

You can see in the details of Kristin's story any number of possible learning outcomes imbedded in the children's play. As Kristin says, "right in front of my eyes" the children were counting, learning language from each other, exploring scientific concepts, solving problems, and inventing new ideas and actions. By closely observing the details of the children's play, Kristin had opportunities to assess and plan for math, language, science, multicultural education, and social skills. But an equally important aspect of this story is Kristin's reflection on her own attitudes and feelings. Rather than succumbing to discouragement, she sees her power to follow the children's interests and reframe the requirements so they include the joy and complexity of these unfolding activities. Kristin is bringing herself—her beliefs, values, and passions—to her work, which fortifies her to claim her power and take responsibility for creating more meaningful experiences for the children and herself.

PRINCIPLE   Think Through Your Actions

Young children spend almost every waking moment working to make sense of the world. Endeavors like the ones in Kristin's group happen all the time. But too often teachers are distracted, focused on requirements, problems, or the schedule, and thus miss the incredible opportunities germinating around them. To take advantage of these openings for deeper joy and learning, you must stop to examine what is influencing your thinking and consider possibilities for the actions you might take. The daily work of early childhood teachers is complex, with ever-changing dynamics related to program parameters and the group of children and families, as well as your own views and background. Within this context you move about your day reacting and responding to what is unfolding around you. Responsive curriculum requires slowing down, making conscious decisions, and staying alert to what unfolds. To be purposeful, you must be aware of the various things that influence your behavior.

Know Your Teacher Scripts

In *Developmentally Appropriate Practice in "Real Life,"* Carol Anne Wien (1995) suggests that it is "teacher scripts," learned from your own experiences with teachers, that determine your actions with children. Because you are making multiple decisions, thinking on your feet all day long, you often respond from these "scripts," or unexamined views of what teachers do. The following is a list of typical teacher scripts:

- Make sure children follow the rules and routines and stick to the time schedule.
- Intervene when children are in conflicts or are displaying risky behaviors.
- Plan learning activities to keep children busy and meet standards.
- Help children stay on task and complete a project.

Certainly, most of these behaviors are a necessary part of working with children, particularly groups of children. There are rules, requirements, routines, and activities to complete. Yet limiting yourself to the role of "preschool police," which many of these behaviors suggest, is unpleasant for both teachers and children. Lilian Katz (1998, 36–37) analyzes teacher behaviors in her comparison of Reggio Emilia schools with those in the United States:

> The content of the relationships between our [U.S.] teachers and their pupils tends to be dominated by information about the child's conduct and level of performance. Thus, it seems that the content of relationships between teachers and children in our early childhood settings, when not focused on mundane routines, is about the children themselves. In contrast, my impression of Reggio Emilia practices is that to a large extent the content of teacher-child relationships is focused on the work itself, rather than mainly on routines or the children's performances on academic tasks. . . . Adults' and children's minds meet on matters of interest to both of them. . . .

A program has intellectual vitality if the teacher's individual and group interactions are mainly about what the children are learning, planning, and thinking about, plus their interest in each other, and only minimally about the rules and routines.

This seemingly simple observation from Katz presents many challenges for how you think about your role as a teacher. Rather than emphasizing curriculum activities and routines, your actions could be guided by your own curiosity and an eagerness to meet up with the children's hearts and minds. You could acknowledge what you are seeing and offer ways to keep exploring their interests and ways to connect with other children. When you see your role as learning alongside the children, your actions are very different from when you're thinking of yourself as a conveyer of information, mediator of conflicts, or driver of standards. You use various responses, including the behaviors of a stage manager, a coach, and a news analyst and broadcaster.

Know Your Professional Influences

Many commercial early childhood resources reinforce a limited teacher script approach to teaching. Workshops may offer techniques and catchy acronyms, but these don't help teachers examine the dynamic process of teaching and learning with children. Catalogs promise their packaged activities will help teachers efficiently reach desired outcomes. However, using them with children reveals fleeting satisfaction when they lack context and involve no real investment on the part of the children or teacher. Clearly, professional resources are important to your work, and new ideas and activities keep you fresh and growing; but you should be diligent in choosing resources that challenge you to fully examine the complexities of your work.

Know Your Theoretical Influences

In addition to teacher scripts and commercial materials influencing your work, your images of children, conscious or unconscious, control the actions you take. This reminder is one of the greatest contributions to the field from the educators of Reggio Emilia. Read the words of Carlina Rinaldi:

> Each of us has his or her own image of the child, which is reflected in the expectation that we have when we look at a child. Some focus on what children are, what they have, and what they can do, while others, unfortunately, focus on what children are not, do not have, and what they are not able to do. Some focus more on their needs than on their power and capacity. As a result you have positive or negative expectations, and construct a context that values or limits the qualities and potential that you attribute to children. (Gandini and Edwards 2010, 50)

Before we were exposed to the educators of Reggio, other European child development theorists strongly shaped definitions of best practices in the United States. Perhaps their ideas influence your thinking as well. Drawing on the theories of Jean Piaget and Maria Montessori, NAEYC initially imbued the definition of developmentally appropriate practice with a belief that young children learn best through self-initiated play and discovery, and teachers should foster independence. Wanting to protect children from authoritarian teaching and push-down academics, many teachers have embraced these beliefs and interpreted them to mean that teachers should take a "hands-off" approach. Ironically, these same teachers readily intervene and try to guide children's behavior, with the goal of protecting individual rights and learning to take turns.

Unfortunately, this protective stance and emphasis on individualism is not only culturally biased, but obscures the actual competencies that children have. In the name of developmentally appropriate curriculum, teachers could easily be "dumbing children down" (Gatto 2002). Teachers may think they are protecting children, but perhaps they have a limited view of children's capabilities. In addition, they may well be marginalizing other cultural perspectives that value interdependence over independence and learning in groups over individual efforts and achievements.

Many communities of color in the United States have experienced this as another form of racism. Current experts have urged teachers to re-examine the central role of the social context for children's learning and the important role of adults in scaffolding that process. In fact, this discussion typically draws on the writing of Lev Vygotsky (a white man from Russia) instead of referring to research by U.S. educators of color such as Lisa Delpit, Gloria Ladson-Billings, Lily Wong Fillmore, Cecilia Alvarado, or Zaretta Hammond. As you examine the theories that may be guiding your work with children, take care to recognize the historical and cultural context from which they sprang.

Chew on This

Jonathan started working in the toddler room while taking early childhood classes at the community college. After seeing the lead teacher, Miss Aurora, feeding one of the children, he felt concerned and decided to talk with her during naptime.

"Miss Aurora," Jonathan began, "why were you feeding Ming Gong? He's too young to be using a fork and spoon. He would be much more independent if you just let him eat with his fingers. I couldn't understand what you were saying to him, but I hope you weren't being critical and lowering his self-esteem."

Miss Aurora took a deep breath and patiently tried to explain. "Ming Gong's parents want him to learn

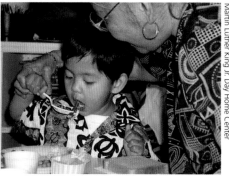

Martin Luther King Jr. Day Home Center

to be careful with food and not waste anything. I was showing him a good way to eat and talking him through it in his home language. Independence is not the focus for Ming Gong's parents. Being careful with food and eating the American way is what they're concerned about. What I'm concerned about is demonstrating that I understand and respect their wishes."

Though they may differ in their definitions of best practices, most child development experts agree that children benefit from a structure and adult actions to support their learning. Sometimes these actions are obvious, and at other times less apparent. For instance, when teachers see the documentation stories of the remarkable in-depth investigations of children in programs inspired by the Reggio approach, they are often left wondering how a teacher or activity got from one point to the other. What did she see, say, or do to make this happen? It's not always clear what role the teachers played to bring out these ideas in children and enabled them to focus and work together so productively. It's tempting to think, "My kids could never do that," or "I would never be able to pull that off with all the other things I have to get done," because these stories usually omit many details of the invisible structure and implied teacher actions that make their work so significant. It is often hard to translate how this work could support and deepen learning related to standards. This is one of the primary purposes of this book and the curriculum framework—to help you think through your actions to support deeper learning experiences, especially when you have others prescribing what your curriculum should be.

Helping Hand

Here's a description of an ordinary moment in a toddler room and how three teachers responded to it. Read the story and then notice how each teacher has a different approach to what is unfolding.

Sixteen-month-old Savannah is playing at the sensory table when her child care teacher begins moving around the room cleaning up the toys and singing, "Clean up, clean up; it's time to get ready for outside." The teacher has twelve kids to get ready for the group's turn on the playground. The teacher approaches the sensory table where Savannah is diligently working to lift the lid to close up the table. Savannah is having difficulty because her body is in the way. Another child, Kyle, is standing close by watching Savannah's efforts. As you read each teacher's story, consider what influences might be shaping the teacher's response.

Mountain School

Maya's Response

Teacher Maya doesn't acknowledge Savannah's attempt to help with cleanup. She's worried about how much time it will take to get the rest of the group ready, and she wants to make sure the children get enough time outdoors. She takes Savannah's hand

and leads her away, closing the sensory table herself. Maya says to Savannah, "It's time to go outside; let's get you ready. You too, Kyle; I'll help you put sunscreen on."

Listen to Maya

"It always takes so long to get the kids ready for the next activity. Today we almost missed our scheduled outdoor time because the children wanted to keep playing, and they dawdle so much during our transitions."

Reflect

Maya seems to be influenced by the clock and schedule in this moment, rather than considering Savannah's point of view and the learning possibilities in this situation. Maya may be working from an unexamined teacher script of helping children follow the routines and get to the next planned activity. Playing outdoors is an enjoyable and important activity for the children, and Maya may have wanted to make sure the children had enough time for that. Teachers regularly have to make choices about how to use their time. But Maya could have verbally acknowledged Savannah's work, even while making a conscious decision to move her along in order to stay on schedule. She might have said something like, "Wow, you're working so hard to close that table. Thank you. Now let's get ready to go out." If Maya verbally recognized Savannah's attempt to close the table and made a mental note to involve her in lending a hand in the future, their relationship would be strengthened, and Savannah's hard work would be acknowledged and supported.

Tanya's Response

Tanya thinks to herself, "How cute! Savannah wants to help with cleanup, but she really doesn't know how to close the lid." She moves closer to help. "Here Savannah, let me do that for you." She lifts the lid herself as Savannah and Kyle watch.

Listen to Tanya

"I got such a kick out of Savannah trying to close the sensory table today. She is such a cute little thing. I was worried as I watched her struggle with that lid, and I thought she might pinch her fingers. I made sure I helped her before she got mad and frustrated or, even worse, hurt if the lid fell on her."

Reflect

Tanya finds Savannah's attempts endearing, but she doesn't seem to take her seriously, perhaps because she is influenced by her view of the limitations of Savannah's age and lack of spatial awareness. Rather than seeing Savannah as competent and able to do this task, she worries about Savannah getting hurt or frustrated and feeling bad about herself. Yet if Tanya observed more closely, she would understand that Savannah sees herself as capable; this is why she attempts the task and keeps at it. If Tanya brought this more competent image of children to this moment, she might have acted differently. She would see how Savannah would continue to see herself as capable if her efforts were encouraged, and come to see herself as a contributing member of this community.

Phillip's Response

Phillip closely watches as Savannah uses great focus and determination to try to get the lid on the table. He gives her a few minutes to work on her own and then decides she might benefit from some coaching. Phillip moves to her side and says, "Savannah, you are working hard to lift the lid of the table so you can close it. May I show you what I know about how to make this job easier?" Noticing that Kyle has been watching all along, Phillip invites him to learn too. "Kyle, you might be interested in this too. See? I stand at the side so my body doesn't get in the way. Then I use my strong muscles to lift up the lid, and it turns over as I close it." Phillip demonstrates as he describes his actions. He invites Savannah to try, and because the lid is a little heavy for Savannah, he suggests they all work together. "Kyle, you stand over on that side with Savannah, and I'll stand on this side. Here we go!" They lift the lid together and the job is done.

Listen to Phillip

"I was so impressed with Savannah's determination to help with cleanup today. I see this all the time with my group. They know about our room and routine, and they want to help. I try to take their efforts seriously and use every opportunity I can to teach them to do things. It may take a while, but eventually they really do learn. I want to encourage their strong desire to be contributing members of the group. Most people would never believe how amazing these very young children can be."

Reflect

What could be influencing Phillip's decision to stop and take time for this moment with Savannah and Kyle? Phillip has identified the role he wants to play in children's learning—he looks beyond the schedule and planned curriculum activities to the value of this moment. He knows the demands of the group and the need to have a consistent routine, but he also believes that moments like this are also part of the curriculum, holding possibility for meaningful learning. Because he sees these children as competent, he takes the time to coach them and, in turn, helps them live into their competence.

Obviously, you cannot always take advantage of every possible learning moment with each child. You must balance what individuals deserve with the needs of the group as a whole and the value of consistent routines. However, even when there isn't time to engage as fully as Phillip did in the example you just read, you can avoid responding from unexamined teacher scripts and interacting with children primarily about rules and routines. You can notice and acknowledge their efforts and interests, and you can see them as competent and curious. As you make choices about how to use your time, you can think

through what is influencing your actions and commit to making more purposeful decisions. Acknowledging the unfolding moments in your group invariably creates more possibilities. These instances are not events in between your teaching, but rather, central to deepening your relationships with children and enhancing the teaching and learning process. Once you begin to approach your work this way, you will see the abundant opportunities for strengthening relationships and learning all around you. The challenge then becomes choosing what interests to follow and expanding your repertoire so that unfolding moments grow into meaningful curriculum.

Your Turn

Choose a morning to keep track of what unfolds as you work with the children. If possible, do this with a coworker. Notice the flow of the day, what the children were involved with in general, and some specific times when you interacted with individual children or directed the group. At the end of the morning, write down what occurred in enough detail to jog your memory when you later reflect on the following questions:

- How did your curriculum activities and daily schedule affect your actions and decisions?
- When might you have followed the children's ideas and interests, but didn't?
- How did your image of children and their capabilities influence your actions?
- What other factors (environment, family/culture/community, media, biases, mandates/policies) might have influenced you and this situation?
- When did you claim your power to help create more meaningful experiences for you and the children?

PRINCIPLE   Cultivate a Mind-set of Receptivity

As teachers, we need to create a climate of receptivity, which does not mean merely the willingness to listen carefully or patiently. It has to do with quieting your state of mind as you prepare to listen. It means not pressing on too fast to get to something that you think you "need to get" as the "purpose" or "objective" of the conversation. There's something about silence and not being in a hurry that seem to give a message about receptivity. Children need some reason to believe that what they say will not be heard too clinically, or journalistically, or put to use too rapidly, and that the gift they give us will be taken into hands that will not seize too fast upon their confidence, or grasp too firmly, or attempt to push an idea to completion when it needs to be left open, incomplete, and tentative a while.

—Jonathan Kozol

As Jonathan Kozol suggests, the way to start in our work with children is to stop! Teachers must slow down in order to take in the moment, see what is afoot, and give the situation time to unfold naturally. On the surface, stopping and waiting doesn't look like action, but it is the primary place to begin when supporting in-depth work with children. The first action we take is within ourselves. We make it our practice to observe closely so we can see the details of what is happening. Silence and not being in a hurry tell children that we are open to being changed by their ideas. This is the basis of true conversation and learning. As we stop to look and listen, we are absorbed in our own learning process to understand the children as well as reflect on our interpretations of the situation. When we stop and wait, we communicate respect to the children and honor the possibilities inherent in ordinary moments. Paying closer attention to these moments increases our delight in the children as we gain a profound respect for their insights and abilities. We come to trust them as partners in the teaching and learning process and love the work we are doing. Working in this way requires cultivating a very different mind-set. You come to see yourself as a researcher, intellectually engaged in what is emerging. You are able to live with uncertainty and work together with the children, trusting that your shared pursuits will be meaningful and useful.

Ramp It Up

As you read the next story, notice the details of teacher Cindy's receptivity to the big noise and action of the children in the block area and what unfolds as a result.

A group of children in Cindy's child care room have been passionate about building ramps with blocks. When the construction is complete, the children zoom small cars down the ramps, causing them to fly all over the room. Their work is loud and boisterous and involves big body action as they try to get the cars to fly as fast as they can. The flying cars crash against the walls and windows, and sometimes they get very close to other children. Cindy redirects the children's actions, warning them of the dangers of the flying

they worked. I was thrilled that the children took this work seriously and followed the guidelines I set out. It was exciting to watch them learn about the physics of speed. I'm so glad I followed my hunch that speed was their real interest, not random, wild play."

Reflect

Many teachers would jump right in and stop the noise and the potential danger of this play. But Cindy's mind-set of receptivity enabled her to wait before jumping in with her adult agenda. She allowed the children's interest to unfold and grow and then used their passion to prompt them to go deeper with their learning. Rather than waiting for the children to inadvertently learn about the physics of gravity and speed through their random play or stopping it altogether, Cindy challenged them to continue exploring in a way that became more purposeful.

cars. *"Keep the cars on the ramps to get them to go fast. It's too dangerous to throw them like that."* *Rather than taking the cars away and stopping the play, Cindy responds to their quest for speed and brings them some golf balls. "I have a new idea. These golf balls can go really fast. I'll let you use them if you roll them. If you throw them, they will be really unsafe and I'll have to put them away." The children eagerly begin to build ramps and live up to Cindy's guidelines about rolling them. And indeed, the children are able to get the golf balls to race down the ramps at exciting speeds, without throwing them.*

Listen to Cindy

"As I observed and listened to the children, I kept asking myself: 'What are they trying to accomplish here? What is so thrilling?' I realized that they weren't just being loud and crazy, but instead trying to get the cars to go as fast as they could. I think I was brave to decide to offer them golf balls to help them accomplish their speedy goals. I thought it would motivate them to pay more attention and use some control as

Use the Thinking Lens® Protocol

Area for Reflection: Know yourself

- What is your usual response to loud, active play in your classroom, when things are flying all over and hitting the walls?
- How does Cindy's approach to the children's big play deepen your thinking about your response?

Area for Reflection: Find the details of the children's competence that engage your heart and mind

- What is your response to Cindy's offering of the golf balls and guidance to use them safely? Do you believe children are capable of using coaching like this to focus their behavior?

Area for Reflection: Consider other perspectives

- What do you think the children are learning from the ramp and ball play? How might you explain the value of these experiences to a parent?

No Ordinary Moment

No child was meant to be ordinary and you can see it in them and they know it too. But then the times get to them and they wear out their brains learning what folks expect and then spend their strength trying to rise over those same folks.

—Annie Dillard

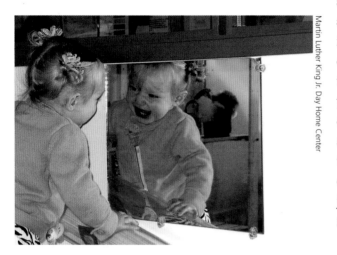

Martin Luther King Jr. Day Home Center

Study the look on Hannah's face and how it symbolizes this quote by Annie Dillard. Hannah sees herself and this moment in her life as extraordinary. Her own image reflected back to her in the mirror brings her absolute pleasure. When was the last time you looked at yourself in the mirror this way? Can you remember why you stopped? If we still looked at ourselves and experienced life in this way, we might see others similarly, and that could transform how we live together on the earth. We can choose to notice and learn from young children's point of view or sadly, as Dillard suggests, be one of "those folks" that children must "rise over."

PRINCIPLE   Seek the Child's Point of View

When you watch young children closely, you will note their intense focus and determination, curiosity, and delight. Whether happy or sad, angry or tired, young children are naturally optimistic and eager for every encounter. This drive ensures that their brains will develop faster during the early childhood years than at any other time in their lives. The estimated number of brain connections that develop throughout this period can be as many as a staggering 250,000 per minute (Shonkoff and Phillips 2000). During this time there are no ordinary moments!

The child's perspective can influence your decisions and actions and is critical to understand if you are to engage children in a deeper teaching and learning process, and at the same time, enhance your own experience. It takes practice to look and listen attentively. You must suspend for a moment any agenda you might have for what the children should be doing. Instead, put yourself in their shoes to understand the experience from their point of view. Spiritual masters around the world know that the practice of being present in the moment can bring peace and joy to people's lives as well as infuse it with profound meaning.

Fabrics Galore

When Carline, an infant caregiver, saw a colorful pile of beautiful fabric, she immediately knew her group of seven- to eighteen-month-old children would love it. She decided to play with the fabric herself to learn about it, and she imagined what the children might do with it. She wrapped herself in the fluffy cloth and waved it in the air. She thought about how the children would love to dance with the fabric, and play hide-and-seek. She tried to imagine what her

Burlington Little School

little ones might experience and think about. "If I cover my head, will I be able to see you? Can I find you? Will you be able to see me? When I wrap myself in the fabric, I'll feel safe and comfy." She knew the children would be drawn by a sense of wonder as they explored the textures of the fabric. "Is it soft or hard? How does it smell? Can I eat it?" With these thoughts in mind, Carline couldn't wait to see what her group of children would do with the giant rainbow of colors.

A Bounty of Bracelets

In the following story, discover with Deb how attentive her one-year-old children are when she stops to consider their point of view.

Deb offered a collection of colorful, sparkly bracelets packed in clear plastic containers with lids. The children examined the bracelets closely, noticing how they sparkled in the light. They were fully engaged in putting the bracelet rings back into the cups and fitting the lids on. Oscar immediately knew what the rings were for, so he spent a very long time putting every bracelet he could get ahold of onto his arm. When Deb pointed this out, the other children seemed to understand the importance of this work for him and let Oscar have more bracelets so he could complete the task. At one point, Kiran began throwing the rings onto the ground in front of him and then watching them as they spun around and around like a top until they slowly lost momentum and wobbled to a stop. When Deb noticed what Kiran was doing, she called the other children's attention to his idea. This captured their interest, and along with Deb, the children all began playing this new game of throwing bracelets and watching them spin.

Listen to Deb

"I immediately knew from my previous observations of the children that they would love the plastic sparkly bracelets I found at the dollar store. As I observed them with these materials, they were absorbed in using them just as I predicted. They focused intently on putting the plastic rings back into the cups and carefully putting the lids on. I'm always so intrigued by how seriously toddlers take this kind of work. When I saw Kiran deliberately throwing the bracelets, my

initial reaction was to jump in and stop this behavior. One of my ongoing goals is to help the children see how to care for our materials. Fortunately, before I jumped in, I stopped to look at the situation from his perspective.

"What I realized is that Kiran had discovered that if he threw the rings just the right way, they would spin around and around like a top and then slow down and stop. I was thrilled to learn this new way to explore the bracelets and called the other children's attention to Kiran's idea. I'm so glad I stopped to see Kiran's point of view. I was just amazed that he figured this out; he's only fourteen months old! His discovery is now a part of the learning games we play with the bracelets, and the children are getting quite good at controlling this small aspect of the science of physics."

Reflect

Deb stops to observe the details and conscientiously works to consider Kiran's point of view. Her analysis of the situation allows her to respond in a way that furthers his study of the spinning bracelets. She sees the possibilities for collaboration, as she invites the other children to learn from Kiran. As you reflect more on this story, we invite you to get curious about other details you've read.

- How do these very young children come to respect and learn from each other when their verbal ability is so limited?
- Why do toddlers find exploring containers with lids so fascinating?
- Do the children feel the satisfaction of conquering a tricky puzzle when they succeed in putting on the lid?
- Do you think they are soothed by knowing that some things in the universe can be put together just right?

Getting curious about the children's point of view will keep you intellectually engaged in your work.

Taste Tests

How often do you jump to conclusions about what is happening with your group? In the following story, notice how Neda realizes her initial impressions of a child's communication were missing the child's point of view.

Neda offered her toddlers an array of fresh fruits and plastic knives for cutting. When they would cut open each fruit, Neda pointed out what was inside, sharing in the children's delight and surprise of each unique fruit. Along with discovering the fruits' internal beauty, the children eagerly began taste testing. As Anna tasted the lime slice, her face puckered and she called out a disgruntled sound. Neda acknowledged, "Yes, limes have a sour taste, don't they?" Anna wasn't satisfied with this response. She kept pointing to the lime with an animated face of concern. "You don't have to taste that one," Neda offered. Still dissatisfied with the response, Anna went to the sink, climbed the step stool, turned on the water, and proceeded to wash the lime. As Neda observed these actions, she exclaimed with surprise, "Oh Anna, now I think I understand. Are you trying to wash that sour taste off the lime? Try tasting it again. Did washing work?"

Urban Village Two Neighborhood House Head Start

Listen to Neda

"I love to plan activities for my toddlers that offer them new experiences. Watching their amazement at what they found inside each fruit helped me to see the fruit in a new way. Through their eyes I noticed the interesting shapes and textures and the gorgeous array of colors. The children showed me how to immerse myself in the fragrance and savor every bite. I had a delightful surprise when Anna came across the taste of the lime. She kept making faces, and I tried to tell her she didn't need to eat it. When she went on a mission to wash off the lime, I finally saw her idea. It was a shock to her that I would give her

something that tasted so nasty and a revelation to me that such a young child could be such an independent, competent thinker."

Reflect

Because Neda's approach to this activity was to observe from the children's perspectives, she was looking for the details that showed their thinking. This mind-set allowed her to consider Anna's theory: that her teacher wouldn't have given her something that tasted bad, so the lime must have something on it that needed to be washed off. Rather than trying to "teach" her about the fruit, Neda invites further investigation of Anna's theory when she offered her the logical next step, to test out her theory by tasting the lime again. This story is a powerful reminder that even very young children are theory makers, working to understand and communicate their ideas. Neda's thoughts and actions are a good model of how to look beyond our adult viewpoints to really understand those of the children.

Your Turn

When you seek the child's perspective before responding, rather than just focusing on behavior, you choose an action that will expand the learning experience. To gain insight into what the children might find interesting in a material, try exploring materials before offering them. Choose a material you think the children will find engaging. Think about your group and make some guesses about what they might be drawn to and what they might notice. Play with the materials yourself and notice your own discoveries. These explorations will alert you to language you can offer the children as they use the materials. As you prepare yourself through these explorations, you get ideas about possibilities that might unfold, but you stay open to surprises that you didn't anticipate. Offer the materials to the children and then use the reflection and action questions list on page 145 to observe, make meaning, and respond to their points of view.

PRINCIPLE   Notice the Details to Discover More Possibilities

As a teacher, you can uncover the children's point of view by noticing the many small things that are occurring within the group. Children look closely at details that adults often take for granted. Adults are usually quick to assign a meaning and a label to what they see. Yet when you just summarize or make generalities from your observations, you don't have much information to use for making meaning. To capture the specific details of what you hear and see, you can use a variety of simple tools: a clipboard and pen, a sketch, an audio or video recorder, or a camera. Your role is to highlight the details of the unfolding moments, not only for yourself but for the children as well.

Sand Scientists

As you read the following story, ask yourself what might have emerged if the teacher had noticed the details of what the children were doing. What guesses do you have about children's theories and understanding based on the details in the story?

In a program designed for children identified with special needs, two four-year-old boys played near each other in the sand. Hector seemed to be on a mission to fill a plastic plate with sand. Over and over again, he piled the sand on top of the plate and then used the back of his shovel to slap the sand and make it flat and even with the rim of the plate. He used significant force as he pounded the sand with the shovel. At one point, he moved near Sam who was also playing in the sand. Hector watched Sam for a few minutes, noticing that he, too, was working to flatten the sand. However, instead of using a shovel, Sam used a plate and in a single motion, flattened his sand mound. Hector waited until Sam put the plate down; then he picked it up and, with obvious satisfaction, copied Sam's method. Sam began to whine and complain, saying, "He took my plate." Teacher Julia moved in quickly and made Hector give the plate back to Sam, suggesting that he wait his turn. The conflict was settled, and Hector was redirected to another area to play.

Listen to Julia

"Sam and Hector got into it again in the sandbox today. I'm glad I was nearby to help them figure it out, so their disagreement didn't get out of hand like it often does."

Reflect

Julia didn't see any of the details that could have led her to respond differently. Let's take a closer look at the what happened and the missed opportunities in this situation. Can you see Hector's purposeful efforts as he explored the properties of the sand and invented tools to accomplish his goals? He learned

Desert School

from watching Sam and then successfully applied this new learning for his own purpose. Seeing these details could enhance the image of Hector as a competent learner, rather than only viewing him as a child in a program for children with special needs. The teacher also missed an opportunity to point out Sam's good idea and how Hector learned from him. Rather than reinforcing Sam's complaining, she might have suggested he practice being a coach by showing and describing his ideas to Hector. Imagine how encouraged the boys' parents would be if the teacher shared the details of their skillful ideas and interactions in this situation. Instead, these opportunities were lost as the teacher moved in to resolve the conflict.

Obviously, the work of a teacher is complex. As a teacher, you don't often have time to sit back and look for all the details. But this story is a reminder of how important it is to plan for regular opportunities to capture details. Doing this will help you see that each situation has multiple perspectives and possibilities for interpretation and help you to respond with this in mind.

Use the Thinking Lens® Protocol

Area for Reflection: Know yourself

- How would you assess your ability to observe closely and capture the details of children's experiences?
- What insights have you had about yourself and the role you play in children's learning when you realize that you missed some important information and responded to children in a less-than-helpful way?

Area for Reflection: Find the details of the children's competencies that engage your heart and mind

- What behavior or activity in children have you once viewed as bothersome but now want to reconsider in light of the children's competency and how to provide for it?

PRINCIPLE   **Share Conversations Following the Children's Lead**

Fortified with the children's perspectives and careful observations of their work, teachers are ready to share conversations with children. Children are "doers" who don't often reflect on their activities. Talking about what you see points children's attention to the properties and characteristics of materials, people, and actions that they may not have noticed or do not yet have the words to describe. Describing to the children what you see unfolding offers the possibility that they will go further with their investigation. And it just might encourage their thinking to move to a new level.

These are not just casual conversations; instead they require teachers to practice using the details and children's viewpoint in conversation. The difference between these kinds of interactions and those that interrupt children's pursuits is that the focus stays with the child's current actions or interests, extending rather than shifting. Following the children's lead, you can help them connect their interests to the larger world, extend their vocabulary, and further develop their receptive and expressive language skills. You can remind them how what they are doing connects with something they have done previously with you or with their family. You can also advance the learning process by authentically engaging with children around your own life experience, sharing your ideas and views on their interests.

Authentic conversations that follow the children's lead look very different from teaching techniques that lack a give-and-take process. You might view it as the "dance" of teaching and learning with children. It is a complex set of rhythms and turns, requiring sustained attention and sturdy shoes, but the added significance and pleasure you will gain in your work is well worth the effort.

Dough Dances

As you study the following simple conversation between teacher Janie and Tomas, picture the warm body language between them and the ease with which Janie gives value to Tomas's work. Her words are limited, but one action builds on another, and the connections Janie is making are layered with meaning for both of them.

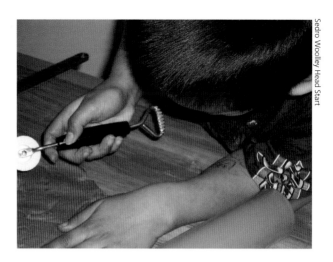

Janie is sitting at the playdough table next to four-year-old Tomas in her Head Start classroom. The other children have gone off to play elsewhere, while Tomas diligently continues using a crimping tool along the edge of his playdough hearts.

Tomas: "After I do all of these cookies, I'm going to bake them."

Janie lights up as she looks at his work: "You have done a lot of work here. I see marks all around the edges of each heart."

Tomas, too, lights up: "I'm going to show you how to do it."

Janie: "Okay, show me."

Tomas demonstrates how to carefully make marks around the edge of the dough with the crimping tool. He seems to relish the role of teaching as he points to the hearts and says: "You do the small ones, and I'll do the big ones. You have to follow the lines all around."

Janie leans in, showing she takes his instructions seriously. "Okay, I followed the lines. Now what do I do with them?"

His interest seems piqued and Tomas decides what to offer next. "I have to take the side off." He cuts an edge off one of the hearts and then leans in to examine what he has done. "I made a medium size."

Janie looks curious about his repeated reference to size and adds an additional thought. She asks, "How do I know which are the medium? Do we have to measure?"

Tomas: "You do it this way." He takes his crimping tool and makes a line from edge to edge—bottom to the top, and side to side. This divides the dough into quarters.

Janie, imitating what he did: "You mean like this?"

Tomas: "You have to make it bigger."

Janie watches Tomas closely and imitates his actions again.

Janie: "I see what you are doing; you made it smoother."

Tomas: "Here, let's do this."

He works on his own design with the tool. Janie follows his lead and shows him the design she's made on her dough.

Tomas: "It looks like a boat."

Janie: "Where do you see a boat?"

Tomas, pointing: "There is the bottom and those are the sails."

Janie: "Oh, I see it now. I didn't have that in mind, but it did come out looking like a boat."

Tomas keeps working. He shows his new design. "Look, I made a star."

Janie: "Yeah, it looks just like a star. I see the lines and the points." She points to these features as she describes them. They continue enjoying each other's company like this until the call for snacktime.

Listen to Janie

"I love to talk with children and hear what they think and have to say. I believe if they can express themselves, they will feel comfortable to speak up and learn from that. I use my own curiosity to talk with them and to notice together: 'What happened?' 'How are we going to solve this?' 'What will we do next time?' It is so much fun to be with children in this way. You never know what will happen or what new discoveries or learning will take place."

Reflect

It's not unusual for children and teachers to sit together at the playdough table, but the care with which Janie conversed with Tomas is more unusual. She pays close attention to his ideas and actions, naming what she sees, imitating him, asking him for further clarification, and sharing her ideas in response to his. She trusts the direction he takes to be most pertinent for his learning. With her comments, Janie doesn't try to teach Tomas about measuring, but instead provokes him to think through his own ideas. As he does this, he is challenged to build new concepts and vocabulary. Through this experience, Tomas is discovering that he has important ideas to express and can help others learn. This easy exchange fosters Tomas's relationship with Janie. Knowing this task is important to Tomas, she wants to challenge him to recognize the ideas he is pursuing and to take them further. Within this trusting relationship, he will feel safe to take up any new challenges Janie may offer for his learning.

Martin Luther King Jr. Day Home Center

Tender Tommy

Oona has recently transitioned from the baby room to the toddler room. Tommy instinctively knows what's needed. He joins Oona at the window, and sharing their two-year-old perspectives, they begin to form a friendship.

Tommy: "I'm two and a half."

Oona: "I'm two."

Tommy: "You want to play at my house?" He gently puts a hand on her shoulder.

Oona: "My mommy says you can come to my house too."

PRINCIPLE   Support Children's Connections with Each Other

Children have a huge capacity for offering support and also for accepting and benefiting from the gifts of others. Human beings are born with an instinctive drive to reach out and connect with one another. Yet teachers often try to learn as many skills and strategies as they can to manage children's behavior and then focus on teaching children how to behave and get along. Imagine, instead, what would happen if you saw children as already possessing the gifts for developing relationships and your role being to help them express this. Children are compelled to connect with one another and are genuinely fascinated with one another's words, ideas, and actions. This presents ripe opportunities for developing in-depth curriculum experiences.

We can turn to the theories of Lev Vygotsky to support the idea that relationships are a source of energetic learning processes. This involves making meaning together, rather than merely acquiring facts. The study of meaning involves children and adults working together to explore ideas and processes so they can come to shared understandings. Approaching learning in this way is dynamic and often spicy, as the group may have disagreements while they learn to work with multiple perspectives and negotiate their differences. Diving in together helps children see that there are many ways of thinking and expressing themselves, and that different perspectives are worthwhile for solving problems and creating new thinking. The group comes to see that learning can be exciting and fun.

Teachers can call attention to different points of view among children. You might describe children's words and work, highlighting how their ideas and approaches are similar and different. You can also suggest that the children talk about one another's work, ideas, and assumptions, inviting challenge and negotiation. When a child has accomplished something meaningful and shows pride in her work, ask her to show and tell another child how to do it and what she figured out. All of these actions enable children to share what they know and, in the process, better understand it themselves. Many teachers work in multilingual, multicultural classrooms where it's especially important to help the group see and understand each other.

Bubble Experts

As you read Sheila's story, notice how her acknowledgment of the details of the children's actions fostered connections among them.

One day at the water table, the children were immediately drawn to the soapy water and, even more so, to the eggbeaters, spending a long time trying to figure out how they worked. They paid close attention to the different ways they could turn the handle, watching the blades spin as the handle was turning. As they worked, their teacher, Sheila, restated what each child said and pointed out what they were doing.

"Look, Raul is showing us his beater turns really fast."

"Lilia says hers is easy to turn."

"Many of you see that the blades stick when you turn the handle too fast."

Sheila's attention seemed to bring out the children's curiosity so that they kept trading beaters and excitedly telling and showing each other how the beaters worked.

"Mine is really fast. Look how I do it."

"Mine has this kind of handle. I turn it and the wheels move."

After about ten minutes of play and discussions on the workings of the beaters, the children turned their attention to how the beaters changed the soapy water. Roberto put the eggbeater directly into the water and turned the handle to see what would happen. He did this a few times and then put the beater into one of the bowls filled with water and turned the handle again. He showed the other children the bubbles he was making.

"Look at this," he exclaimed as he turned the handle and watched the water change into a pile of bubbles in the bowl.

Sheila imitated his actions, asking, "Is this how you do it, Roberto?"

Many children began to do this as well and repeated the action several times, until Roberto said, "I'm going to make a lot and a lot and a lot and a lot of bubbles—watch." As he worked, Sheila asked him if he could slow down and show each thing he did so the other children could learn how to do it too. As he demonstrated, Sheila named the steps he was taking for making the bubbles.

"Step one, you fill up a bowl with the soapy water.

"Step two, you put the beater into the bowl.

"Step three, you begin to turn the handle."

As Roberto turned the handle, he said, "You have to go really, really fast to make a lot and a lot of bubbles."

He squealed with delight as his bubbles began flowing over the side of the bowl.

The entire group focused on Roberto's steps and were able to follow them because Sheila had put them in the spotlight. The children were so pleased to be able to share this discovery, and Roberto was grinning from ear to ear as the children kept asking him, "Roberto, is this how you do it?"

Listen to Sheila

"I'm always looking for ways to help the children see themselves as learners and also as teachers for each other. There are a mix of languages spoken by this group: Spanish, Russian, and English. Since I have been pointing out their actions, they are building more connections with each other. They are beginning to thrive on being a group and supporting each other. I love that I can help them."

Reflect

Sheila uses close observation of the children's actions to help them see their own thinking as well as learn from one another. Children don't automatically reflect on their actions, so teacher talk that illuminates children's actions will often provoke self-awareness. Becoming self-aware and thinking about your own actions and ideas is the foundation for learning. Strategies for learning increase as children begin to see each other's ideas and approaches. In fact, children often learn more from one another than from adults, so referring them to one another is a worthwhile approach. Sheila is aware of the importance of this as she works with her group.

Babies with Babies

Cristina works with very young children. How does her scaffolding reveal the remarkable insights these early toddlers have?

Cristina observed her group of one-year-old children playing with the baby dolls and related props in the room. They imitated the actions from their own experiences, such as trying to fit the bottles in the dolls' mouths and covering the babies with the blankets. Cristina observed them closely so she could imitate their behavior and play alongside them, describing the details of what unfolded among the group.

"Kiran is feeding his baby a bottle."

"T'Kai is gently putting his baby to bed."

"Hannah is rocking her baby to sleep."

"My baby is crying. I'm going to give her a hug."

The children paid attention to Cristina's comments and tried out what they saw her and one another do. Oona, one of the older children, extended her play to a sequence of actions as she fed her baby, wrapped it in a cloth, and then rocked it to sleep. When she noticed the other children were following her, she repeated this play script over and over.

Listen to Cristina

"It has been delightful and fascinating for me to watch the children imitate the familiar caretaking activities from their own lives with our dolls and props. I love to make guesses about what they might be thinking as they play. As I describe the details out loud, the children seem to pay more attention to one another's play and often try what I have pointed out. Today I saw something new. As the children began playing together, they were watching and interacting with one another more than usual. I know it is a stage in their development to move from parallel to cooperative play, but it seems that my broadcasting of their actions helped them make a leap in their thinking. I particularly noticed this with Oona's play. The other children eagerly followed her lead as she was playing

with her doll. She noticed the other children's attention to her, and I think it enabled her to see herself and her actions in a new way. A dreamy look came into her eyes and a satisfied grin came over her face. She seemed at that moment to understand the power of her imagination. It was such a profound experience to witness her growing awareness of her ability to create her own magical world of make-believe."

Reflect

Cristina isn't just using a teaching technique, but rather bringing her own enthusiasm and curiosity to her interactions with the children. Along with Cristina, we can wonder about the remarkable development going on with her group.

- Is this baby play beginning symbolic representation of children's family experiences?
- Does watching one another's pretending introduce the children to the power of their imaginations?
- Is it the foreshadowing of dramatic play that will bring them such delight later?

- Are we witnessing Vygotsky's theory of social constructivism in action?
- How does commenting on their play help deepen the children's experience and enable their collaboration?

When you immerse yourself with the children as they play, you can illuminate for them the amazing process of human development you are witnessing.

PRINCIPLE   Take Action on Behalf of Children's Strengths

It occurred to me that we are teachers not by chance, but because we are exploding with intentions. Just like children and babies, we are seekers of meanings. Making meaning is different from acquiring knowledge. While knowledge is static, meaning making is the process that moves us to act. What are we going to do after we gain knowledge? Although this way of being with children liberates us from having "the right answers," as we embrace uncertainty and open ourselves to dialogue, we gain a sense of freedom, but with this freedom comes responsibility— the responsibility to act and to change. —Iris Berger

As Iris Berger suggests, at the heart of responsive teaching is a dive into what is happening with the group, making meaning of it together, and using what you create to learn and live more fully. Young children bring this open, eager disposition to your life, and your challenge is to figure out how to offer your adult wisdom without taking over in the learning journey you are taking together. At the center of the meaning-making process is the belief and understanding that children have a deep desire to show their competence and make a contribution to their community. This is how they develop a positive identity and learn what they need to know to function in the world. Teachers can best support this process by paying attention to children's competence.

The task is to look for and highlight children's participation and "know-how." This responsive relationship is a cycle that builds on the children's and teacher's strengths. If you come to see the children's competence, you will take the time and develop the patience to coach them. When you do, the children come to see their own abilities and positive attributes. The foundation of this cyclical process is the belief that all of us can live up to our fullest capacity for working in partnership toward a common good. Could there be a more important purpose for education in today's world? These may sound like lofty goals, but opportunities for living this way are in the everyday moments you have with children.

Binkie Love

As you read the next story about two eighteen-month-old children, notice how the teacher works with the children's capacity for sharing and helping each other instead of jumping in to solve their problem.

Today as she got absorbed in her play, Wynsome dropped her binkie and forgot about it until she saw the one in T'Kai's mouth. She went up to him, yanked the binkie out of his mouth, and put it in her own mouth. T'Kai started to complain loudly. Teacher Sandy responded to this bumpy moment by suggesting that the children work together. "T'Kai, let's go find Wynsome's binkie so you can have yours back." T'Kai accepted this idea readily, and they searched the play area together. When they found Wynsome's binkie, Sandy suggested they go to the sink to wash it off. Wynsome, listening to the exchange, eagerly joined them at the sink, bringing T'Kai's binkie with her so it could be washed too. Wynsome willingly gave the binkie back to T'Kai and with the binkies in their rightful owners' mouths, the children spontaneously gave each other an exuberant hug.

Listen to Sandy

"T'Kai and Wynsome both love their binkies and would chomp on them all day and night if it was okay with their mamas. From my earlier observations, I have come to understand that these two children share a strong connection around their binkies. They know firsthand how important binkies are and must associate their own feelings with the other. I've seen them offer a binkie to each other when they are playing side by side. I also think that sometimes taking the binkie from the other is about trying to get closer by climbing inside each other's experience. It seems as though Wynsome wants T'Kai's binkie rather than *a* binkie or *her own* binkie. It was such a sweet moment when they hugged each other. I've heard that children this age are self-centered, but when I think about what is underneath their behavior, that just doesn't ring true. The reason Wynsome willingly gave T'Kai his binkie back was her interest in sharing the task and being connected with him."

Reflect

Many teachers in this situation would try to help Wynsome learn she shouldn't take other people's things or teach T'Kai to "use his words." Sandy doesn't mediate this conflict by responding to the children's self-centered behavior to have their own binkies. Instead she calls on the children's innate desire to be in relationship when she suggests to T'Kai they find Wynsome's binkie. Wynsome shows that Sandy is on the right track when she eagerly joins in. This story challenges Piagetian ideas that children are egocentric and unable to take another person's perspective. When we offer a way for children to live into their positive attributes and abilities, we reinforce their social skills.

Martin Luther King Jr. Day Home Center

Traffic Jam

It's important to cultivate your mind-set and ability to see children's strengths and offer them strategies for learning to use them. Sometimes it takes strong intervention and perseverance, as the next story demonstrates. Notice the intentional and consistent action Ann takes on behalf of the boys' potential to play together cooperatively.

In the block area, it wasn't clear what Juan and Joseph wanted to do because they just started pulling all the blocks off the shelves and throwing them on top of each other in a scramble on the floor. This seemed exciting to them as they added explosion sounds to the crashing of the blocks as they hit each other. Seeing this, teacher Ann quickly gathered a basket of trucks and cars and asked, "Are there any road build-ers here today to make a place to drive the cars and trucks?" Juan and Joseph immediately began lining up unit blocks end to end.

Joseph: "Let's make it a really long road, all the way there . . . long, long."

Juan: "Here, here; go here."

Joseph: "No, no; it needs to go long here. I want it to be long here." He took some of Juan's blocks and put them at the end of his growing road.

Juan screamed in protest: "NO! NO! HERE! HERE!" He kicked apart Joseph's road, scattering the blocks.

Ann quickly offered a clipboard and said, "I'm drawing the road you made out of blocks." She then handed the clipboard and pen to Joseph. "Will you draw some of the blocks for our map? That way, we can remember how the road goes. We can use this as a map to help us rebuild. Our drawing tells us where the blocks should go."

When Joseph was done, Ann stood the clipboard with the finished drawing up on its side and Juan looked at it repeatedly as he began replacing the blocks end to end.

Ann: "Let's add cars to the map. Can you two work together to draw some cars?"

The boys negotiated their own turn taking and their drawings soon showed not only the road but the movement of the cars, and they also told the story of the boys at play.

Listen to Ann

"This was a loud and volatile situation as the boys' conflict could easily have grown into a big fight. I've been trying to help them see each other's ideas and offer them ways to work together. I try to figure out what they are individually trying to accomplish and then help them work with the ideas they share. Their first reaction is to bump up against each other, but if I stay with it, I can usually help them work together."

Reflect

Ann takes clear actions that support her belief that these children are capable of working through their differences and collaborating. Rather than approach-ing this potentially volatile situation by offering techniques for turn taking, threatening time-outs, or banning their use of the materials, she sees their initial energy as a sign that they are enthusiastic about working together. She seeks to capture the boys' collaborative spirit by inviting them to connect their ideas and actions through the challenging and focused task of building and drawing a road for their cars. Through this work, the boys come to see their own and each other's competence and feel the reward of working on a shared task.

Your Turn

Observe children working together in a popular play area of the room and document their activities through taking notes and photos with the following focus:

- What specific things do the children do and say that indicate they are connecting with each other and building relationships?
- How do they use the objects or materials in their play to communicate their ideas?
- What challenges or conflicts occur? What do the children do and say to resolve their differences?

Use your documentation to make a homemade book with a title such as *We Know How to Work Together*. Include photos and descriptions detailing what the children say and do that reflects what they know about working together. Regularly read this book with the children and invite them to add more ideas over time.

Use these questions to explore what you've learned:

- What am I seeing that reinforces my view of children as eager to connect and capable of working through their differences?
- How does revisiting their experiences help their ideas and actions change and grow?
- What other ideas do I have for illuminating children's relationships?

6 Coach Children to Learn about Learning

But it's not just learning things that's important. It's learning what to do with what you learn and learning why you learn things at all that matters. —**Norton Juster**

One of the most rewarding outcomes for an early childhood teacher is when the children in a group initiate their own play, work well together, and keep at it for an extended period of time. Teachers often feel proud when learning is so focused and fun that the children don't really need them. When you value these experiences for children, you might become adamantly opposed to interrupting the children's play with your or other people's agendas. Or perhaps you might be puzzled about what your role should be when children are involved in sustained play. To feel like a "real teacher," you might feel obliged to seize upon emerging themes in children's play and plan a "curriculum unit" around them.

The value of child-initiated play can hardly be overstated. This understanding has been at the heart of early childhood education since the beginning of our profession. Children thrive when they have a lot of time to pursue their own ideas through play using open-ended materials. Elizabeth Jones and Gretchen Reynolds (2011) say that children who have these opportunities will become "master players," which they assert is one of the most crucial outcomes for early education, since master players are motivated and successful learners.

In discussing the importance of teacher actions, we never want to inadvertently diminish the vital importance of sustained child-initiated play. Rather than interfering, taking over, or overwhelming them with too much instruction, the actions you choose should *support* children's learning. Instead of insisting that children do things your way, for example, offer helpful suggestions. Teachers walk a delicate line between challenging children to work at the upper end of their abilities and frustrating or discouraging them. Lev Vygotsky identified this as the "zone of proximal development," which he defined as the distance between what children can do at their current level of development and what is possible for them with support from adults or peers (Berk and Winsler 1995). He called this support (the actions teachers can take to help children reach the next level of possibility for their learning) "scaffolding." Engaging in this process with children is one of the greatest rewards of teaching.

Coaching children to *learn about learning* is an important part of the scaffolding process. And this process is most successful when you coach children to build upon familiar experiences or offer the next step after long periods of open exploration. When you see children involved in activities where they might benefit from mastering a skill, those are teachable moments. Yet you need to believe they are capable and deserve more support, or it won't even occur to you to offer something more. After each coaching session or demonstration occurs, children will need opportunities for practicing a new skill to make this a part of their own repertoire for learning.

In the previous chapter, we explored how teachers can notice and enhance ordinary moments as part of everyday curriculum. In this chapter, we will examine more fully the teacher's role in extending children's activities by offering ideas, know-how, and

wisdom. You can use the following principles to help children go further as you coach them to learn about learning.

Principles

- Help children see learning as a process with distinct components they can practice.
- Invite children to assess their own learning.
- Coach children to use tools and strategies for learning.
- Plan coaching sessions separately from playtime.
- Help children use reference materials to support their learning.
- Teach children to look closely.
- Teach children to draw in order to see more clearly.
- Offer stories and dramas as tools for coaching.
- Support children to learn from their friends.

Burlington Little School

Teach Me Something

While sitting next to Deb at the art table one day, four-year-old Priya (who had been in Deb's preschool program for a couple months) said, "I really like coming to preschool and all of the things that we play with here, but when are you going to teach me something, Deb?" This wasn't the first time Deb had heard this sentiment from a child. Children who had graduated from her preschool class and returned from kindergarten for a visit would proclaim how much they were learning now that they were in "real school." Deb tried not to be defensive when hearing these comments but instead tried to understand the child's point of view. Eventually, Deb came to understand that the children's attitudes were similar to many adults who had thoughts such as "You don't learn when you play. You learn when you go to 'real' school and the teacher teaches you something." These

experiences got Deb thinking about how powerful it would be for children if she could help them learn about their own learning. From that day on she worked to develop strategies and engage in conversations to explore with the children how and what they were learning through their play.

PRINCIPLE Help Children See Learning as a Process with Distinct Components They Can Practice

Have you ever wondered what young children think about learning? They absolutely understand that they don't have as much information or as many skills as adults and older children. Yet they continually strive to reach the next level and proudly let others know of their growing abilities. You often hear two-year-olds fiercely say, "I'm not a baby anymore!" Preschoolers claim their size and age with bravado, knowing that those who are bigger and older have more power and privilege in the world. What if you harnessed this self-assurance and drive for competence, and steadily helped children take charge of their own learning?

Teachers plan for children's learning, but adults rarely let children in on their thinking. Children don't often get to see the "why?" behind what you do. It takes reflection to understand what is happening and to see all ways you might extend and deepen learning. But the daily life of providers and teachers allows little time away from children to do this reflection. In addition, when you do make time to revisit your work, you seldom investigate what the learning experience was like for children. Instead, you might make general evaluations about the children's interest in your curriculum and whether you met "your" teaching goals. But what if you invited the children to be part of your reflection process, becoming your partners in identifying what is worth learning and the best way to go about it? When children can say, "I know how to learn something," they see themselves as capable, become more confident, and don't get as easily defeated by setbacks.

To help children see how learning unfolds, you can draw on the theories of "multiple intelligence" (Gardner 2011), "the hundred languages of children" (Edwards, Gandini, and Forman 2012), "social constructivism" (MacNaughton and Williams 2009), and "making learning visible" (Project Zero and Reggio Children 2001). As you incorporate understandings from these resources into your teaching, you can introduce them to children as a natural part of your classroom culture and learning practices. How might this look?

As children play, adults can call attention to the many ways they are learning. You create an expectation and awareness that they are here to "get smarter" not by reminding and instructing, but by describing and inquiring about what is unfolding. For instance, a teacher might make comments and ask questions like these:

"When you do _____ , you are learning about _____."
"What are you thinking about when you do _____?"
"As you work, how will you know when you are done?"
"If you want to learn more about _____ , here is what you might do _____."

You can include concepts of learning theories in your interactions with children. Children naturally use multiple approaches to learning as they play, but they aren't necessarily aware of their process. When you offer children a framework for thinking about their actions, they can decide how to pursue their learning. They see what works best for them and are challenged to try new things. Over time, children come to know this is the way they learn. Your time with children will be better focused when you make the following concepts explicit:

- When you want to learn more about something, look closely at what you have done and think about your ideas.
- You can let someone know about your ideas through a conversation, by directly describing them, or by creating a story.
- You can teach someone what you know or the steps you followed.
- Writing our ideas on a chart or in a book reminds us what we have been learning. Then we can come back to these ideas again later without having to start from scratch.
- Another way to learn more is to create drawings of our ideas and actions.
- We can use different materials to explore the same idea. We could build or sculpt how something looks, create a dance, write a story, or make up a drama about it.
- Inviting others to join us in thinking will help us learn more. Our friends, our families, people in the community, or books might give us more ways to think about our ideas.

Here are some specific comments you might say to children to incorporate these ideas into your teaching.

- "Tell me your ideas, and I'll write them down."
- "Tell me the story or the steps. What comes first? Then what?"
- "Let's make this into a book or a chart."
- "Let's draw what you have been doing or making. I see _____. What else can you put in the drawing?"
- "Let's find some other materials to use for making this same thing."
- "Who else can join us to explore this idea?"
- "Are there books or other people who might be of help?"

A look at preschool teachers incorporating these concepts into their daily curriculum will shed light on how to help children learn about learning.

Learning with Legos

In the following example, observe the ways that Kirsten helps the children see how they can keep learning by using their passion for building with Legos.

After many days of shared excitement over building with Legos, Kirsten approached the children with a clipboard and a pen. She told the children that she could write down their stories about the things they had built. Josh was the first to take up her offer and dictated a story as he pointed to the parts of his Lego construction.

Kirsten: "You've been working on that a long time, Josh. If you tell me the story of it, it will help you learn more."

Josh, pointing to each part of his structure: "This is the garden that my dad made in our yard. These are the trees and plants. My dad is mowing the lawn. This is me. I'm riding on a sled at the back of the yard."

Kirsten: "Let's look closer and see if we can draw it."

Burlington Little School

Kirsten repeated the story that Josh had told her as she carefully drew each part. Josh gave her directions, suggesting more details as she worked on the drawing.

Josh: "I have a hill back there that I ride my sled on."

When she invited Josh to draw his own Lego structure, he declined, saying he didn't really think he could do it. Kirsten assured him that he would keep learning and maybe later take up this challenge.

After a couple of weeks and many experiences of talking about his Lego structures and watching the teachers draw them, Josh became quite skilled at drawing the details of his Legos. He eventually loved re-representing his Lego constructions, initiating the drawings on his own.

Burlington Little School

As Lego mania continued in her room, Kirsten kept offering new ways for the children to make their work more complex. When some of them began flying Lego rockets around the room and pretending they were pilots talking over their radios, Kirsten put out butcher paper and drew roads and land forms, offering this as the landing pad for the rockets. As the children took up this suggestion, an extended drama unfolded over the weeks that followed. The children used markers to add their own ideas to the landing pad and a detailed airstrip was created.

On another day, Kirsten suggested the children make rocket ships out of recycled materials. A number of children spent the day working on this challenge. In the coming days, the children incorporated straws and flubber (a borax, glue, and water mixture sometimes called "gak") to design and build a fueling dock for their Lego drama. The flubber became the fuel and straws were used as hoses for fueling the rockets.

Listen to Kirsten

"Many of the children in my group spent a big part of our playtime sitting next to each other and building with Legos. Sometimes they would talk or play together around their Lego constructions, but that was as far as their play would go. My first instinct was to try to get them to move somewhere else to play so they could be exposed to more tools and materials. Instead, I decided to try to use their competence and interest in Legos to challenge them to work together and learn something more. At first I wasn't comfortable taking such an active role when the children played. I have learned not to interrupt their play. But I found if I stayed focused on the details of the children's work, urged them to think and talk about their interests, and encouraged them to join their ideas through a shared task, they jumped right in with me and each other. This has become an ongoing habit for all of us now; as the children play, we all pay attention to the details and use them as the source for more conversation, activities, and learning."

Reflect

Have you found yourself worried about children in your group who play in the same area with the same materials day after day? Kirsten's story shows how to use the children's obsessions to expand their play and introduce multiple strategies for learning. Did you notice the language and suggestions Kirsten used to encourage the children to see and expand on the learning that their play offered? As Kirsten works with the children over time, talking about their ideas and helping them explain their actions to each other, she offers additional materials to revisit their work, She also helps them learn how they can keep learning while pursuing their own interests and passions. Utilizing multiple strategies for learning becomes central to the daily life in this classroom for individual children such as Josh, as well as the larger group. What better outcome could we hope for children than developing the skills and dispositions necessary for being independent, as well as cooperative, lifelong learners?

Burlington Little School

Use the Thinking Lens® Protocol

Area for Reflection: Know yourself

What are your thoughts about the tension between child-initiated activities and teacher action to scaffold children's learning? What role do you most often play when children have initiated their own play activities? When do you intervene and when do you step back? How do Kirsten's actions to extend the children's play resonate with or challenge your beliefs about the teacher's role in children's self-initiated activities?

Area for Reflection: Find the details of the children's competencies that engage your heart and mind

- Identify all of the skills and competencies the children developed as a result of Kirsten's challenges.
- How does your view of children's competence affect the role you choose to play in their learning?

Area for Reflection: Consider multiple perspectives

How would you assess your current understandings and practices related to Vygotsky's theories about scaffolding learning and the zone of proximal development?

PRINCIPLE   Invite Children to Assess Their Own Learning

Another strategy for focusing children on their own learning is to work with them in assessing what is worth putting into their portfolios, displaying in the room, or sharing with parents. With some guiding questions, children can begin to reflect on their work and how it does or doesn't represent things they are learning. Questions to consider when looking over work samples and documentation of their efforts could include the following:

- Which of these shows us what you have been trying to figure out as you've played this week?
- Does one of these (pictures, stories, papers) capture something you have been trying to learn?
- Do you see something here that makes you know you are learning things while you are here?
- When you look over these collections, can you think of something you would like to learn next? How could you go about that?
- Who knows about this and might help you?
- What will you do tomorrow to get started?

Whose Learning Is It?

Read the following story of the routine that teacher Brian uses in his class to help the children assess and appreciate their own learning.

Each Monday morning, Brian displays a collection of the work his group of four-year-olds completed during the previous week. He places observation stories, photos of the children's play, and artwork on a table for review. Brian sits at the table during playtime, working with small groups of children as they eagerly come to hear the stories of their time in child care. They look things over and talk about what they did and what they learned. It's the children's job to decide what work to add to their own portfolios. The children spend time with their current work, but also love poring over the many other items that have been collected throughout the year. Brian suggests that the children study the current items carefully to determine which work best represents how they have been learning.

Listen to Brian

"I used to feel so overwhelmed by the emphasis our program places on assessing children's learning. Filling out checklists and doing observations for each child's portfolio took so much of my time and took me away from relaxed time with the children. This changed dramatically when I started to think of ways to involve the children in this process. After all, it is their learning that I am tracking, and they should be a part of that. What I do now is make my observations and assessments of their play into stories with photos for us to study together. We have come to love this activity as a routine for starting our week. We constantly talk about learning, and these conversations have become a vital aspect of our time together."

Reflect

Can you imagine how powerful it is for children to engage in an ongoing reflection of their own learning process at such a young age? After all, a young child's entire life is about learning. Brian's weekly routine

takes advantage of this simple fact, offering children insight and ownership of the learning process. Children need a variety of experiences in order to learn, and reflection on those experiences brings about the deepest learning. And as you can see in Brian's story, children are eager to hear about themselves and their friends, so this activity also encourages collaboration and infuses a sense of joy in the learning process. Additionally, involving the children in this process helps Brian enjoy a task that he dreaded in the past.

Now I Know What Learning Really Is

When children spend their preschool years learning about learning, they come to new realizations. Priya, the four-year-old from earlier in this chapter, is one example.

Burlington Little School

At the end of the school year, Priya had another conversation with teacher Deb. Deb was bringing closure to their preschool experience by asking children to reflect on the year. She asked a number of questions, including: "Can you tell me what you've learned that you didn't know at the beginning of the year? What do you want to remember about your time here in preschool?" Deb reminded Priya that at the beginning of the year, she had said, "I really like coming to preschool and all of the things that we play with here,
but when are you going to teach me something?" Deb wondered what Priya thought about that now. Priya responded, "Oh, that was before I knew what learning really is."

Your Turn

As you reflect on your group of children, do you know how much they understand about their own learning process? What tells you this? How often do children talk about a plan for what they want to do? How is new learning acknowledged in your group? Do the children notice it or do you point it out?

Use your answers to these questions to begin conversations with the children about their learning. Try developing a simple learning plan with individual children or a small group, and then work together to document and assess what happens.

PRINCIPLE   Coach Children to Use Tools and Strategies for Learning

As you make the learning process visible to children, you can further their learning by coaching them to use tools, materials, and specific strategies. Children are keen observers of the adult world, and they are eager to learn and become better at making their ideas and actions understood. Historically, child-centered teachers in the United States have been reluctant to coach children in this way, offering models or demonstrations, for fear of limiting children's creativity. *Discovery* has been our mantra, and our sacred guideline has been to let children figure out what works and what doesn't. Exploration and discovery *are* an important part of children's learning. Nevertheless, some kinds of learning require instruction, support, and challenge. It's unfair to ask kids to communicate ideas without showing them how to use tools to do so. When we take the mystery out of tools, skills, and processes for learning, children will gain the confidence and ability to pursue their interests.

The following stories show different teacher approaches to coaching children.

Scissors Skills

This story reminds us that even the youngest children want access to the power of tools. Teacher Deb offers the children in her group scissors to cut flubber. What is your reaction to her decision to teach babies to use scissors?

One day when her toddlers were exploring flubber, Deb remembered her work with preschool children and how easy it was for them to cut flubber with scissors. She decided to try teaching her one-year-olds how to use scissors. The children watched her demonstration in earnest, as she showed them how to hold one part of the scissors in each hand and move them back and forth to cut the flubber. The children were captivated by this serious task, concentrating hard to practice what was demonstrated. Deb held up the flubber so it dripped down in a long drop, and the children worked at using the scissors until they were able to successfully cut the flubber. Oscar watched Deb's demonstrations of the two-handed way to use the scissors. He then confidently took the scissors in one hand and set about cutting with ease, even turning his wrist and hand to meet the task.

Martin Luther King Jr. Day Home Center

Listen to Deb

"Every day the toddlers I work with surprise me in the things that they can do. They are always so interested in the adult world and the tools I use in the room. They love to clean with the sponges and want a broom to help sweep when they see me sweeping. I have responded by having enough tools for them to participate in the real work of our room. Today I took this a step further. One of the things they are enticed by is the scissors. They always seem to find the scissors that I keep in the room for adult use. Today when we were exploring flubber, I remembered my work with preschool children and how simple and satisfying it was for them to cut flubber with scissors. It occurred to me at that moment that I could teach these one-year-olds to cut. At first I giggled to myself and thought about what most people would think of the idea of giving scissors to a one-year-old. (Those same people often worry about giving very young children substances like flubber!) However, I've come to know the children's determination and abilities, and I stay right with them during activities that need supervision, so I decided to go for it. When I suggested we could learn to use the scissors, the children seemed astounded. They remembered that I usually take scissors away. They watched me with intense concentration, then worked diligently to learn to cut. I had another shocker when I showed Oscar the two-handed way to use the scissors. He looked at me like I was nuts, took the scissors in one hand, and proceeded to cut like a pro. I've had four-year-olds who couldn't do what this twenty-month-old did with the scissors. I've come to see that children of this age

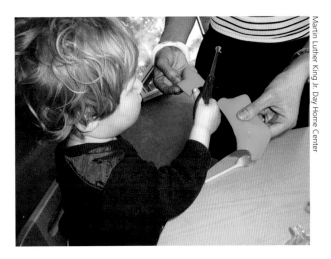

Martin Luther King Jr. Day Home Center

haven't yet been convinced that they are incapable of participating fully in the world, and I am finding out that they are right! I will continue to take seriously the challenges they offer me."

Reflect

To become a coach for children's learning, you need to believe that children are capable and deserving of the skills and information that adults have power over. Deb's belief in her group spurred her to take the time to break down the task into steps that the children could manage, clearly demonstrating what they needed to learn, and then watching and waiting patiently. Her story is a clear example of Vygotsky's theory of scaffolding. The children (except Oscar!) needed support to be able to use scissors safely and with success. Their eager attitude and determination, along with their growing small-muscle skills, created a zone of proximal development that allowed the children to work at a higher level with Deb's help. Challenge yourself to consider what new skills the children in your group are eager to learn and capable of learning with your coaching. Imagine the children's and your own satisfaction when you spend your days together working with increasing challenge and skill.

Memory Lane

Coaching children to use thinking strategies can also help them take on more complex learning. Here Ann coaches Kierra to use her memory as a strategy for mastering a game she is playing.

Kierra spent most of one morning playing a lotto matching game. She laid out the cards of children's names in long rows. Then she dove into the effort of finding cards that matched, turning over one card, then another, and another, and another, until finally—a match! Other children would join in but then quickly leave the game, intrigued for only a short while by the playful element of searching for the hidden surprise of a matching card. After watching this unfold, teacher Ann decided to offer some coaching to the one child still playing the game.

"Kierra, I'd like to play this game with you," Ann said. "Will you teach me what you know about how to play this game?"

"You go two times; then it's my turn," replied Kierra. "We hafta find a match. But first we gotta fix the cards, because they got broke. They hafta go in a

Parklake Two Head Start

line." She gestured toward the cards that were lying helter-skelter on the carpet. Together Kierra and Ann straightened the cards, arranging them in neat rows, creating order from the chaos.

Kierra let Ann have the first turn. Ann flipped over one card, then another, reading the names aloud; they didn't match, so she set them back in their original places in the row, commenting, "I'm going to put these right back in their places so I can remember where they are next time."

Kierra took a turn and was careful to set the cards back in their spots, echoing Ann's words: "That's Alex's place. That's Ana's place."

Back and forth they traded turns, searching for pairs of cards that matched. Ann offered, "Okay, Kierra, remember that Jonathan is right here—we may need him later to make a match!" Later, she said, "Hey, we saw another Prudencio already—do you remember where he was?" Name by name, they matched up the cards, working their way up and down the neat rows until all the cards were paired.

Listen to Ann

"As I watched the children play this game, the cards became more and more jumbled; kids lifted a card to see what it held, then set it back down in any random spot on the carpet. Most of the children soon tired of the random 'hide-and-seek' quality of the game and left it to Kierra, who was stalwart in her efforts to master this game. I wanted to expand the possibilities that the game held for Kierra by suggesting strategies for playing the game that would deepen the intellectual effort involved. I hoped to move the game from 'hide-and-seek' to 'remember-and-find.' Kierra quickly embraced the strategy I offered, keeping the cards in well-organized rows and paying close attention to the location of each name. I was thrilled that with this strategy, Kierra mastered the game, brilliantly maneuvering through the long rows of black rectangles, finding cards exactly where she'd put them, creating a game of memory and skill."

Reflect

Consider how Ann asked for Kierra's thinking about this game as the launching point for the coaching she wanted to offer. You can see from Kierra's comments that she had her own understanding of this game and could clearly describe it. Ann picked up on Kierra's description of the game being "broken" and used that as the place to begin her suggestions. Ann played right alongside Kierra, talking out loud to coach her toward the thinking strategies that would enhance Kierra's learning as they played the game. It takes close observation, a strong desire to understand children's perspectives, and lots of practice to determine the most effective ways to coach children toward deeper thinking. As you can see in this example of Ann and Kierra, the outcome is deeply satisfying for children and teachers.

PRINCIPLE Plan Coaching Sessions Separately from Playtime

If you want children to initiate their own activities and play collaboratively, show them possibilities for using tools and materials. But rather than interrupting their open playtime to offer coaching, set aside separate times for these special lessons, perhaps during a small-group time or as part of your circle time. During these coaching sessions, show children the many possibilities for using everyday materials such as blocks, paint, playdough, and manipulatives, and then give them time to work with the materials, try out what they learned, and add their own ideas and actions. Don't insist they do it your way, but instead suggest the many possibilities with the emphasis on how they can invent more. As children work with the materials on their own, take photos and write down their words, turning these into pages for binder books to be kept in the related area of the room. Continue to document and add these documentation pages to the binders. You can even keep the same binder in the room over a number of years so children can revisit what they did when they were younger or see what their siblings did when they were in preschool.

Blocks and Bridges

Here is an example of how Cindy coaches children in using blocks through carefully planned lessons.

The children enthusiastically gathered around the tables and block platform for block-building lessons. Cindy began by describing the kinds of building she had observed the children doing lately. "I have noticed that a lot of you have been building roads by putting the blocks on the floor, connecting them end to end to make a long line." She demonstrated what she had seen and showed some of the photos she had taken. "Today I wanted to teach you how you could build a bridge with these blocks to add to your roads." A few of the children confidently claimed that they already knew how to build a bridge. Cindy said, "Great, you can help me teach the others." As a

part of the demonstration, she held up each different block, asking the children to name what they noticed about the shape and size. She described and demonstrated how the children might fit the various blocks together to form a bridge and other structures. After this ten-minute demonstration, Cindy invited the children to jump in and try bridge building. They eagerly worked, copying what Cindy had done, but also adding their own ideas, calling out, "Look what I did!"

Listen to Cindy

"The children have been excited about our block-building lessons and very eager to try out the new ideas I offered. Because they have gotten really good at building roads with the blocks, I wanted to demonstrate the possibility of adding bridges by building up and attaching tunnels and archways. The children feel so confident in their block-building abilities that they think I'm silly for trying to teach them more. But I notice that these lessons really do help them

strategies that connect to the children's current work. You can see how this immediately leads the children to use the blocks in new ways. Cindy's demonstrations, the children's hands-on work, and the binder book are all concrete tools for coaching the children to learn and practice these new skills and concepts. Along with these rich experiences, you can see the literacy learning available as the children follow a series of steps and practice reading as they use the binder book as a reference tool.

Boss of the Paints!

Here is another story of coaching lessons, this time in the art area. Deb decides that because the children have had many opportunities to explore paint on their own, offering a lesson in mixing colors would be most helpful.

Deb created a chart showing the steps to follow in mixing paint and planned a lesson to teach the children how to use the chart. Deb started the lesson by saying, "I'm going to teach you how to be the boss of the paints." Deb explained this could happen if the children used the steps in the chart, so they would have control of the paints, rather than watching the colors blend together in the jar. She used a paintbrush and paints to carefully demonstrate the sequence on the chart of "wash, wipe, dip, mix, paint." After this demonstration, Deb invited the children to try. They dove right in, excitedly calling out their new discoveries to each other: "Look, I made orange." "Wow, look at this! I turned it into green."

use the blocks in new ways. The children often start with what I demonstrate, but then add their own ideas and inventions. I believe that their familiarity with the blocks propels them to new understandings and actions, so these coaching lessons are the perfect thing to do. I've created a binder book that highlights each of our lessons and shows the remarkable roads, bridges, and tunnels the children have been making. I'm excited to see them regularly use this book as a reference during playtime."

Reflect

Cindy's story shows how the children's ideas and actions can become a source for coaching them new skills and strategies. In her coaching lessons, Cindy breaks down and describes the different methods she has seen the children use in their constructions and then builds on this by offering information and

Listen to Deb

"I knew that the invitation to be 'the boss of the paints' would get the children's attention because they are always so interested in the power of being a boss. They felt really good about themselves as they successfully followed the sequence on the chart. But I was shocked when the children were so surprised with the results of their paint mixing. They have been painting all year and mixing is their favorite thing to do. Their reaction was like they were making an amazing new discovery. From that day on, the children have been revisiting the idea of mixing colors, at first to discover the control they can have over the change, but now they are carefully mixing the color of paint they specifically want for their work."

Reflect

The children were delighted and amazed that they could mix paints to create new colors. Although they had mixed paint colors repeatedly in their own explorations, they had never thought about controlling the process. This story shows how coaching and documenting has the power to enhance the children's skill and confidence, leading them to extended explorations. In addition, when children are coached to follow a series of steps and a process, they gain an important tool for learning to learn.

Your Turn

To learn how to coach children in using new materials and tools, gather together some basic supplies for working with wire as a sculpting medium. You will need 18- to 22-gauge wire, wire cutters, and tools for shaping the wire. You can use masking tape, clay, or Styrofoam as a base to hold the wire, but that's not essential. All these supplies can be found at craft or hardware stores.

Sit down and explore the properties of the wire—how it feels to work with it in your hands and the different strategies you can use to create shapes with it. Think about individual skills, information, techniques, and terms that would help children use the wire and tools successfully.

Reflecting on your experience with wire, plan a coaching session or demonstration that you can offer children. This might include a chart with steps for becoming "the boss of the wire," guidelines for safety, and vocabulary related to the tasks of engineering, sculpting, and working as an artist. Try this out with children, noticing what happens, and revising the way you might coach in the future.

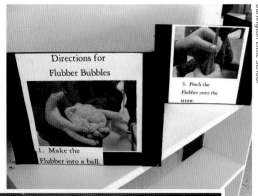

Flubber Bubbles

Children find blowing bubbles with flubber fascinating. It is a challenging undertaking, and often only one or two children are successful flubber bubble blowers, while others struggle. To help the children in her group learn the best strategies to use, teacher Anna Maria worked together with the children to document their discoveries and create a book of photos and step-by-step instructions (dictated by the children) on how to blow flubber bubbles. This year, two different methods for blowing flubber bubbles were identified, so they have two books of directions, to which the children regularly refer for help. Through this effort, the children are beginning to see each other as resources for new learning, as well as learning to use reference books.

PRINCIPLE   **Help Children Use Reference Materials to Support Their Learning**

Pictures, directions, and charts can spark ideas in children and can show them steps and practice skills for using materials. Following a pattern or a diagram to accomplish something is both challenging and satisfying for children, but hard to do without some initial coaching. Study the following stories to see how these teachers offered reference material to encourage children's learning.

Stone Sculptures

Sometimes just including a reference book as part of an invitation will serve as an entry point for some further coaching. Notice how Miss Dee Dee accomplishes this with an interesting book on the playground.

One day Miss Dee Dee placed a book about stone sculptures in with some of the rocks on the playground and stood back to see what would happen when the children discovered it. Jamilla and Rochelle were the first to pick up the book. They held the book upside down but showed no sign of realizing this. They studied the pages and exchanged some words that Miss Dee Dee couldn't hear so she approached the children and asked what they were noticing.

Martin Luther King Jr. Day Home Center

Jamilla: "They got some really big rock pictures."

Miss Dee Dee: "Yes. Look at those tall rock structures. Actually, if we look closely, we can see that an artist took some smaller rocks and stacked them on top of each other to create these big structures."

By this time, Samara had joined in, peering over their shoulders.

Samara: "I'm an artist. Watch. I can make those stack up."

Samara spent the rest of the outdoor time experimenting with different ways to create towers of rocks that wouldn't fall. At various points, children would come to watch her, and she would describe what she was discovering.

Samara: "The big ones are easier. Those little ones don't stay. See, these got more flat parts. You gotta get the flat parts to line up. The most I got so far is seven."

Listen to Miss Dee Dee

"I'm often looking for interesting books so children will come to see them as references for their ideas. Books that connect children's activities with the work of artists are especially appealing to me. Putting the Goldsworthy book next to some actual rocks was a useful strategy to provoke their interest and offer an example for the children to pursue. They often use the rocks for building and design, so I thought this book would be very helpful for them. I loved how they connected with each other and worked together around this interesting activity."

Reflect

You can see Miss Dee Dee's goal for the children's use of the book come to life in the story as the children eagerly moved between working with the book and working with the rocks. By explaining that the book reflected the work of an artist, she helped the children connect to the bigger world and see themselves in this way. Samara displayed this when she confidently proclaimed, "I'm an artist." It's also easy to see how this activity can meet learning outcomes in math, science, and spatial relations as the children study the shapes and sizes of rocks, and try out strategies for balancing their rock designs.

The Challenge of Using a Model

In the next story, Shauna sees how the children step up to the challenge of following a model to enhance their block play.

Shauna noticed the children's avid interest in and their attention to the details of the small, different-shaped blocks they had been working with for over a week. She decided to introduce some diagrams that came with the blocks to suggest a new way the children could use them. They immediately focused on the details in the diagrams and the blocks, determined to make what was illustrated. Shauna pointed out to the children how the illustrations had taught them more about the blocks and suggested that they make illustrations of their own work. The children gladly took up this task, drawing diagrams of the structures they had created. Shauna put these drawings together in a binder to leave on the shelf near the blocks for the children to refer to.

Listen to Shauna

"I learned in my early childhood classes never to give children a model to copy. When diagrams came with the Legos, I threw them away to ensure that children drew on their own creativity. What I realize now is that when children have lots of open time to play, they are ready for new challenges. Working to replicate a complicated model can be extremely rewarding. I gave the children a wonderful collection of small blocks of different shapes and sizes, which came with diagrams for building, using the unique features of the blocks. After the children had played with the blocks for over a week, I thought it was time to challenge the children by offering the diagrams. I was excited to see how engrossed they became in duplicating the patterns and structures in the diagrams. What was even more impressive was their willingness to make their own diagrams!"

Reflect

Can you see the difference between leading children through an activity where everyone copies a model of, for example, the same paper plate bunny and using the kind of complex diagram for enhancing block play described here? All too often, professional guidelines become rules that teachers follow without thinking. Our purpose in offering stories like this one is for you to see the powerful role you can play in children's learning when you thoughtfully use your wisdom and skill to help children understand and then further develop their competencies.

Models and diagrams offer children opportunities for careful study, for learning to follow steps and sequences, and for working through complex problems. Reference materials with pictures and diagrams give young children concrete experiences in literacy development as they practice reading and using symbols for their thinking and learning. Think about the children you work with—identifying a challenge and working through it successfully is among the most satisfying learning experiences for them.

Gather books or reference materials from your current collection of adult or children's books that could be used as a tool for children's learning. Review the books with the following questions in mind:

- Do these books have inspirational and clear pictures that show possibilities?
- Are there diagrams or steps to follow that the children can understand?
- Could children use these books or reference materials on their own or would they benefit from some coaching in how to use them?
- In what ways could the books or reference materials be useful if you added them to areas of your room?

Choose one of these books or reference materials and combine it with some related materials as an invitation for children's discovery. As you observe the children using the reference materials, notice what teacher actions might be helpful. Take action and then reflect on what happens.

PRINCIPLE   Teach Children to Look Closely

If your goal for coaching is to enable children to become self-directed, cooperative learners, then they need to sharpen their observation skills. Children are typically inclined to notice details, and you can help make use of this for their learning. Paying attention to what is around them will help children with their collaborative undertakings, reading body language and social cues, and discovering others' ideas and perspectives. Coaching children in observation skills taps into their eagerness to sort, classify, and see how things are alike and different. Noticing details will benefit their spatial relations, drawing, and literacy skills. Coaching children to observe closely will also help them read facial expressions and body language (emotional intelligence), distinguish letters on a page (literacy learning), and observe objects under a microscope (science learning).

A camera is another good tool for coaching children to notice what they see. Because children regularly see adults taking photographs, they are eager to use the camera themselves.

Children First

Through the Looking Glass

Using a magnifying glass or jeweler's loupe is a useful way to teach children to look closely. The advantage of a loupe is that it is held right up to the eye and blocks out all other distractions. Whichever tool you use, children benefit from some initial coaching to help them recognize when something is in or out of focus. *The Private Eye: Looking and Thinking by Analogy* (Ruef 2005) offers a curriculum using loupes, including a companion guide to introduce prekindergartners to the process of looking, drawing, and theorizing with 5x loupe magnifiers. The author suggests that teachers initially use a slide projector or overhead projector to teach the concept of "blurry versus clear." Then you can move on to coaching the use of loupes or a large magnifying glass that comes with legs. Encourage the children to describe what they are seeing when they look through the loupe or magnifying glass and what it reminds them of. Have them draw what they are seeing. For instance, children looking closely at a leaf have said the veins of the leaf remind them of bones in a hand. If these drawings are put on transparencies, they can be projected on the wall to change the scale and help the children identify new details.

Zoom Lens

In the following story, Amber has a camera dedicated to the children's use. What insights do you get from this story about how children see the world?

"Can I take pictures?" the children in Amber's classroom frequently asked as they saw Amber take photos of their work. She decided to get a digital camera exclusively for the children's use. When given the camera, the children often used the zoom feature for close-ups of textures and angles of different items around the room. They also took close-ups of different parts of people. They loved looking at each photo on the LCD screen on the camera right after taking a picture. Because she wanted the children to notice and describe what they were drawn to, Amber created a routine of downloading the photos onto the computer and then talking about them with the children.

Blake couldn't wait to show Amber the details he had captured with the camera. He and Amber turned viewing the photos into a game where Amber had to try to figure out what the image was by looking closely at the textures, colors, and shapes on the screen.

Blake: "Amber, look at this, look at this!"

Amber: "What am I seeing? I see translucent colors and different shapes."

Blake: "Yes, yes, and this is the open part of the glass. Can you tell what it is? Come over here." He took Amber by the hand and pulled her over to the table where the color blocks were located. "See, I took a close picture of these."

They continued this game with every photo. After viewing all the images, they erased the photos on the camera and Blake eagerly started the game again.

Listen to Amber

"I had always been curious about the images that ended up in my camera after one of the children had used it, so I decided to get a camera that the children could use throughout the day so I could study their photos more closely. I notice that the children consistently take close-up photos of discrete items, like a wheel on one of the toy cars or the weave of the carpet. They also take a lot of photos of faces and body parts, using the zoom lens so the parts are almost unrecognizable. I haven't been sure if the children are purposeful in what they select to photograph or if they just like using the zoom. Today, Blake gave me some insight when he invented a game where he took close-up photos, and I had to guess what they were. He was very purposeful in his picture taking and loved showing me these distorted views."

Reflect

Amber's descriptions of the children's photography, and Blake's photos in particular, present interesting questions to consider. How do children see the world around them? Do they notice the smaller details more than the fuller picture that adults see? Is this another sign that while adults tend to make quick meaning of what is around us, children have the ability to be present to the many possibilities? When we offer children the opportunity to use cameras and explore what they see around them, we can coach them in heightening their awareness and their ability to see, and in the process we can share in their rich view of the world.

PRINCIPLE Teach Children to Draw in Order to See More Clearly

In addition to giving children plenty of open-ended time for drawing and painting, we can use these activities for learning to look closely. The goal is not to create exact representations, but rather to help children see details for their learning. Mona Brookes (1996) offers useful strategies for this. In *Drawing with Children*, Brookes provides worksheets to help children practice copying shapes. The notion of copying a drawing has been traditionally discouraged in early childhood education, but here it is used as a coaching strategy for how to see, rather than produce, art. Helping children notice the elements of design—lines, shapes, sizes, and patterns—increases their aesthetic development and their ability to represent.

George Forman (1996) describes the value of drawing to learn about something. When children work to transfer onto paper what they see as a three-dimensional object, or represent an idea they have in their mind, they are confronted with problems to solve. Simple drawing lessons will help children in these ongoing endeavors.

The stories that follow provide examples of how teachers have worked with children to draw the details of what they are seeing.

Burlington Little School

Look a Little, Draw a Little

In this story, notice the direct ways Cathy coaches the children to draw. Her goal for them is not only drawing, but also understanding how to observe closely and how to work with thought and purpose.

Every week Cathy offers a drawing lesson. She gives the children special drawing pens that are used only for these lessons. She begins her coaching by suggesting that the children look closely at the details of the object while she describes what she sees as she moves her finger over an object. For example, when they were drawing self-portraits, Cathy said, "I see this oval shape that outlines your face. At the top of your oval face I see some of your hair. Can you see a row of hair growing above your eyes? Those are brows, and yours curve down a little. If I look closely at your eyes, I see a round, dark shape in the middle, your pupil, and then another circle around that." As they work on their drawings, Cathy coaches the children to look a little and then draw a little, and then look and draw again.

Listen to Cathy

"I have not been trained in art and I don't see myself as an artist, but I have always had a great desire to learn to draw. Recently I read that in the Victorian era, everyone had instruction in drawing and was expected to learn to draw. You weren't considered well educated unless you could render the human figure and draw a still life. This information led me to the idea that the children and I could learn to draw together. I've studied various books about drawing, some geared toward children and others toward adults, and I've attempted to share the lessons from these books with the children. What I notice is that children's work is always unique to them. We may all be drawing the same flower, but children emphasize the different aspects of what they see. The drawing lessons direct their attention to looking closely and their drawings always reflect the details they are seeing. We often revisit our line drawings with watercolor paints, so we add the aspect of color to what we are seeing. Or we will work with watercolor alone. I'm always amazed at the beauty, care, and attention the children give to this work."

Reflect

Most children love to draw, and it is an easier way for them to represent their ideas than writing or even talking. Even the youngest children can use drawing to communicate movement, experiences, and feelings (Kolbe 2005). But drawing with children, as Cathy describes, is more than art and creative expression. If children gain skills and confidence to draw what they see around them, they will be able to express ideas, tackle problems, and learn through their drawings. Children can develop their skills by drawing particular objects that they can easily see, such as ladders, bicycles, and pussy willows. The goal of these drawing lessons isn't just to learn to draw, but to coach children in looking closely to learn more.

Colorful Coral

Black-and-white drawings help children capture details. In this photo, however, teachers Fran and Nicole also help the children notice and represent the colors of the sea life present in their community.

To begin their investigation of sea life, the children looked through a reference book featuring images

of the Great Barrier Reef. The glossy photographs of the colorful coral were alluring, and the children were eager to talk about the colors, shapes, and interesting names of these coral formations. The teachers offered a palette of brightly colored chalk pastels alongside images of various coral species. They helped the children notice shape and color, and make choices about the coral pieces they preferred. The children took care to blend the chosen pastels to achieve the desired hues they saw in the coral. Fran and Nicole helped the children notice each other's blending techniques, which ranged from using several fingers together to merge larger blocks of color to delicately smudging color and line with a pinkie fingertip.

Your Turn

To help children cultivate their ability to see, you must develop your own keen awareness of the details around you. Try "drawing to see" using the following guidelines.

- Find an object to draw that has simple lines, shapes, and textures, such as a flower with a stem.
- Place the item where you can see it, but far enough away from your pencil and paper so you have room to draw.

- Looking only at the item and not at your paper, draw the details of what you see. Allow your pencil to draw what your eye notices, rather than trying to draw with a particular idea of the item in mind.

For more practice with this kind of contour drawing, turn to the book *Drawing on the Right Side of the Brain* by Betty Edwards (2012).

PRINCIPLE   **Offer Stories and Dramas as Tools for Coaching**

You can coach children by telling stories and using props to convey ideas you want them to grasp. Stories captivate children's attention, and playing out the details with dramatic play and props helps children internalize the concepts and strategies. Read about how teacher Sarah invented "teacher theater" for this purpose.

Dino Theater

As you read the children's responses to Dino Theater, notice how many social skills and strategies they come up with. How might Sarah use their ideas in the real conflicts that occur in the classroom?

At one morning meeting, Sarah acted out a story using three rubber dinosaur toys. In her story, two of the dinosaurs were building a castle out of blocks when a third dinosaur came along, hoping to join their game.

The first two dinosaurs said, "No, you can't play with us," and the third dinosaur felt sad and didn't know what to do.

At that point Sarah stopped the story and asked the children what they thought the dinosaurs could do to solve their problem. The children came up with a host of ideas, which Sarah then had the dinosaurs act out. Sarah had the dinosaurs "talk" about their own thoughts and feelings as they interacted. Here are a few of the suggestions the children made:

Tess: "They could change their mind and let the other dinosaur come to the party."

Elaina: "The one could go ask his mother for help."

Taylor: "The longneck won't like them."

Maria: "The longneck could build its own castle."

Siri: "The longneck could ask if they could come over to her house. They could play a little while at her house and then they could go to the castle. Then they could connect them."

Ruth Mabel: "The longneck could ask the dinosaurs if they could move over a little bit."

Maile: "Maybe they could go to a party—all the dinosaurs. That yellow one could say 'There will be a really big cake with five candles,' and they could sing 'Happy Birthday' to the yellow one."

Alex: "If they change their mind, they could join her in their game."

Ira: "Maybe they could go to a movie about dinosaurs called The Dinosaur Movie, *and they could watch the longneck."*

Ezana: "Dinosaurs don't eat the same food."

Kintla: "He could talk: 'Please can I play?'"

Sarah left the animals out for the rest of the day so the children could play and replay the various scenarios on their own.

Listen to Sarah

"Teacher theater is a tool I use often to coach the children to work through common issues or problems that arise in the classroom. The kids are full of good ideas and creative solutions to help the protagonists in the dramas. They particularly love it when my coteacher and I act out a situation for them to consider. I choose the topics for teacher theater in response to a particular or recurring interpersonal issue that is happening in the classroom. By having teachers or animals act out the situation, the kids involved can revisit their problems and receive some coaching without feeling singled out or criticized. Teacher theater is tremendously popular, and the kids always ask me to replay the scenario again and

Hilltop Children's Center

again and again. Replaying the drama with the props we leave out is also very popular. It's fascinating to watch the children act out what they have learned from the story and discussions."

Reflect

Whenever children are invited to pretend, they seem to be able to access skills and concepts that are more difficult for them to grasp in the middle of a real situation. The practice of teacher theater helps children to think constructively about how to solve social problems, because the issues are one step removed from the emotion and intensity of their own play. Teacher theater also shows children how to collaborate on generating ideas and offers them words and solutions to try the next time they find themselves in a similar situation.

For a more in-depth view of coaching kids through stories and dramas, consider the book *Kids Like Us: Using Persona Dolls in the Classroom* (1999) by Trisha Whitney.

PRINCIPLE   **Support Children to Learn from Their Friends**

Children learn not only from their teachers' demonstrations and coaching, but also from their peers. In fact, Vygotsky's theory of scaffolding points out that children often learn more working side by side with friends who are operating at the top end of a similar zone of proximal development (Mooney 2013). Children often use similar language and understand things in the same way, so coaching them to learn from each other is a useful approach. To support children in how to learn from one another, you can plan specific opportunities for children to help each other or work together, and suggest that they teach the other children what they have done or know about.

Be My Friend

In the following story, notice how Benny's teachers help him share his good idea and become a teacher for his peers. Pay attention to how Ann continually finds opportunities to refer children to each other.

Ann, a consultant in a Head Start classroom, watched with amazed delight as Benny turned paper towels meant for cleaning up splashes from the water table into pouches for holding water. Impressed with his ingenuity, she took the photos on the right to capture the steps Benny took as he made pouch after pouch full of water. She planned to use these photos to revisit this work with Benny and to highlight Benny's work to his friends, teachers, and family.

Ezra, Benny's teacher, and Ann alerted the other children to Benny's good idea about the water pouch and asked Benny to teach the other children how to make pouches. With splashing, laughter, and joyful pride, the children followed Benny's step-by-step instructions on how to turn paper towels into sturdy water pouches.

Soon after witnessing Benny's invention, Ann visited another center run by the same Head Start agency. There, Cedeena was playing at a table full of birdseed. Ann told Cedeena the story of Benny's invention and said, "I wonder if Benny's idea would work with birdseed?" She showed Cedeena the photos she'd taken of Benny's work. Cedeena eagerly accepted the challenge and soon invented a pouch for birdseed! She practiced and practiced filling a paper towel with birdseed and lifting it up without spilling the birdseed.

"Benny ought to know about this!" Ann exclaimed to Cedeena. "You could write him a letter to tell him about your invention." She helped Cedeena start her letter: "We can begin the letter by writing, 'Dear Benny,'" Ann said. "Then what should we tell him about the pouch you made for birdseed?" Cedeena dictated words and Ann wrote; then Ann handed Cedeena the pen so she could draw her pouch so Benny could see it.

Parklake Head Start

Ann delivered Cedeena's letter to Benny and his teacher, Ezra. Benny was delighted, laughing a big belly laugh and eagerly gathering a marker and paper to write a letter back to Cedeena. After dictating a letter to Ezra, Benny added a diagram of the birdseed invention, a way of letting Cedeena know that he understood her idea.

When Cedeena received Benny's letter, she hurried to her journal where she drew a picture of her friend Benny. Then Cedeena practiced making her birdseed pouch some more. Cedeena thought about Benny while she worked with birdseed.

"Does Benny like to go fast on the tire swing?" she asked Ann.

"I don't know," Ann replied. "You could write him a letter to ask." And she did.

"Does Benny like my blue skirt?" Cedeena wondered as she wrote her letters.

"I don't think Benny knows what you look like," Ann answered.

"I'll draw him a picture so he knows who I am," Cedeena decided.

Parklake Head Start

Benny and Cedeena's correspondence planted the seeds for a friendship that continues to grow. Their teachers have arranged a field trip for the two children's classes to meet at a park near their school, a park with a tire swing. Benny and Cedeena can cement their friendship with the joy of speed!

Listen to Ann

"A core value in my teaching is to nurture relationships among children. I watch for opportunities to help children grow connections with each other, ways that I can invite them to see each other in new ways, to collaborate, and to deepen their friendships. Benny was new to his classroom and hadn't made many connections with other kids yet. I wanted to help the other children see his competence and creativity, and experience his leadership. And I wanted to help Benny see himself as a good buddy to other

---

Use the Thinking Lens® Protocol

Area for Reflection: Know yourself

- What is your reaction to this story of Ann's actions to build relationships among the children?
- Do you think she intervened too much? Why or why not?

Area for Reflection: Find the details of the children's competencies that engage your heart and mind

How did showing the children the details of their competence encourage them to take up Ann's challenges to go deeper in their learning and to take other perspectives?

Area for Reflection: Seek the child's perspective

After hearing Ann's interactions with the children, what new thinking do you have about how children's perspectives can help you plan meaningful opportunities for learning?

children, able to offer them his ideas and inventions. When Ezra and I asked Benny to teach the other kids how to make pouches for water, Benny stood a little taller; his pride was tangible. He didn't say much, but demonstrated each step. His demonstrations engaged the other children—who spoke a number of languages—and launched the whole group into a shared adventure. And the shared adventure of making—and popping!—pouches full of water strengthened the relationships among this group of children.

"My decision to share Benny's story with Cedeena also grew from my core value about growing relationships between children. It was powerful for me to see two very young children (both these kids were barely four years old!) grow a solid connection to each other without meeting, by sharing their stories in writing and images. This experience affirmed the power of literacy—writing and drawing—as a tool for relationships."

Reflect

Ann's coaching offered abundant opportunities to incorporate literacy, sequencing, and representational work into Benny's and Cedeena's learning. But there are larger implications in this story. As Benny and Cedeena heard about each other's pouch making, they began to imagine the other person's experiences, taking each other's perspectives and wondering about each other. Building from their shared experience of pouch making, they invited each other into other games—pushing each other on tire swings, using blocks together, being *friends* with each other. As they came to know the other person, they also came to know themselves more deeply—as inventors, teachers, writers, and friends. Their offerings of warmth and friendship radiate from their exchanges. This shows how coaching is more than teaching techniques. It can foster genuine interactions that deepen our relationships and the quality of our lives together.

Engineering Teams

Cindy and Vicky decided to challenge the children in their group to learn from each other by outlining a specific activity and selecting the children who would work together as a learning group.

Because most of the children in their group constantly played together in the block area, Cindy and Vicky wanted to challenge them to use their ideas and skills to teach each other more about block building. They separated the children into three "engineering teams." Each team had a different set of building tools and a different goal—to build a horse arena, an airport, or a ramp. The teachers decided on these activities based on the building they had observed during playtime. After a few moments of adjusting to the fact that they would be working with kids they didn't typically play with, the children took up the challenge and began to show each other what they knew about how to build with the blocks. When the building work came to an end, the teachers asked the children to take their building one step further by drawing a picture of what they had created. Using clipboards and pencils, the children began to draw. Some of them drew the constructions by looking at them. Others drew by tracing the blocks. The children compared their strategies for drawing and building as they showed their drawings to each other.

Listen to Cindy and Vicky

"Most of the children in our preschool group have been very focused on building and construction over the last month. Each of them uses the blocks in unique ways, and as a result, they have mastered different skills. We wondered if we could help the children see and learn from each other's work if we gave them a few challenges and encouraged them to work with new partners. We directed the formation of the groups and helped the children work through their bumpy times. After the team building projects, we challenged the children again and asked them to draw their structures. Our goal was to introduce the idea of depiction, that you can translate a three-dimensional idea into a two-dimensional one. The children were thrilled to take up this challenge. Later in the year, we'll ask them to draw their structures before they build them. We might even suggest that they do a collaborative drawing. We are excited about this idea of putting the children into smaller groups to coach one another about their ideas and skills. It provided a wonderful opportunity to build new relationships and collaborate. And they really did teach and learn from one another!"

Reflect

Many teachers think that child-centered curriculum means that teachers don't direct anything. You can see in this story that Cindy and Vicky's plans all revolve around the children's interests and ideas. But they are also claiming an active role to challenge the children to work at a more complex level in their relationships and with the materials and activities. You can see the careful thinking and planning in the structure for teamwork that they offered the children. This created a purposeful space and time to coach children in problem solving and conflict resolution. Unlike during "heat of the moment" conflicts, the children anticipate the teacher's coaching because they have been alerted ahead of time that working with new people might be difficult. It is also apparent how closely the teachers observe and listen to the children so they can use these details to build on their ideas and strengths. These teachers have tentative plans for future challenges, which indicate additional possibilities for the children's growth as well as their own.

Your Turn

Observe the children you teach and note the different skills each has mastered. Look for an opportunity to arrange for one child to teach new skills to someone else. You could have the child talk another child through the steps, make a chart with the sequence

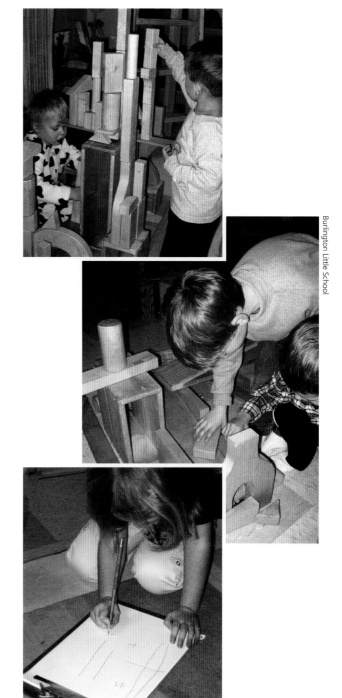

Burlington Little School

to follow, or offer a demonstration to the group and have the group make the chart. Afterward, reflect on how this process worked and what changes you might make to incorporate this into your ongoing teaching practice.

7 Dig Deeper to Learn with Children

What if we were to assume that children came to school more, rather than less, able to communicate their thinking about the world? Why not assume that when the child enters school, he or she presents us with an enormous number of innate tools to acquire knowledge? What effect might this assumption have on our approach to what the languages of learning are?
—**Karen Gallas**

Throughout *Learning Together with Young Children*, we have urged you to draw on children's strengths and competencies as the focus for the teaching and learning process. Karen Gallas (1994) reminds us that children bring "innate tools" to this process. If you believe this to be true, how will it affect the way you respond to children's actions? Rather than seeing children's self-initiated pursuits as a distraction from planned curriculum, you can use these pursuits as a vehicle for deeper learning. Children constantly communicate as they play, sing, use their bodies, engage in dramas, build and construct, and make up games. The challenge is to notice the details of how children are communicating their thinking, so you can support them to go further. Sometimes this might mean telling the children about an idea related to what they are exploring. At other times, teachers may challenge children to re-represent their idea with another material, such as drawing their block structure or using objects from the natural world to explore a concept. When Gallas speaks of "the languages of learning," we are reminded of the renowned poem "The Hundred Languages of Children" by Loris Malaguzzi (Edwards, Gandini, and Forman 2012), which has inspired the world to see

children as remarkably competent. Both Gallas and Malaguzzi remind us that the way children express their knowledge and tools for learning should not be limited to adult agendas and narrow academic goals.

Working with children's natural approaches to learning isn't a new idea in the early childhood profession. However, the role of the teacher in child-centered curriculum reflects a continuum of interpretations and practices. For example, many Montessori programs advocate for carefully crafted materials and teacher instruction to help children learn a way of doing something and then encourage independent work for them to master an experience. On the other end of the continuum are passionate play advocates who believe adults should stay out of almost all children's activities. We, the authors, advocate for teachers to see the complexity in the teaching and learning process, and to make decisions based on careful reflection of your values, goals, and knowledge of the individual children as well as their cultural and the community context.

Teaching with deep respect for children's competencies requires you to engage your mind with theirs. You notice what is unfolding and then determine the support and challenge that will invite them into deeper study. Depending on the child and the setting, support might involve holding back your own thinking or perhaps describing what you are seeing. You might decide some coaching is needed on ways to approach a problem, use a tool, or find a resource.

If you favor co-construction of knowledge, or side-by-side learning with children, consider the work of an improvisational theater artist who must develop a scene with other actors without a script to follow. Improvisational actors approach each idea offered as an invitation they must accept. Their rule of thumb is to respond to each invitation with "yes, and . . ." For instance, picture the following situation.

Actor 1: "Oh look, it's raining."

Actor 2: "Do you want a peanut butter sandwich?"

Do you see how offering something totally unrelated to rain, like peanut butter sandwiches, leaves no direction to go? Now consider another response.

Actor 1: "Oh look, it's raining."

Actor 2: "Let's jump in these puddles."

Here actor 2 uses the "yes, and . . ." rule. "Let's jump in these puddles" acknowledges that noticing the rain is an offer worth taking up and adds new and interesting possibilities to keep the scene going. Bringing this simple "yes, and . . ." mind-set to your teaching repertoire suggests that you are looking for the children's thinking. You take their ideas seriously and believe they can handle new challenges. How might this look between a child and a teacher?

Child: "Yeah! It's raining. There's a puddle I can jump in."

Teacher: "Stop—don't jump into that puddle; you'll get all wet and might catch cold."

Do you see how this response stops any possibility for using the child's idea for a deeper experience? Consider another response.

Child: "Yeah! It's raining. There's a puddle I can jump in."

Teacher: "Let's find your rain boots so you can jump in every puddle you can find."

This teacher says yes to puddle-jumping, challenging the child to do more with her exuberance, while helping her to stay dry and comfortable.

This chapter is designed to help you consider the innate tools and passions children bring to the learning process by giving you examples of teachers saying "yes, and . . ." to expand the children's experience. Can you see how the "yes, and . . ." rule is another way to think about Vygotsky's theory of scaffolding children's learning (Berk and Winsler 1995)?

The following principles will help you know what comes after the "yes, and . . ." as you accept children's many promising offers.

Principles

- Challenge children to go a step further in their pursuits.
- Help children represent their ideas with multiple materials.
- Tap into children's love of songs and music.
- Draw on children's deep fascination with drama and magical thinking.
- Build on children's attention for the natural world.
- Explore children's theories for deeper learning.
- Reflect children's ideas back to them with documentation.
- Engage in teacher research to enhance your teaching practices.

PRINCIPLE **Challenge Children to Go a Step Further in Their Pursuits**

To uncover what children are thinking and challenge them to dig deeper, you must look closely at their actions and try to understand the ideas they are exploring. This work is part improvisation and part research. As you work alongside children and reflect on your observations, you can discover their interests to spark further investigation. Children's behavior and words also help you see what they already know, and you can use this awareness to support them in taking on new challenges. Sometimes children have inconsistencies, gaps, or "soft spots" (Duckworth 2006, 184) in their thinking that can be taken up for further study. It is best to offer only one next step, aligned with the children's pursuits, rather than rushing in with numerous activities or a unit to study.

Opening the Doors to Learning

In the following story, notice how each of Bekah's small challenges grows her moments with the children into a longer investigation.

Bekah set out geo boards with rubber bands, encouraging the children to make geometrical shapes and patterns by stretching the rubber bands across the nails on the boards. Three-year-old Sage found them fascinating. Sage used the rubber bands to form a rectangle and announced, "Look, Bekah, I made a door."

Bekah said, "You did make a door. I bet you could draw a door too." Bekah moved her finger along the rubber band lines, outlining the rectangle shape, and explained, "See, you can make lines with a marker that look just like the rubber band lines."

Bekah found a marker and paper and showed Sage how to draw the lines. Then she handed the marker to Sage, who took up the challenge. With much deliberation, even looking back and tracing the rubber band lines with her marker, Sage drew a door.

The older children next to Sage became very interested in her work, proudly declaring that drawing a door was really easy. Bekah responded, "Here's some markers and paper. Go for it!" The group all began drawing doors, showing each other their completed work. This went on for the rest of the afternoon and continued into the next week. Making doors became a shared activity for the group. The children drew pages and pages of doors.

At one point, Bekah challenged the group of door makers in another way: "What's behind all these doors?" The children immediately wanted to figure out how to get their doors to open. Bekah responded by offering X-Acto knives and coached the children to carefully cut open the doors with the knives, using necessary safety precautions. Once they mastered cutting the doors, the children spent the next few days drawing pictures of "surprises" that were behind the doors.

Listen to Bekah

"When Sage announced that she had made a door, it launched an interesting exploration with the entire group. The fact that she discovered and named her shape a door made me think she might be interested and able to learn to draw the door. The older

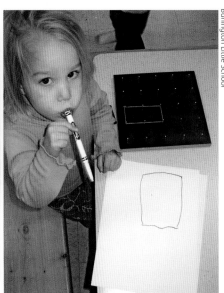

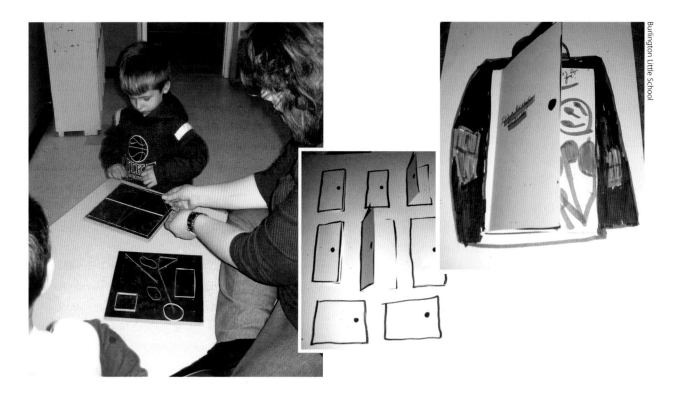

children usually have all the ideas and take the lead, so I wanted to challenge them to follow Sage's lead to see where it went. I was delighted with how this opened the door for all the children, both literally and metaphorically. As I think about this, I am seeing many more possibilities for the door as a metaphor to offer back to the children. What is so interesting about doors? Why have the children been drawn to them? What else can we do to keep thinking about doors?"

Reflect

Bekah's story illustrates how the use of appealing, open-ended materials and teacher actions aligned with children's interests can connect children to each other and expand their learning process. Making a door with rubber band lines and then drawing it gave Sage and the other children experiences with symbolic representation. Bekah believed the children were capable of safely using an adult tool and she carefully demonstrated and coached them in the process. This expanded their skills and investigation. Think about what might have happened if Bekah chose, instead, to focus solely on teaching Sage

the name "rectangle" to identify the shape she made with the rubber bands. Consider what might have occurred if Bekah had suggested that Sage make something else with the rubber bands. The timely comments and suggestions Bekah offered built a bridge to each new activity and encouraged collaboration among the group. The questions Bekah poses at the end of her reflection show teacher research in action. What strategies or materials could she offer next to learn more about the children's thinking related to doors?

Even the youngest children in your program benefit from challenges to pursue their ideas and questions. In the next story, notice how the teacher's attention to the simple actions of a child reveals opportunities for enhanced learning.

Floating Leaves

Julia's ordinary moment of exploration on the playground led to a deeper investigation when her teacher noticed and took her actions seriously. How might you pay close attention to these kinds of details with your group?

While on the playground one morning, Ann watched Julia act on her appetite for scientific exploration. Julia found a leaf and put it into the tube on the fence and then looked to see what would happen. The leaf didn't move. Then Julia blew into the tube, but the leaf still didn't move. Julia put more leaves into the tube. She blew into the tube again—and this time, one of the leaves swooped out of the bottom of the tube. When they went back inside the classroom, Ann offered Julia another tube and some leaves to continue her exploration. Julia put a leaf in the new tube, and it didn't go through this tube either. Julia blew hard on the tube, but the leaf still didn't budge. Ann demonstrated an idea. She held a leaf on the palm of her hand and blew on it. The leaf floated to the floor. Julia put a leaf in her hand and blew on it. The leaf floated to the floor, and Julia clapped her hands.

Listen to Ann

"Julia loves to blow bubbles. From bubble-blowing experiences, she knows that the power of her breath can move things through the air. Did she draw on this knowledge today as she explored the leaves and tubes? How do we make meaning of Julia's interactions with the leaves and tubes, and how might we extend or challenge the thinking she did today? Can we understand her work as an investigation of cause and effect? Our hypothesis is that, indeed, Julia's

work with the leaves today was an inquiry process. *What happens when I blow on leaves—through tubes and on my hand?*

"To honor her inquiry, we'll offer Julia other objects with which to experiment—objects that move easily with breath, and objects that will resist breath. We'll arrange materials near our heater vent so when the air moves up through the vent, it will move the materials. As we continue to watch Julia's encounters with these invitations for further inquiry, we will challenge her to carry on her pursuits, and we'll learn more about her understandings and questions."

Reflect

Do you see how Ann's action of demonstrating the consequence of blowing on the leaves was in line with Julia's initial pursuit? If Ann hadn't seen the essence of Julia's experimentation, Julia might have gotten frustrated or abandoned her inquiry. Notice how Ann poses questions to herself to better understand the meaning of this play for Julia. She draws on her observations of Julia's previous experiences blowing bubbles to determine the next challenge. She plans the next step to "honor" Julia's quest and to find out more, not just to teach Julia a physics lesson.

PRINCIPLE   **Help Children Represent Their Ideas with Multiple Materials**

As teachers discover children's underlying interests and understandings, they can routinely invite children to explore their ideas by representing them in various of ways. In the larger educational arena, students often represent their learning with a paper, a test score, or a demonstration of mastery. However, representing what children know doesn't only demonstrate their learning; it also enhances it. Different mediums such as drama, drawing, or sculpting provide children with additional perspectives to reflect on an idea or understanding and then confront what isn't yet clear (Forman 1996; MacNaughton and Williams 2009). Each medium helps children practice different skills and recognize different aspects of the ideas they are exploring. As they

University of New Hampshire Child Development Center

study a representation together, observant teachers can guide children in recognizing their ideas. When you view children's representations of their thinking with different materials, you can begin to see what they are trying to figure out. From there, you can offer new avenues for additional inquiry. The stories throughout this book reflect a curriculum approach that continually highlights and revisits experiences to enhance learning.

Facial Relations

As you read the following story, note how teacher Maya tries to see what the children find so fascinating about their faces and the innovative ways she offers different materials for them to represent their interest.

Face-painting materials are always available in the art area of Maya's preschool room. Several times a week, a number of the children were using the mirrors and oil pastels to paint their faces. They worked carefully, looking at themselves for a long time in the mirrors and studying the many photos Maya took of them. They focused on covering particular areas on their faces instead of painting a mask or a design.

Noticing the children's interest, Maya printed large black-and-white photos of the children's faces and offered these for them to paint on. The children eagerly took up this work, asking for multiple copies of the black-and-white photos to keep painting. Again their focus was on painting over distinct spaces and lines on the photos of their faces. At one point, the children decided to add to their work and paint on each other's photos.

The next week, Maya gave the children wire and demonstrated how they might follow the lines and shapes of their faces by bending and shaping the wire. This was a difficult task, but the children were challenged to revisit these interesting aspects of their faces, so they kept with it.

Maya continued to offer different materials for the children to re-examine their interest in the spatial aspects of their faces. She introduced them to Picasso's

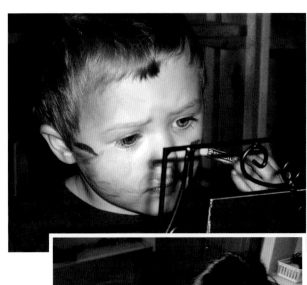

unusual paintings that highlight and distort facial features. The children delighted in these, which led to cutting up the photos of their faces and gluing them back into different configurations.

This work continued off and on for a number of weeks. There was a long stretch where the children used mirrors and fine-line pens to draw pictures of their faces. In this work, they began to represent the details of their faces in their drawings, which depicted eyelashes, eyebrows, and ears.

Listen to Maya

"This year a few children in my room were captivated with painting their faces. It was evident that they took

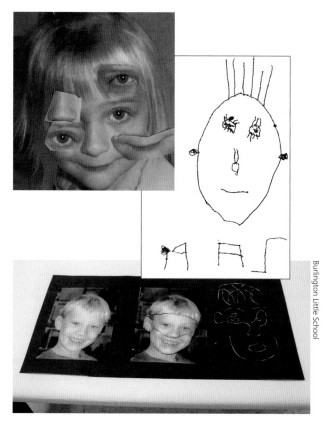

Burlington Little School

this work seriously and delighted in exploring their faces in many ways. They loved to show each other what they had done and have a photo taken of their altered faces. When I printed out the photos and studied the collection of them, I got really curious about the children's face painting. I found it interesting to look closely at each of their faces to see the purpose and detail in their work. It was fascinating to see the different facial expressions the children had behind the face paint in each of the photos.

"The photos reflected the children's deliberation and careful work with design, shape, and color. I began to ask myself what they were exploring as they used the paints in this way. Did they feel the magic and power of altering their identity? Were they revisiting the contours and spaces of their faces by coloring over them? I decided to give children more opportunities to explore this fascination with their faces. And they dove right in with everything I offered. They continued to study the spatial aspects of their faces for a long while, but with each new material, their study shifted to other aspects of their

faces. I loved how they worked with each other's faces too. I'm certain that these extended experiences of re-representation allowed them to look deeply into human faces and see many things."

Reflect

Maya didn't jump in and turn the children's interest into a unit on faces, but instead looked for the underlying fascination the children demonstrated through their work. As a result, she focused on offering different materials for children to re-represent their focus on the spatial aspects of the shapes and lines of their faces. As you reflect on this story, think about what other materials you could present to continue the children's re-representation and study of faces. What guesses do you have about how the children would respond and what they would do with this new offering?

Sink Surprises

The following story from teacher Jacob reflects the in-depth project work of a group of three- to five-year-olds who spent weeks and weeks exploring how a sink works.

The kids began the project thinking that they knew the answer to how a sink works, and the teachers invited them, through long dialogues and studio sessions, to share and develop what were very, very incorrect assumptions. They sketched sinks and water

Hilltop Children's Center

fountains from all over the school. They played with sets of real plumbing pipes to explore the physical aspects of what they were discussing. These kids imagined desalinization machines hooked up to their sinks, underwater Ferris wheels, and oceanic waves that sent water to their taps. And do you think they ever figured out how a sink functions? Absolutely not! But they did use their imaginations, represented and re-represented their ideas, shared and listened, and learned about the scientific process.

Listen to Jacob

"In-depth investigations are emergent, child-centered, and more akin to lengthy investigations than planned projects. To me, the most inspirational aspects of these projects start with a simple premise or hypothesis that gets turned on its head. In-depth investigations are a perfect example of reflective practice enriching curriculum. The teachers must lead even though they don't know where they are going. They supply the means, not the drive or the inspiration. If they think they know where they are going, then they must hope to be proven wrong, because by making an assumption, they have already closed their minds to many unpredictable experiences. What part of learning is better than surprise? You think you know something, and then you go a little bit deeper and, surprise! Our role as teachers is to let children practice exploration, rather than force them to learn about plumbing, and in that way they achieved success."

Reflect

Teaching in this manner harnesses the motivational power of children's innate curiosity and gets them thinking scientifically about the world. Lilian Katz (2015) emphasizes the difference between this and purely academic goals. She describes the latter as "concerned with the mastery of small discrete elements of disembodied information, usually related to pre-literacy skills in the early years, and practiced in drills, worksheets, and other kinds of exercises designed to prepare children for the next levels of literacy and numeracy learning"(2). In-depth study work is aimed at intellectual goals like reasoning, practicing the scientific method, forming creative ideas, and running with those ideas until they lead somewhere.

This kind of work stimulates the young brain in ways that clinging to factual knowledge can't. That isn't to say we don't want to raise children who understand facts—of course we do—but that sort of learning is best built on a strong intellectual disposition and a love of learning

Drawing on the work of Vivian Paley, teachers can use story dramas to help children re-represent their ideas in many different ways. Story dramas invite children to go through a process of dictating a story, drawing it, and acting it out as a drama. This creates a habit of mind for thinking in multiple ways, which can be carried over into other activities. It's an especially useful tool for children who are less inclined to draw or dictate their ideas.

Story Dramas

In the next story, notice how story dramas spread like wildfire in this child care program. Can you see how the children were motivated to participate by the prospect of acting out their story with their friends?

From the beginning of the year, Deb's group of three- to six-year-old children were passionate about acting out dramas with whatever tools or materials they happened to be using. In order to frame and further this natural interest, Deb decided to introduce them to story dramas, an activity she adapted from inspiration from Vivian Paley. Every week in Deb's class, she set aside a table for creating story dramas and invited the children to participate. At first a number of the younger boys didn't show much interest. But once they understood that they would be acting out their drawings, they dove right in.

One day the children eagerly visited the table and each drew a picture of a story they wanted to tell.

Some of the drawings were simple illustrations and stick figures. Other drawings were very complex, depicting every detail of the story. Next, the children dictated the story to go with their drawings while Deb wrote down their words. The last component of the process was for the children to act out their stories.

All of the children gathered around the stage. One by one, the playwright-actors went up on the stage with their story and drawing and chose the part they would play. The story was read carefully for the group to notice each of the roles before the rest of the cast was selected. Deb helped cast the parts, making sure everyone who wanted to be involved had a role to play. The children eagerly raised their hands to be the flowers, grass, sun, and ocean as well as the animals and people in the stories. The group did a quick dress rehearsal where Deb invited the children to demonstrate and practice actions, sounds, or words that depicted their part. Then they quickly and exuberantly acted out each story.

Listen to Deb

"The steps the children follow for story dramas spill over into other parts of their day. They are more willing to draw, engage in dramas, and talk about their ideas. Even the children who are the most reluctant to hold a marker or pencil work earnestly on these story drama stories because they know what's coming—they get to act them out! Over time, I have seen the children's drawing skills grow by leaps and bounds. I have also discovered that dictating stories really helps the children learn language and the form and function of reading and writing. The younger children who are just beginning to work with these concepts learn that they must slow down so I can write each word. The older children, who understand initial concepts about literacy, practice phonemic awareness as they carefully pronounce the sounds of the words that they dictate. I have delighted in the way they play with their understanding of what makes a good story through the words and phrases they choose for dialogue, action, and the passage of time. The children love to put each other into their stories, and I can see the influences they are having on each other's story lines.

"Acting out the drama is the most engaging aspect for most of the children. It is usually very short, sometimes chaotic, but always exciting. The children have been adding props from our classroom to enhance the dramas, and they often take up the story line of one of the story dramas in their free play. The children have powerful feelings as a result of seeing their words and drawings come to life through their friends on the stage.

"I have continued to add other elements of re-representation to this activity. Sometimes the children draw their pictures onto transparencies and then we project them on the wall above our stage with an overhead projector. The drawings become the scenery that the actors use in the drama. To extend this process to other media, I have begun to ask children to dictate a story about their Lego constructions or block structures, and then we cast the parts and act them out."

Reflect

Deb's story includes many layers of learning through representation and re-representation. Can you see how language, literacy, creative expression, math, and spatial skills as well as significant cooperation and problem solving all surface through the use of story dramas? When children draw or illustrate their ideas and the actions involved in their stories, they are confronted with many challenges. They must decide the most important elements of the story and the relationships of the characters to the action. They must work with spatial and visual concepts as they depict the details. In the story development and dictation process, they come to understand that letters make up words and that words become sentences and then whole stories can be read back and enjoyed. All of these actions are foundational for learning to read and write.

The children's work in these story dramas portrays the struggles that all human beings have with good and evil, love and hate, fear and bravery, danger and rescue, allegiance and betrayal, and life and death. The stories usually have happy endings where the good guys come back to life, and evil is defeated as the hero saves the day. Working out feelings of fear and powerlessness through dramatic play has long been considered important for children's emotional development (Hoffman 2004).

Your Turn

To better understand the value of having children re-represent their ideas in a different medium, try this activity adapted from one invented by Tom Drummond.

Step 1: Gather together a few friends or coworkers, along with an object that you are familiar with but about whose inner workings you don't know much. Possibilities include a kitchen timer, fax machine, staple gun, windup toy, or Jacob's ladder folk toy.

Step 2: Without peeking inside or dismantling the object, explore how it works and makes note on what you are curious about.

Step 3: Make a quick list of questions that come to mind about this object.

Step 4: Discuss your theories about how this object works with the others in the group.

Step 5: Make individual drawings showing your theory.

Step 6: Compare your representations and see if they explain the inner workings or if there are still questions that remain.

Step 7: Decide on another material (such as blocks, recycled materials, wire, or clay) to create a collaborative representation of your theory about how this object works. Refer to your drawings in the process and note any new insights that occur as you translate your theory from your drawing to a new material.

Step 8: Use your drawings and new representation to explain your theory and discoveries to someone else. As you consider your learning process, consider whether you have deepened your understandings of the following concepts:

- exploring to learn (physical knowledge)
- hypothesizing to learn (theory making)
- drawing to learn (symbolic thinking and consolidating knowledge)
- collaborating to learn (social constructivism)
- making thinking and learning visible through multiple representations (multiple intelligences)

As you think about the new understandings you gained through this activity, what will your next step be? How can you incorporate what you learned into your curriculum planning?

PRINCIPLE   **Tap into Children's Love of Songs and Music**

Listen to preschool children at play and you will often hear them humming a familiar tune as they work. When you turn on music, watch a toddler's body move in time to the beat. Children are naturally drawn to the rhythms and sounds of music. They easily remember lyrics because they tell a story and are connected to a melody. Why not draw on this enthusiasm for music to help children take pleasure in learning? As Tom Hunter suggests in the next section, don't just use songs for the purpose of teaching a lesson. Instead, offer music for the joy and liveliness it can bring to life.

Listen to Tom and Sing a Lot

The following words of wisdom about using songs with children are from Tom Hunter.

"We turn songs into teaching resources too quickly these days. In a way it makes sense—children learn a lot when they sing, so why not teach them using songs? The problem is the delight of the song itself gets lost to whatever it is we want to teach children. The song no longer exists as a song inviting a range of responses. It's become a lesson, one-dimensional, often with the vitality wrung out of it. Teachers should sing a song with children many times before using it to teach anything. Play with it—faster/slower, louder/softer. Wonder out loud about it. Change the words. Let it belong to the children and become part of their lives with all the connections they will naturally make. Then it becomes even more valuable, the learning it brings coming not only from what teachers want but what the children find.

"Children surrounded with lively oral experiences (songs, finger plays, nursery rhymes, conversations) will likely master early literacy skills fine. What's the bottom line? Sing a lot so the song is first a song and then a teaching resource."

Enticing Fred

Family provider Billie loves to sing with her children, who have become mesmerized by the story line and rhythm in a song about a turtle. Read her story of how the children take serious steps to re-create the song for their own lives.

"My Turtle, Fred" (Hunter 2004) is a song that Billie and her kids listen to and sing often. It tells the story of a stray turtle that wanders into and eventually out of a child's yard. One spring, three of the school-age boys in Billie's program decided they were going to create a turtle habitat that was so inviting that Fred couldn't resist and would end up wandering into their yard. They did some research and came up with what they thought turtles needed to survive, and then set

about creating "turtle paradise," as they called it. They dug little ponds, created shaded areas with pine branches, and built lovely rock gardens, tree-bark climbing apparatuses, and other features that only turtles could fully appreciate. The final touch was when Billie took them to the pet supply store and they picked out several turtle replicas (made of resin and stone) to place strategically around the habitat. Their reasoning was that if Fred should wander into the yard and see all these other "friends," then he would be more likely to stick around for a while.

Listen to Billie

"The story and melody of 'My Turtle, Fred' seemed to touch something deep inside these boys in my group. They listen to the lyrics and take them very seriously, worrying about Fred and where he might be living. Their concern for Fred has led them to this wonderful collaborative project to create a habitat to lure him to our yard. I think on one level they understand that Fred won't really come to live with us. But they also believe he will. So far, we haven't spotted any visitors to our turtle paradise, but the children haven't given up hope that their carefully thought-out plan will eventually work . . . and neither have I!"

Reflect

Billie uses songs in her program all the time because she knows their power to reach children at a deep level. She takes the children's interests seriously, tapping into their love of this song to explore many opportunities for joy and learning. The music and lyrics of the song inspire the boys to expand their thinking to take the perspective of the turtle, asking themselves, "How can we create a beautiful place where a turtle would like to live? Who would the turtle like to live with?" Their answers show that they recognize the significance of relationships and understand the importance of protective habitats. What is your response to the boys' tenderness, creativity, and ability to make plans and carry them out

as they design, construct, and sing about this habitat for Fred?

Using songs to revisit ideas and information draws on one of the multiple intelligences that children can bring to their learning (Gardner 2011). The following story reminds us, even if we don't have any formal musical training, that music can become an integral and lively aspect of our daily life together.

Silly Songs

As you read the story of Deb's approach to songs and music, think about the music you enjoy in your own life and how you can bring this to your work with children.

Deb sings all the time with the children in her child care room. They sing songs that other people have written, but they also make up their own songs. Deb spontaneously invents operas during moments

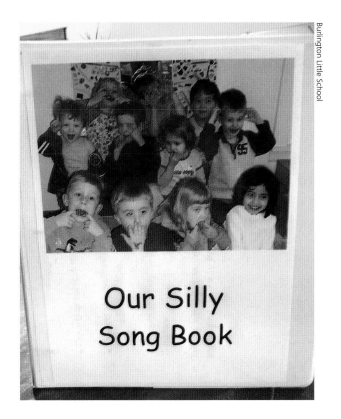

Burlington Little School

Our Silly Song Book

of adventure on the climber or when children are expressing themselves in the drama area. They sing greetings to the sun and the rain and the changing of the seasons. And they make up ditties to go along with their daily routines. One year, the songs about routines were particularly delightful to the children. Because the children were making up and singing out so many verses to the songs as they worked, Deb suggested they make a songbook with words and illustrations. The children turned it into a silly songbook as they laughed uproariously at the zany lyrics they created about their routines.

> *"Go to your cubby . . . and take a shower."*
> *"Turn on the lights and . . . don't get in fights."*
> *"Look for your lost underwear . . . in your hair."*

The children looked through the book each day, singing about the simple pleasures of their days in funny, new ways. The book was over three inches thick by the end of the year.

Listen to Deb

"One of my favorite childhood memories is my dad's singing. He would sing in the shower and sing along with the radio, and the best part was singing together with me. He never had any formal music training and neither have I, but this hasn't stopped me from enjoying music in my life and in my classroom. Following my dad's example, I sing all the time with the children, who are learning so much from their love of singing and making up songs. They draw pictures and dictate the silly lyrics all the time for our songbook. I see them reading it to each other throughout the day. But more importantly I know that I'm passing along the same pleasure and wonderful memories that my dad's singing gave to me!"

Reflect

As Deb suggests, the songbook she and the children created is an excellent example of literacy learning. As the children dictate the lyrics, they begin to understand that words and sentences can be used to write songs and books. The children come to see that print has meaning and is useful and enjoyable for their lives. Additionally, did you notice the phonics practice they engaged in when they made up lyrics that rhyme? You can also see in this story the power of humor to enhance children's thinking. The unrelated images and words the children invent and put together for the lyrics show they understand that when they contrast two opposing but interesting ideas, it can be funny. When children work at shifting their perspectives in this way, it boosts their cognitive development (McGhee 2003).

PRINCIPLE   Draw on Children's Deep Fascination with Drama and Magical Thinking

Young children's use of make-believe play and magical thinking to make sense of the world is a delightful aspect of spending our days with them. Children regularly act out dramas and offer profound observations, relating their own experiences and view of the world to other people, animals, and even objects. The technical terms for some of this thinking are "animism" or "anthropomorphism," which refer to giving human personalities, thoughts, or movements to natural or inanimate objects. Rather than seeing this worldview as merely cute or dismissing it as undeveloped, why not draw on children's unique perspectives to extend the learning process?

Teachers can create dramatic play opportunities that specifically reflect children's interests and encourage them to represent and deepen their understandings. Whenever children say, "Let's pretend," a new landscape of possibilities for learning is revealed. When children pretend, they try on new feelings, roles, and ideas. They stretch their minds along with their imaginations.

Bird-Watching Park

Study this story from Australian colleagues Fran and Nicole describing how adding dramatic play props related to the children's deep interest in birds extended the study and learning over a long period of time.

Providing one reference book about birds was enough to invite four-year-old Lewis and his peers to become engrossed in the world of ornithology, and they began researching birdlife at every opportunity. Responding to this interest in birds, teachers Fran and Nicole set up a small area in the room that included several other reference books and storybooks along with sticks, stones, feathers, bird figurines, and a real nest. The children immediately took this interest to the outdoor area. They became avid bird-watchers, using the reference books to help them in their bird hunts.

The teachers then decided to create an outdoor dramatic play area to facilitate further exploration and extend the play. Soon the children were checking in to the bird-watching office the teachers created and taking binoculars and clipboards on their hunts to record their findings on identification charts. The drama extended to using tents and turning the outdoor BBQ area into the "Earlwood Bird-Watching Park." The children eagerly immersed themselves in the play. However, it soon became apparent that there were not many birds in the area to actually find. The children decided that it must be because the birds could see and hear them coming.

The group decided they needed a bird-watching house, and so Fran, Nicole, and the small group of friends worked on converting the existing outdoor cubby house into a bird-watching house. They attached bamboo to the exterior of the house and painted it in tones of brown and green in order to camouflage their position. They discussed plans for their new bird-watching house as they painted, excited about the prospect of seeing a wide range of birdlife once they were suitably concealed within this new vantage point. Riley also decided that leaving birdseed out might draw the birds to the area—he sprinkled seed with the other children and eagerly checked on the progress of attracting birds. The children also sketched colorful parrots in chalk pastels, which were laminated and mounted around the bird-watching park as another lure.

Listen to Fran and Nicole

"The power of the peer group is remarkable. The passion friends have for a particular subject matter can become infectious within this community of learners. We came to understand that the children certainly possessed a wealth of knowledge about birds, which became the basis for their practical ideas about what would attract birds to the area. The most popular suggestion was the bird-watching house, which became a focal point of play for this group of bird enthusiasts for many, many months."

Reflect

This story reflects something very different from traditional prop or theme boxes that teachers offer arbitrarily for children's play. Can you see how the children's appetite for fantasy and the addition of these particular dramatic-play props launched this group into more study and collaboration around something they were already engrossed with? The children took this "make-believe" play seriously, as they knew the possibilities it held for engaging their minds and emotions. The children didn't just play or learn facts about birds. Instead, they used the props to express and construct new understandings about birds and many other things.

Through their bird-watcher play scripts, the children became more careful observers and skilled at using reference materials. They developed skills for recording and analyzing their findings and practiced problem solving to meet the challenge of how to attract birds to the outdoor area. The children used the props to invent and construct the bird-watching house and stretched their thinking by taking the birds' perspectives. Along with all of this, they strengthened their identity as learners and collaborators. The teachers, Fran and Nicole, took this dramatic play seriously as well, offering support and adding complexity to the drama while marveling with the children at the ongoing possibilities for this pursuit.

Planning opportunities for children to draw on their innate tendencies toward animism is another way to engage them in complex learning processes. Children eagerly engage and learn with a character they can have a relationship with. These characters invite them to pretend and explore in ways that teachers can't.

Rat Habitats

The following story shows how Lindsay helped her group learn to care for their pet rats by helping them talk together. What is your response to the children's point of view about the rats? Can you see why they would be drawn into a relationship with these energetic creatures?

The children in Lindsay's child care room gathered in small groups near the rat cage to hold the pet rats and to talk about them. As they watched, the children spent a lot of time talking about the rats' point of view, what they might like and not like about how the children treated them and their cage. Lindsay extended the children's interest in the rats' perspectives by making stick puppets from photos of the rats and inviting the children to have a conversation with them.

Furry rat: "I like it when you hold me gently and most of all when you let me run around."

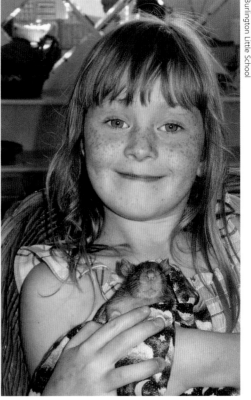

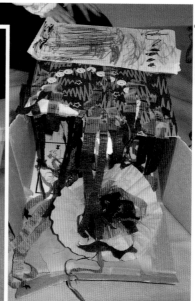

Burlington Little School

Zoe: "We have to make sure we hear the cage click; otherwise, you will get out and chew the cords and you can break the electricity and climb on wire fences."

Furry rat: "I do like to chew on things."

Olivia: "Is it why your eyes are so big, 'cause you're scared?"

Furry rat: "Sometimes I get scared when you bang on my cage."

Zoe: "Can you climb big poles and swim in the water? I heard that on a show about rats."

Furry rat: "I do like interesting things to climb on. And yes, I can swim."

After many discussions between the rat puppets, Lindsay invited the children to think about what they learned in the conversations to design and build habitats for them. As the children used recycled materials to build the habitats for the rats, they talked about how the rats' perspective influenced their work.

"The rats like colors, so we have to have many colors in the habitat."

"They run around a lot. That's why we need to make it big."

"The rats love to be in cozy spaces. They need a blankie. They need a carpet to be soft and cozy."

"I'm putting in two chairs to sit in. Rat chairs. Cozy chairs."

"The rooms the rats need are a living room, eating room, hallways, and a bed in a bedroom."

"They need doors between the rooms so they can get in the room."

"I'm using this screen for the door, so the air can get in and the rats can breathe."

"All of the rooms in the habitat need air holes."

"Remember, they like it best when they get to run around."

"When we put all of the rooms together, the rats have lots of room to run around."

"We can make windows in the tops of the rooms so we can watch them in the habitat."

Over a few weeks' time, the children created an elaborate habitat for the rats. They watched the rats closely in their new habitat and continued to remodel it based on their observations.

Listen to Lindsay

"Since the beginning of the year, the children in my group have been infatuated with the rats living in a cage in our child care room. Their shared interest in these small, friendly creatures has led to a big, collaborative project. The children lit up when I introduced the rat puppets. I was surprised at the genuine way they took up the conversations with the rat puppets. They seemed to be able to think more creatively when they pretended to talk with them. We could see the children's amazing ingenuity for using what they observed and understood about the rats in order to make them a comfortable, beautiful, and fun habitat. They were so excited to show the rats their new habitat and knew they must introduce them to it in a calm and gentle way to keep the rats safe. I've noticed that their tender concern for the rats has spilled over into their interactions with each other. As they are thinking about what it takes to make friends with the rats, they are making friends with each other."

Use the Thinking Lens® Protocol

Area for Reflection: Know yourself

How comfortable are you sharing in children's fantasies and magical thinking like teacher Lindsay did with the children's ideas about rats?

Area for Reflection: Find the details of the children's competence

What details do you see in the children's words and actions that show their empathy and sense of responsibility toward these living creatures?

Area for Reflection: Seek the child's perspective

What can you learn about the children's home lives as you study their words and ideas for what the rats need to be comfortable?

Reflect

Can you see how the children's magical thinking about the rats led to serious scientific investigation and study? Their imaginary conversations with the rats motivated them to closely observe the rats' behavior and then led to rigorous thinking about

the design and construction of the elaborate habitat. Lindsay didn't respond to the children's interest by offering lessons or facts about rats. Instead she extended their conversations, knowledge, and work by inviting the children to make believe they could really talk with the rats. Her actions encouraged them to use their imaginations to boost their interest and learning.

To see the world the way that children do, teachers must be able to hold on to their adult view of the world and at the same time use children's logic to offer new ideas. That may mean practicing magical thinking yourself by applying your human thoughts and feelings to objects and creatures and joining with the children in exploring the possibilities. In the following story, the teachers invite the children to bring their unique perspectives to learn more about the physics of water.

A Water View

In this story, notice how easily the children are able to use their view of the world to immerse themselves in new understandings. As you study the children's ideas, try out their way of thinking about the water to see what you learn.

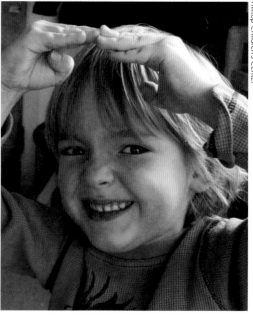

During their play at the water table one morning, four children began articulating and drawing their theories about why some objects sink and others float.

Jonah: "Rocks make things sink."

Lucy: "Because they don't have enough air."

Eric: "Right, rocks don't have enough air in them and then they sink."

Felix: "My Lego boat floats because the water is strong enough to float it."

As they talked, the children tried to make their theories visible to each other, offering each other the rock and the boat to hold and weigh, pointing out the way the rock fell quick and sure to the bottom of the table, and bending close to the water's surface to study the way the boat floated on the water. Teachers Nick and Ann met regularly with the children over several months to investigate their original, loosely formed theories and to explore new theories that they developed as they worked with a range of materials and a tub of water. After a few rounds of prediction, experimentation, and analysis with objects, Nick and Ann decided to ask the children to think about the experience of sinking and floating from the water's perspective. They posed various questions to provoke the children's thinking. Ann began the exploration

Hilltop Children's Center

of the water's perspective by taking on the voice of water in a story about a lake's encounter with a rock and a pinecone. As she told the story, she invited the children to help her describe the water's thoughts and feelings.

Ann: "How do you suppose the water feels as the rock lands on its surface?"

Jonah: "The water would feel tired."

Ann: "And when the pinecone lands, what would it feel then?"

Lucy: "That felt nice, because the water could feel it scratch where it had itches."

Eric: "When leaves go on the water, it feels tickled."

This story launched the children into thinking more broadly about the water's perspective:

Jonah: "Do you know how to say 'sink' in sign language? Like this." He scrunched his face into a grimace of effort and clenched his hands tight, making his arms shake. "That means the water is so strongly trying to hold something up that is very heavy. It's just too heavy. The water has to work hard but it can't do it."

Ann: "And what is the sign language word-sign for 'float'?"

Jonah lifted his hands above his head and smiled. "That means that the water held it up! It was easy for the water, and the water was happy that it was so easy."

Listen to Ann

"As we watched the children's focused investigation of sinking and floating, we wanted to encourage their theory making and testing. We tried to challenge them to move their thinking into ever more complex terrain. We decided to invite the children to meet formally as a 'work team,' a group experience in our program where children and teachers come together to investigate a question over time. In the children's initial play around the water table, Felix had suggested that water has an active role in sinking and floating when he'd said, 'The water is strong enough' to hold a Lego boat. This sparked our decision to help the children think about this idea some more by exploring the water's experience, to take an unfamiliar perspective and to examine the theories they'd been sharpening through a new lens."

Reflect

These teachers' intention wasn't to "teach" the children about sinking and floating, density and water displacement, or other elements of physics. Instead, they wanted to invite the children into a cycle of investigation and inquiry, creating an opportunity for the children to revisit and revise their initial theories about air and weight, and to develop new theories based on further study. The simple story of a pinecone, a rock, and a pond of water sparked insightful consideration by the children and a new way to understand what it means to sink and float. They willingly let go of the perspective of the objects in the water and took up the invitation for a new way of seeing. They built a relationship with the water, acknowledging its effort, extending compassion for its experience of being overwhelmed by a heavy object, and celebrating with a grin and arms outstretched its experience of holding an object lightly on its surface. The children's understanding of "sink" and "float" became more complex, and they certainly did learn about physics. The invitation to take the water's perspective deepened the children's investigation by engaging their emotions and their intellect more deeply.

PRINCIPLE   Build on Children's Attention for the Natural World

The ongoing movement to connect children to the natural world led by the Children and Nature Network and Richard Louv promotes the vital importance of nature for children's well-being. The natural world is also a significant source of learning and expression for young children (2005). Mud, sticks, and stones are often used by children to create constructions, dramas, and whole new worlds for relationships and negotiations. Howard Gardner added the naturalist intelligence to his theory of multiple intelligences (1999). Thoughtful, observant preschool teachers immediately understood his reasoning. Most teachers have known children who never miss a tiny creature in the vicinity of their play. They have firsthand experience with children who learn through their instinctive understanding and deep relationship with nature. So, rather than viewing the outdoors as only a place to let off steam, you can see it as a place for rich investigations and opportunities for revisiting and re-representing concepts from other learning domains. Here is an example from teacher Cassie, who used the children's deep interest in living creatures to extend their learning outdoors.

What's Outside of Our Play Yard?

The children have taken an interest in the area outside the fences of the play yard. They point out the many things they notice, such as boats on the canal, people running or biking past, and animals and plant life. Recently, the children animatedly pointed at something across the canal.

One child called out, "Look! Way over there, do you see the dinosaur?"

Several children looked and looked, but couldn't seem to find it.

"Way over there. Look!"

One child peered across the canal, and her eyes widened. "There's a dinosaur! Look, a green dinosaur!" She called to others, "Look! Do you see it!"

Once they had all seen the dinosaur, which was a plant sculpture made of ivy across the water and near the bridge, they began looking for other things. Looking straight up into the tree, the children noticed a dark lump high in the branches.

"It's a bird nest!"

"It's their house where birds live."

Cassie decided the following week to take the children on a walk on the canal path outside the fence so they could take a closer look at the things they had spotted and possibly make some additional discoveries. It was a bright, beautiful sunny morning as they started their walk. The children came to a bench and sat down for a while. They looked at the water for a long time, talking about the many animals they 'saw.'

"I see a big angry shark!" one child said.

"I see an octopus," said another child.

"I see a fish jumping!" added another.

Of course, they couldn't really see these animals, but it gave the children just as much joy to pretend they could! They laughed together as they kept thinking of different and exotic animals they imagined living in the canal water. After a while, the group continued their walk down the path.

Listen to Cassie

"I was a magical thinker as a child. I loved hunting for imaginary creatures, running from giants, and playing all sorts of games about them. My parents also showed me the 'magic' of real elements in my surroundings, tadpoles in a pond, birds' nests, and all the many beautiful and fascinating plants around our house. The dance children do between the real and the imaginary world is a profoundly special and important one. How we react to their visions or games about imaginary things tells them a great deal about the importance of play and imagination in their life as a learner. I watched quietly, not interrupting or correcting them, as the children talked freely together about the things they saw, regardless of whether or not they were 'really' there. I chose to do this because of my own history of joyful make-believe, but also because I see the amazing thinking that happens during uninterrupted imaginative play. The children named as many animals as they could, and when they ran out of animals, they kept walking, in search of even more sights and opportunities for make-believe play. All the time the children were talking, I saw them engaging together with humor and silliness, allowing one another to throw ideas into the pot until they had created a frenzy of laughter.

"The natural world is one of the best teachers we can offer a child, and the best way to get to know a teacher is laughing together! This experience has set a bar of excitement for the outdoors that continues in all of our time on the canal. We've parlayed this type of walking excursion into deeper thinking in dramatic play, hiding from monsters behind big rocks or trees we find, as well as real-life examples of weather phenomenon such as wind and rain, and the effects they have on the canal. My role as the teacher takes different forms, depending on the children's questions or the path of their game. On some days I find myself answering many questions about types of rain, and on others I'll be silent for a long stretch of time, watching a game unfold in the imaginary world."

Reflect

As you read Cassie's reflections, you can hear the deep values she has about the natural world based on her own wonder-filled experiences and the strong desire she has to share this with children. You can also hear her careful thinking about the role she wants to play in extending the children's learning. She seeks the children's magical perspectives and sees the joy and competence they bring to this experience. Cassie wants to protect this time for them by being a keen observer and a witness who marvels with them rather than thinking she must always be teaching them something.

Reflecting in this way is an active role you play as a teacher. The decision to stand back is as powerful as the decision to move in. The children's continued interest in the natural world that Cassie describes reflects the power of the role she is playing both behind the scenes and in view of the children. What deep values do you want to share with children? How do you move in and out of children's play and learning? How does the role you play communicate to the children the importance of their play and learning?

Millions of Pods

Children can learn much from the natural world beyond just studying nature for itself. Indeed, nature provides an abundance of loose parts with interesting textures, colors, shapes, and sizes. Wanda takes advantage of the learning possibilities when the children in her group begin collecting pods that have fallen from the trees on her playground.

Nolan, Zoe, and teacher Wanda were walking around the play yard when they noticed numerous tree pods on the ground, reflecting the wonderful fall season. The children wanted to collect them, so Wanda gave them plastic bags for pod gathering. The group had conversations about what these pods were and how they got to be so big and wet. The children described the colors, textures, and shapes of the pods, noticing these aspects as they found each one. It took them the rest of the afternoon to complete the pod-gathering task. When it was time to go inside, Wanda suggested they would continue to explore the pods.

The next day, Wanda set up a table with trays filled with pods and baskets for sorting. The children quickly remembered their interest in the pods and began sorting and counting and continuing to discuss the texture, weight, and dampness of the pods.

One of the children said, "I think we should keep these forever."

There was a chorus of agreement but then many recognized that if they were to keep the pods, they must dry them out. The ideas the children came up with to dry the pods included baking them in the oven or heating them in the microwave. They had many questions and theories about what changes would happen to the pods as they heated up.

Burlington Little School

"What will happen when they are in the microwave?" Wanda asked them.

The children replied:

"They will get kind of big and they will get small slopes on them."

"They will turn into fries and cakes and ice cream."

"They will get bigger bristles around it."

"They will get drier because of the heat."

"They will get powdery, because they will get puffy and explode."

Then Wanda asked, "What will happen when they are in the oven?"

"They will get a little bigger with bigger bumps."

"They will get dry, bigger and dry."

"They will burst in the oven cause it's hotter."

A number of the children were fascinated watching the time count down on the microwave oven. They counted with it and also kept suggesting that more time needed to be added. When they finished heating the pods, they examined them closely and discovered that they had not changed very much. Some of them were less soggy, but not much. For the rest of the afternoon, the children continued to sort and classify the pods on the table with a variety of sizes of baskets and tongs.

Listen to Wanda

"The children were excited about the many pods creating a beautiful, natural carpet in our yard. These interesting natural materials were soothing and satisfying because of their sensory qualities and the sheer abundance of them. The children's close attention to the specific features of the pods was apparent in their predictions about heating and drying them. Most of the children seemed to think that the heat would cause the pods to get bigger. Is that because they have watched things rise as they bake in an oven? This was truly emergent curriculum growing from the children's interest in these natural items. The wealth and splendor of the natural world presented an incredible learning opportunity for individuals, the group, and for me as a teacher."

Reflect

This serendipitous event with the pods was rich with learning because Wanda challenged the children to pursue and go further with their exploration. She created an opportunity for the children to explore mathematical knowledge when she offered baskets for sorting, classifying, and counting the pods. She encouraged science knowledge through inquiry, collaboration, and problem solving when she invited the children into the kitchen to make predictions and test out their theories for getting the pods to dry out. As you read their predictions, what guesses do you have about the children's understandings and theories? Can you see at each juncture how Wanda used the children's love of the sensory wonders of the natural world to create more opportunities for investigation?

In the past, spending time outdoors was a huge part of childhood. Most of us remember the visceral, sensory aspect of nature such as feeling fresh air on our skin or seeing the sunlight shining through the buildings in the city where we lived. We remember feeling powerful and adventurous as we climbed a tree or rode our bikes down a steep driveway. So much of our identity came from the landscape where we grew up. This is less true for children today. As children spend less time outdoors, their ability to learn is impaired, and they experience many ailments that older generations did not. Understanding this problem, teachers can take advantage of children's natural curiosity and connection to the natural world to engage with them in learning.

Your Turn

Think about an outdoor place from your childhood where you loved spending time. Then find some materials from nature that will help you tell the story of your experiences in this place. Share this with someone, letting the natural materials speak along with your story. Offer these same materials to a group of children and observe what they do with them.

PRINCIPLE   **Explore Children's Theories for Deeper Learning**

Children are constantly trying to figure out how the world around them works. When you observe them closely, you can see how their actions are really a way to try out their theories about how the world works. Their continued desire to uncover and rearrange the world so they can understand it can motivate them toward deeper learning. When you tap into children's thirst for understanding by helping them uncover their theories and make them visible, the work becomes fascinating for both you and the children. You can ask children to explain their theories, offer materials to help children tell the story of their theories, or suggest they use different media to re-represent a theory to expand their thinking. As you work with children to help them pursue their theories, you will gain new insight from their unique perspectives.

How Do Phones Work?

In this story, Emily undertook an exploration with the children in her child care class to discover their theories about how landline telephones work.

Aidan asked his mom the thought-provoking question "How do phones work?" Aidan and his mother brought this curiosity to school and shared it with Aidan's teacher, Emily. Emily wondered if other kids might be interested in this idea as well, and so she decided to take a small group of interested kids into the studio to explore what they knew and see what direction they might take to uncover their theories. Aidan and Emily checked in with other kids to see who else might be interested in learning about how phones work. Gabriel, Eli, Cecilia, and Brooke were attracted by the question and decided to join the group.

As they arrived in the studio and found a cozy space on the floor, Emily set the stage for the conversation: "We're all wondering about how phones work. What are your ideas about that?"

Aidan: "My mom said that the voice goes through

"The wires go into another house. The wires are attached to the phones. One wire's attached to the Seattle phone, one wire's attached to the Washington, DC, phone." —Cecilia

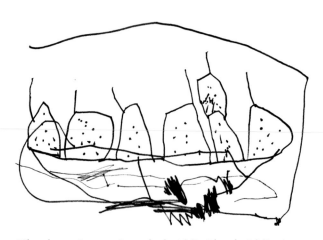

"The phone stays on. It needs electricity. The electricity stays in. It's inside the tank." —Brooke

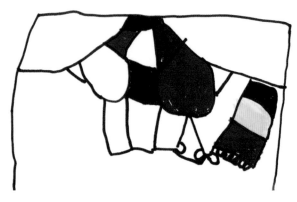

"This electrify is underground. I'm making what underground looks like." —Eli

a wire into another wire into another phone and the voice goes into another ear. Then another person's voice goes into another wire."

Cecilia: "And you can hear it."

Aidan: "And you can hear it. After they put back the phone down, the electricity goes out and . . ."

Cecilia: "The voice goes out."

Aidan: "Then the voice goes out. Voice is electricity. The electricity is on when the voice goes inside the ear."

Gabriel: "My dad said that phones really use electricity so other people could use them. You have to put something down so you can hear other people on the phone."

Teacher Emily: "What about Cecilia's ideas?"

Cecilia: "I can dial because I have a piece of paper that has the numbers."

Aidan: "I don't talk on the phone because I'm three . . . I mean four!"

Gabriel: "I'm four and I can talk on the phone."

Gabriel (to Cecilia): "How do you know what numbers to push?"

Cecilia: "You have to match the piece of paper to the numbers."

Gabriel: "How do you know what numbers are on the paper?"

Cecilia: "I look at the numbers on the paper; then I dial them."

Gabriel: "How do you know which number you're calling?"

Teacher Emily: "Are you wondering how she knows who she's calling?"

Gabriel: "Yeah!"

Cecilia: "The paper has the name on it."

Teacher Emily: "So, it sounds like to help a phone work, it needs electricity, wires, and you can dial numbers. What else do we know about phones?"

Aidan: "When the phone goes into the other ear from the first phone, I notice that it burns the whole house off the ground like a rocket ship."

Cecilia: "I don't think so."

Aidan: "Well, that's what my phone does at home."

Eli: "Does it turn into a space shuttle?"

Teacher Emily: "Eli, what are your ideas about how phones work?"

Eli: "Electricity comes from the wires."

Teacher Emily: "Do all phones have wires?"

Everyone: "No."

Cecilia: "I have 164 wires."

Aidan: "Do you want to know how many wires I have? . . . ONE HUNDRED!"

Eli: "I have twenty hundred and seventy thousand."

Brooke: "I have a phone that doesn't have a wire."

Eli: "It's just pretend, you know."

Teacher Emily: "How does a phone work that doesn't have wires?"

Gabriel: "Your voice goes through the air in the sky and goes into the other telephone."

Next Emily suggested that the children continue this conversation while drawing pictures of their ideas. As they drew their ideas on paper, they added details to their theories about how phones work.

Listen to Emily

"The children brought a lot to this exploration—their real-life experiences, their theories, their imaginations, and their ability to be fantastical. Drawing their theories gave them time to absorb and sort out the ideas that came up in their conversations. I thought that seeing these ideas on paper might serve as a visual communication tool for each other's ideas, stimulate some further language, and extend their thinking. These intricate ideas and their drawings provide a window to the serious thought and developing understandings that children can uncover through a process together. The children each brought their unique ideas into this investigation, developed theories based on those ideas, and bounced those theories off each other. They added layers of thinking by continually contributing to the process and listening to each other. I plan to bring this group of imaginative kids together again in the coming weeks to consider what might come next to extend this experience for them."

Reflect

This story shows how excited children can be when thinking through their ideas. Their excitement leads them to a greater investment in the learning process. They want to stick with the task because they are so innately invested in figuring things out. Look back over this story and study teacher Emily's questions and comments. Notice how her responses help the children revisit their ideas, stay focused on the conversation, reinforce their thinking, and challenge them to think and say more. Try analyzing the children's comments and drawings representing the theories each child has about how the telephone works. Where do you see their life experience influencing their logic? Where do you see them run into blocks in their thinking that lead them to magical explanations?

PRINCIPLE   **Reflect Children's Ideas Back to Them with Documentation**

In chapter 5, you saw examples of teachers placing books, posters, and photos from their documentation around the room for children to revisit their work. Using documentation with children coaches them in learning skills, steps, and processes. Revisiting experiences helps them become self-reflective. Reflecting on experiences provides the most effective learning for both adults and children (Project Zero and Reggio Children 2001). Showing children documentation of their work not only reinforces the children's identity as learners, but gives teachers an opportunity to learn more about the children. Showing children their previous ideas sparks further interest, brings up new questions, and stimulates more action.

Documentation for the children to revisit can be placed throughout the room. You can create an appealing display with notes and photos next to the materials that were used in the story. Or you might print photos of the children and their work onto transparencies and project them on the wall where children can use these larger-than-life images of themselves to launch new interests and explorations. A simple computer slide show of images from an investigation can be playing as the children begin the day, which encourages them to pick up where they left off the day before, rather than start from the beginning.

A slide show of images playing at the end of the day allows children to revisit their learning with their families when they arrive for pickup. All of these opportunities for seeing themselves involved in the learning process reinforce and increase children's knowledge.

Inventing Our Own Language

Even very young children benefit from reflecting on their experiences. In this story, one-year-olds experience a powerful impact when they see and revisit their ideas.

Deb kept a daily journal and took lots of photos of the unfolding activities that were significant to her and the toddlers she worked with. She studied the photos and notes for her own learning and also began sharing them with the children and their families. Telling these stories to the children and showing them the photos of her observations had positive influences on their play skills. The details from her journal entries about the children's study of flubber demonstrate the power of using observation stories and photos with children to learn from revisiting experiences.

One day as the children worked with flubber, Deb narrated their actions and pointed out the things they were doing.

"Oh look! When Kiran puts his finger in the flubber, he pokes a hole.

"And Oona is using the comb to make dots and lines all over the flubber.

"See how T'Kai is carefully putting the lid on the cup."

As she described and pointed out these actions, the children copied what they saw and heard. They also

stayed at the flubber table a little longer than usual.

A few days later, Deb showed the children a home-made binder book containing photos of their flubber explorations. She read the book to the children when they came to the flubber table to play. They were engrossed in the story about themselves and the flubber. When she was done reading, a number of the children looked through the book again. The children continued to explore the flubber, trying out the tools and actions that were in the book. As they worked, Deb continued to refer them to the photos and describe their actions. They stayed at the flubber table even longer this time.

Later that day, Wynsome was sitting by herself looking at the flubber book and imitating the poking action that Kiran was doing in the photo. She was poking the photo with her finger just like he was.

When Oscar and Hannah worked with the flubber, Deb used her observations and photos to show them back their work. As they played, she continued to describe what she saw them doing and pointed out their actions. After she took a number of photos, she immediately downloaded them onto the computer and invited the children to look at a "show" about their work. Many other children came over, fascinated

to see themselves on the screen. They pointed excitedly, saying each other's names.

Oscar was very interested in seeing a photo of himself making an imprint in the flubber with the edge of a plastic container. As he looked at the photo, he made a grunting sound and pointed, indicating that he had pushed hard to make the imprint. Deb suggested that he show this action with the real flubber.

Many Ways To Play
With Flubber

This time as he pushed hard to make each imprint, he intentionally made the same grunting sound. Hannah showed that she caught on to Oscar's meaning right away. She demonstrated by pressing her hands together really hard and squinting her face as she made the same grunting sound. Both of them continued to make imprints in the flubber, grunting as they worked.

Listen to Deb

"I invited the children to begin a study of flubber over an extended period of time, because it is a substance that moves and flows and responds to the children's actions. I had used documentation successfully to enhance preschool children's learning, but I wasn't sure what impact this practice would have on my work with one-year-olds. The children eagerly engaged in revisiting their ideas and actions with the flubber through my descriptions and the photos. As I examined the children's responses to the documentation, I wondered if it helped them develop symbolic representation of their actions in their mind. I was thrilled when Hannah and Oscar shared an understanding about making flubber imprints. I believe that the work I have been doing encouraged the children to create a shared language for the hard pressure needed for imprinting. I saw this event as important for the development of their symbolic thinking and language, but I also saw a bigger significance. I got to witness the miraculous process humans go through to develop language."

Reflect

Deb's story shows the power of revisiting documentation with children over a longer period of time. This sustained study extends the children's learning as they practice these skills and concepts through their actions and see these same actions in the documentation. And indeed, as the children have these experiences and come to represent the action of applying pressure with a grunting sound, they develop a construct in their brain for pressure and then don't have to see it or do it to remember it. Tracking the children's work over time demonstrates their progress as well as enables Deb to see the impact of showing children the documentation.

Learning Alongside Children

In the following fascinating story, teacher Nadia offered children a unique way to show them back their ideas. As a part of her documentation of studying Piaget's schema theory, Nadia decided to share the theory with the children to see how it would affect their work, thinking, and learning.

Since the beginning of the school year, the teachers have noticed the children's deep engagement in using blocks, magnetic tiles, and loose parts. The children used complex communication skills and teamwork as they developed innovative ways to use the materials. The end results were always different. Nevertheless, the same themes from Piaget's schema theory kept showing up in this complicated work: sorting, positioning, trajectory, enclosing, enveloping, and transporting. While studying photos and observations of the children's work at a team meeting, the teachers discussed the value of sharing with the children the learning that was happening during this type of play. They agreed that inviting the children to take a closer look at their work with their teachers would be a wonderful way to collaborate as partners in this study of schema.

At a morning classroom meeting, teacher Nadia introduced the concept of schema theory. She showed the children photos of some of the schema work the teachers were seeing in the classroom. She said, "Did you know that when you are making these type of creations, you are learning and your brain is growing? The work you are doing is so important that there is even a name for it: schema. There are lots of different kinds." Nadia named the types of schemas reflected in the photos and showed the children a list of the other possible schemas. "We have been watching you work closely, and we are really excited to learn about

Pacific Primary School

schema together with you! Your families are invited to learn with us too!" The children were very excited to join their teachers in this investigation, and it was the beginning of a meaningful collaboration.

Since then the children have taken their work to another level. After creating something, they take a close look at their work and ask a teacher, "Is this schema?" The teachers study the list of schemas with

the children. "Oh yes, we can see enclosing, positioning, and sorting," Nadia might say while pointing to the details of their work. They also take photos for further study. To support this inquiry, Nadia has dedicated an entire wall to ongoing documentation. Each child has a panel where they post photos of the work they are doing. The children often help choose the photos and tape them on their panel.

Listen to Nadia

"It has been really meaningful to see children examine photos with a teacher, a peer, and with family members. Children have also been engaging in conversations about schema on their own. In the middle of their work with blocks, tubes, and rocks, children often shout out, 'Wait guys, wait! I see schemas! Look! We made an enclosure and patterns.' Children will pause to a look and agree, 'Let's keep going and make more schemas!'

"It is amazing to have learned with the children that schema can happen anywhere, and you realize it in places where you may have least expected it. One day, Nate poured yogurt on his crackers and added a blueberry to each one. Caleb noticed this and pointed out, "Look—it's schema; he's connecting and making patterns." Children have now begun to independently identify schemas. They closely observe the work of peers and their own work both at school and at home.

"We have invited families to share observations and photos from home. We share these at morning meeting. I received an email from Caleb's mom with a photo attached. 'Caleb said, "Please take a picture of this and send it to Nadia. You HAVE to do this; it's very important!"' It's immensely gratifying to work as close partners in this study of schema. The competence of these children amazes me, and I look forward to what else will spark in this wonderful collaboration."

Beyond Paper and Sounds

As you experiment with digital ways to keep children and their families connected to your documentation, consider the following story about teachers provoked by the children themselves to investigate useful technology for this purpose.

During an investigation of paper and its many different folding attributes, children in my class began to create cuckoo clocks. I captured the creation of the children's ideas through pictures and video. As children played with their voices and sounds to create noises that went with their creations, they asked to have their sounds recorded. The children in preschool 1 had worked with sound recorders in the past, but the devices only recorded ten seconds of sound and allowed no visual. I challenged the children to think past recording just the sounds, which led to this conversation:

Ms. A: How could we make these motions and sounds of our cuckoo clocks visible?

The children suggested I record them doing their sounds and actions using my smartphone.

Gretchen's House Early Learning Children's Community

Ms. A: How will our families and friends see these videos?

The children immediately had ideas: Stand next to the clocks and show each person the video. Or put your phone next to our clocks. One child suggested gluing the videos next to their cuckoo clocks, and another suggested having a button to push to make the video appear on their parents' phones.

Our teaching team was intrigued by this idea of parents using their phones to see the video and began researching how this idea could be put into practice. Their questions included: How can we include a video without access to a screen or way to display for each child's creation? How can we include a video that would pop up on another person's device without having to send each person the file?

We learned about QR codes and used a smartphone to record the children's images and sounds. Each child was assigned a unique QR code that went with their specific cuckoo clock. So, all documentation viewers had to do was scan the code using their phone with a QR reader app.

I took each child who had made a cuckoo clock out in the hallway to see the documentation and let them explore the technology (QR code and reader via the smartphone). They practiced using my phone to scan the codes, push the buttons, and view videos. The children soon spread the word about this new device, telling their parents and others, encouraging them to scan the codes to play the video of them doing their actions and sounds. —Ms. Allison

Listen to Ms. Allison

"Taking the children's questions and thoughts seriously led us to learning about QR codes. Through this process, we were able to extend a paper experience to include video and sound when a screen or computer isn't present. Beyond just seeing themselves in the documentation, the children were able to explain and explore the use of technology as it related to a project they were involved in.

"I see no limit to what the use of QR codes can do since a QR code is similar to a barcode, and it links you to content through the Internet. There are so many ways QR codes can be used to provide easy access to all kinds of content. I feel we have just touched the surface of possibilities."

Reflect

Ms. Allison's story reminds us that we never know where using documentation with children may lead. This is a beautiful example of how taking children's ideas seriously can prompt new learning for everyone.

As early childhood educators continue to wrestle with how much technology is appropriate to include

What is a QR code?
A QR code is similar to a barcode, and it links you to content on the Internet. For example, a QR code could provide a link to websites, articles, documents (such as Word, PowerPoint, or PDF), photographs, videos, voice recordings, and so on with just the scan of the code.

How can I use a QR code?
To use a QR code, you must have a smartphone/device equipped with a camera and a QR code reader/scanner application. Many newer smartphones and tablets come with such an app installed.

What if I don't have a QR code scanner on my phone/tablet?
You can download any QR reader app on your phone or tablet from your app store. Most QR reader apps are free.

How do I use a QR code scanner?
Make sure the app is open, and hold the guides so that you can see the QR code image in them. This will scan the code and the content will pop up.

in children's environments, it is wise to consider the guideline offered by Chris Bayes, a preschool teacher in New Zealand: "We must ask ourselves, does this technology offer value that isn't otherwise present in our environment?" Incorporating QR codes into documentation displays of children's work is a lovely example of value-added technology.

Your Turn

Offer a group of children some interesting materials to play with. While the children play with the materials, here are some things to do:

- Observe closely with a clipboard, pen, and camera. Capture specific details of what you see and hear.
- Ask the children to describe what they are doing and their ideas.
- Point out each child's work and ideas to the others.

Look over your notes and photos and analyze them by considering the following questions:

- What did the child (or children) do and say? Use descriptive words about specific things, including any quotes from their conversations.
- What were they learning? Compare your documentation with a learning domain list, schema theory, or perhaps an assessment tool you use.
- What were you curious about? What do you value in this?
- What ideas does the child's family have about this?

Create a homemade book or digital document for the children using the detailed information you collected and the photos you took. Offer this to the children along with the materials that are depicted. Observe, document, and photograph how the children respond to this documentation of their work.

What ideas does this give you for what to do next?

PRINCIPLE **Engage in Teacher Research to Enhance Your Teaching Practices**

At its core, using reflective teaching practices means being curious and intellectually engaged in the teaching and learning process with children. When teachers view their work as researching everyday moments, planned curriculum experiences, and connecting these to current learning theory and research, their teaching practices become more responsive and meaningful for the children and themselves. Teachers can focus informal research on problems or dilemmas they face or things the children do that they are curious about and delight in. Rather than relying on teaching techniques and standardized approaches, reflective teachers study and consider the many possibilities for understanding children and the role they play in their learning. The following stories show reflective teachers at work, digging deeper to learn more ways to enhance and sustain learning for the children and themselves.

You're Wasting Your Time Not Drawing

Teacher Veronica recognizes the many roles reflective teachers play in extending children's learning. As you read how she worked to support children's drawing skills, notice the strong values and high image of children's competence she brings to her work, along with her keen observation skills and in-depth analysis. Veronica offers reflections on the roles she plays in the children's engagement with her and each other.

When Michael said, "You're wasting your time not drawing," to me this morning, I remembered when he transitioned from the younger class to our class this fall. Back then he was not interested in anything at the art table. He didn't even want to write his name! Michael has come a long way, and he's not the only one. Other children, who would only occasionally come to the art table, are so much more immersed in art these days too. Michael's words drew me to reflect on how the children went from being weary participants to making constant requests for different art

materials and drawing anything they can see. When I think back to how this interest began, I come back to a few key elements: interest, relationships, and observation.

Although the children were not always creating art, they were always observing art. They were often mesmerized by the artwork that the teacher sitting at the art table was working on. I believe the children's sense of wonder and the relationships they have built with us creates a bridge between them and the wonder in art. As they became more active in creating their own art, they also observed their friends' artwork to gain inspiration, and art became a part of their relationships as they worked together.

The children's sense of wonder and interest is a key component in all of this. In my role as an educator, I have to ask myself, should I draw alongside the children to my full capacity? There are several different thoughts in regard to this question, but I believe it is a matter of knowing your children. Some educators will draw with their children, drawing abstract shapes and scribbles; others will not draw at all; and some, as

I have done this year, will draw to their full potential along with the children.

In the past, I limited myself to drawing scribbles and abstract shapes because the children saw my drawing as an impossible standard to reach, which would lead to frustration. I edited my drawing so that children could learn from my technique. However, the children in the classroom this year see wonder and a challenge in my work. They want to rise to that level, while understanding that their drawings will not look exactly like mine because I've had years of practice.

Relationships are the foundation for fluid conversations between people. Mimi can be found at the art table at least once a day. She loves art! At the beginning of the year, her drawings were primarily of her and her sister, which she drew using triangles as the bodies and circles for the heads. Back when I had set up books to provoke children to draw book characters and the covers of their favorites, I sat with them to draw. Mimi watched me as I drew, and said, "I want to try it. How did you draw it?" I simply told her that I looked at the lines and followed them as I drew. She took that advice and drew her own fantastic drawing. Our relationship and the proximity to someone who was being supportive helped her hone her drawing skills. She's been making complex and detailed drawings ever since. One day, I asked Mimi, "How did you become the fantastic artist you are today?" Mimi replied, "Well, I practiced, and I practiced and then it made perfect, but I still have to practice." I could not have agreed more.

It is not only relationships among children and teachers that help drawing thrive, but also the deep relationships peers have formed with one another. When Porter's baby brother was born, we had a picture of Porter holding the baby. Porter immediately stated, "I'm going to draw it." He was not alone. Michael also drew the baby, while Benny watched nearby. Benny's interaction of simply watching is as valuable as Michael's interaction of drawing. Observation is the foundation to children becoming interested in experimenting with different art forms and interpretation. Benny and Porter spend so much time together and their relationship has blossomed. Benny now becomes interested in Porter's drawings and creates his own interpretations of them.

One of the most valuable and unexpected outcomes of this work was the amount of self-assessment and constructive criticism between the children. Their deep interest in drawing has led to deep self-assessment. As Mimi draws, I often hear her talking to herself, guiding herself through her work. When she is done, she always discusses how she feels about her finished artwork and her intentions behind the piece. It is astonishing to hear her take a step back when she is unsatisfied, and say, "I need to make another one. But I need to make one that's better." The way the children speak about their peers' artwork is equally impressive. Instead of just comments like, "That's a good drawing," or "That doesn't look like ____," the children are thoughtful in what they say to each other. Michael and Porter drew pictures of candy over the course of a few weeks. While they were drawing, they would comment on each individ-

ual piece of candy. When drawing jelly beans, Porter looked at Michael's and said, "They almost look like jelly beans, but they need to be less of a circle," in reference to the indentations on beans. Michael then took a careful look at the jelly beans and decided to change his drawing. Their relationship and their experience drawing made that a successful execution of constructive criticism. If the relationship had not been there, this could have been grounds for a serious argument.—Veronica

Listen to Veronica

"Knowing the group of children I have this year, I will continue to draw alongside them throughout the year to challenge and motivate them. I believe that if they have made so much progress in relationship building, curating and nurturing deep interests, building on observational skills, and developing self-assessment, then peer constructive criticism can only lead to deeper thinking, communication, and strong confidence. These are skills we often seek within ourselves as adults, so imagine how far they can go when children already possess these skills at four and five!

"As we move forward, I want to use children's artwork as provocations. Children will then become more a part of the process of planning, giving them greater ownership of their drawings, and hopefully getting them to motivate other peers to join in their provocation. I want to continue to get the children excited about their art and the art of others."

Reflect

Early childhood teachers are often told to never draw for or with children to avoid squelching the children's self-esteem and creativity. Veronica's story reveals a different idea about this "sacred" early childhood rule. She has examined her reasons for drawing with the children. And because she believes in the children's competence, she wants to offer a challenge and communicate that learning to learn to draw takes time and practice. Veronica has come to know her group well, and they respond to her offering with enthusiasm and a willingness to dive deeper into drawing on their own and with each other.

Veronica's story shows the power of reflective teaching to fully engage children in the learning process. Reflective teachers avoid looking for a "right" way to support children's learning, but instead think of themselves as a teacher-researcher who considers at any given moment the many possible roles to help children dive in to continue their excitement about learning.

Discoveries about Crying

Abhirami's journey to become a teacher researcher has been strongly influenced by her desire to understand more about what infants are communicating when they cry.

The more time Abhirami spent with infants and the adults who worked with them, the more she realized that her team needed to study crying together. Teachers in the program were told to help the crying child first. But often three children would cry at the same time. Which crying child gets helped first?

Abhi decided to read articles in order to gain a deeper understanding of infant crying and her responses to it. She also began to closely observe the crying children and reflected on her own feelings about their crying.

She learned that crying is an infant's primary way to communicate. For Abhirami, this meant that she needed to treat crying as a language that had to be deciphered. She decided to listen and observe when infants cried so she could respond and not just react to their crying. Responding instead of reacting meant that she would critically think about her own behaviors and plan a sequence of behaviors to follow when she hears an infant begin to cry. She began to identify and ask questions about the different types of crying she was hearing. Was this a protest, involving loud cries and restlessness? Was it a cry of despair,

involving monotonous cries, along with inactivity and withdrawal? Or was it detachment, where the infant was withdrawn and had seemingly lost hope that the caregiver will provide comfort?

Initially, Abhirami and her team had more questions than answers, but eventually they developed a better understanding of infant crying. They began talking to interested families about what crying behaviors they observed at home. During team meetings, Abhirami facilitated discussions about crying by reading sections of research articles. With her new understanding, she decided to create a documentation display that would communicate the team's written plan and bring visibility to their intentional behaviors for supporting crying infants.

Listen to Abhirami

"Learning about crying as a form of communication began to influence my responses to crying children. For instance, when I identify that a child is protesting, I move closer to let them know that I am available to them. From my readings, I learned how the caregiver's response can support or undermine how babies develop a sense of trust. I also recognized that infants need partners to learn and develop self-regulation. For observers, I concluded that it was very important to make visible a written plan of my intent for supporting crying infants.

"For the documentation display, I partnered with my teaching team and one of our parents, Bekah Galer. She is a gifted artist who envisioned her son as her model for the portrait. I provided her with a black-and-white photo I captured of her son crying in the Infant Room and she used crayons to create a portrait of her crying son. According to Bekah, she applied orange and yellow around his face to capture *her* feelings of anxiety and stress when her son cried. She chose blue for his tears to express her son's feelings of pain and sadness. Collaborating on this project not only strengthened my relationship with Bekah, but also deepened my understanding of crying infants.

Gretchen's House Early Learning Center, art courtesy of Bekah Galer

"For teachers, observers, and visitors, the documentation display functions as a reminder of the importance of partnering with crying infants. With each new discovery, our plan will continue to evolve and continue in shaping our understanding of crying."

Reflect

Because listening to crying can be excruciating, often adults rush to stop crying behavior before attempting to understand what the child is trying to communicate. Yet understanding the need behind the crying and then addressing that need often allows children to self-soothe, calming their bodies on their own. Adopting the curious mindset of a teacher-researcher can help us become more tolerant of crying and begin to see the details of children's efforts to communicate thoughts and feelings through crying.

Abhirami assessed her early reactions and sought out resources to learn more about crying. She took initiative by talking with families and her teaching team to develop new insights in the classroom and at home. Then she collaborated with a parent to create an artistic documentation display, which incorporates the language of color, adding further dimension and visibility to the understanding of crying. Using this holistic approach, teachers acknowledge that infants are competent communicators capable of expressing their thoughts, feelings, and needs through crying. Your interactions with children, their families, and coteachers can be enriched as you become a teacher-researcher and share your findings through documentation.

Your Turn

Consider taking up your own informal teacher research project. Choose a focus based on problems or dilemmas you face, theories children have, or things they do that pique your curiosity. Develop a couple of research questions related to the focus.

Then, gather observations, photos, and notes over a period of a few weeks. Study this documentation on your own and with colleagues. Add or adjust focus questions as you uncover new insights and understandings. Finalize your research by reflecting on what you learned about children, yourself, and the teaching and learning process. How will you use what you learned in your research to transform your teaching practices?

8 Adapt the Curriculum Framework for Different Settings

The best in life comes from a center, something urgent and powerful, an ideal or emotion that insists on its being. From that insistence a shape emerges and creates its structure out of passion. If you begin with a structure, you have to make up the passion, and that's very hard to do. —**Roger Rosenblatt, via Margaret J. Wheatley**

The structures and regulations that shape pre-K and early childhood programs have very little to do with the passions children and teachers bring to their work. Requirements are intended to move children toward standards and teachers toward compliance (Wagner 2002), not mobilize their passions. Nonetheless, when you commit yourself to "teaching with fire" (Intrator and Scribner 2003), you will find ways of working around the barriers in your setting. Your passion and the resources you seek out will help you invent structures that support more in-depth learning for you and the children.

As you've studied *Learning Together with Young Children*, have you found yourself periodically thinking, "Yes, but in my setting, we can't . . ."? The barriers to using the curriculum framework presented in this book may initially seem formidable. The daily demands of your work don't lend themselves to slowing down and being reflective. Required curriculum components, learning outcomes, and assessments may dominate the focus of your limited time. There are constraints related to the logistics of your space, schedule, budget, and staffing patterns. Perhaps your children represent a wide range of cultural and linguistic backgrounds or have families challenged by issues of poverty, violence, or the legacy of racism. You may have children who attend only part time or

a few days a week, or you have double sessions with two full groups of children and teachers who alternately share your space.

Some teachers experience isolation as the only one in their program with an interest in analyzing or writing up documentation stories. Do you find it difficult to choose a focus for curriculum when so many interests are emerging? What about different perspectives and conflicts that have to be negotiated with coworkers, parents, monitors, or coaches assigned to your program? The list of challenges teachers face goes on and on, and they are all real. But if you remember why you wanted to be a teacher in the first place, you tap into longings that unleash other possibilities. You can transform frustration into determination. When you taste how your days with children could be different, you will refuse to settle for less. In this spirit, we offer you another challenge: move beyond your self-imposed limitations and fears, claim your power, and invent your own way to deepen children's learning with our curriculum framework.

Claiming your power will look different in each setting. You must engage in a continual process of examining and negotiating the real lives and interests in your classroom with the standards and regulations you're handed (Wien 2004). Ask yourself questions such as these:

- How can my documentation support children's learning while also helping me uncover where standards are being met and what else I might do?
- What other possibilities and perspectives will deepen my thinking?

- Is there an aspect of my work that I might research more to discover how theory shows up in real life and my real-life teaching practices can inform theory?

Here are some principles to guide you in adapting our curriculum framework for your particular setting.

Principles

- Focus your documentation on a process.
- Invent new ways to meet requirements.
- Expand possibilities for prescribed curriculum.
- Document everyday experiences that meet standards.
- Make assessments relevant and meaningful.
- Seek different perspectives to inform your planning.
- Learn from conflicting ideas.
- Encourage coaches to engage in research with you.

PRINCIPLE   **Focus Your Documentation on a Process**

When you make documentation available to children, they see themselves and their peers exploring, discovering, inventing, and learning. This is especially valuable when you are trying to engage children in extended investigations when they attend your program on a part-time basis. In-depth investigations or projects are difficult to keep going if you don't have a consistent group of students who regularly explore questions together, challenge each other, and learn from each other's ideas. Children who attend part time may have difficulty following the threads of a project topic, feel out of sync with others in the group, or lack consistent relationships to hold their interest. When different groups of children attend on different days, they may develop dissimilar interests or go in different directions with a topic, making it hard for the teacher to know how to focus the overall project.

In part-time programs, teachers may find it more useful to focus long-term projects on the *process* of an investigation, rather than a topic. When you show children documentation of the process different groups are engaged in, you connect them with something familiar and help them see how they have shared experiences even though they aren't exploring together each day. A process lends itself to deeper learning because it allows children to engage from their own perspective, rather than try to play "catch up" with what they've missed when they weren't there. As you review with children documentation of what others have been doing, you as a teacher aren't focused on a topic, but on getting the group to "see" each other and invest in a process together.

Mix It Up

If you are an after-school teacher, you are probably with your group of children for only a few hours each day, and the children may often arrive to your program wound up or burned out from their school day. Does it make sense to pursue in-depth curriculum in this situation? As you read about Rhonda's approach, notice how her choice to focus on a process rather than a topic opened a new line of thinking for her and the children.

Rhonda has named her group "The Explorer's Club" to reflect her approach to providing curriculum a few hours a day for children who come to her after school. Some children come every day, others only a few days a week. Rhonda's curriculum is environmentally based with a wide range of interesting things to do around

painting. Rather than just appreciating that, Rhonda decided to experiment with the idea of focusing extended project work on a process rather than a topic. She began offering an invitation each week that focused on an aspect of color mixing, keeping a daily journal of observations, and creating displays of the efforts of different groups, drawing the attention of the children to each other's work. The children began staying at the color-mixing table for longer periods of time, trying to replicate or take further what they saw other children doing in Rhonda's documentation. This created shared connections between children who rarely saw each other in person.

Several months into this open-ended investigation of color mixing, Rhonda decided to introduce specific instructions for mixing colors to get different shades and hues. After discussing her documentation about these efforts, Rhonda then suggested the children create a full color palette with documentation of the formula for making each color to share with children who were not present. This sparked an ongoing connection between different groups as they studied and expanded on each other's color palettes.

Listen to Rhonda

"Until this color-mixing project, I was beginning to think it was not possible to sustain an interest in a project topic when the group of children changes each day. Finally, I realized I had to let go of my preconceived notions of what this was supposed to look like and redefine the concept of in-depth projects for my situation. Because color mixing offered so many possibilities for investigation and theory making, I realized that these were the elements of in-depth project work, even though it wasn't a topical theme to pursue. Using my documentation and the same materials with each group could provide a thread to weave between the groups. And this could support my values of helping children experience connections over time and across different groups.

"What I didn't anticipate was that using my documentation with the children would address my

the room. Some materials are always available while others are special invitations she sets out for them to explore for only a few days.

Rhonda has mastered the art of observing the details of children's activities, but she struggles with how to offer in-depth project work when children are with her on such a limited basis. Her coworkers are content to just hang out with the kids and show no interest in collaborating with Rhonda to figure this out. Still, Rhonda's disposition is to be persistent in gathering documentation because she delights in revisiting what the children have been doing. She began noticing that more than anything else, most of the children in her program gravitated toward process activities, such as working at the sensory table or

own hunger to have someone to talk with about the details I'm seeing. Indeed, these conversations with the children have provided me with more perspectives, deeper understandings, and ideas about other strategies for extending their thinking and connections with each other. This color-mixing project has reminded me that I don't have to give up my longings for more in-depth work and collaboration. I just have to think outside the box."

Reflect

Instead of letting go of bigger expectations for her work, Rhonda let go of the idea that there is one right way to do in-depth investigations with children. Her values and solid practice of creating engaging invitations in the environment, along with her persistent disposition and attention to observing the details in children's pursuits, enabled her to leap over the barriers she was experiencing. Using her documentation with the children was a critical factor in helping them build relationships that influenced each other's investigations. Even though many of them couldn't talk with one another or compare their explorations side by side, they were able to relate the process they shared through the photos and Rhonda's stories about the work. This approach also helped Rhonda overcome her own isolation and sense of failure in meeting her expectations. Rhonda's story helps us see in action what might otherwise be abstract theories: co-constructing knowledge and pedagogical documentation.

In the Comfort of Friends

When planning to start a two-and-a-half-hour, two-day-a-week toddler play group, Deb encountered reservations and skepticism among colleagues. As you read her story, how would you describe what in-depth curriculum looks like for this age group and under these circumstances? Notice how Deb's documentation focused on the process of building relationships.

Martin Luther King Jr. Day Home Center

Deb is masterful at setting up environments where children encounter wonder and delight, and the room for her toddler play group is no exception. But she knew that for children twelve to twenty-four months old, any interest in her engaging environment would hinge on the children and their families feeling secure and comfortable. As part of her plan, Deb encouraged the parents to linger with the children for as long as possible before leaving the room on the first day. The environment would be new and different for the children, so Deb worked to include many things that would feel familiar for them.

The first "curriculum plan" she developed was to take photos of the children: a close-up photo of each child's face, a photo of each child with his or her family, and a photo of each child with Deb. By the time the children arrived for their second day, Deb had put the photos in little books for the children to look at. The children were also given a picture of themselves with Deb to take home and post on the refrigerator. Deb added pictures of the children with their families in frames and in homemade books around the room.

In the coming weeks, Deb placed larger photographs around the room that focused on the children's exploration of the room and each other as playmates. One day she printed the photos on transparencies and watched the children point with recognition and squeal with delight as they recognized themselves, family members, and new playmates up on the big screen. Seeing Kobe's picture projected on the wall, Aiden noticed he was absent that day. "Where Kobe?

Where Kobe go?" he asked. The children were clearly making connections with one another. They were also making connections between activities they saw in the photos and what was available in the room. When Sasha saw Shaelyn rolling a ball down the ramp in a photograph, Sasha took a few balls from the basket herself and scrambled up the ramp to roll them down. Soon the children were sending other things down the ramp and in the coming weeks continued their experiments with different possibilities for ramp play.

Listen to Deb

"I was so thrilled to be returning to work with toddlers, and I had so many ideas I wanted to try. But I have to admit, I was a bit worried, as I shared my colleagues' concerns. Would the children be secure enough to part with their parents and enjoy the environment I was so carefully planning? Was the time between days in my program too long for them to recognize it as a safe and secure place? Would they forget about their playmates or have trouble bonding with me? I'm a strong believer in the value of open-ended, self-directed play—valuable in and of itself—so I had to keep asking myself, 'Why would you care about developing some in-depth curriculum?' My initial idea about curriculum was to foster comfort and security with lots of familiar images. Seeing themselves in pictures not only met this outcome, but led to stronger connections among their playmates. I know this isn't how teachers or parents typically think of 'curriculum,' but I have no doubt that helping the children form relations is the essence of in-depth curriculum for this age group. I'm reminded that despite prevailing notions about toddlers, they are capable of sustained attention and have a keen eye for details. They are eager to be together, not just parallel players. Doesn't this suggest that curriculum for them can be far more engaging?"

Reflect

Deb's story brings to life the research findings on attachment theory and brain development for toddler curriculum. Because she drew on the idea of emotional and social intelligence (Goleman 1995, 2006), Deb demonstrates that in-depth curriculum for this age group goes beyond planning activities. Instead, she focuses on the process of building relationships. Making common threads of experiences visible to children not only deepens their relationships but also enables them to build on each other's ideas. When you see your friends doing things in pictures, it reminds you of what you know. Children will usually enjoy a couple hours a week in a fun environment, but Deb's view of curriculum involves more than short spurts of entertaining activities. She focuses on the foundational idea that deeper involvement in learning comes from secure relationships and revisiting familiar experiences to make new connections.

PRINCIPLE   Invent New Ways to Meet Requirements

Many child care providers and early childhood teachers feel they cannot deviate from a standard approach to curriculum planning because of licensing regulations, NAEYC accreditation criteria, requirements that come with public funding, or efforts to receive a high score on an environmental rating scale (ERS such as ITERS/ECERS), or an assessment tool such as the Classroom Assessment Scoring System (CLASS). However, if you are conscientiously planning and have documentation of your work, you can negotiate with monitors and evaluators, and demonstrate how you are meeting the intent of the requirements. Do you feel confident that you can articulate clearly why you do what you do? Do you see yourself as an inventor, risk taker, or challenger of the status quo? If not, you may want to cautiously begin to integrate some of the ideas in *Learning Together with Young Children* and most likely this will generate interest and curiosity from others. Sometimes simple changes can lead to big things.

From Parent Involvement to Engagement

Head Start has long been known for its parent involvement component and many state-funded preschool programs are mandating this as well. Typical documentation of this requirement gathers data on the number of parent volunteers, parent education meetings, and home visits. Too often this ends up in an archived file, rather than becoming a vital part of the program's history that is kept alive through storytelling.

Director Karina takes a different approach, engaging families in gatherings with agendas centered around building relationships and continuing a sense of shared history together. During one of the first gatherings, Karina and her team offer a slide show highlighting the story created by staff and children of the previous year's significant events and activities families had been involved in. This is followed by a question for the families gathered: "What is the story you want to help us create?"

Each subsequent gathering follows a similar format with opportunities for mutual exchanges to continue getting to know each other and celebrate traditions and accomplishments. Part of each meeting is a "community café discussion." Here are some of the questions they have explored:

- *What are some memories you have of you or your family going to school?*
- *What is the meaning behind the name of your child?*
- *What resources would you like to see us offer at family gatherings?*

At each of their gatherings, families have the chance to create something either for their child or for the program. For instance, at a fall gathering, the parents used leaves and watercolors to write something they were thankful for about their children. These get read to the children later at the center and the children, in turn, sent a message back about why they were thankful for their families.

Photo documentation of the agendas and family gathering activities are put into slide shows and printed as a way not only to meet requirements mandated by their public dollars but also to keep their history visible.

Listen to Karina

"When we first adopted this idea of Parent Gatherings, we didn't really know how it would unfold. Our program was getting ready to go through the journey of QRIS for our state. We needed to have documentation of work that is done with families, but we wanted it to be done in a holistic way that aligned with our values. We have a common space, where families are able to build community, learn from each other, and share their deep understanding about their culture and their child. Our family gatherings happen once a month. I started to notice that families were interacting with each other, and it didn't matter that English wasn't the common language. I felt very proud that we were giving the families the same opportunity that we give our children.

"One moment that I will always remember was when we were exploring the topic of 'my child's bucket list' (the dreams they have for their young children); I can still hear the sentences clear as day in my head. As a daughter of Mexican immigrants, I know the importance of school and the impact that

Southwest Early Learning Center, a chapter of Sound Child Care Solutions

CRISTIAN

Meaning of Cristian is "Follower of Christ" We chose this name because we wanted a name from or related to the bible. In our family we follow a Christian life. ♥♥

we have had on these families. There are times that these types of questions about hopes and dreams do not get asked. We understand that rough patches will happen in life and some of these children might not have the same opportunities as their fellow classmates, but giving the parents a chance to create dreams and become advocates is the least we can do. Parents were in tears sharing their dreams. For me, our photo stories are a beautiful way to document the way we organically work with our families while meeting the million requirements.

"As our funders come and review our information, it isn't the quantity of data they get from us, but the content and quality of data that we are able to share with them. This is impactful because they can see the significance around the work we do and how we stay true to our mission and values, which sometimes is very hard when you have to juggle many grants."

Reflect

Karina strives to have her center's work with families parallel what they are offering the children—opportunities to learn and create big dreams for their lives. She doesn't equate poverty, language learning, or new immigration status with a deficit in who they are. As an administrator, she works with her teachers to intentionally focus on the quality of her documentation, wanting it to communicate how they are genuinely engaging with families.

Transforming the idea of meeting requirements to developing a visible history together with families is an innovative way Karina has built the culture of her center. Approaching her work this way holds a deeper meaning and provides new vitality, rather than stress, as she fulfills requirements.

What ideas does Karina's approach give you for working more closely with families in your program? What steps can you begin to take to invent new ways to meet any requirements that come with your funding?

Making the Leap

It's easy to be held captive by someone else's interpretation of licensing regulations. But if you understand the *intent* of the requirements, you can demonstrate how you are meeting this intent in a different way. Notice how Marilyn, a licensor, encourages providers to stand up for what they believe is appropriate. Can you imagine doing what she suggests?

Marilyn always approaches her licensing visits with keen eyes, open ears, and her state's licensing codebook in hand. Her job, as she sees it, is not only to ensure the health, safety, and well-being of children, but also to encourage innovation and exceed the minimum licensing requirements. Marilyn isn't just looking for violations, but appropriate variations on how teachers are keeping the children's best interests in mind. As she walks around the inside and outside of a building, watches interactions with children, and reviews required documents, you will hear her making comments like, "I can see that you have kept our code in mind when you added this new area to your play yard."

When Marilyn doesn't initially see evidence of something that is required, she uses this as an opportunity to raise questions, not jump to conclusions. "Can you tell me how you go about meeting our requirement for posting curriculum plans for children?" Sometimes this question opens up a fruitful discussion about the intent of a regulation or a possible variation of how it could be met. As a licensor, Marilyn sees her role as not only a monitor for quality, but a motivator to think through the why and how of important quality components. Her visits are not dreaded by programs. Rather, the staff members appreciate the new eyes and ears she brings, and her openness to their ideas, even as she holds them accountable for standards.

Listen to Marilyn

"Licensing administrative codes are legal requirements for child care providers. However, if you read our codes, they are usually very broad. I always tell providers that the key is to be able to articulate and document what they believe, do, and plan for children. Sometimes when providers feel they are being stopped from doing what they want, it is not due to a licensing code, but someone interpreting it in a very limited way. This is when the confident and knowledgeable provider needs to be able to say why she does something the way she does, and justify that she is meeting the codes.

"If you feel you are not being allowed to do what you know is appropriate for children, go to a supervisor in licensing. Do not be afraid to do this. One emergent-curriculum–styled program fulfilled the requirement of posting curriculum by hanging large pieces of paper on the wall where the teacher webbed the day's activities with the children. Her only change in practice was to save those papers for the licensor and to date them. Now, if a licensor could not make that leap, then I would engage a supervisor."

Reflect

Licensing and QRIS monitors, along with Head Start review teams, all have an important role in holding programs accountable to quality standards. Marilyn's approach parallels the NAEYC accreditation process in that she encourages programs to self-reflect and set goals for their own improvement. If your monitor is more rigid in interpreting regulations, what could you offer to open this person's mind?

Start with the assumption that you can have a discussion. Think in terms of friendly negotiations and raising the monitor's awareness of other options. Show evidence of your careful thinking, not just your defensiveness. When all else fails, if you believe what you are doing is truly beneficial for children, follow Marilyn's advice and talk to a department supervisor.

Teachers often tell us they struggle to make required record keeping meaningful in their actual work with children. This is especially true when you are required to fill out curriculum planning forms and turn them in long before the actual days of implementation. If you are using your observations to guide your planning, new ideas may be emerging from the children that will influence the direction of your curriculum. Depending on your comfort level with challenging requirements, you may want to explore new ways to document your curriculum to more closely align your required paperwork with your practice. Or, you may choose to just fill out the required form but not let it hinder your responsive to children's emerging interests.

Digging beneath the Surface

Striving to be in compliance with all the requirements, many programs often have teachers create multiple documents with the same information. Dayle's story demonstrates that when teachers are supported to find a way to streamline this process, they can get to the heart of what is most important and meaningful. Notice how satisfying this experience was to both Dayle and the parents.

Dayle's infant and toddler program requires teachers to do individual planning for their infants and toddlers. These are based on observations that get documented in several places, creating a frustrating amount of paperwork for teachers with the same observations repeated on daily sheets, placed into the child's curriculum plans, and then used again on

the Desired Results Developmental Profile (DRDP), an assessment tool used by the program. Dayle approached her director and got encouragement and strong support to start experimenting with a new way to document these individual plans.

Listen to Dayle
"I found myself struggling to create authentic curriculum plans while addressing all the requirements. How was I going to dig beneath the surface and bring children's true interests to light? I started experimenting with new ways to document my plans for each child with these three goals in mind:

- bridging the gap between families and our classroom
  I felt that this goal could be achieved by adding photographs to the curriculum plans. This helps families more clearly see their child's plan and provide more feedback.
- including standards without overshadowing the children's existing competency
  Prior to this, I organized my observations by developmental domains and used a checklist to ensure that children were meeting each measure. I shifted my thinking by changing my starting point for planning. Instead of looking at the standards and how the children met them, I put the children first and then applied the standards to what they were naturally doing.
- incorporating my voice as a colearner alongside the children
  I tried to meet this goal by asking questions, offering my reflections, and posing plans for further investigation.

"The following pages show how my old model looked, followed by my new one.

Original Lesson Plan Form

Toddler Two: Mateo 8/31/15–9/4/15

Teacher Dayle McLeod

Daily Observations and Reflections:

Bella picked up Mateo's stuffed animal. I said, "It's Mateo's. Give it to him." She walked over and handed it to Mateo. Mateo said, "Thank you." Bella walked over to me and repeated, "Thank you." (Language as well)

Mateo walked around the room crying. He laid down on the blue cushion in the position that he sleeps in. Mateo followed me to the sink. He laid down on the floor mat in the same position. I then offered him milk and he fell asleep.

Social Emotional Development

List ways you will set the stage to enhance Social Emotional Development

- Follow Mateo's cues to know when he is tired
- Reflect language, give scripts of "mine" while pointing to hand or "give back"

Daily Observations and Reflections:

Mateo picked up each marker from the table and made a mark on his hand. He stated each color as he made the marks.

Creative Development

List ways you will set the stage to enhance creative development

- Provide markers
- Reflect colors

Daily Observations and Reflections:

While helping Mateo with sunscreen he repeated "un-keen" (sunscreen) several times.

Language and Literacy Development

List ways you will set the stage to enhance language and literacy development. Minimum of 30 minutes per day.

- Mateo has been repeating many simple phrases; continue to reflect and give simple scripts

234

Experimental Lesson Plan
Teacher Dayle McLeod

Date Observed: 1/11/16–1/15/16
Date Implemented: 1/19/16–1/22/16

Approach to Learning & Self Regulation
1/14

Alejandro was shaking the bells with Colin and Andrew. As Alejandro followed Colin around the room, Colin held the bells up to his ear. Alejandro mimicked this action and brought the bells up next to his ear. Alejandro looked at Colin and smiled.

Mimic Alejandro's actions when with him to observe his response — look for other children he may be imitating through out the week.

> ATL-REG3: IMITATION

Social and Emotional Development
1/15

Alejandro was sitting at the breakfast table. He heard Emeric crying and pointed at Emeric while vocalizing. I stated, "Emeric sounds sad." Alejandro pointed and vocalized again. Greyson stated, "Emeric's crying." Alejandro nodded his head yes.

Alejandro pointed to another child when they were crying and was wanting to be near them — I wonder what it is about the child crying that intrigues him. Is it the sound? Is he wanting someone else to attach the emotion to the crying? I will continue to observe this interest in crying.

> SED2: SOCIAL AND EMOTIONAL UNDERSTANDING

Language and Literacy Development
1/15

Alejandro was sitting at the breakfast table. He heard another teacher and child talking about cars. He vocalized and began to walk away. I stated, "You can use a car when you're done — right now you're eating breakfast." Alejandro put his dishes in the bin and walked over to the trucks.

Continue to reflect on Alejandro's actions and vocalizations. Offer one word scripts for him to use.

> LLD1: UNDERSTANDING OF LANGUAGE (RECEPTIVE)

Cognitive Development
1/12

Alejandro explored snow in the sensory table this morning. He seemed eager to taste it and feel it on his face. Alejandro used a small strainer to scoop the snow up and into his mouth.

I wonder if Alejandro would use the strainers in a similar way with a different material in the sensory table (a tool for eating)? I will attempt to offer the strainers with a variety of materials again next week.

> COG11: KNOWLEDGE OF THE NATURAL WORLD

Physical Development – Health
1/12

Alejandro was eating bagels with jam at breakfast. I looked closely at how he was holding onto the bread as he dipped it into the jam. Alejandro held the bread in his right hand, holding it between his thumb and pointer and middle finger.

Offer varying writing utensils (markers, crayons, pencils) to observe how he is holding those. Continue to offer tongs when serving meals for Alejandro to become more comfortable with using them (pinching).

> PD-HLTH4: FINE MOTOR MANIPULATIVE SKILLS

Parent Reflections

New Lesson Plan Form

Teacher Dayle Mcleod

Alejandro's Lesson Plan
Dates Observed: 5/2/16–5/12/16
Dates Implemented: 5/16/16–5/26/16

Alejandro has been recognizing his own name when he hears others say it. He points to himself and states, "me andro." He has also been stating "me andro" when he sees a picture of himself. I wonder what his response would be to looking at himself in the mirror.

<u>Sed1: Identity of Self in Relation to Others</u>

Alejandro approached the table and stated, "paint." I offered him a smock. He told me "no" and pointed to the chair. I was surprised as Alejandro typically will put on a smock. I then looked at the chair next to me and I had set a smock on the back of that chair. Alejandro proceeded to paint while the smock sat on the chair.

<u>Atl-Reg3: Imitation</u>
<u>Vpa1: Visual Art</u>

Alejandro has shown an interest in vehicles — especially construction trucks and busses. While outside, he seems to be able to recognize the sounds of the different vehicles as they drive by. In this photo Alejandro turned quickly as he heard the sound of a bus driving by on Capitol. How would Alejandro respond to a walking trip to watch buses drive by on Shiawassee?

<u>Cog9: Inquiry through observation and investigation</u>
<u>Hss2: Sense of Place</u>

Alejandro saw that I had taken my shoes off while in the sandbox. He sat down and took his shoes off, too. He proceeded to use the spoon to scoop sand onto my feet. He tapped my foot gently with the spoon. I wonder what Alejandro would do with the animals in the sandbox? Would he try to bury them too?

<u>Atl-reg3: Imitation</u>
<u>Sed3: Relationships and Social Interactions with Familiar Adults</u>
<u>Cog9: Inquiry through Observation and Investigation</u>

Plan for the next two weeks:

- Construction hats added to dramatic play
- Plan a walking trip with three other children
- Continue to reflect on Alejandro's language "Your name is . . ."
- Add books with busses
- Use large safari animals from T1 in the sandbox
- Offer similar painting experience without smocks already at the table

Family Feedback:

The new approach to documenting lesson plans seems to be really appreciated by our parents, with this example of feedback:

"'I am a busy parent of five who, like many parents, would love to know more about my child's day and what he is learning. But to be honest, I don't always have the time to read through lesson plans or identify what or who he is engaged with at school. I am very attracted to the pictures displayed in the new lesson plans, as they catch my attention and let me in for a second to see what my child was doing, his facial reactions, and body language. The added standards provide me with comfort in knowing my child is receiving the best education possible through intentional experiences. I appreciate the questions Dayle asks in each section because it allows me to think more deeply about what my child is doing and why. The questions also provided prompt new inquiries of what my child is interested in and how to best support him at home. I enjoy looking at this layout, as it provides me with the information I want to know while offering me the comfort I need and the curiosity to ask "why?" It allows me to become invested in my child's learning while assisting in my understanding of my child's growth and development.'"

Reflect

While it's important to individualize planning for infants and toddlers, this process can be time consuming and redundant for teachers, a "busywork" task, taking time away from genuine reflection. Dayle recognized that to be meaningful, it was important to connect observations, planning, and assessment in her documentation. Rather than assume a position of powerlessness, she took initiative to approach her director for support and began to experiment with new forms of documentation based on her specific goals. Rather than just meeting a requirement, Dayle wanted her documentation to genuinely engage families with specific examples of what their children were doing to show their competency and meet the desired outcomes in developmental profiles.

Choosing to include her questions and reflections provides a window into her thinking and an invitation for families to offer feedback and dialogue.

Shuffling the Boxes

A teacher can often initiate change by working within a required system rather than challenging it altogether. Notice how Kristin's efforts to meet requirements around lesson plan boxes gradually shifted her thinking as well as the expectations of parents and her coworkers.

Kristin's Head Start program has a lesson plan form that all teachers must post. During her first year of teaching there, she dutifully filled in the little boxes and tried to conform to the thematic and learning domain focus the form is centered on, even though her approach to curriculum was more emergent than these forms suggest. As she grew in confidence, Kristin had a number of conversations with her education coordinator and director, seeking permission to try something new. While they weren't willing to let her abandon the essence of the form, her supervisors gave Kristin tacit permission to do some experimenting.

She started including new boxes on her form and adding questions to take up with her coworkers at the end of the week when they would sit down to plan. As she began doing more observing and photographing, Kristin's documentation replaced her activity books as the primary source for ideas about what to do next. Over the next few years, she moved some of her documentation into the little boxes themselves as evidence of what her thinking and the children's learning was focused on that week.

Listen to Kristin

"After my first year of learning the ropes and going along with everything in my program, I started playing around with the layout of the lesson plan form, as well as the required information it asked for. Initially my supervisor and I made some minor changes, like replacing the word *theme* with *focus*, and then I added

Kristen's Experiment with Planning Forms

PHASE I: TOPIC EVALUATION

What has been happening in the classroom and our community?
How did this topic come to our attention?

In classroom, the children have been very interested in painting. They have been talking a lot about colors. They have been mixing colors to make new colors, and adding glue and collage materials.

What is the underlying interest in this topic? Why is it meaningful to the children?

magical—the new colors they make, satisfies curiosity, the way it feels—textures: smooth, rough

How does this topic support the values of the teachers, parents and our program?

Supports science exploration, art appreciation and expression, vocabulary acquisition, respect for others (taking turns, making choices about paint and materials)

What possible directions could this topic take? Make a planning web:

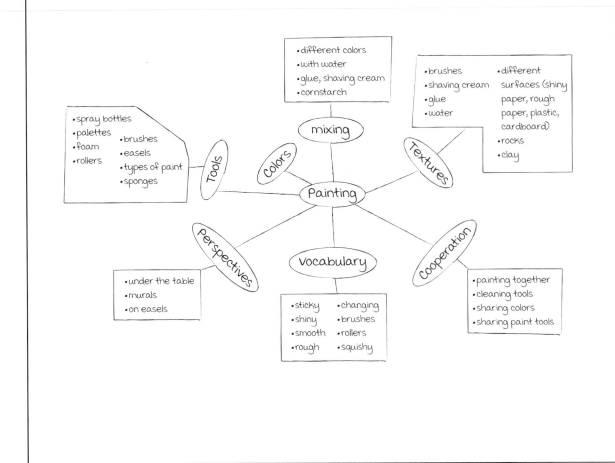

Kristen's Experiment with Planning Forms

Our Investigation _Paint!_

Large Group Meeting: How was your weekend? Revisit documentation panel from painter's visit. movement!	movement! Story: the Pot	Review painting with tools—what was that like? movement!	Review hand-washing week-in-review. movement!
Small Group Meeting: explore new paint tools: rollers, spatulas	explore new paint tools: rollers, spatulas	Review painting tools and add new surfaces—easels, the wall	Paint on vertical surfaces— easels, the wall

What did we find out? _Children are excited about making big paintings—covering space._

What next? _Offer long rolls of paper, butcher paper, offer paint outside?_

the word *investigation*. I experimented with reducing the number of boxes that had preplanned activities and adding boxes that would be filled in with environment changes. Over time, I continued to play with the form, with collaboration from my direct supervisor and a careful eye from the education director, and it evolved along with my own understanding of curriculum. Eventually, I added space for reflection, which I titled 'What we found out' or 'What we discovered today.' I added questions like 'What do we want to know about this?' and 'What do we need to help us in our investigations?'

"The boxes were ever present, of course, and I was still required to write in activities. But those evolved from preplanned activities that had a predetermined outcome, to small-group activities that were more invitation focused. Soon those boxes were filled in with things like 'explore clay' or 'review documentation from our field trip.' At the end of each week, I invited my coteachers to review documentation with me, and we would discuss where the children might go next, and write in the boxes the invitations we would offer next. After four years, I finally stopped filling in the boxes altogether and started putting pictures and stories in those spaces with narrative about what was happening. The parents and teachers all loved it because it was so clear what was really happening in the classroom."

Reflect

Translating a cycle of reflection and action onto a form is a difficult endeavor because it is hard to capture the complexity of this dynamic process on a flat screen or piece of paper. The process easily loses its vitality and life if you try to put it in little boxes. The challenge is to invent a representation of your thinking so that your written plan communicates the mind-set of a researcher even as you acknowledge learning goals for the children. If you are saddled with a standard form, do your best to integrate your thinking into the words you put in the little boxes. When you write out plans in advance, you easily

forget to pay attention to the learning process itself.

Kristin shows us how a teacher's experimentation can enhance her own understandings as well as those of others. As she tried to make her curriculum planning form more genuinely reflective of her own thinking process, she was better able to engage others around her. Kristin's shift to using invitations in her activity times with the children became opportunities for the teachers to reflect together with the children about their new discoveries and insights. Her coworkers and the children's families let her know that posting documentation stories had far more meaning for them than words with the names of a song or activity she was planning in advance.

Even if you are required to use a prescribed curriculum with lessons and projected outcomes someone else has designed, you can demonstrate possibilities for deeper learning, as Kristin does in the above story. Keep focused on the *intent* of a particular lesson or desired outcome, and consider how to connect that with what is meaningful to the children. Your ongoing observations of children can guide you in this process.

Listen to Jean

Jean, a child care licensor, shares her thoughts about how to meet requirements:

"Our licensing code calls for evidence of staff planning. In my mind the important part is the planning, not the form. It can be a web, a chart, a list, a blog,

Hilltop Children's Center

Objectives for Development & Learning

Social–Emotional

1. Regulates own emotions and behaviors
   a. Manages feelings
   b. Follows limits and expectations
   c. Takes care of own needs appropriately

2. Establishes and sustains positive relationships
   a. Forms relationships with adults
   b. Responds to emotional cues
   c. Interacts with peers
   d. Makes friends

3. Participates cooperatively and constructively in group situations
   a. Balances needs and rights of self and others
   b. Solves social problems

Physical

4. Demonstrates traveling skills

5. Demonstrates balancing skills

6. Demonstrates gross-motor manipulative skills

7. Demonstrates fine-motor strength and coordination
   a. Uses fingers and hands
   b. Uses writing and drawing tools

Language

8. Listens to and understands increasingly complex language
   a. Comprehends language
   b. Follows directions

9. Uses language to express thoughts and needs
   a. Uses an expanding expressive vocabulary
   b. Speaks clearly
   c. Uses conventional grammar
   d. Tells about another time or place

10. Uses appropriate conversational and other communication skills
    a. Engages in conversations
    b. Uses social rules of language

Cognitive

11. Demonstrates positive approaches to learning
    a. Attends and engages
    b. Persists
    c. Solves problems
    d. Shows curiosity and motivation
    e. Shows flexibility and inventiveness in thinking

12. Remembers and connects experiences
    a. Recognizes and recalls
    b. Makes connections

13. Uses classification skills

14. Uses symbols and images to represent something not present
    a. Thinks symbolically
    b. Engages in sociodramatic play

Integrating Values with Mandates

Luz, director of a program with multiple publicly funded contracts that come with many mandates, has this to say about how she crosswalks her center's values and philosophy with the complexities of working bureaucratic requirements: "Along with our values, we integrate three approaches to planning for children in our program—inspiration from Reggio Emilia, *Soy Bilingue*, and with our funding requirement to adopt a research-based curriculum, *The Creative Curriculum®* and *GOLD®* assessment system. Nothing goes into a child's journal without some observation notes and the teacher's reflections. In the journal are learning objectives listed to guide teachers and parents in recognizing them. Selected parts of the child's portfolio are merged into *GOLD®*. With new teachers, we demonstrate how to include the voices of the children and their families in our documentation and learning stories."

or journal notes, as long as the teacher's thinking is made visible. Names of songs and activities in boxes don't really show thinking. I push again and again for a window into the teacher's thinking to demonstrate evidence of planning. This ultimately raises the issue of whether they get paid planning time. We have to show these connections. Teachers can't think about the best interests of the children without planning time. This is part of their job, not something they should be expected to do on their own."

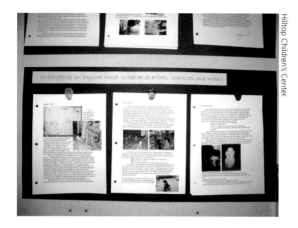

Hilltop Children's Center

PRINCIPLE   Expand Possibilities for Prescribed Curriculum

Even when teachers have a prescribed curriculum they must follow, there are ways to use our suggested repertoire of teacher actions to enhance the teaching and learning process. Some programs are using a thematic curriculum to teach particular content topics while others have specialty curricula for literacy, math, science, and so forth. When you consider the principles we have offered in *Learning Together with Young Children*, most of them can help you think about how to make mandated curriculum more meaningful for you and the children you teach. Most of the teacher actions we recommend work well in any setting.

If you are working with a mandated curriculum with a scope and sequence to follow, your challenge is to make it meaningful for you and the children. You can do this by drawing on different core practices of the curriculum framework and teaching repertoire this book offers. Find other colleagues to brainstorm ideas with. Continue to refine your ability to clearly describe how what you are doing and what the children are learning meets requirements and standards. Take heart from the following stories.

Retrieving Old Bear

Pat, a consultant hired to train teachers on using a mandated literacy curriculum, helped the teachers use their observations of children to make the lessons more meaningful. Though this is initially just a small expansion of the curriculum, do you see how it could lead teachers to do more reflecting and not just use the curriculum in a lockstep fashion?

When introducing the new literacy curriculum, Pat found the teachers were initially excited about having a tool to help them navigate the waters of the increasing pressure for literacy outcomes. The selected curriculum includes a scope-and-sequence, day-by-day prescription of lessons to use with the children. It combines learning the alphabet and phonemic awareness along with using particular storybooks to enhance language development and introduce literature to children. Teachers are to read the books in sequence, highlight particular vocabulary, and follow a script of questions with each book. In her trainings, Pat emphasizes the need for reflection on each lesson. The teachers felt this was impossible because they

Home Away from Home

had no planning time to prepare beforehand or talk afterward about what happened. And literacy is but one of their desired curriculum outcomes. Pat was discouraged that the teachers just did the minimum of what was required, rather than making the lessons their own and planning for more possibilities.

Instead of just giving up on the idea of using a more reflective practice, Pat created an observation form and introduced this as part of the planning process. The form asks teachers to first read each of the storybooks themselves and identify themes that might be relevant to the children. Next she suggests the teachers use their observations to identify specific situations in which the children's play relates to a theme in one of the books. As they take up the particular questions and vocabulary lessons for that book, the teachers then tell specific stories of how they have seen children's activities that relate to the story line. For instance, in the book Old Bear *by Jane Hissey, the animals are trying to work together to solve the problem of retrieving Old Bear. Using her observations, a teacher can tell stories and invite conversations about the times she has seen the children working together to solve a problem. Follow-up activities can build on their experiences as well as use the lessons from the book. With this expansion of the curriculum, Pat breathed new life into literacy teaching for the teachers and the children.*

Listen to Pat

"What I think would help teachers is not a script to follow, but a format they can use to create their own lessons and make them more meaningful. Because I want observations of the children to be a central feature of all teaching, I decided that introducing a form like this could be universally adapted for any of the storybook lessons. I hope that this approach will carry over into other areas of their curriculum planning and that the teachers will come to see the value of observations for making lessons meaningful for children."

Reflect

Pat's approach doesn't disregard the goals of this particular curriculum, but goes beyond its limitations. She devises a simple form to set a protocol in motion for reflection and action based on everyday observations of children. When a teacher introduces a storybook selected by someone other than herself or the children, she can still personalize the content with related stories featuring the children and their playmates. Each of these little ways of claiming your power to do something deeper and more significant in your teaching leads to bigger things.

Inching their way along, some dedicated teachers and early childhood programs have created supportive structures that unleash tremendous possibilities for teachers to take their work with children into extended, in-depth investigations. Ann Pelo (2017) is one such teacher, and she offers the following guidelines for planning investigations to uncover children's ideas. Her biggest caution: Don't plan an activity; plan how to find out more about the children's thinking.

- Create a protected corner or studio space where children can pursue an investigation away from distractions and where materials can be left out for work to continue over a span of time.
- Revamp your "small-group time" practices to form evolving work teams or project groups of children chosen for their different but complementary strengths to contribute to a study or an investigation.
- Organize your staffing so that the same teacher can work with the children on the project and also have time to meet with at least one other person to study the documentation you gather during the process.
- Formulate questions and gather materials that lend themselves to children re-representing their ideas about different aspects of the focus you are

investigating over time, moving from individual to group work.

- Save work to revisit with the children, along with your documentation and evolving story of what the group has been exploring and discovering.
- Have the project team regularly report on their work to the whole class, making use of your documentation and their representational work.
- Invite the children's families to study your documentation with you, adding their insights and resources.
- Strengthen your technology resources and skills to include work with a digital and/or video camera, sound recorder, computer, scanner, and printer. Stay current with evolving software to economize your documentation work.

Your Turn

Take some time to review ways you could expand the possibilities for your teaching, whatever the restrictions you may experience. On a large piece of paper or blank computer document, create three columns. Write "Current Practice" at the top of the left-hand column, "Intent" at the top of the middle column, and "Other Possibilities" at the top of the right-hand column.

In the left-hand column, make a list of the current practices and requirements that you feel are restricting your teaching. In the middle column, next to each item in your list, write your understanding of the intent behind this practice or requirement. For instance, if you are required to turn in lesson plans a month in advance, in the middle column you might write, "Make sure teachers are planning for children's learning." In the right-hand column, consider other ways to meet this intent. Here you might write, "Put brief observation notes with a question and next step for further exploration." Once you have come up with some options for expanding the possibilities for your teaching, choose one as a goal to work on. Determine who you need to talk with about this possibility. Who might offer you support, encouragement, or resources? What reservations might you expect and how will you address those? Plan a way to gradually makes these changes.

- What could you shift on Monday morning?
- What changes might you have in place in the next four months?
- How do you want to start the new school year differently in September?

PRINCIPLE Document Everyday Experiences That Meet Standards

With the growth of publicly funded preschool programs, early childhood teachers find themselves increasingly required to work with prescribed standards and learning outcomes. Gone are the days when the standards for early childhood programs were primarily focused on health and safety. Wider educational trends, along with our own efforts to professionalize the early childhood field, now require teachers to know more about learning domains, working with diversity and dual-language learners, and a host of other considerations that require expertise. This is not inherently bad, but it is certainly complex. In the absence of a clearly defined set of values and educational philosophy, teachers can easily be swept into teaching practices that aren't meaningful for children or for themselves. On the other hand, standing on a firm philosophical and pedagogical foundation, teachers should be eager to gain clarity about learning domain content.

Numerous resources are now available to help teachers understand standards and how to integrate them into curriculum practices (Seefeldt 2005; Gronlund 2014). Many commercial curriculums come with their own assessment programs. In selecting the approach you want to take, ask yourself, "How can I nurture children's imaginations and intellectual growth while incorporating specific content into curriculum experiences?" The challenge of meeting standards can become an excuse for not approaching curriculum in a more emergent, child-centered way. However, when you see yourself as capable of innovation and draw on teacher actions in the curriculum framework this book describes, you'll find many ways to document how standards and learning outcomes are being met.

Math Snacks

Marsie, a teacher in a public-school program funded for low-income families through Title I, offers several examples of how her teaching approach meets her state's math standards. Do you see how close observation and documentation contribute to her success?

Marsie y Marta su compañera de trabajo. Desarrollaron una mesa con "un bocadillo matemático" después de leer un articulo titulado "Math at the Snack Table" por Linda Meriwether. Los estudiantes de Meriwether eran de kindergarten, pero Marsie y Marta esteban confiadas en que sus estudiantes de cuatro años del preescolar podían comprometerse con esto como una experiencia de aprendizaje extendida a través de todo el año. Ellas sintieron que esto podría cubrir los estándares de matemáticas que requiere el estado y al mismo tiempo ofrecer múltiples oportunidades no solamente para contar, si no para resolver problemas, aprender a reconocer grupos de hasta cinco objetos sin contar, y enfrascarse en socializar conversando acerca de lo que están haciendo. Así como también ayudándose unos a otros.

YATZEL MAKES
THE MATH SNACK MENU CARD

Los bocadillos están disponibles diariamente dentro del salón. Usamos una tarjeta para el "menú" donde los niños pueden "leer" para aprender la cantidad y tamaño del bocadillo ofrecido. Las maestras facilitan y apoyan la "lectura" del menú al principio del año por varias semanas facilitando en la lectura del menú. Cuando los niños empiezan a aprender el concepto del menú, las maestras les pasamos el proyecto a ellos, incluyendo decidir la cantidad diaria de cada bocadillo, y escribir el menú. Las maestras piden voluntarios para escribir el menú. A menudo los niños se toman su tiempo para dibujar con lujo de detalles y escoger los colores cuidadosamente. Algunos de los voluntarios eran niños que usualmente no escogían escribir durante otras actividades. En representaciones simbólicas ellos estaban en una etapa muy temprana. Los dibujos de las galletas algunas veces eran líneas algo circulares y algunos garabatos a través del papel. Esta experiencia evoluciono al punto que los niños podían pararse a un lado de la mesa de los bocadillos y interpretar sus dibujos para los demás. Los niños pasaban la información unos a otros y se abrían a la diversidad de formas para representar ideas en estos menús. Los niños que escribían estos menús se sentían capaces y querían hacer menús en las siguientes semanas. Conforme lo hacían ellos empezaban a sostener el lápiz con tres dedos y comenzaron a escoger escritura en otras áreas del salón.

Conforme el año avanzaba varios reconocieron grupos de hasta cinco cosas sin tener que contar. Esta experiencia autentica ofrece practica en dibujar círculos, cuadrados, y triángulos. Algunos de los niños escribían los números en los menús. También pudieron tener muchas experiencias midiendo. Un niño que no puede contar usa su mano izquierda para sostener la parte de arriba de la tarjeta que muestra diez uvas. El después usa su mano derecha para poner una uva en su plato. Él mueve su mano izquierda a la siguiente uva y con la derecha agrega otra uva hasta que tiene diez. La sonrisa en su cara conforme mira su plato lleno muestra confianza y satisfacción "¡Si, yo lo puedo hacer¡"

Marsie and her coworker, Marta, developed a "math snack" table after reading an article by Linda Meriwether entitled "Math at the Snack Table" (1997). Meriwether's students were kindergarteners, but Marsie and Marta were confident their four-year-old preschool students could use the math-snack table as an extended learning experience throughout the year. They felt it would address their state's standards for math while offering multiple opportunities not only to count, but to problem solve, learn to recognize sets of up to five objects without counting, converse socially about what they were doing, and help each other.

Snack is an everyday choice in this classroom. They use a "menu" card that the children "read" to count out and to measure their snack. The teachers worked with the children supportively for several weeks at the beginning of the year, facilitating the "reading" of the menu. As the children began to understand the concept of the menu, the teachers turned the project over to them, including allowing them to decide on the amount of each snack item for the day and writing the menu. The teachers asked for volunteers to write the menu. Many children took time to draw the menu in great detail, carefully choosing their colors. Some of the volunteers were children who did not usually choose to write. They were in the very early stages of symbolic representation. Their menus were, for the most part, an attempt at a circle with lines drawn across the page. These children would stand at the snack table and interpret the amounts of the snacks to take to the other children. Children would pass the information along to one another and were very content to read the more difficult menu that the children had made. The children who wrote these menus felt successful and wanted to make menus in the following weeks. They began to use the pencil with a correct grip and started to choose the writing area to work in.

As the year progressed, many children recognized sets of up to five without having to count. With a meaningful purpose, they practiced drawing circles, squares, and triangles. Some children were writing the numbers on the menus. The children also had many experiences with measurement. One child who could not count used his left hand to pinch the top of the card displaying ten grapes. He then used his right hand to put one grape on his plate. He would then move his left hand to the next grape on the card and, with the right hand, add another grape to his plate until he had ten grapes on the plate. The smile on his face as he looked at his full plate showed self-confidence and a sense of "Yes, I can do it!"

Escuchen a Marsie

"Nuestro programa se esfuerza para traer las ideas de Reggio Emilia a niños de bajos recursos económicos, donde la mayoría hablan español. Los estándares y regulaciones pudieran sentirse como barreras pero, si nosotros creemos que el niño es competente y en nosotras como maestras, podemos ofrecer experiencias que pueden ser usadas a lo largo de la vida y ofrecerlas en el aprendizaje diario. Esto puede implicar el juego autodirigido, invitaciones que como maestras brindamos, o la forma en que arreglamos la rutina diaria en el salón.

"Nosotros nos deleitamos al descubrir lo entusiasmados que los niños están y lo creativos que pueden ser en su pensamiento. Comer bocadillos es un tiempo para que todos socialicen, incluyendo a las maestras. Nosotros consideramos esto como una extensa y profunda experiencia que ofrece interminables posibilidades. Que forma tan grata de cubrir los estándares de matemáticas, literatura y lenguaje, desarrollo social y emocional, y ciencias. Y, si, al final del año los niños pudieron usar los números correspondientes uno por uno para contar hasta cinco cosas de los bocadillos ofrecidos y algunos contaban hasta el veinte.

"Hemos documentado las experiencias acerca de la mesa de los bocadillos matemáticos con fotografías, paneles de documentación y con libros que incluyen series de fotografías, en una página los niños están escribiendo el menú y en el lado opuesto

esta el menú original que ellos escribieron. Nosotros usamos estos menús a través del año. El libro de menús se pone parado sobre la mesa de los bocadillos para que los niños lo lean. Escribimos dos páginas resumiendo todos los estándares que cubrimos con esta experiencia. Los administradores y padres inmediatamente pueden ver el aprendizaje que se lleva acabo y los estándares que estamos cubriendo."

Listen to Marsie

"Our program strives to bring the ideas of Reggio Emilia to low-income children, most of whom are Spanish speaking. Standards and regulations can feel like a barrier, but if we believe in the competent child and in ourselves as teachers, we can come up with meaningful experiences and embed them in everyday learning. This may involve self-directed play, invitations we bring as teachers, or the way we set up ongoing routines in the room.

"We were delighted to discover how enthusiastic the children were and how creative they could be in their thinking. Snack is a very social time for everyone, including teachers. We find it a broad, deep experience that offers endless possibilities. What a great way to meet standards in math, literacy and language, social and emotional development, and science. And yes, at the end of the year, the children could all count from one to five and many to over twenty.

We have documented our math snack experiences with photos, documentation panels, and a menu book in a ring binder showing a photo of the child writing the menu on one page and the actual menu on the opposite page. We use these menus a number of times throughout the year. The books stand up on the math snack table for the children to read. We wrote a two-page summary of all the standards we are meeting with this experience. Administrators and parents are immediately able to see the learning that is taking place and the standards we are meeting."

Reflect

The story of math snacks reveals an almost seamless relationship between everyday activities and meeting learning objectives. This accomplishment stems from the teachers' high regard for children's abilities; their relaxed, easygoing schedule full of self-directed choices, including snacks; and their recognition of all the learning that unfolds when children are given meaningful tasks to do. When they put documentation of the children's process of making menus alongside the menu itself, the teachers are showing that they value the process as well as the final product. Taking the time to write a two-page summary of how this activity addresses standards awakened other adults in the room to the learning that is taking place. It also strengthened their own ability to connect what they are seeing to the professional data on math as a learning domain.

PRINCIPLE   Make Assessments Relevant and Meaningful

Assessing children's learning has become a significant focus in today's early childhood programs. As with resources on meeting standards, you can find any number of tools to guide the assessment process (Gullo 2004; Gronlund 2014). Most assessment tools include some kind of developmental continuum or checklist. Tools that rely on portfolio collections and anecdotal records to interpret development progress claim to be "authentic assessment" because a work sampling system (Meisels et al. 1994) draws on a range of experiences children have with everyday curriculum, rather than relying on a periodic, out-of-context test to assess children's competencies.

From our point of view, developmental checklists are of limited value, because they fail to acknowledge the complexity of the learning process. Similarly, teachers tend to narrow portfolio collections of work samples without including documentation of the learning process itself. For assessments to genuinely represent whether young children are meeting learning standards, they need to paint a picture of how children are playing and working, with specific indicators of their thinking in their actions. Teachers must sharpen their understandings of how children develop the dispositions and skills needed for academic learning, so they can plan for this and assess progress accordingly.

Felipe's Car Makes Daily News

Children bring a range of experiences and interests to their early childhood programs. Sometimes children are far more passionate about an activity or investigation than the curriculum teacher's plan. Learning to shift your focus to what interests children can lead you to find new avenues to engage them in academic pursuits. As you read Pauline and Marsie's story, do you see how they took advantage of Felipe's fascination with fast cars to document his grasp of math concepts? Notice the meaning their daily journal has for the children's families.

Con el apoyo del administrador en una escuela del distrito, en un salón de educación preescolar para niños de bajos recursos económicos. Pauline, una maestra de arte y recursos, Marsie, la maestra líder, y Marta la ayudante, crearon un ambiente hermoso en el salón que incluye una área que ellas le llaman un "estudio." Notando que Felipe estaba muy interesado en los autos, Pauline le ofreció un libro de referencias de autos que mostraba muchas marcas y modelos de autos. Felipe estaba fascinado con las diferentes velocidades que alcanzaban varios autos. El notó en cada página donde estaban escritos los números de las millas que cada auto alcanzaba por hora y empezó a buscarlos cada vez que volteaba de página en el libro. Trabajó para figurar si el número era más pequeño o mayor que el anterior.

Pauline lo invitó a dibujar algunos de los autos que le gustaban. Juntos Felipe, Pauline, y Marsie crearon un libro acerca de sus dibujos e ideas. El regreso al libro de referencias en el transcurso de varios meses

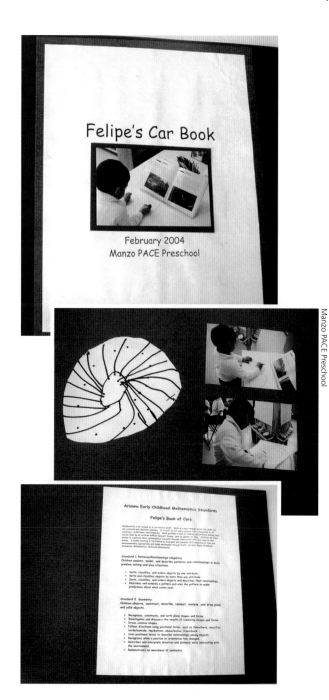

Felipe's Car Book

February 2004
Manzo PACE Preschool

visitaron pudieron ver en esta documentación del proceso del libro de Felipe y en el diario del aprendizaje que está pegado en la pared.

With support from their administrator in a school district early childhood classroom for low-income children, Pauline (a studio and resource teacher), Marsie (a lead teacher), and Marta (a coteacher) created a beautiful classroom environment that included an area they call a "studio." Noticing Felipe's interest in cars, Pauline offered him an adult reference book about cars featuring many makes and models of sports cars. Felipe was fascinated by the difference in speed of the various cars. He noticed where the numbers for miles per hour were located on each page and began to look for them as he turned the pages. He worked to figure out if a number was smaller or larger than previous numbers.

Pauline invited him to draw some of the cars he liked. Together Felipe, Pauline, and Marsie created a book about his drawings and ideas. He went back to his book over the course of many months, drawing more pages and looking at the resource book (expository text), comparing details in it to his own work. This experience met many math standards, language and literacy standards, and social emotional standards as he shared the book with his family and friends and built a strong sense of self-identity and self-confidence. When other parents and visiting administrators saw Filipe's book and the daily journal posted on the bulletin board, they were able to see how his work met a number of standards.

dibujando más páginas y mirando en el libro de referencias comparando detalles del libro con sus trabajos. Esta experiencia cubría muchos de los estándares de matemáticas, lenguaje, literatura, y socio emocional conforme el compartía el libro con familiares y amigos el desarrollaba un fuerte sentido de identidad propia y confianza. Otros padres y administradores que

Escuchen a Marsie

"La historia de Pauline iniciando una investigación extensa con Felipe es un ejemplo de cómo nosotros creemos que proveyendo experiencias significativas para los niños continuamos alcanzando los estándares que el estado nos pone enfrente. El aprendizaje de Felipe era evidente en su libro, y así lo mostramos en nuestro diario del aprendizaje.

"Nuestro Diario del aprendizaje empezó después de que visité una escuela preescolar inspirada en Reggio, esto fue en otro estado, ahí vi los diarios de sus clases. Sentimos que un diario del aprendizaje pegado a la pared enfrente del lugar donde se firma seriá una gran manera de comunicarles a nuestras familias acerca del aprendizaje de cada día. Nosotros usamos fotografías que diariamente tomamos con una cámara digital y escribimos en ingles y español acerca de las experiencias que ahí se están llevando acabo. Nuestro diario es escrito a mano con él fin de que mi asistente Marta y yo lo mostremos lo más pronto posible, usualmente al siguiente día. Ingles es mi primer idioma entonces si yo lo escribo en casa conforme edito las fotografiás, podría resultar en una versión de ingles impresa mientras la versión de español seria escrita a mano por Marta. Nosotros queríamos que los dos idiomas tengan la misma importancia y no que la versión en ingles pareciera más oficial así que decidimos escribir todo a mano.

"Siempre nos emociona mucho cuando vemos que las familias leen el diario conforme llegan o cuando recogen a sus niños. Frecuentemente ellos traen a otros miembros de la familia para que vean las fotografiás y también lean el diario. Los niños se ven en las fotografiás y le piden a los adultos que les lean lo que ahí esta escrito. Esto produce muchas reflexiones de las experiencias de aprendizaje y conversación acerca de lo que aremos enseguida. Esto refuerza la identidad de nuestros estudiantes que están aprendiendo el idioma ingles y también los hace estudiantes competentes. Conforme los días van pasando, ponemos los diarios en una carpeta de argollas y desplegamos los diarios nuevos. Los familiares que no pueden venir muy seguido al salón, pueden sentarse y leer la carpeta del diario y saber lo que ha estado pasando. Los visitantes y administradores también leen los diarios. Ellos pueden ver que nuestro aprendizaje inspirado en Reggio promueve pensar profundamente y cubre todos los estándares de aprendizaje del estado para la niñez temprana."

Listen to Marsie

"The story of Pauline launching an extended investigation with Felipe is an example of how we believe we can provide meaningful experiences for children and still meet the standards our state puts forth. Felipe's learning was clearly evident in his book, and we also highlighted it in our daily learning journal.

"We began our daily learning journal after I visited a Reggio-inspired program in another state and saw their daily journal posted on the classroom wall. We felt that a daily learning journal posted at the sign-in board in our classroom would be an excellent way to communicate with our families about the learning taking place each day. We use daily photos, taken with a digital camera and printed each night, and write in both Spanish and English about the learning experiences taking place. Our journal is handwritten so that my assistant, Marta, and I can get it posted as speedily as possible, usually the following day. English is my first language, so typing the journal at home, as I edited the photos, would result in a typed English version, whereas the Spanish version would be handwritten by Marta. Since we wanted the two languages to be equal in importance and not have the English version appear more official, we have chosen to write it all by hand.

"We are always very excited to find the families reading the previous day's journal as they pick up or drop off their children. Frequently they bring in other family members to read the journal as well. The children see the photos and ask to be read what is written. This produces a lot of reflection on learning and conversation about what we might do next. It strengthens our English-language learners' identities as competent learners as well. As the days progress, the previous week's journals are put in a notebook as new postings are made. Family members who are not able to come into the room often are able to sit and read the notebook journal and catch up on all that has been going on. Visitors and administrators also read the journals. They can see that our Reggio-inspired learning promotes deeper thinking and meets standards."

Reflect

Pauline and Marsie used Felipe's fascination with cars to propel his learning to a deeper level. Rather than just giving him cars to play with, they took his interest seriously by offering him an adult reference book. They invited him to draw the cars he liked and gave him this opportunity again and again so he could keep developing his ideas. Recognizing how this activity was meeting not only the math standards, but also the literacy and social/emotional domains, they spread this news to others by posting it on their daily learning journal board.

And notice the care Marsie takes to honor the home language of Felipe and most of his classmates. They post activity updates in Spanish as well as English and make sure that both languages are presented with equal value.

Pauline and Marsie's daily learning journal brings alive what Margaret Carr (2001) calls "learning stories." Carr and her colleagues developed this narrative form of assessment to address the Aotearoa/New Zealand government's requirement that teachers provide documentation to demonstrate and support the reciprocal relationships between people, places, and things. In their learning stories, teachers are trusted in their judgment about how to bring forth the strands and aspirations of their national curriculum, Te Whāriki, with goals for children centered around belonging, well-being, contribution, exploration, and communication. They capture significant moments throughout their days with children and then use photos to tell the story of the child's learning and how the teacher understands that.

Much like the story of Felipe's engagement with the book of his drawings and ideas, the Aotearoa/New Zealand learning story approach aims to create a strong identity for children as learners, creators, problem solvers, and contributors. Learning stories become a tool for children to build relationships, memories, and connections between ideas and experiences, home and school. Parents are invited to contribute to learning stories in their children's portfolios by adding their perspective on a story or offering a related story from home. These contributions are often referred to as "Parent Voice" in the portfolio.

Inspired by New Zealand's use of learning stories as a narrative assessment, teachers around the world have been experimenting with different formats to use them for this purpose. After extensive study of the New Zealand system, U.S. teacher educator Tom Drummond has developed an extensive website with recommended writing conventions and numerous examples to study and learn from. (We have included some of these materials in appendix F, available online, and you can find more on his website.) Learning story conventions have four basic components that can be enhanced with the Thinking Lens® Protocol. These include the following:

- what happened—a lively description of what unfolded
- what it means—the meaning the teacher makes of this from knowledge of the child(ren), the context and history, child development knowledge, and the teacher's own experience
- opportunities and possibilities—some initial thinking about opportunities and possibilities that have emerged and decisions for next steps
- the family's perspective—questions to seek the family's input and point of view

Because educators in Aotearoa/New Zealand, strongly believe that teachers are important protagonists along with the children in constructing learning, teacher voices are encouraged in learning stories as a way to promote their own self-reflection and invite dialogue.

Arranging a Marriage

Teacher Elida worked with mostly low-income students and children of color. Read how she addressed her concerns about assessment.

Elida felt stressed with so many mandated tools but also disturbed that she had to use tools with children whose culture was far from connected to the assessments. Instead, she wanted to pay close attention to children and engage with them through play and conversations, and also focus on her own journey as a teacher. Elida learned that most of the families she worked with had trouble understanding the assessment documents and checklist due to their limited use of English or understanding of the child development language in the assessments. Many families did not understand ECE terms and vocabulary or know why the child was expected to be at a certain developmental stage.

When she read articles and books about the Aotearoa/New Zealand learning story approach to formative assessments, Elida was fascinated by the idea of telling a story about a child's engagement and learning, along with aspects of the teacher's learning from the story. She thought, "This sounds like early childhood education development not only for the child but also for the teacher and the families." Soon after, she started working as a center director and had the opportunity to mediate required assessments with the approach of writing learning stories and documentation in a way that allowed the teachers and the children to learn, grow, and mentor each other. She called this "arranging a marriage."

Listen to Elida

"I learned that evaluating children and writing documentation does not have to be done in one particular way. Neither does it have to be stressful for teachers, unclear for the families, or so irrelevant for the children. One of the components I love about the learning-story approach is that it encourages teachers to think about their relationships with the children and how they are learning from children. Making that component part of the writing process helps teachers become more reflective, always trying to find a child's strengths and deeper meaning under what they are observing in children. When teachers acknowledge their own delight, curiosity, or puzzlement in studying an observation, they almost always find a more meaningful story to write.

"This approach of 'arranging a marriage' brings hope and meaning to the lives of children and the journey of the teachers. It's true that the assessments, checklist, and lesson plans are ways to track some aspects of the development of children, but they should not be the core value of the classroom. We use the assessment tools as guides, but we are aware that for many children these assessments are irrelevant because the children have their own cultural identity and their own unique way of learning. Many have not had the experience needed to meet these expectations. I want our educators to use a reflective lens to evaluate who and where children are from the minute they walk into the classroom. I believe this can happen through closely observing and finding learning stories to share. Writing stories about children invites an opportunity for teachers to reflect and plan where we might take children from that point, how the family plays a role in this process, and what we as teachers need to learn to better teach these children. This raises hope for cultural democracy, not just for the teachers, but also for the children and the families who deserve to participate and gain empowerment through their knowledge about pedagogy related to their children."

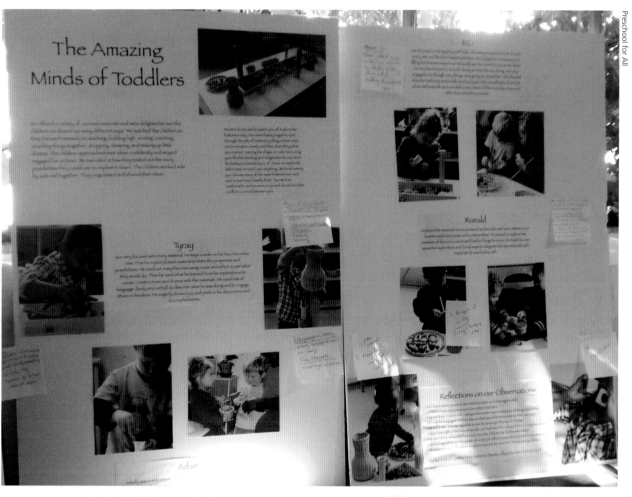

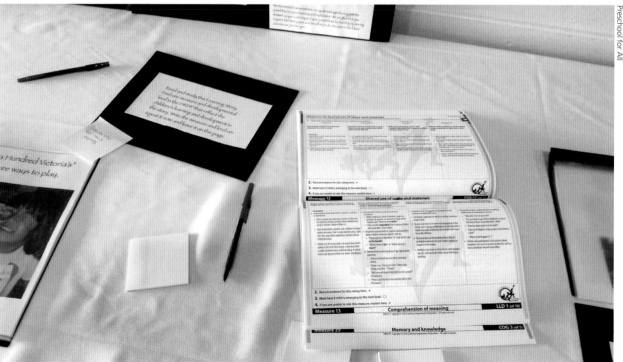

Reflect

Elida challenged herself to stop complaining about required assessment tools and instead invent ways to make them more relevant and less stressful for teachers. Her critical thinking about the lack of cultural relevancy of some of the assessment tools led her to develop some innovative practices. She modeled for others how to be an advocate for cultural democracy in striving for equity. Elida's idea about "arranging a marriage" between requirements and the narrative approach of learning stories encouraged her teachers to become more enthusiastic as well as thoughtful.

Many teachers in the United States drawn to using learning stories are experimenting with how to integrate them with a particular required assessment tool, such as Teaching Strategies Gold (TS Gold),or California's Desired Results Developmental Profile (DRDP). Using the four components for writing a learning story (what happened, what it means, opportunities and possibilities, and the family's perspective), you can easily reference learning goals met by discussing both the goals you hold for children and those called for by mandated assessment tools.

In writing learning stories, teachers may weave questions in, for both the child and the parents. With no pretense of being objective, learning stories not only describe the children's actions, but make the teacher's feelings and interpretations visible as well. Notice in the following story how the teacher writes to the child in the first person, describing what she has seen and what she thinks about it. You'll often find that parents do the same in return.

Emerson the Eclectic Artist

What Happened
February 4, 2016
Emerson, I observed as you painted during open areas. You were mixing the colors together and placing them all onto the white canvas. You would paint using strokes that went up and down or side to side. Once the color covered the majority of the sheet, you

began to mix it around with your fingers and hands. I then saw you using your nails to create streaks all around. It was a moment that definitely caught my attention because of how engaged you were with your painting. I could see your eyes expand as you watched the streaks change the format of your creation. You would move your hands so fast, which led me to curiously watch and wait to see all of your ideas start being reflected through art.

February 9, 2016
Instead of "puppy" play during open areas, you went and watched as teacher Maribel painted the recyclable tower that's in the classroom. You asked if you could join her and a couple of other students. Once they left, you stayed behind and painted over all the brown spots of the tower. I could see the different strokes and how you held specific material down so that it wouldn't fall over as you painted. I also observed as you used a variety of colors and paint-

Opportunities and Possibilities

This could serve as an opportunity for you to be the "teacher" in regards to art and projects. You can bring in ideas or experiences with different materials and teach your friends and teachers about the proper way to use them or how you believe they are most entertaining. We can also plan lessons accordingly so that they begin to incorporate more color and mess. This way, there's something different that lures you in and engages you as a student.

From this observation, I can easily show on our TSG Assessment tool that you are meeting the desired child outcomes for preschool: 7a, 7b, 11a, 11d, 11e, 29, 33. —Cristina Medina-Azpeitia

Listen to Cristina

"Writing learning stories allows me as an educator to learn more about the students and take a look into their interests based on a perspective that they give me. A moment occurs during classroom observations where I can take a step back to view what they're genuinely interested in and see who they are as individuals. During this moment, I'm taking written notes and pictures so that I can capture important moments in our classroom.

"In choosing what to write, I always remember to highlight the interests of the child. I want their personality to be captured in the story. When I start my writing process, I am able to reflect and assure that the curriculum objectives are going to meet the child's learning, as opposed to the child meeting the objectives. It is helpful to have conversations with other teachers about the children's interests and opportunities that would help further develop learning for the student. With Emerson's situation in this story, perhaps something that provides a creative and artistic experience. This whole process of studying documentation means that I am learning right alongside the children."

brushes, experimenting with different sizes and textures in order to give you new results. Your eyes didn't wander off to view what your other friends were doing. You stayed engaged on this painting project for a long period of open-area time. It was a special opportunity for me to witness you fully occupied with an activity in which you were alone. Your passionate energy was one that I was able to experience and delight in.

What It Means

I've seen that when you get the chance to explore with art, your attitude shifts and it becomes relaxed and quiet. You can be doing these projects by yourself and not be distracted by everyone else playing around you. I have also witnessed how art has been a way to grasp your interest when learning about a variety of topics. If you have the opportunity to cut, paste, color, or draw, you're more inclined to sit for longer periods of time until you believe your product is finished.

Reflect

Cristina shows us that when teachers find those moments to step back and observe, they will discover so much about who the children are, their disposition, and their approaches to learning. With such detailed description, she paints a picture of what caught her attention and how it provoked her to talk with her coworkers about what she might offer next. She recognizes that these details keep her focused on the children, not an assessment tool with required curriculum objectives. With inspiration from Cristina, how might you begin to carve out moments for observing details and having conversations with your colleagues? How might you incorporate the learning-story approach into your assessment requirements?

When coaches, administrators, and college instructors support teachers to use the learning story approach, they return some of the independence and excitement about learning that mandated curriculum and assessment tools often rob them of. Teacher Aunica discovered this approach in her college course work with Dr. Annie White, at California State University–Channel Islands, and as she practiced writing learning stories, Aunica included the voice of her cooperating teacher and field supervisor, along with referencing the required documentation of the DRDP for California.

Mud Fun

courtesy Dr. Annie White

Information: Theodore, age seven months, 11/24/15

Observation

Dear Theodore,
Today was the first time I saw you exploring the outdoors since you started crawling. It was surprising how *adventurous you were. You crawled right over to the grass area and began putting your fingers in the mud. You looked at the mud on your index finger with a curious expression on your face. You noticed that there was a tin in front of you. I was surprised that you didn't become aware of the dirt and worms that were also in front of you. You scooted yourself over to the tin and reached for it. You grasped it with your hands and began to put it in your mouth. You also lifted it up and turned it in different angles while you looked at it closely. You started crushing the tin with your body, as the weight of your body was on top of it. You began looking intensely at your little muddy fingers again and closed your fist to feel the texture of the mud in between your palms.*

courtesy Dr. Annie White

What It Means

Theodore, as you explored the outdoors, you learned and supported many areas of your development. You used your fine-motor skills as you reached for, picked up, and put the tin in your mouth. You also boosted your gross-motor skills as you army-crawled and scooted your body closer to the tin to be able to reach it. You demonstrated social-emotional learning as you explored with your hands and examined them, building your self-awareness. This is a part of your identity of self in relation to others. You also showed your expression of emotions, as you had a curious look on your face as you noticed the mud and how it felt on your fingers. You are developing an understanding of spatial relationships as you lifted up the tin, turned it around in different angles, and put it in your mouth.

Opportunities and Possibilities

To further support your inquiry and development, I will continue offering opportunities for you to explore the outdoors. I will offer you different textured areas like concrete, grass, and sand to see how you explore and discover different surfaces. I wonder how you will respond to these different surfaces.

Response 1

Jenn, Cooperating Teacher

Dear Theodore,

I love to watch you following your curiosity and interests as you explore outside. It is fun to see you discovering the texture of mud—I know you will have a lot of fun investigating this further as you grow. It does not surprise me that you were drawn to the tin that Aunica shared because I have observed how much you enjoy exploring shiny and reflective things! Anything that catches the light is sure to catch your eye. I think we will put some pie plates outside so that you can continue to explore objects that are metal.

I am curious to see what you might discover. —Jenn

courtesy Dr. Annie White

Response 2

Bridget, Field Supervisor

Theo,

You have developed an interesting way of exploring items. I have seen this before and in this exploration of the tin. You lie on your stomach and explore the toy, then roll with it in your hands to lie on your back. In this position, you can explore the item on your stomach, and then you roll again. You are motivated by this internal drive to explore and need very little from teachers during these experiences. You explore contentedly with your hands and fingers.

I truly enjoy watching the discoveries you make during these planned experiences. —Bridget

DRDP- *ATL-REG 4; COG 1; COG 9; COG 11; PD-HLTH 2; PD-HLTH 3; PD-HLTH 4*

Listen to Dr. Annie White

"After participating in several study tours to Aotearoa /New Zealand, I returned to my home state of California to do more research on the learning-story approach and incorporate it into my work, first with Head Start teachers and family providers and then as part of my courses when I began to teach full time at one of our universities, CSU–Channel Islands. Now learning stories are used with students as part of their field work, children's assessment, child care program assessment, and student self-assessment. As I watch my students dive into this approach, I see them surprised to find the ease and joy in developing their learning stories. I find the task of writing a learning story sharpens observations skills, builds closer connections with the children and families, and leads to more authentic curriculum practices. Encouraging student teachers to write directly to the child and to include their own delight in and interpretation of what they are seeing really engages them. It becomes another tool for their own learning.

"To ensure students can confidently continue using the learning-story approach in their ECE workplaces, I teach them how to write learning stories in conjunction with using the DRDP required children's assessment tool. This process makes completing the DRDP less daunting and, in some ways, more connected to their daily experiences with children. When students use this approach in their fieldwork, their cooperating teachers, field supervisors, parents/guardians, family, and community members are often so taken with the details that they, too, contribute their voices to the story. My hope is that this sparks an interest in adopting the learning-story approach center-wide. Aunica's story is a good example of how university students use learning stories as a pathway for deeper connection and more authentic relationships with children, families, and community, far beyond what the DRDP offers."

Your Turn

Whether or not you are required to assess children with a particular tool, you will want to be following and communicating children's learning and development process. To make this more relevant and meaningful for you, the children, and their families, begin by spreading out some collected documentation. Then invite at least one coworker or classmate to join you in studying your photos and notes. Practice using the Thinking Lens® Protocol in your conversation, which sets the stage for writing a story. In deciding what to write up as a learning story to display, put in a child's journal, or use as a required assessment tool, consider your values and goals for the children and the significance of this particular activity. In appendix B (page 296), you'll find a guide sheet that helps you use the Thinking Lens® for writing learning stories.

PRINCIPLE   Seek Different Perspectives to Inform Your Planning

If you work in a program with diverse families, children, or coworkers, use this diversity to enrich your perspectives and planning. When teachers begin to study their documentation for possible curriculum projects, they often identify a number of topics or learning outcomes they could pursue with the children. This is a critical moment, because too often a teacher's agenda can take over and cloud what a child is actually curious about or the ideas he is exploring in his play. You might also be overlooking the

different viewpoints and contributions parents can offer. Before jumping in with a series of plans and resources for the children, take the time to explore different perspectives on what your documentation has actually captured. First and foremost, try to find the children's perspective. You can show them some piece of your documentation and invite them to say more about its meaning. You can talk with your coworkers and the children's families. Their perspectives can illuminate yours. If you like using the Internet, find a related Facebook page or a blog where other early childhood professionals are eager to discuss and explore the meaning in children's conversation and play. As you plan, take one step at a time, with a focus of discovering more about the children's thinking, so that you can determine what scaffolding is needed. Your plan should be shaped around inquiry, some form of research or investigation for you *and* the children.

Don't Bug Me

Linda's initial efforts at using an emergent approach to curriculum involved trying to develop curriculum plans around "themes" the children seem interested in. For instance, when she and her team noticed the children interested in bugs, they developed an extensive curriculum plan centered on different kinds of bugs, with activities related to this theme.

Recently, as she thought more about the idea of looking for what was really capturing the children's attention, Linda realized that she had totally overlooked a little girl's close interest in the wings of a ladybug. The child was investigating how the wings were sometimes hidden and then appeared. But at the time, Linda and her coworkers didn't pay attention to this and just focused on the idea of bugs in general. "We totally missed it!" she exclaimed in hindsight. It was a great relief to her to hear that this is common for teachers who are just starting to think in new ways about deeper curriculum experiences for

Lakewood Coop Preschool

children. She realized that even teachers she admired and held up as role models once struggled with what to do. "Sometimes I see someone so advanced, and I don't think about the fact that they had to learn how to do this too."

Follow Their Hearts

Rukia, a child care teacher, discovered the power of studying her observations to gain new perspectives. As you read her story, look for Rukia's desire to be responsive to the parents' perspective about school readiness, even as she seeks their son's perspective on the meaning of his block play.

Peter, a child in Rukia's room, lives with his two dads, who are very keen on ensuring that his teachers are getting him ready for school. Rukia noticed that Peter's main interest is building with blocks, and he prefers to do this more than anything else. She decided to pay closer attention to this block play, hoping to get more insight into Peter's fascination. Initially, she wondered if his talk about creating big dinosaurs hinted at a fascination with issues of power. But as she kept watching, she noticed Peter was carefully creating small piles of blocks all around his big dinosaurs.

Rukia was hesitant to post her documentation, concerned that Peter's dads would think she wasn't mov-

ing him into more academically oriented activities. While trying to determine what action to take, she gathered the photos she wanted to display and took her notes to meet with her director. As they examined each of the photos, they concluded Rukia should try to find out more about the little piles of blocks Peter was consistently making each day. Rukia returned to Peter with photos of the little piles of blocks and told him she was so curious about them.

Peter: "Those are eggs. And (pointing to the bigger block structures) these are dinosaurs who want to be daddies."

Rukia: "Tell me more about these eggs."

Peter (shaking his head slowly as if lost in thought): "They just have to follow their hearts."

When she returned to share her documentation of this conversation with her director, Rukia realized that Peter's perspective was grounded in the context of his family and adoption. His block representations had deep meaning for him. She felt his dads would appreciate her documentation now and, indeed, they did. They were touched and appreciative of her close attention to their son's play. Rukia used their conversation as an opportunity to also describe more about how she sees Peter as on track for school readiness and the ways she intends to support his continued learning.

Listen to Rukia

"One of the most profound changes that I have made as a professional is in my image of the child, and thus my image of the teacher. My work with young children has evolved, and my effort to honor the perspectives of Peter and his dads is an example of that. I think my role as a teacher is to support, to challenge, to research, and to give hugs. Peter's ongoing fascination with blocks made me curious, but at the same time, I wanted his fathers to know that I heard their concerns and I, too, wanted him to be successful in school.

"At first I thought my task was to document and show his dads all the learning Peter was engaged in as he played with blocks. I was also looking for where I could introduce some learning concepts in a developmentally appropriate way. I believe children can benefit from that. However, as I observed with learning goals in mind, I realized my research approach was flawed. I needed to understand what Peter was doing from his point of view, not from our adult goals for him.

"Getting my director's perspective helped me focus in on those little piles of blocks he was making. I might have missed that, assuming the dinosaur theme or some academic learning was what I should pursue. At the core of my evolution in teaching has been listening to and connecting with the children, and then talking with others about possible meanings for what I am seeing. I was so moved by Peter's words that the eggs 'just have to follow their hearts.' He was thinking so deeply about how he came to his family. Children are capable of exploring complex ideas and emotions. I never want to minimize them with some teaching agenda I have."

Reflect

This story provokes opportunities to enhance an inquisitive disposition. Where does Peter's phrase "follow their hearts" come from? Is it language his dads have used or is this his own expression? Either way, we get a glimpse into how loved Peter knows he is. When parents are quick to emphasize their academic goals for their children, play-oriented teachers may think they need to inform the parents about developmentally appropriate practice. Because you are an educator, you may think you know more than the parents. But Peter's words remind us to seek both his point of view and that of his dads. Even if parent perspectives create tensions, you must keep in mind that parents, like you, want the very best for their children.

Rukia is a responsive teacher, using the perspectives of the children, their families, and other professionals to challenge her own thinking. Because she paid attention to details while gathering documentation and took time to study them with her director, Rukia was able to suspend her teacher agenda and discover what was really significant for Peter and ultimately for his dads. She didn't, however, suspend her goals of ensuring Peter will be ready for school. She will continue to be alert to opportunities to teach content and skills in developmentally appropriate ways.

Use the Thinking Lens® Protocol

Area for Reflection: Know yourself

What in your background and values is influencing your response to this situation and why? Is there something in Rukia's approach that inspires you to rethink your practices?

Area for Reflection: Find the details of the children's competence that engage your heart and mind

What delights, surprises, and challenges you in considering Peter's block building and conversation?

Area for Reflection: Consider other perspectives

How do you deal with parent perspectives when they are different from your own?

Area for Reflection: Consider opportunities and possibilities for action

How does Rukia inspire you to seek collaboration in studying your documentation for deeper insights?

PRINCIPLE   **Learn from Conflicting Ideas**

Many teachers who want to start teaching differently often struggle to convince their coworkers to try out new ideas. A teaching approach that attempts to follow the children's lead can be challenging on many fronts. You have to not only rethink how you want to handle conflicts among children but also clarify your values and goals. Conflicting ideas may arise between you and your coworkers or you and the children's families. When you aren't working with a scripted or scope-and-sequence curriculum, you are always doing a bit of a dance. And sometimes you step on toes, especially when there are different ideas about who should be leading and what steps to take. Teachers love working with colleagues when the dance is simpatico, and they see eye to eye on most things. Yet even compatible teachers have perspectives that eventually bump into each other, often ruffling feathers and raising tensions. How do you shape these moments with children or other adults as occasions for learning rather than judging? Consider the following two stories.

Exercising Empathy Muscles

Out on the playground, Eddie approaches his teacher with tears streaming down his face. Pointing across the playground, he cries, "He yelled at me and punched me. I want him to say sorry!" Matt, the accused, has already checked in with Eddie and asked if he needed anything to feel better. In anger, Eddie shouted "No!" so he has been left alone.

Teacher Chelsea describes her thought process: "I try to prepare Eddie. Matt may not be sorry. And if he is not sorry, I am not going to make him apologize. As much as they want it to, 'Sorry' will not heal a wound; it will not demonstrate any comprehension of what is wrong. An apology that isn't backed up by actual remorse isn't going to build any understanding or empathy within either child. There are other ways to truly fix this: an ice pack, a hug, a promise to try to use words next time. As we talk, Eddie shares more of the story. 'Well, I was running, and I bumped him like this.' He bumps one foot against the other. 'But I'm not going to say sorry.' I ask him, 'Are you sorry?' 'Yes, but I'm not going to say it because he's not saying it to me!' Oh goodness, I am not sure what to do. Both boys are ready to talk again; one not sorry but willing to engage, one sorry but struggling too. I fight the urge to take over. It takes some time, but we come to agreement. The boy who punched will try to just use words next time. Eddie apologizes for bumping and asks, 'Are you okay?' With those peace-making offerings, they are fine to play again. A few minutes later, Eddie runs and bumps into me. 'Sorry, Chelsea!' And he's off."

Listen to Chelsea

"There is nothing like an apology from a genuinely remorseful friend. But what do my students gain from the quick, autopilot apology that has no follow-up or follow-through? Nothing—no one is really held accountable and no one is really cared for. I know that my students learn best when they are engaged in meaningful ways, whether it's those traditionally academic skills like writing or social-emotional skills like empathy. My three- and four-year-olds live in such a black-and-white world, but they are still capable of thoughtfulness and real friendship. With scaffolding and a clear expectation from the adults in their lives to resolve these issues, conflicts in the classroom become opportunities to exercise these empathy muscles. Handled with understanding, you can help create a sense of justice for every child to tap into the next time they get that feeling in the pit of their stomach that tells them something isn't quite right."

Reflect

When Chelsea says, "Oh goodness, I'm not sure what to do," she shows us what a masterful teacher she is. Rather than immediately plunging into a conflict management technique, she is carefully assessing what this moment of conflict holds for the children's learning. She doesn't try to find a quick fix, but

instead trusts in the children's ability to be thoughtful in their friendships, even if their social skills haven't fully developed. She is seeking bigger, more lasting goals—growing the children's empathy muscles and a sense of justice that they can draw on in the future.

Use the Thinking Lens® Protocol

Area for Reflection: Know yourself

How does being around conflict make you feel? What do you see as your role when conflicts arise between children?

Area for Reflection: Seek the child's point of view

When you listen to Eddie and consider why he doesn't want to tell Matt he is sorry, how do you understand his perspectives on what's fair? Why do you think he later apologizes to teacher Chelsea for bumping into her?

Hilltop Children's Center

Our Canadian colleague, author Carol Anne Wien, reminds us that "emergent curriculum requires a toleration of error as teachers feel their way to creative solutions. Such ways of working require all the authentic and fruitful resources of thinking and feeling that teachers can bring to the classroom: the result is that teachers demonstrate vitality, energy for learning, and remarkable new ideas."

Wien brought us the following story about Bobbi and Annette when we raised this question with her: "What do you see teachers do when they don't share the same idea about a strategy to try with children?" She tells this story from her perspective as a weekly educational consultant and participant observer in the Peter Green Hall Children's Centre in Halifax, Nova Scotia, where Annette is the art specialist and assistant director and Bobbi is the teacher in a classroom for four-year-olds. We zero in on one small feature of the story to introduce how one teacher's idea of discovery is another's fear of contamination.

Discovery or Contamination?

Inevitably there are times in the life of a project investigation when it is not clear what to do next or how to resolve a problem. In such instances, when ideas for solutions are generated, no one is sure how they will work or whether they are the "right" moves that support the children's developing sense of an idea and how they might participate in it. In the following story, notice the interaction between Bobbi and Annette as they negotiate what materials to use and the role of the teacher. What do you see as the source of their emerging tensions?

One day in the four-year-old classroom, Ahmed made an offhand comment about playdough being "sculpture." Bobbi, his teacher, wondered about this, talked to the children about their ideas, and found them very interested in pursuing the idea of sculpture. As a result, she provided more playdough, which led to more sculpture—mostly little lumpy animals. Bobbi was concerned by the children's frustration with the

playdough, which kept breaking and drying out, preventing them from getting the detail they wanted. She consulted with Annette, an art specialist in the program, but was skeptical when Annette suggested using Plasticine. Bobbi had previously found Plasticine unpliable and unresponsive to children's efforts to mold it. In this instance, the debate between Bobbi and Annette centered on different understandings: the experience of the material told Annette that Plasticine was a solution, and Bobbi's previous experience with the children told her it wasn't.

They agreed to try the Plasticine, and Bobbi was pleasantly surprised to find that on this occasion it was the right material. The children settled into producing "sculpture" with increased focus, more details, and a wider range of subject matter, from human figures to sunflowers. Then a new problem emerged. Bobbi noticed the children's seemed worried that their objects wouldn't "stand up." Annette interpreted this as the classic problem of struggling to move from two dimensions to three dimensions and offered to demonstrate what artists might do, using clay and a wire armature wrapped around a rock. The children were fascinated, enjoyed bending the wire into lively shapes, and produced very effective sculptures by pressing lumps of clay around their bent wire. Annette did two demonstrations with different children during small-group times, and she and Bobbi then provided lots of rocks, wire, and clay on the art shelves for the children to use when they wanted sculptures to "stand up."

These materials, however, were not touched. Bobbi and Annette were perplexed. What had gone wrong? The children were still interested in sculpture, enjoyed the display of what they had made, but continued to choose Plasticine—thus repeating of the problem that things wouldn't stand up—rather than the new materials on the shelf. Annette thought perhaps she and Bobbi had missed a step, that the children needed a chance to explore wire by itself to understand it more as a medium with its own "language," as Reggio educators would say (Edwards, Gandini, and Forman

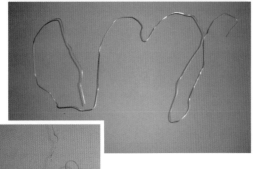

2012). So Annette invited the children to draw squiggles on paper and to bend wire to match their squiggled lines. Several children grew intrigued with the possibilities of wire and created marvelous sculptures, such as one called "the dancing mammoth." Still, no one returned to the wire armatures waiting on the shelves. Bobbi and Annette let it go.

The children continued to take part in different sculpture activities, such as taking walks to discover sculpture in the community and looking at art books of sculpture, but the problems of working vertically persisted. One day Bobbi walked into the classroom after an interview with a parent and found Annette showing the children how to wrap a wire shape with paper and tape on the wrapping board to create three-dimensional forms. "What are you doing?" Bobbi asked, horrified, because she thought the demonstration too directive, bypassing possible discovery and research on the children's part. She thought the children might lose the ability to discover connections on their own as they explored sculptural processes. She did not think the children were ready for this sort of move and saw it as "a disconnect." She and Annette had not had time to discuss Annette's activity beforehand due to the practical realities of scheduling many activities in a complex organization. Bobbi's comment "stopped Annette cold." Annette wondered if she'd "blown it." Annette was afraid she had "really screwed up badly." She finished the activity with the children and put the materials away, but she really regretted her enthusiasm to teach the technique so quickly.

Listen to Carol Anne

"I pondered the source of the apprehensions here. Both Annette and Bobbi struggle constantly in their work with the tension between letting children discover (but not have to 'reinvent the wheel') and something they call 'contamination.' By contamination, they mean reducing the children's confidence in their own ideas, in their capacity to figure things out, and to express their understanding in their own ways. To them, a child who asks an adult to draw something for her because she can't do it is someone whose confidence has been 'contaminated.' Simultaneously, they believe that techniques in using materials need to be demonstrated to children, so they have some possibility of using various media with competency. They find the line between demonstrating a technique to increase children's sense of possible moves with a material, and the worry that children's ideas will be hampered or 'put down,' a frequent source of tension. Our ongoing discussion about this tension is a reminder that uncertainty always resists easy resolution, and new spirals of thought continuously open out."

Reflect

It isn't possible, nor really desirable, for teachers to always agree on a course of action. Do you relate more with Annette's or Bobbi's perspective in this story? Teachers must negotiate different ideas, just as children do. This story brings us a challenge: rather than being intimidated by differences or, conversely, feeling your ideas are "the right" ones, how can you use conflicts as opportunities to reexamine your image of children and the role of a teacher with them? Teaching is a dynamic process and learning often involves disequilibrium. You learn to teach by reflecting on your own ideas and thinking hard with other people. Be curious about what others are thinking and invite conversations around differences. When you have to name your experiences—what you know and believe to be true—your own understandings are strengthened. Trying on other perspectives helps you grow as well.

PRINCIPLE   Encourage Coaches to Engage in Research with You

Publicly funded pre-K programs and QRIS systems increasingly assign coaches to work with programs on quality improvement. This role, as with the education coordinator position in Head Start agencies, is typically conceived of as providing technical assistance for improving scores on a rating tool or implementing a prescribed curriculum. Teachers, eager to receive good scores, are often anxious when coaches enter their classrooms. Some are more than willing to comply with whatever is needed to meet the standard, while others are resentful that an outsider is judging what they do without understanding their context, constraints, or program values. An excellent way for teachers to build a good relationship with their coaches is to invite them to view upgrading the quality of the program with an "action research mind-set." The following two stories from coaches who have approached their work in this way reveal different possibilities. Eliana and Deb provide a model for action research as they observe how positively children respond to teacher interactions that are assessed on the CLASS tool or how materials indicated on an Environmental Rating Scale (ERS) can engage children in deep learning. When teachers and coaches engage in research together, they both see new possibilities and gain deeper meaning from the intent of rating scales and assessment tools.

Monkey Bar Magic

As a coach, Eliana works with many state-funded programs. She met Ms. Margaret in one of these programs. The two of them quickly formed a partnership. Ms. Margaret, like many other supervisors, is under multiple pressures to perform well on assessment tools and to serve an increasingly diverse population of children and families. Instead of focusing on the assessments, Eliana and Ms. Margaret uncovered Ms. Margaret's own professional goal: to develop additional skills to better serve the growing population of Spanish-speaking immigrant families and children at her site. How could she, as a monolingual English speaker, foster meaningful relationships with the children and families? What skills, strategies, and dispositions could she cultivate to become a more effective educator to all the children? With these guiding questions in mind, Ms. Margaret and Eliana set to work.

Eliana thought that using learning stories might support Ms. Margaret's goals because they are often written to the child and family, and can help connect families to the school environment. She also saw Ms. Margaret's goals as an opportunity to highlight aspects of the recent "Powerful Interactions" trainings Ms. Margaret had attended and her upcoming CLASS assessment. As a coaching strategy, Eliana started documenting the positive interactions she saw and turning these observations into learning stories—one for Ms. Margaret and one for the child. Eliana used the four components of learning stories and the practice of writing it directly to the person.

Learning Story for Ms. Margaret

What happened

It was amazing observing how you worked with Angel today. I saw him attentively watch the children who were actively using the monkey bars. He seemed very tentative at first. But as he watched your enthusiastic celebration of other children's successful crossing, he moved to the front of the line. You saw him . . .

I mean, you really SAW him, Margaret! Your eyes met, and you gently encouraged him to give it a try. He understood that you were ready to support and help him. You started to coach him, to show him with your gestures and your body language that you would help him practice this new skill. When I studied the pictures later, I saw the pride in his eyes. And can you believe how fast he learned how to cross the monkey bars?

What it means

You and I have talked so many times about the challenges of being monolingual in English while working primarily with Spanish-speaking families. You expressed a strong desire to develop more skills and dispositions that would support your dual language learners. Well, today I felt like you were teaching us how to do this! You started by observing Angel's interest and by supporting him and valuing what he wanted to accomplish. Remember when we started

discussing the Powerful Interactions *book? You took the three steps needed for a powerful interaction: 1. You* were *present. I could tell from your smiles, from your encouraging gestures that you were right there, joyfully sharing the children's interests. 2. You* connected *with Angel. You showed Angel that you saw that he was interested and that you were ready to spend time with him. 3. You waited for the right opportunity and then you* extended *his learning by encouraging him to take a risk and refine his large-motor skills. You used body language and several easy words and expressions such as "You can do it," "Great," "That's it" to help him understand your support. You also introduced him to new words such as "alternate" and "hang." Angel is so lucky to have you as a teacher!*

Opportunities and possibilities

As you and other teachers continue to celebrate Angel's accomplishments, he will become more and more comfortable at school. Aren't nurturing and supportive relationships the base of the pyramid

courtesy of Eliana Elias

courtesy of Eliana Elias

Learning Story for Angel

What happened

Yesterday, I took pictures of the joyful children playing on the monkey bars. I noticed that Ms. Margaret was having fun too. She clapped her hands and laughed enthusiastically every time a child crossed the bars. I noticed that you watched Ms. Margaret's excitement from the top of the platform. At first, I thought you were just waiting for a turn. But then I realized that you were a little hesitant to try that activity. Ms. Margaret noticed you too. She knows you well by now, and she knew that you had been thinking about trying to go across for a long time. I heard her when she called your name and gently encouraged and coached you to try. She first talked to you about it, and then she held your legs a little. Your face lit up when you figured out that you could hold your body and hang from the bars! You smiled and practiced with Ms. Margaret for a while. After lunch and nap, you returned to the playground and eagerly ran to the monkey bars . . . and you surprised everyone by going across all by yourself! I am wondering how it felt for you. Did you feel powerful and strong? Did you feel proud and excited?

What it means

After Ms. Margaret and I talked about your pictures, we realized so much learning was happening during those moments. You were so brave to try this big challenge, and you practiced and practiced until you succeeded. That is called "perseverance." So, when something is hard, we know that you can try and try until you master it. Good for you, Angel! Your body is growing and each day it is getting stronger. Your muscles need to practice all kinds of skills so that you keep building them up. Fresh air and exercise will also help you be a good learner and a healthy child. It is fun to feel powerful in your body, isn't it? We also talked about the fact that you and Ms. Margaret are beginning to understand each other. Ms. Margaret can say a few things in Spanish, and you are learning

model? By nurturing your relationship with him, you will be helping him build a strong base for his success at school. I can see many possibilities and opportunities here. What do you see? For instance, Angel might really enjoy other physical challenges. As he takes on these challenges, he can demonstrate how capable he is, even if his English abilities are still developing. I wonder if you could set up some additional physical challenges outside. How about an obstacle course? A balancing beam? Do you think Angel would like that? What other ideas do you have?

The family's perspective

I am also wondering if Angel's family would like to see these beautiful pictures and share with us some of the physical challenges Angel likes to take on when he is at home or in outings with his family. Could Ms. Maria translate a brief conversation so you can share the memories of this great day with Angel's family?
—Eliana

English fast! Mostly, you still rely on each other's body language. When you see her smiling, you know that she is encouraging you. When she sees you watching attentively, she knows you are curious. But slowly you are beginning to understand the words Ms. Margaret is using like "Hang," "Great," and "That's it." We are working on finding many strategies to continue to help you learn English while you continue to speak your beautiful Spanish with Ms. Maria, your family, and all your friends. I am also noticing that you and Ms. Margaret really like each other and that she wants to encourage you to keep learning new things at school. It is great to be at a school where you have such encouraging teachers, don't you think?

Opportunities and possibilities

You are already so comfortable at school, Angel! You only started a few weeks ago. I am wondering what other types of outdoor activities you would like to practice and try. Do you like the bikes? Should we try setting up some other challenges, such as a balancing beam? Do you do challenging things when the teachers take you to the park?

The family's perspective

To Angel's family: It was so wonderful watching Angel so engaged at school. Tell us more about how you might want to promote his physical abilities. If possible, bring us pictures of fun outings you are doing with him, where he gets to challenge his muscles. Also, share with us some of your thoughts on how we can continue to promote Angel's perseverance. We are off to a wonderful start! — Eliana

Listen to Eliana

"While Ms. Margaret's program was fairly traditional with children sitting and 'receiving lessons,' it did not take long to see that she was a special woman—committed to the children, to her work, and to her community. Her many challenges did not stop her from formulating a very complex goal for herself. For instance, we talked a lot about the wider sociopolitical context of her setting, not the friendliest towards any minority. In our coaching relationship we started with baby steps, working hard on the physical and social environment. I started demonstrating the observation process to give her a taste of its value for her work. Besides modeling an example of a child's learning story, I wanted Ms. Margaret to experience what it was like to have someone point out details of the terrific things that she is doing."

Reflect

As a coach assigned to a publicly funded early childhood program needing to improve developmentally appropriate practices, Eliana approached her relationships with genuine respect. Rather than focusing on compliance issues, she uncovered Ms. Margaret's aspirations and challenges. She did the side-by-side work of noticing and describing the details of what the children were doing. Through the use of the learning-story format, Eliana put a spotlight on the real strengths she saw in both the child and the teacher. What particular details in Eliana's learning stories stood out for you? How is this coaching approach similar or different from the one you are familiar with? What do you see as a first step in developing a coaching relationship similar to this?

When you are called upon, as a teacher, to help improve a rating score related to materials in the environment, this doesn't mean you have to spend money buying one-purpose materials from a catalog. Instead, use this as an opportunity to research with your coach, director, or education coordinator what the content area is about and how children are already pursuing learning about it. Cultivating the mind-set of a researcher and the skills of observing and documenting promotes reflection and enthusiasm that goes beyond meeting compliance.

Loose Parts Math Learning

Deb's coaching work often involves bringing a combination of non-traditional materials (such as those described in chapter 3 of this book), some technology for gathering documentation, and a handout related to concepts to be explored. She finds this is particularly effective in improving scores related to mathematical learning. A typical coaching session might look like this:

Deb and the teachers spend a few minutes exploring how the materials might be offered to interest the children and what teacher talk might be useful. Alongside the teacher, Deb takes photos and notes of what the children do with the materials, and then they meet to study their documentation, referring to the handout, which helps them understand how the children are using math concepts like these drawn from Clements and Sarama (2005):

1. *Classifying: organizing materials by attribute*
2. *Exploring magnitude: describing and comparing the size of objects*
3. *Enumerating: saying number words, counting, instantly recognizing a number of objects, or reading or writing numbers*
4. *Investigating dynamics: putting things together, taking them apart, or exploring motions such as flipping*
5. *Studying pattern and shape: identifying or creating patterns or shapes, or exploring geometric properties*
6. *Exploring spatial relations: describing or drawing a location or direction*

Little Eagles Child Development Center, a chapter of Sound Child Care Solutions

By the end of Deb's coaching session, teachers typically recognize that when interesting, open-ended materials are offered to children, math learning unfolds everywhere. They see they don't need a lot of commercially produced "math" materials, but rather can find many different possibilities for math learning with loose parts from thrift store finds.

Listen to Deb

"It's remarkable how excited teachers are to see children learn the skills that they feel so responsible for teaching. They marvel at how they don't need to offer math lessons or kits, but instead can provide interesting combinations of non-traditional, open-ended materials to engage children's exploration of the concepts. Teachers also come to recognize that they may be limiting children's learning because they have a narrow idea about teaching academic skills. Recognizing that children are naturally able and eager to learn these skills helps teachers feel more confident about meeting the standards and talking with families about how children acquire academic skills. This coaching approach of offering interesting materials and guiding teachers to observe and document what children already know about academic content supports both the children's and teachers learning."

Reflect

Whether you are a coach, education coordinator, director, or lead teacher, you can work with teachers to see themselves as researchers, moving beyond a compliance mind-set to one that is eager to learn

---

Transcend the Scores

"We all know that receiving government money comes with a host of requirements and regulations. While public funding may provide more resources, you also face more restrictions. As a coach for teachers in a state-funded program, I ask myself on a daily basis how to support teachers so they will continue to feel a sense of autonomy. I want them be more reflective as they continue to enjoy their work. I try to place requirements in a larger context. Even though some of the values and standards in the CLASS assessment sound a lot like elementary school for pre-K, I encourage teachers to see how aspects of it could fit into our existing frameworks of child development and action-oriented curriculum. When terms are foreign to the ECE context, such as 'instructional learning formats,' I reframe them: 'having deeper conversations with children.' I encourage teachers to see this as another tool in their toolbox. This may not be our first choice of terminology, but it is a technique we can learn and use in the context of having deeper conversations. We can count up all our puzzles and books and house-corner materials in the assessment categories, but is that the endpoint or the beginning? It should create a platform for children's explorations and those explorations should be where our attention goes after using a rating scale like the ERS. Being eternally focused on satisfying requirements, counting our equipment, or the number of words spoken, does not create quality teaching over the long term.

"We could satisfy the requirements because they are mandatory, but how can we make them serve our purposes as thoughtful practitioners? What else can we mine from rating scales and assessments? Just as we make invitations to children, we can invite teachers to see new possibilities from new tools.

"Some years ago there was a spectacular ice dance team who scored perfect marks in their Olympic routine, an unheard-of achievement. When practicing, they didn't stop at the end of their four-minute dance but immediately started over for another complete routine. Where you set your goal has a great deal to do with how strong and energized you will be. I encourage teachers to set goals for themselves that transcend the scores."
—Joan, ECE coach

about the intent and knowledge base underpinning items on a rating scale. Consider questions for your coaching session like these:

- What are math materials?
- Where does math happen?
- What role do teachers play to extend and scaffold learning?

Your Turn

Having read how a number of teachers, coaches, and monitors are using the principles in this book to guide them in adapting our curriculum framework for their settings, which of these methods do you want to take on in earnest as a next step for yourself? Review the list of principles at the beginning of this chapter (page 226) and make a plan for yourself. Consider these questions as you take up this challenge:

- What change in your attitude holds the most promise for improving your practice?
- How can you expand possibilities for using your documentation?
- Where do you see openings for more flexibility in interpreting regulations, rating scales, and performance standards?
- Which of your coworkers challenge your thinking in the most helpful ways?

9 Claim Your Responsibility to Live Fully and Teach Well

Teaching as an ethical enterprise goes beyond presenting what already is; it is teaching toward what ought to be. It is walking with the mothers of children, carrying the sound of the sea, exploring the outer dimensions of love. . . . Teaching of this kind might stir people to come together as vivid, thoughtful, and yes, outraged. . . . The fundamental message of the teacher is this: You can change your life. Whoever you are, where you've been, whatever you've done, the teacher invites you to a second chance, another round, perhaps a different conclusion. The teacher posits possibility, openness, and alternative; the teacher points to what could be, but is not yet. The teacher beckons you to change your path. **—Bill Ayers**

Getting inspired by new ideas can bring on a rush of excitement and an initial flurry of activities. Perhaps you are the kind of person who dives in and spends an extraordinary amount of time and energy trying to implement a number of changes. Or, you might be someone who feels cautious, overwhelmed, or uncertain about where to begin in applying what you are learning. If you are to move forward with the curriculum framework proposed in this book, you must create a sustainable plan for yourself, one that keeps you learning and advocating for change.

Sustainability is a key word here. You will need nourishment and companions on the journey.

When you look for ongoing professional development opportunities for yourself, carefully think about what will offer you sustenance and renewal. Consider forming a study group focused on the theoretical framework, pedagogy you are pursuing, or the leadership skills you want to develop in yourself. Look for programs to visit that already use the approach you are interested in. Find a mentor, and become involved in mentoring others. Each time you consciously extend yourself to help an adult or a child learn something, you become more mindful of the dynamics involved in teaching and learning.

As we witness in children, early childhood educators who embark on lifelong learning alternately feel exhausted and invigorated, discouraged and inspired, afraid and courageous. When you make a commitment to refuse less than what children, families, and you deserve, you become part of a tradition of warriors for justice and champions for change. To claim your responsibility to live fully and teach well, study these principles and draw inspiration from the spotlight stories this book offers.

Principles

- Find colleagues to support your learning.
- Use an anti-bias and equity lens for all of your work.
- Take risks to try new things.
- Visit inspiring programs.
- Explore the question "Why?" to challenge thinking.
- Take leadership for change.

Martin Luther King Jr. Day Home Center

PRINCIPLE Find Colleagues to Support Your Learning

Ideally, you want to be working in tandem with coworkers in your program, but if you find that to be slow going, make connections with other early childhood professionals who share your passion. Consider going to a workshop or conference focused on the ideas and practices you are pursuing, and make it a point to try to find someone interested in an ongoing discussion of these issues. Explore other programs or organizations in your community where you can find colleagues and form alliances. It is not uncommon for early childhood organizations to be dominated by people who aren't practicing teachers or home providers, so you may need to challenge these groups to reach out to those working on the floor with children. While there are many online groups and resources, there is no substitute for face-to-face meetings where you can practice the risk taking involved in a dialogue across different perspectives. Being an educator or change agent requires ongoing learning, refining of your vision, and leadership skills.

Puget Sound ESD Head Start

There are many ways to help yourself feel less isolated and more connected. Read how Julie, a Head Start coordinator, took action to overcome her isolation as the only person in her agency with a different vision for what children and families deserve. She created a lifeline for herself. Here's how she explains her solution to isolation.

"I moved to this city to take a job as a coordinator of a newly built, Reggio-inspired site that I hoped would become a model program. Immediately, I found myself isolated because no one in my agency had the exposure to or experience with the ideas that I had, and I had a big vision guiding my work. To connect with others, I put out a flyer calling people to join me in a Reggio Roundtable where we could study and talk together, visit each other's sites, and offer support. The response was really good. People in this roundtable group were my lifeline when I found myself drowning in a sea of paperwork, pressures, and lack of understandings about my vision

back at my agency. When that stuff gets you down, you have to reach out to others. You need that to keep growing and not fall back yourself."

Your Turn

If you find yourself working in isolation, try to answer these questions for yourself:

- Who would be interested in hearing about an observation that puzzled me?
- Who might share in my excitement about what just happened with the children's investigations?
- Who would challenge me with a different perspective on what I'm seeing or thinking?
- What book would I like to study and discuss with others?

Then, using your answers to these questions, contact some of the people you identified and suggest a monthly get-together, or set up a blog to regularly share your observations and questions and gain other perspectives and challenges. A valuable resource for these kinds of undertakings is *Reflecting in Communities of Practice: A Workbook for Early Childhood Educators* (Curtis et al. 2013).

PRINCIPLE **Use an Anti-bias and Equity Lens for All of Your Work**

As you begin to deepen your understandings and leadership in behalf of living with cultural democracy in a diverse world, your curriculum practices will go beyond exposing children to multicultural artifacts, food, and holidays. Whether you work in a diverse or homogeneous program, opportunities abound for you to explore what children are already thinking about differences and fairness, which will help you determine which anti-bias goals to pursue. Taking up these opportunities is a courageous act and provides new learning for children, teachers, and families. It sets the stage for activism to grow.

Rich and Poor

Consider this story from Sandra, an after-school "Big Kids" teacher in a center of mainly white, privileged children and families with a stated anti-bias philosophy.

Over the last couple of months, Sandra's team noticed that the idea of wealth entered into some of the Big Kids' games. In the summer, Sandra remembers watching a few girls pretend to be "rich," donning fancy clothes and jewelry. Some children have also pretended to be "poor," with mentions of worn clothes, hand-built houses, and little food. The team began collecting information about when and how this theme showed up, and what the children expressed about what it meant to be rich or poor. They wondered why this idea was intriguing to the children— was it a way of "trying on" different socioeconomic roles?

Hilltop Children's Center

Seeing an opportunity to build on the students' interests and address the team's anti-bias goals, the teachers decided to keep trying to learn about students' understanding of rich and poor. At their team meetings, they discussed their observations and made some guesses about what the kids would want and need to learn. The Big Kids' idea that a person's belongings correlate to their wealth made Sandra think of images she had seen in Peter Menzel and Faith D'Aluisio's book Hungry Planet: What the World Eats. *This book features a photojournalistic survey of thirty families from twenty-four countries and the food they eat during the course of one week. Sandra made a plan to share these photos with the children. She wondered what they would notice in the pictures and how they would respond. Would they notice the similarities and differences between the structure, home, and diet of the pictured families and their own family? Would the idea of wealth come up in this conversation?*

For her first look and discussion, Sandra chose seven photographs, intentionally selecting diversity of family size, skin color, homes, and food. At this point, her goal was to spark a conversation and collect more information about the children's ideas of wealth. She planned to keep her voice (and opinion) as absent as possible—speaking only to encourage discussion, looking closely, and clarification.

As the photos were passed around, the children were immediately interested and began commenting on what they noticed.

Frankie: Look, these people didn't eat much.

Jagger: Maybe they're poor.

Tate: And they don't have much food.

Jahleel: And they just made their own house.

Jagger: And their clothes are just old.

Kendal: They're totally poor.

Jahleel: These people ate a lot, even pizza.

Teacher Rilee and Sandra asked the kids to explain how they knew whether a family was rich or poor.

Maggie: When you look at this family, they eat a lot of meat. They're rich. I think this one's the richest cause there's lots of meat and vegetables.

Jack: This one's the richest 'cause they eat the most meat.

Jahleel: I think this one because they have a lot of food.

Frankie: I think this one is the poorest 'cause this is a week and look at how much food they have. It's not that much. And their house is just a tent and a campfire. It's all from the wild.

Teacher Rilee began challenging their thinking by asking, "Is there just rich and poor? Is there anything else?"

Frankie: Everyone's normal or poor. Not rich.

The team of teachers was excited to continue gathering information about what the children think about the differences and similarities between rich, poor, and "normal." They plan to have the children help them create a mind map of the children's understandings to help everyone see what's most important to them and how their ideas are connected.

These topics are thought provoking, multilayered, and "spicy," so they'll have many discussions and activities to help students learn from and challenge one another, grow in their understanding of wealth and the world around us, and take the perspective of others who may be richer, poorer, or living somewhere different from them.

Sandra and her team expanded their investigation to the children's families and sent a request home with the children.

"Families: At this early stage of this investigation, your input is especially helpful. We would love to know more how these topics are present in conversations in your home. What curiosities have you noticed your child possesses about wealth? What have you shared with your child about what it means to be rich or poor? As you read this document, what did you notice? What do you think are themes we should track down? What do you hope your child takes away from this work?

"We welcome your feedback and your ideas about next steps and further plans. If you were a teacher in our room, what mediums, discussions, or activities would you begin next? How could you invite the children to stretch their thinking and take a different perspective? Please share with us by replying to this email or by chatting with one of us at pickup."

Listen to Sandra

"It can feel risky or uncertain to step with families into such a big, complicated topic like wealth. While children's thinking is still developing, adults come with a lifetime's worth of values, opinions, and experiences. Writing stories like this one is one way to share curriculum as it emerges and make our antibias goals more visible, which can generate support from families. This partnership benefits everyone involved, helping to expand understanding and foster new perspectives as we study children's conversation and play, consider their understanding, and plan next steps."

Reflect

Sandra took a risk, not only in opening up a conversation about wealth with the children and their families, but also in starting to explore the complexities of power and privilege. In her center, teachers' salaries are not even a third of that of most of the families enrolled, creating the possibility for tension. Anti-bias goals are not just for children, but for teachers as well, adding another layer of risk taking in our self-examination. When you consider using anti-bias practices, what goals do you have for your own learning?

Use the Thinking Lens® Protocol

Area for Reflection: Know yourself

- How comfortable are you in talking about economic inequities around you?
- Where do you place yourself on the continuum of privileged to disenfranchised?
- What in your background and values is influencing your response to the children's play and words, and why?

Area for Reflection: Examine the physical/social emotional environment

- What do you think might be influencing the children's recurring play about rich and poor?
- What kind of social emotional environment allows both children and teachers to take up these "spicy" discussions?

PRINCIPLE   **Take Risks to Try New Things**

As you continue to develop as an early childhood educator, you will discover how taking risks can enhance your understanding of the teaching and learning process, as well as help you form closer relationships with others. What do you know about yourself as a risk taker? Who could serve as a role model for you? It might be someone you know or one (or more) of the providers and teachers who have contributed stories to this book. Taking risks on behalf of something you really want to learn or accomplish nearly always increases your self-confidence, and often your humility, whether or not you feel completely successful.

Play a Few Chords

Consider this simple yet bold risk that Billie, a family provider, took with the children in her care.

After years—decades actually—of wanting to learn to play the guitar, I am finally taking lessons and being brave about my clumsy, awkward efforts in front of my kids. For so long I have been the teacher and although I certainly have learned a great deal from the children, I never quite got the feelings that come with being the learner, at least not since college many years ago. Letting myself trust these little ones with my ineptitude and fear has been so freeing and has created a new kind of bond between us. When I try to play a few chords of "Go Tell Aunt Rhody," they give me a standing ovation and their support is sincere. When I get frustrated because I can't get a chord to sound right, they remind me that it just takes practice and that I'll get it sooner or later. How often could I have been more patient with a child who didn't understand a concept that seemed so obvious to me? Now I get it! Being a learner right along with them

Heart and Home Family Child Care

has made me more aware of how often we direct children rather than trust them to figure out what works best for them. I am so thankful for their patience as I figure this out in my own time. Being part of this community of learners has made me a better teacher.
—*Billie*

Let's Get Focused

Consider this story about Marisol and her experiences.

Coming into a new center in a different state, Marisol was very excited to begin working in a center that shared her teaching philosophy and valued documenting children's play. She was especially pleased to learn that each teacher is given time outside the classroom during the week to plan and work on their documentation. Unlike what happened at her previous center, teachers are also paid to attend monthly all-staff meetings. She looked forward to working as part of a team of dedicated teachers with a director who seemed very supportive.

After a few months, however, Marisol found herself feeling a bit lonely and isolated. Having time to work on her documentation was great, but she really wanted to hear other ideas she should consider as she studied her photos and notes. Sometimes she was puzzled by the meaning of the children's play or conversations. Other times she was eager to share something remarkable she uncovered while studying her documentation. In the monthly all-staff meetings, the agenda was always packed, and she wasn't sure if there was time to ask for help with her documentation. Her previous center had begun to use the Thinking Lens® Protocol and while she was now using it on her own, she thought it would be a helpful tool for more focused all-staff meetings. If she went to the director to offer this suggestion, was she too new to be taken seriously? Despite her hesitation, she mustered up her courage and approached the director to share some of her thinking.

Bright Minds Early Learning Center

Listen to Marisol

"I love so much about this center and I don't want to jeopardize my relationships with anyone. They are all great teachers. As someone new to the center, I'm not sure I have any right to suggest changes, but I've experienced the value of collaboration and the focus a protocol can bring to the process. I'm always weighing the risks of speaking up and the risk of lost opportunities when I remain silent. In deciding to go to my director I took the approach of sharing my hesitations and asking if she would be open to hearing about my experience and what I was eager to offer. I'm so glad I took that risk because she was very receptive and started making changes at our next staff meeting. I think she appreciated someone thinking about the whole staff and how we could better learn together. Directors, too, experience loneliness with all the things they are responsible for and are expected to 'fix.'"

Reflect

Finding a place to work that shares your philosophy, has a supportive director, and provides work time for documentation and staff meetings is like a dream come true. So often these support systems are missing. But when you've experienced an even more satisfying way of working, you risk losing your heart and ability to bring your best self to work when these elements are missing. Marisol was able to consider the perspectives of others in her center and approach her director with self-awareness and sensitivity. In the end, she recognized that directors often long for a "leadership team" to suggest new ideas to improve their centers.

When Risks Are Right

Working cross-culturally, especially with the legacy of racism and the dynamics of power and privilege, is perhaps one of the greatest risks educators are called to take. Consider how Kelly, a white woman, recognizes how this risk taking unfolds as she works with an African American colleague.

Taking a risk is determined by an internal alarm. Something dings or rings or screams and says, "This isn't comfortable; this is beyond my skill set; I can't do this—or I shouldn't do this"—or some other message that says, CAUTION. I've been delivering professional development sessions for years now—there is no internal alarm as I reach a stage and address hundreds of people for a keynote. There's excitement and energy, for sure, but it doesn't feel risky.

But recently, I've had the opportunity to work with another professional development facilitator, Ijumaa Jordan, an African American woman, who has invited me to work with her to write articles and create and deliver professional development sessions that explore play equity issues, the racial identity development of young children, and the negative impact of the colorblind approach. Let me be clear, working with Ijumaa is not a risk, as she is a thoughtful, supportive, intentional friend and mentor—but the content can feel risky to me, as a white woman who has been surrounded by privilege. Exploring these ideas out loud and for publication in early childhood journals feels risky. It feels risky but it also feels right. It feels right because, as I deepen my understanding of the impacts of systemic racism, I realize that people of color take risks nearly every moment, and white people need to

understand that and not always play it safe. It feels right even though I know my risk is not the same risk Ijumaa takes when she talks about them. And even as it feels right, I worry that even in writing this, the focus is on my feelings about the work, rather than decentralizing white experience in anti-racism work. It feels hard and complicated and there are times where I feel ill-equipped but my comfort is not more important than young children's healthy and supported racial identity development. So I take a deep breath, and I dig in—to the ideas, the questions, the pain, the beauty, the impact. I embrace the risk because the word ally *can't just be a noun and I (and we) have work to do.* —Kelly

Your Turn

Reflecting on the stories from Billie, Marisol, and Kelly, consider something you have been longing to do but haven't yet worked up your courage to begin. Then take some time to assess yourself as a risk taker. When it comes to trying some new actions, which of the following statements feels most like you?

- I avoid taking risks and tend to put my head in the sand when something new is required.
- When there's something new I want to learn, I'm willing to go through the discomfort to learn it.

courtesy Kelly Matthews

- When I feel something really needs changing, I'm willing to stick my neck out.
- I'm always ready to challenge the status quo, to speak up, or to advocate for something that obviously needs changing.

Are you satisfied with your current relationship to risk taking? Do you want to make any changes?

PRINCIPLE Visit Inspiring Programs

Visits to other programs are professional development opportunities. You get a firsthand look at how others are translating their philosophy and values into practice. Making such visits is also a way to develop new relationships for ongoing dialogue. You can learn from but never replicate what others are doing. Each program has its own environment, resources, and challenges.

Sí se puede (Yes We Can)

Linda Irene has been teaching for over twenty years and is always in search of new ideas and professional development for herself. After hearing about a bilingual program in another city that was moving away from traditional, theme-based curriculum, she arranged a visit. For two days she observed in the classrooms, attended a professional development training they were holding, and met with individual teachers and the director. These experiences helped

José Marti Child Development Center

her reflect on her current practice and struggles in her teaching, and she returned to her program with new energy and ideas to offer.

Eschuchen a Linda Irene

"En contraste con lo que sucede en mi centro educativo, donde nuestro director da libertad a los profesores para elegir su propio currículo. En el centro educativo que visité todos parecían estar enfocados en la misma dirección. Por lo que todos estuvieron muy emocionados en recibir invitaciones. Cuando caminé, desde los salones de clase pasando por la bodega, para la reunión con el personal pude observar el contraste de la transición que iba ser llevada a cabo, es decir, desde materiales dirigidos a un aprendizaje tradicional para la niñez temprana hacia materiales más creativos y culturalmente vibrantes. Ellos dijeron que usar las ideas de invitaciones los había dispuesto más a compartir tanto materiales como ideas. Ellos parecían tener más confianza en poder desenvolver este plan acerca del currículo en una manera más significativa, y no sólo convertirlo en simple papeleo.

"Aprendí mucho hablando con una maestra acerca de cómo ella integra sus valores con esta idea de invitaciones. Ella identificó sus valores como sus raíces indígenas, sus valores familiares, la unidad, la paz y la libertad, el respeto y la educación. Yo pude observar cuando ella demostraba eso con los niños. A ella le gusta trabajar con frases o dichos como ¡Sí se puede! Ella ha observado cómo estableciendo invitaciones con los materiales permite que los niños aprendan mientras juegan. Ella siempre incluye opciones relacionadas con escritura porque quiere que los niños obtengan esas habilidades tan importantes, pero quiere que esto suceda de una forma natural.

"Su director les ha brindado el apoyo para estos cambios y ella ha realizado los preparativos necesarios para enviar a los maestros semanalmente a reuniones de desarrollo en su centro educativo. Ella esta animando a todos los profesores para continuar con su educación. Los que carecen de habilidades o educación del idioma Inglés obtienen ayuda, no solo a través de clases, sino también con un ambiente de apoyo brindado por sus colegas. Ella reconoce que los maestros más capaces pueden guiar a los otros, de este modo ella expande la base de liderazgo.

"Regresando a mi centro educativo ahora tengo mucho en que pensar en términos de innovar ideas. Estoy tan inspirada con mi visita y ahora tengo ideas acerca de cómo salir adelante. Yo sé que se puede hacer. ¡Sí se puede!"

Listen to Linda Irene

"Unlike my center, where our director gives teachers freedom to choose their own curriculum approach, everyone at the center I visited seems to be on the same page. And they are so excited about setting up invitations. When I walked from their classrooms to their storage room to the staff meeting, I could see the contrast from where they've been to how they are making this transition away from traditional early childhood learning materials to more creative, culturally vibrant ones. They said that using the ideas of invitations has made them more willing to share both materials and ideas. They seem to have more confidence that they can figure out how to do this curriculum thing in a meaningful way and not just have it be about filling out paperwork.

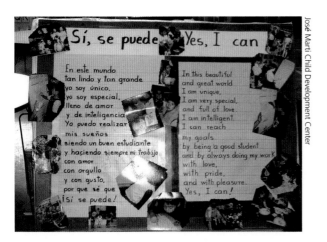

José Marti Child Development Center

"I learned a lot from one teacher about how she integrates her values with this idea of invitations. She identified her values as her indigenous roots, her family values, unity, peace and liberty, respect, and education. I could see her demonstrate those with the children. She likes working with slogans or mottos like ¡Sí se puede! (Yes we can!). She sees how setting up invitations with open-ended materials allows the children to learn while they are playing. She always includes options related to writing because she wants the children to get those important literacy skills, but this happens in such a natural way.

"Their director is so supportive of these changes, and she has made accommodations to get teachers to weekly professional development meetings in their center. She is encouraging all her teachers to continue their education. Those who lack English-language skills or education are getting help, not only by going to classes, but from the supportive environment of their coworkers. She recognizes that the stronger teachers can mentor the others, so she is expanding the leadership base.

"Going back to my center, I now have a lot to think about in terms of making changes. I'm so inspired from my visit and now I have ideas about how to move ahead. I know it can be done. ¡Sí se puede!"

Reflect

Do you have moments of discouragement or confusion in your current setting? When this happens, many teachers begin griping, blaming, or burning out. Linda Irene was able to avoid falling into a rut or negative mind-set about the struggles she was having in her own program. Instead, she took the bold step of using her professional development hours to visit another program known for its excellence in bilingual education and openness to new ideas and practices. As a result, both her heart and mind were nourished and renewed.

PRINCIPLE   **Explore the Question "Why?" to Challenge Thinking**

If you are an early childhood teacher trying to implement the ideas of *Learning Together with Young Children*, sooner or later you will want these practices to go beyond your own room. When your supervisor is on the same track, you'll probably have support for what you are doing. But if your room is to be more than an anomaly in your program, you'll want to provide more leadership in transforming the whole organization. You start, of course, by modeling with your own work how to translate a philosophy and set of values into everyday living and learning with children. And, you invest time in building relationships with the children's families, your coworkers, and your administrators.

The more you "think out loud" with them, the better they'll understand the "why?" behind what you are doing. If you decide to change your approach to daily routines (for example, no longer focusing circle time on the calendar or enforcing rules that limit how many children can play in a particular area), explain the values or philosophy these changes reflect and what you are trying to accomplish. This process of making your thinking visible is important for teachers and administrators alike. It is also important to do if you are assigned a coach to work with you as part of QRIS or another funding stream.

Thinking Together

Working on a teaching team with someone who had more traditional views of the teacher's role, Deb found that continually asking "why?" in their planning meetings led to some new understandings and practices that then spread to other teachers in her program.

Kirsten, my new coteacher, followed a very traditional approach to curriculum planning. She was eager to plan entertaining, cute, and fun activities for the children. Rather than squishing her enthusiasm, I used her suggestions as an opportunity for us to think together. When she wanted to make a rain forest and hang it from the center of the room, I asked, "Why would we want to do this? Where does the idea come from?" I wanted us to practice the thinking we need to do underneath the activities we planned.

Kirsten was unsure of her role in an emergent approach to curriculum. I gave her a clipboard and pen and set her to work observing the details of children's play. I steered her toward children she didn't feel a connection with. In our discussions, we explored the why or meaning of what the children were doing. I suggested she show children the photos and sketches

Refugee and Immigrant Family Center, Sound Child Care Solutions

she had of what they were doing and ask them why?

I knew this coaching role was giving Kirsten a framework for thinking when I overheard her having a conversation with another teacher in our building. She was asking why they didn't do documenting and storytelling with the children like we did in our room. Kirsten had made this practice her own and was now coaching others to explore the why of their practice.
—Deb

Be More Authentic

Luz works as the director of a center with blended public funding streams, each of which has numerous regulations. Her main focus, however, has been to steadily develop her center to embrace a set of shared values to guide the program. These values are regularly referenced and guide the design of their environments, policies, and interactions among the teacher, children, and families.

Luz views professional learning not only as a process of mentoring individuals, but also as a way to develop a learning team that can achieve collective goals and tasks, which includes documenting how they meet all the standards and requirements. In the process, Luz uncovers the "why?" behind each standard and creates systems and structures for the work that needs to be done. She meets with the coaches assigned to her to make sure they understand what her team is doing so that another outside agenda

doesn't step in to change the approach she is taking to quality. When a monitoring review is scheduled, she doesn't want anyone to experience the stress of a last-minute scramble to get things in order. She says, "If you believe that these regulations are a foundation for quality, why would you wait until the last minute to do that? Why would you want to distract the attention of the teachers from their important work with children and families each day?"

Listen to Luz

"We have many grants and contracts with requirements, but we stay focused on our values and learning in a more human way than just assessments. In my work with teachers, I stress this is not about assessments, but about a critical time of life when brains are developing and a love of learning can be developed. Together we learn about how to see children, the role of the environment and the teacher, and establishing relationships with children and their families. We want children to drive the classroom and what we do. When people come to monitor us, they can see right away this is a high-quality program, even though we often do things differently than what they expect to see. When they express any concerns about accountability standards, I always ask, 'What is the intention of collecting this data? How can you help us be more authentic as we do it?'"

Reflect

Luz shows us that when you guide teachers to keep the center's values in the forefront of considering regulations and assessment tools, they become intentional in their work. Asking "why?" is an ongoing part of her conversation with teachers and monitors alike. Luz is clear about where regulations help them improve their quality and where they must be questioned as an obstacle to the values they hold for children and families. Luz reminds her teachers that when the monitors come to assess their program, she wants them to see staff expressing their values in practice, instead of worried about the paperwork. What in Luz's story helps you rethink your work?

Dissolving Boundaries

Judy, a community college instructor, tells a remarkable story of five child care providers who advocated for more meaningful education to enhance their professional development. Their actions not only resulted in improved education for themselves, but ultimately benefited other students who were eager to become bilingual as well.

We have to use bridges to dissolve boundaries. The demographics of our communities are changing. This means our current assumptions must change with them. Five Spanish-speaking child care providers approached our department with a request for training to improve their understanding of developmentally appropriate practice and state licensing regulations. We established a cohort for primarily mono-Spanish speakers; eleven have successfully completed courses that meet CDA competencies. Because others wanted to be bilingual as well, we have recently opened the cohort to include mono-English speakers. . . . We are now in the second year of providing early childhood and family study college courses with a bilingual format of instruction. It has been exciting to participate in a safe learning environment where people are sharing and discovering ways to communicate and discuss common interest topics. —Judy

PRINCIPLE   **Take Leadership for Change**

The ideas in *Learning Together with Young Children* stand firmly in the tradition of progressive educators who have come before us, who believe as we do that education should be a vehicle for social transformation, not perpetuation of the status quo. If this is true for you, consider ways you can become a stronger leader for change.

Be Brave and Confident

In this story, Elidia, a coach in a state QRIS system, explains how she encourages ECE teachers to think beyond compliance or scores on rating scales.

When we try to be in compliance, we often forget about the larger goal of education. I encourage teachers to be brave in a sense of taking risks as innovators, trying new ways of teaching and learning, taking a different perspective rather than hoping others will innovate first. I believe being an innovator is also being an advocate for children, and it is a rigorous job. If you just settle with what you have, you lose the opportunity to create new roads and critical ways of thinking.

I believe teaching is social justice work because most of the schools in the United States use inappropriate assessments to evaluate children's performances. While we do need a way to evaluate the teaching and learning process, when teachers are mandated to maintain fidelity to these assessments, more attention is given to the numbers rather than to children. Teachers worry whether their scores are meeting the outcomes and then pressure children to assimilate to the learning styles of the assessment tools, ignoring who the children are in their own cultural identity. We stop ourselves from thinking about innovating and nurturing children's imagination. Then, we as educators or institutions become the oppressors of children's rights. If we undermine these aspects of the teaching and learning process, we marginalize children as well as great teachers who really want to make a difference in the life of children.

I urge teachers to be brave and confident with their knowledge and experience. Advocacy for children is needed, taking the risk to be an innovator even when it becomes painful. The teacher's voice can start making children feel valuable, validated, and visible. The teacher and the child's relationship and their voices can provoke change to create new learning, new questions, and new thinking.—Elidia

Transformation must start within each of us and then ripple out into wider and wider circles. We must change attitudes, practices, organizations, and policies. Each of us has a role to play in creating this paradigm shift. Rebecca New (1997) reminds us that "organizational principles, physical environments, and pedagogical strategies all combine to play an overt advocacy role for young children's rights." She further states that "the heightened emphasis on leadership and advocacy among American early childhood professionals reflects a sense of heightened need—not for resources, but for resolve. The contrast between our nation's ability and its will to care for its youngest citizens has never been so clear."

New's words are reminiscent of how Loris Malaguzzi described the history of the remarkable schools of Reggio Emilia that have inspired the world. Referring to the early years, in the late 1940s, when they began to re-create schools out of the disasters of fascism and war in their region of Italy, Malaguzzi (1998, 50) said: "Finding support for the school in a devastated town, rich only in mourning and poverty, would be a long and difficult ordeal, and would require sacrifices and solidarity now unthinkable. . . . Some of the schools would not survive. Most of them, however, would display enough rage and strength to survive."

In today's climate of regulatory and data-driven mandates, the task before us is to mobilize our resolve and display enough rage over the current lack of attention to the rights of children. Current trends and policies are devaluing and standardizing their childhoods, and robbing them of more meaningful educational experiences. Simultaneously, we must display our strength, individually and collectively, in ways we have yet to imagine.

Our Work Is More Than Our Job

With a job in a large, complicated ECE organization with many bureaucratic regulations, Kristie has found a way to stay faithful to her work. Here is her story.

I find a great difference between my job *and my* work. *My job is about tasks that I complete. It's laid out in my job description. My work is about purpose. It informs me how to do my job. There are many tasks that need to be completed. They are not necessarily*

in line with my passions, but they do open up avenues for my passions to be engaged and flourish. For example, I may not be passionate about writing reports. However, the reports help inform our funder about the work that we do. They help to bring recognition and continued funding. Both are essential for the work that I love to continue. My task is to complete the report. My work is to improve the early childhood experience for teachers and children. When I am firmly grounded in my work, my task is no longer a necessary evil. It becomes a necessary component to make sure that my work can continue.

Compliance sets the stage for the beautiful wonders that occur in early childhood settings. The issue is not to view compliance as the finish line. My work always compels me to continue the race. I start with compliance and keep running towards quality. That's what it means to be faithful to our work.

We are required to measure our success. The question for me is: Does assessment equal accountability? For many it does. Measurement is not bad. The issue is that we only look at measuring one way or one aspect of impact. We must hold ourselves accountable to the impact that we are making, but we need to broaden our lens. It's about more than measuring skills attained. What about citizenship, belonging, connection to the world, and a sense of joy? These are all factors that impact lifelong success.

We have to see that part of our work is to be change agents. We can't stay silent when we see things that aren't right. We have to be informed, open, and not blind. Our work is to call out where the battles really lie. We have to call out how we see things such as racism and white privilege embedded in our system. For instance, we have to recognize how we have been viewing young black male children. We can no longer allow the mentality of "We gotta get this child right." We have to see the need for a paradigm shift. We need to see teachers as an integral piece to this puzzle for change. Instead of the mindset that focuses on correcting the child's behavior, the focus shifts to the teacher's perception of the child.

As an organization, do the work of defining purpose. Think about your identity as an organization. What is your culture and how does it set the climate? Who are you, and what do you want to be known for? How much of your focus is truly on the children and their families? Then, spend some protected time reviewing your purpose at key times throughout the year.

"This is how your work can inform your job."
—Kristie

Moving Forward with Progressive Education

As we complete revisions for the new edition of this book, we are heartened by the many thinkers, leaders, and groups raising challenges to the standardization and regressive trends in how the United States is moving forward with early childhood education. An online search will uncover many examples of research and advocacy supporting the curriculum approach we offer in *Learning Together with Young Children*. Regular articles appear in the media about the dangers of robbing children of learning through play and their active bodies. You'll find blogs and active groups of parents and educators calling for a recalibration of what early childhood education must do to help children be successful in school and life. In our minds, any discussion of quality needs to also include issues of equity. While there are any number of worthwhile groups we could recommend, in the United States we especially suggest you follow the work of several important research, policy, and advocacy groups:

1. **Defending the Early Years (DEY).** Make use of their early education activist toolkit. You will find articles, research reports, and inspiring stories of activism. (www.deyproject.org)

2. **Broader Bolder Approach (BBA).** This group, with their regular reporting of research and policy issues, can help you keep abreast of national efforts to refocus the funding and delivery of early childhood education and services. We especially appreciate their focus on the "opportunity gaps" as foundational to address before we can arrive at equity. (www.boldapproach.org)

3. **Empathy Educates.** This organization promotes conversations, collaborations, and mobilizing for actions. The resources they offer and leaders they partner with will continue to inspire, educate, and challenge us. (www.empathyeducates.org)

4. **Rethinking Schools (RS).** This group in Milwaukee has a long history of teacher-led efforts to analyze education with a social justice lens. While their work and resources have primarily been focused on the K–12 arena, with the publication of *Rethinking Early Childhood Education*, edited by our Harvest Resources associate and author Ann Pelo, they have launched a stronger focus on the early years. The analysis they continually offer is particularly helpful for teachers in understanding the larger educational trends that undermine social justice. (www.rethinkingschools.org)

We have been particularly inspired by our colleagues across the seas in Aotearoa/New Zealand, and across the border in neighboring Canadian provinces who provide leadership for a very different way to advance quality in early childhood education. Our colleagues at Harvest Resources Associates, along with those whose work we follow, have been providing terrific leadership examples for creating a more innovative approach to coaching, teaching, advocating, and learning with children. Our hope is that you will be inspired by these efforts to strengthen your own professional practice with children and families, and also to become a leader and agitator for change.

Consider these possibilities, which hold great potential for transforming the early childhood field.

For each one listed, you'll find concrete examples in the appendices, along with a selection of resources carried over from the first edition of this book. Appendices D through G can be found under the Web Components tab for this book at www.redleafpress.org.

- Adopt the mind-set of a curious seeker and action researcher, nurturing your own development through inquiry into the meaning of children's play and their learning process. You can do this as a practicing teacher, family provider, director, education coordinator, or coach. You can share a piece of your research about the teaching and learning process in meetings, at conferences, and on blogs. Perhaps you will go on to publish your work, in the tradition of Vivian Paley and Karen Gallas, or perhaps in *Voices of Practitioners*, the Beyond the Journal web page of *Young Children,* online at www.naeyc.org/publications/vop.

- Integrate the Thinking Lens® and other protocols into your daily reflections about your work and in collaborative settings where you are studying documentation and trying to address dilemmas. While not specifically focused on early childhood, the work of the School Reform Initiative (SRI) offers great workshops and resources on using protocols. You can find more about these by visiting their website, www.schoolreform initiative.org. Our appendices reprints a selection of their resources, along with examples of our own Thinking Lens® Protocol, including a Spanish translation, and ways in which coaches and teachers have incorporated this protocol into their ECE work.

- Invent structures to support and guide reflection on the teaching and learning process. Administrators, education coordinators, and coaches can concretely support the reflective teaching practices described in this book by carving out time and budgeting for teachers to regularly meet to share what they are curious about and learning in their work. While it is a challenge to provide basic off-the-floor "planning time" for each teacher, what teachers really need to grow themselves are consistent team meetings with protocols and pedagogical guidance. More examples of programs that have been working for some time to develop these structures can be found in appendix E and elsewhere on the web. It takes time, inch by inch, but it has to become a priority.

- Explore a shared-services model for pooling together particular aspects of your administrative services to share expertise and resources, which frees up site-based administrators to focus on the people in the program, rather than the running of a business. A shared-services model centralizes management functions to save dollars and build professional management capacity, and provides focused expertise. While a range of examples of shared services can be found at http://opportunities-exchange.org and www.early childhoodfinance.org, we provide a few examples in appendix E.

- Form a Community of Reflection and Practice (CORP) to systematically study the extensive resources offered by Tom Drummond, an emeritus educator of children and adults who offers the essence of his life's work in ECE on a magnificent website. You will find remarkable resources there to inspire you, provoke your thinking, give you specific protocols and strategies for working with a set of democratic values, connecting with and talking to children, best practices in college teaching, studying and writing learning stories, and becoming a strong leader and advocate. In striking contrast to so many commercial ventures seeking to benefit from our under-resourced profession, you are free to duplicate and make use of any of Tom's materials, just not make money off of them. See appendix F for examples of specific materials that will aid you in taking leadership for changing the status quo in early childhood education.

- Consider using an assessment based on a narrative method such as the learning story approach from Aotearoa/New Zealand. Not a commercial product, the learning story approach trusts the judgment of educators about what learning matters. This approach is well substantiated in several primary texts with extensive examples on the New Zealand Ministry of Education's website as well as NZ's Educational Leadership Project's website, www.elp.co.nz/learning_stories.cfm. In the United States, Tom Drummond's website has a full menu devoted to learning stories, tom-drummond.com. Appendix F offers examples from each of these.

- Use current research data in advocating for improved salaries and working conditions for early childhood educators. The Center for the Study of Child Care Employment conducts cutting-edge research and proposes policy solutions aimed at improving how the United States prepares, supports, and rewards the early care and education workforce to ensure young children's optimal development. A brief summary of their work, *The Early Care and Education Workforce: Essential but Neglected,* is found in appendix G, with a fuller picture of their work at www .irle.berkeley.edu/cscce/about/about-us/.

- Become an equity advocate and activist to better support the children, families, and teachers in your community. When you understand that your "work" is more than your job, you recognize how issues of social justice have a direct impact on your aspirations. Depending on your experience and disposition, this work may come naturally or be a challenge for you. To become a leader for change in this arena, you'll need to uncover more about yourself as well as the experiences and perspectives of others. Find resources and colleagues to support and educate you in this work. Some starting places might include www.raceconscious .org and http://member-forums.naeyc.org/group /diversity-and-equity-education-adults-interest -forum. In addition to working to strengthen your leadership for equity, you can also incorporate an anti-bias equity lens for discussions in your staff meetings. A sample staff meeting agenda for this is offered in appendix G.

- Consider joining one of the World Forum Working Groups and talk with others around the world about issues such as children's rights, nature education for young children, peace building with children, men in early childhood education, early childhood in Africa, children with HIV/AIDS, and many more important topics. Connecting with people outside of your own country greatly expands your perspective and offers yet another way to develop yourself as a leader for change. Visit https://worldforumfoundation.org.

Our hope is that you will be both inspired and spurred into action by knowing that many early childhood educators around the world are joining together to provide stronger leadership for social change. While most of the field is focused on compliance, you can provide leadership to keep equity and the real lives of children and teachers on the forefront of every ECE agenda and decision-making process about definitions of quality and how dollars and time should be allocated. Together we are more powerful than we may imagine. Remembering the words of Terry Tempest Williams, let's mobilize our imaginations and our resolve to keep democracy alive.

Democracy is a way of life: the right to be educated, to think, discuss, dissent, create, and act, acting in imaginative and revolutionary ways. The human heart is the first ionic of democracy. It is where we embrace our questions. Can we be equitable? Can we be generous? Can we listen with our whole beings, not just our minds, and offer our attention rather than our opinions? Our future is guaranteed only by the degree of our personal involvement and commitment . . . as we engage the qualities of inquiry, intuition, and love.

—**Terry Tempest Williams**

Appendices Overview

Since the publishing of the first edition of this book, many early childhood educators have been hard at work translating the ideas offered for their particular work settings. We've assembled a selection of examples to help you engage in a similar process. These include documents you can use in staff meetings, PD settings, or college teaching. You'll find examples of how programs are negotiating implementing the ideas here in the context of mandates that come with public funding and samples of organizational structures administrators have put into place to orient and support teachers to work in this way. You'll also find additional appendices online that show a selection of larger professional efforts to advocate for related issues of anti-bias and equity issues, play as a foundation for learning, teacher compensation, and working conditions.

We recognize that over time organizations may morph into a shadow of their former selves, or expand to incorporate new visions. Ongoing research and web-based resources also have the potential to make our appendix out of date. Nevertheless, the examples here and online are offered as a taste of what is possible when people are determined to create meaningful tools and structures to help grow their vision.

APPENDIX A   Tools to Help Clarify Your Current Perspectives and Foundations

Before beginning any new curricular approach, it's helpful to evaluate what is happening now in your program, what values and theoretical framework are already driving your work with children, and what new thinking you might need to undertake.

Appendix A contains four resources to help you consider your starting points as a teacher, administrator, or team, as you examine the relationship between your values, theory, and what you do in everyday practice.

We created the following assessment to help you think about the resources and thinking you already possess, and what new development and support might be necessary to adopt the curriculum approach of *Learning Together with Young Children*.

Assessing Your Foundation for In-Depth Curriculum with Children

Clarifying Your Beliefs and Values
To consider whether you have developed your vision and teaching practice for in-depth curriculum work, please list three words or phrases you typically use to describe children.

_____

_____

_____

In light of these words, please write a brief paragraph for each of your answers to these questions.

- What do you believe children are capable of and deserve?
- What values do you want to shape children's lives in your program?
- How do you demonstrate you value childhood?
- What process have you used to clarify your beliefs and values as an individual and a program?

Designing an Engaging Environment with Interesting Materials
To consider how well you have prepared your environment for in-depth curriculum work, in your journal write a brief paragraph for each of your answers to these questions.

- How have you designed your environment to reflect your beliefs and values?
- How does your environment reflect the lives of the children and their families and the community in which they live?
- What materials do you offer children to
  a. encourage them to make things from their understandings and imagination?
  b. provide for sensory exploration and transformation?
  c. evoke a feeling of magic, wonder, and curiosity?
  d. allow them to feel powerful and active in their bodies?
  e. explore different ways of seeing and being in the world?
- How does your environment give attention to order, aesthetics, and the natural world?

Using Observation and Documentation Skills
To reflect on your current view of the role of observation and documentation in your work, choose which of the following sentences is most true for you. Describe why the statement you chose is closest to your experience.

- Most of the time I do the documentation required, but I honestly don't find it useful.
- I think the process of documentation is very important and useful for my understandings and planning.
- I gather lots of documentation, but I don't know what to do with it.
- I think of documentation as a delightful treasure hunt with many treasures to be found.

What system do you use to gather and analyze your observations of the children?

How do you use your observations in planning for the environment and curriculum activities?

CREATING A CLASSROOM CULTURE FOR IN-DEPTH CURRICULUM WITH CHILDREN

To consider how your daily schedule and use of time support in-depth curriculum, write down your daily schedule, noting the specific amounts of time allocated for each component of the schedule. Add up the exact time for each of the following:

- Child-initiated and child-directed time (children select their own materials and activities to work with alone or with others)
- Teacher-initiated and teacher-directed time (teachers direct children's choices and attention to an activity, including transitions and routines such as meals, sleep, and so on)
- Teacher-led time (teachers offer children choices among activities)
- Teacher coaching time (teachers coach and demonstrate the use of materials, tools, and processes)

Are you satisfied with the balance of time in your schedule? What changes might be indicated?

What strategies do you use to help children and their families make the transition between home and your program, and how do you make them feel connected during the day?

How do you encourage families to collaborate with you in shaping curriculum experiences for the children?

In what ways do you encourage children to notice different perspectives and points of view?

How are children given ownership of your environment and activities?

How are relationships and children's pursuits respected, made visible, and celebrated?

To help you on your journey of *Learning Together with Young Children*, consider these questions from Aotearoa, New Zealand, in a book about their national curriculum, *Understanding the Te Whāriki Approach*.

Origins and Influences

- What do you know about the history of your country in relation to curriculum?
- Which theorists influenced the development of your curriculum?
- Which theorists have influenced your practice and beliefs most?

Vision and Values

- What are the values that shape your practice?
- How do you negotiate values and practices within your early childhood community?

Image of the Child

- What is your image of the child?
- Do you and your colleagues have a shared image of the child?
- How does this image shape interactions and opportunities within your setting?

Weaving a Curriculum Mat

- How might you go about weaving your own curriculum mat in your setting?
- Who might you involve?
- What support would you need?

Valued Outcomes of ECE

- What do you see as valued outcomes of ECE?
- Are these values shared by colleagues, children, and parents?

Used with permission from Wendy Lee, Margaret Carr, Brenda Soutar, and Linda Mitchell. 2013. *Understanding the Te Whāriki Approach.* David Fulton Publishers.

Values, Theory, and Pedagogy

The following chart shows the connectios among values, theory, and pedagogy in the classroom. The left column offers four possible perspectives/values that could guide your thinking. Follow each row across to see the theoretical assumptions, outcomes, pedagogy, and record keeping consistent with each perspective. Use it as a model for creating your own document showing your values about children and teaching, the theory that supports you, and the teaching that results from both.

Clarity on Values and Theoretical Perspectives and Their Outcomes in Practice

Perspective/Values	Theoretical Assumption	Practical Outcomes	Pedagogy	Record Keeping
Readiness/Preparation for the future	Behaviorism (Skinner 1965)	Preparation for school	Teacher directs and controls outcomes	Checklists
Developmental/ Protection	Developmental psychology (Piaget 2001)	Notion of universal child moving through predetermined set of developmental milestones. Teachers plan experiences to meet these.	Teacher guides children through verbal and physical support. Helps with conflict resolution. Teacher facilitates, providing experiences with time and space to extend and challenge children's interests.	Use of child observations linked directly to planning learning experiences.
Foster group and individual identity	Sociocultural theories (Vygotsky 1978; Brofenbrenner 2006; Rogoff 2003; Carr 2001)	Children construct own knowledge through interaction with others.	Teacher scaffolds learning and complexity through play.	Collection of samples of children's work in portfolios with documentation that explains learning goals.
Critical reflection; Multiple perspectives and meanings	Post-modern and post-structuralist, critical science (Dahlberg, Moss, and Spence 1999; Dahlberg and Moss 2005)	Learning happens in particular social and cultural context. Reciprocal relationships with families and communities. Children are co-creators with adults; explore issues of power, social justice, equity iin democracy. Many ways of viewing the world and multiple pathways to learning.	Adults and children negotiate and collaborate in the learning process. Educators reflect, question, and challenge their practice by documenting and analyzing children's experiences and learning.	Variety of approaches, including family and children's input into documentation process and meaning making.

Adapted with permission from *Building Waterfalls: A Living and Learning Framework for Adults and Children (Birth to School Age)* 2006. Queensland, Australia: C&K.

Self-Study Guide for Reflecting on Anti-bias Curriculum Planning and Implementation

Use this tool, extracted from the online Appendix to *Leading Anti Bias Programs*, for self-assessment of your work as an anti-bias educator.

	NOT YET: This is new territory for me / Not applicable to my age group now	SOMETIMES: I have a beginning awareness of this area	USUALLY: But it still requires conscious effort for me	CONSISTENTLY: I do this with ease now	THE NEXT STEPS FOR ME: My goal is . . .
A. RAISING SELF-AWARENESS—TAKING A LOOK WITHIN					
1. Am I aware of my own cultural identity and history? How comfortable am I about who I am?					
2. Am I aware of biases I may hold?					
3. Do I view diversity and exceptionalities as strengths? Do I believe that ALL children can succeed regardless of their race, gender, ethnicity, language, or physical disabilities?					
4. Am I able to give accurate, honest answers to children's questions about differences and am I comfortable admitting when I do not know the answer to a question?					
5. Am I able to intervene with ease when I hear comments that exclude someone, show bias, or are discriminatory? Do I know what to say and how to say it with ease? Do I model ways for responding to bias?					
6. Do I have access to a colleague who can act as a trusted ally in my diversity and anti-bias work?					

Excerpted with permission from Dora W. Chen, John Nimmo, and Heather Fraser. 2009. "Becoming a Culturally Responsive Early Childhood Educator: A Tool to Support Reflection by Teachers Embarking on the Anti-Bias Journey, Multicultural Perspectives 11(2): 101–106. DOI: http://dx.doi.org/10.1080/15210960903028784.

APPENDIX B   Using the Thinking Lens® Protocol

Learning Together with Young Children offers you a Thinking Lens® Protocol with sample questions for each of the areas of consideration involved in reflective practice. This tool can be adapted for many uses, including planning, considering how to respond to unfolding events, studying documentation, writing learning stories, professional learning experiences, and collaborative discussions on dilemmas you may face.

Appendix B contains a starting document with sample questions in both English and Spanish for using the Thinking Lens® as a protocol. Also included are several examples of how the Thinking Lens® has been adapted for different uses. These are offered to encourage you to expand the ways you use this tool as a protocol.

Know yourself

What captures my attention as the children engage, explore and interact?

What delights me as I watch and listen?

What in my background and values is influencing my response to this situation and why?

What adult perspectives (standards, health and safety, time, goals) are on my mind?

Find the details of children's competency that engage your heart and mind

What do I notice in the children's faces and actions?

Where do I see examples of children's strengths and competencies?

What do I think is valuable about this experience?

Seek the child's point of view

What is the child drawn to and excited about?

What might the child be trying to accomplish?

Why might the child be interacting with others this way?

What developmental themes, ideas, or theories might the child be exploring?

Examine the physical/social/emotional environment

How is the organization and use of the physical space and materials impacting this situation?

How could we strengthen relationships here?

How are schedules and routines influencing this experience?

Consider multiple perspectives

How might the child's culture and family background be influencing this situation?

What questions might we ask to get the perspective of the child's family?

Who else or what other perspectives should we consider?

What child development or early learning theories should we consider in this experience?

What desired early learning outcomes do I see reflected here?

Consider opportunities and possibilities for next steps

What values, philosophy and desired outcomes do I want to influence my response?

What new or existing relationships could be strengthened?

Which learning goals could be focused on here?

What other materials and activities could be offered to build on this experience?

What new vocabulary could we begin to use?

Conociéndome a mi misma(o)

¿Qué captura mi atención cuando los niños se envuelven, exploran e interactúan?

¿Qué me deleita al ver y escuchar?

¿Qué valores en mi pasado están influenciando mi respuesta a esta situación y porque?

¿Cuales perspectivas como adulto, por ejemplo, valores morales, salud y seguridad, tiempo, o metas están en mi mente?

Encontrando los detalles que envuelven tu corazón y tu mente

¿Qué tomo en cuenta en las caras y las acciones de los niños?

¿Donde veo ejemplos de la solidez y la capacidad de los niños?

¿Qué es lo que pienso que es valioso acerca de esta experiencia?

Tomando en cuenta el punto de vista del niño

¿Qué es lo que atrae y entusiasma al niño?

¿Qué es lo que pudiera estar tratando de conseguir o alcanzar el niño?

¿Por qué pudiera estar el niño interactuando de esta manera con otros?

¿Qué temas de desarrollo, ideas o teorías pudiera estar explorando el niño?

Examinando el ambiente físico/social/emocional

¿Cómo esta impactando la organización, el uso del espacio físico y los materiales en esta situación?

¿Cómo podríamos reforzar las relaciones aquí?

¿Cómo influyen los planes y las rutinas en esta experiencia?

Considerando perspectivas múltiples

¿Cómo podría estar influenciando la cultura y el pasado de la familia del niño en esta situación?

¿Qué preguntas podríamos hacer para obtener la perspectiva de la familia del niño?

¿A quién mas o que otras perspectivas deberíamos de considerar?

¿Qué teorías del desarrollo infantil y del aprendizaje temprano deberíamos de considerar en esta experiencia?

¿Qué resultados del aprendizaje temprano deseo ver reflejado aquí?

Considerando oportunidades y posibilidades para los próximos pasos

¿Qué valores, filosofía y resultados que deseo, quiero que tengan influencia en mi respuesta?

¿Qué relaciones nuevas o existentes se podrían reforzar?

¿Cuales metas de aprendizaje se podrían enfocar aquí?

¿Que otros materiales y actividades se podrían ofrecer para fomentar esta experiencia?

¿Qué vocabulario nuevo podríamos empezar a usar?

Putting the Thinking Lens® at the Center of Meetings

The Thinking Lens® has been a crucial tool for professional development, curriculum design, and promoting a culture of inquiry at Peabody Terrace Children's Center since 2009 when our center-wide intention for staff was "Reflection." After struggling to use it regularly, we committed to using the Thinking Lens® at every team meeting in each of our eight classrooms throughout the year, with varying degrees of success. To support our practice, we created a large poster of the protocol and hung it in the center as a touchstone for staff and a provocation for families. The protocol enabled us to focus our conversations and minimize interruptions and diversions. As we gained familiarity with the process, our thinking became clearer and more organized, and it was easier for teachers to find deeper meaning in their observations. Soon teams used the Thinking Lens® (with some modifications or deletions) to solve conflicts or answer questions that arose: "How should we approach the stress developing around naptime?" "Where should we move our documentation board?" "How can we get our babies outside every day?" By the end of the year, we were more proficient with the Thinking Lens®, appreciated the value of protocols, and had created curriculum that was more connected to children's spontaneous work and play.

Due to the reality of staff turnover, however, within a few years, the Thinking Lens® became a "sometimes" tool for most teams, and it was a challenge for newer teams to make time for it at all. As an organization, we had various levels of expertise with the Lens, but those of us who knew how helpful it could be searched for ways to use it more effectively. Some teachers felt the protocol took up too much of their limited meeting time, so they wanted to abbreviate it. However, after examining each prompt, there wasn't a single one they wanted to drop. A month or so later, we found the rearranged version of the Thinking Lens®, which was coordinated with the practice of writing learning stories in the workbook, *Reflecting in Communities of Practice* (Curtis et al). This connection with another layer of their work resonated with teachers, and they were better able to relate curriculum planning to documentation through its use as a result.

Another shift took place after we were all trained to use Non-Violent Communication (NVC) and purchased several decks of "Emotions" and "Needs" cards to support our practice with NVC. Using this concrete tool, teachers were able to work through conflicts and difficult conversations with one another and with families in an effective and creative manner. We wondered if we could make the steps of the Thinking Lens® concrete in a similar way. In response to this, our studio teacher, Katie Higgins-White, made sets of beautiful, large index cards, with a prompt from the Thinking Lens® on each one. We still keep a full copy of the Thinking Lens® available but, with practice, the simplified and color-coded prompts are adequate to move through the protocol.

We marvel that just this card on the table or the floor in the center of our conversation has so grounded us. We stray from the protocol less and move through the steps more effectively in a clearer, more fluid conversation. All teachers have equal access to the prompt, and they share the power to move forward, instead of the protocol resting in the hands of one person. We've discovered that even where teachers place their eyes to check the prompt (in the center of the conversation, rather than on their own notebook or lap) invites connection and eye contact. Switching from one aspect of the protocol to the next is more collaborative and even playful.

This small, concrete change has been unexpectedly powerful and parallels our practice with children. Just as with the beautiful and useful environments we provide to support children's learning, the creation of this beautiful, simple, useful material has helped our teaching teams use the Thinking Lens® more effectively and more often.

Contributed by Kendra PeloJoaquin

Thinking Lens® Sentence Starters for Writing Learning Stories

Know Yourself

I was intrigued by _____.

I was surprised by _____.

I had to smile when I observed
_____.

This reminded me of _____.

I want the children to know that I felt
_____ as I watched this
experience unfold.

My reflections on this experience helped me learn
_____ about myself.

Notice the Details of Children's Competency

I was amazed by the child(ren)'s ability to
_____.

I want the children to know that I noticed
_____.

The child(ren)'s face(s) told me
_____.

The child(ren)'s voices sounded like
_____.

It was clear that the child(ren) know about
_____ and understand how
to _____.

Seek the Child's Perspective

I noticed the child(ren)'s particular interest in
_____.

The child(ren) seemed especially curious about
_____.

I wondered if the child(ren) was/were trying to
_____.

It seemed to me that the child(ren) might have been
telling us that _____.

I think the child(ren) might have
been experimenting with the idea of
_____.

It seemed like the child(ren) were wondering about
_____.

I want to ask the child(ren)
_____.

Examine the Physical and Social Environment

As I think about the role of the environment/
materials in this experience, I'm reminded that
_____.

In our curriculum, we try to provide environments/
materials that are _____ and
this experience demonstrates this in action.

This experience reminds me to offer more materials that _____ .

This experience reminds me that I want to create an environment that is _____ .

Seek Multiple Perspectives

Watching this experience drove home the child development/learning theory that tells us _____ .

As I reflect on this experience, I can see how someone might see it as _____ .

I think _____ could offer me a valuable perspective on this story .

When I shared this story with _____ I gained the insight that _____ .

Opportunities and Possibilities

This story has me eager to try _____ .

Children learn best when they _____ and you could clearly see that in this experience.

This experience offered children a meaningful opportunity to _____ .

This experience reminded me of the importance of _____ .

In our curriculum, we emphasize _____ and I can see this happening in this experience.

In our values we promote the anti bias goals and equity and this experiences opens up the possibility for exploring _____ .

Experiences like this will serve these children well as they get older because _____ .

It is especially important that children have experiences like these when they are young because _____ .

I could see this child (these children) growing up to be _____ .

This experience reminds me that I always want to be a teacher who _____ , so I will now _____ .

This experience challenges me to _____ .

Contributed by Debbie Lebo and Wendy Cividanes, Harvest Resources Associates. From *Learning Together with Young Children: A Curriculum Framework for Reflective Teachers*, Second Edition by Deb Curtis and Margie Carter, © 2017. Published by Redleaf Press, www.redleafpress.org. This page may be reproduced for individual or classroom use only.

Adapting the Thinking Lens® Protocol to Address a Dilemma

As a coach in a publicly funded dual-language school-age program I offered a professional development day that, instead of being designed *for* teachers, was designed in collaboration *with* teachers. The educators of Nihonmachi Little Friends (NLF), a bilingual program, located in the heart of Japan Town in San Francisco, California, met with me before our professional development day. We identified one case, the case of Juan, which would give us a great starting point for discussions about cultural differences, language barriers, bilingual and multilingual development, team work, home and family connection, limit setting strategies, and so on. One of the educators wrote the case, and three of them helped me plan the agenda. We also decided that we wanted to strengthen our community, so we emphasized group discussions and carefully chose resources that would advance our content knowledge of the issues illustrated by this complex case. In order to support our reflections, we used the Thinking Lens®, with adapted questions. The results were amazing. All the educators engaged deeply in the discussion, creating a list of suggestions and strategies that resulted in a better understanding of how we would support Juan and many other children like him. For me, this structure presented a meaningful way to use our own experiences as a springboard for our growth as professionals.

We effectively used the Thinking Lens® Protocol to understandings and meet these goals:

- To deepen our knowledge about language acquisition in the context of NLF's community
- To review, share, and develop strategies for enhancing children's language abilities (in English, Japanese, and the child's home language if different than those two)

- To support our fellow teachers and to enhance our ability to work as a team

After we set some agreements for how we would work together to support one another's learning, I offered the idea of using a protocol to analyze an observed dilemma facing the center to harness the experiences and expertise in the room. Case studies or "dilemmas" are issues that impact our practice, and cause us to ponder and question. In the context of our professional development, cases can help us go deeper into issues that affect daily practice and help us connect one another's experiences and other perspectives.

We identified the following questions that were concerning us:

- Why do our Japanese-speaking children start losing their interest in speaking Japanese at school?
- How can we make Japanese more interesting to our school-age kids?

An observation of Juan helped us unpack these questions in the context of a dilemma the staff was facing.

We read the observation and then used the Thinking Lens® as a protocol for deepening our understandings. Then we broke into groups and generated strategies to try.

In this process everyone's voice was heard and we got deeper in our thinking. We were able to "peel the onion" and got to uncover some underlying questions about the purpose of program and how to solicit the perspective of the children's families.

Contributed by PFA Coach and Harvest Resources Associate Eliana Elias

Case Study of Juan

Juan started attending NLF in August. He is four years old and speaks mainly Spanish. He is an only child and his parents are separated, so he sees his dad only every other weekend. His mom is working full-time and going to school part-time. He lives with his mom and grandmother, and they mainly speak Spanish at home, although his mom does speak some English to him as well. His dad speaks mainly Spanish to him.

Juan uses body gestures such as pointing to express himself in English. His vocabulary is not very clear, and it's hard to understand him. He speaks in two- to four-word sentences in English. His Spanish is also delayed for a four-year-old. His mom said she also has difficulty understanding him in both languages but also that his language is getting better. His mom added that Juan is listening better and doing more fine-motor activities since he started coming to NLF.

NLF was not Juan's first school experience. He attended another school where the children were aggressive, so he has his guard up and sometimes will have a delayed reaction to behaviors from other children; for example, if another child pushes him he will push that child back later on, not when it happens. This fortunately does not happen that often.

Juan is very strong-willed, and once his mind is made up, it can be difficult to change. His mom said he is just like his dad.

INCIDENT On a cold day, Juan was asked to put on his jacket so he could go outside in the morning. He refused and was pushing the teacher to get in line to go outside. The teacher told him that it was cold outside. He needed to put on his jacket or he had to stay inside. He kept repeating "no jacket" and "outside." He eventually was put in a chair and was given the same choice—indoors or put the jacket on and go outside. He continued saying "no jacket" and "I outside." He was teary-eyed and mad, and tried to get up from the chair. Eventually (after fifteen minutes or longer) the teacher was able to convince him to do a puzzle indoors. He sat quietly alone for a while.

Adapting the Thinking Lens® Protocol for Case Studies

Knowing yourself

When you hear Juan's case, what feelings and thoughts come about for you?

What, if any, cultural aspects of your own life color the way you react to this case?

Finding the details of children's competency and seeking Juan's point of view

How might you see that Juan's action shows his competency?

In which ways might he be using his "strong will" to cope with the stresses in his life?

What do you think Juan wanted to communicate?

How might we increase communication with Juan?

How might Juan's limitation in understanding or expressing his ideas might be affecting his relationships in the classroom?

What strategies might we use to increase Juan's receptive and expressive language?

Examining the physical/social/emotional environment

How do you think the classroom structure and routine affected Juan's actions here?

What adaptations can we make to the physical space in order to accommodate children of diverse backgrounds?

What adaptations can we make in order to better serve children of linguistically diverse backgrounds?

What strategies can we employ to develop positive relationships with all children in general and with diverse children in particular?

Considering multiple perspectives

What questions might we ask to understand the perspective of Juan's family?

What resources might you use in order to better communicate with Juan's family?

What strategies can we use in order to develop a positive relationship with Juan's family?

What child development or early learning theories should we consider in this experience?

Considering opportunities and possibilities for next steps

How might the NLF team work together to support Juan?

Besides language development strategies, what other strategies might be needed in order to support Juan?

What curriculum planning strategies might be helpful in supporting Juan in learning English and Japanese *and* maintaining and developing his Spanish?

Strategies for Enhancing Language Use at Nihonmachi Little Friends

Group One Ideas
1. Use visual expressions, pictures of feelings and emotions
2. Communicate with families *together* (particularly in the case of Juan), and also include the grandmother
3. Post and use the visual schedule for the day
4. Be aware of small things and details
5. Use physical gestures to communicate
6. Make and use flashcards with pictures and *both* languages illustrating common items such as jacket, bathroom, and so on)

Group Two Ideas
1. Learn a few words in the children's home languages and, in Juan's case learn more about his specific interests (ex: DINOSAURS) and use these words in his language
2. Have a photo checklist, especially during transitions
3. Change the environment to adapt to the children's physical needs
4. Pair children/create a partner system, where two children have to help each other with things like jackets.
5. Ask families to share more of their culture and expose the families' cultures through the environment

Group Three Ideas
1. Put ourselves into his (Juan's) shoes in terms of his cultural values (including food), language environment, unfamiliar environment
2. Ask his parents about their discipline style and what works at home, and use the same strategies at school
3. Repeat, rephrase what he said in sentences
4. Respect his autonomy and independence, but at the same time, teach natural consequences
5. Avoid any excessive emotional stress

Group Four Ideas
1. Use visuals
2. Home routine
3. Use Parallel and Self Talk
4. Have simple, short conversations
5. Use Positive Feedback, affirmations (Positive Descriptive Acknowledgements (PDAs))
6. Learn songs in the children's home languages

Group Five Ideas
1. Teachers should learn common phrases in the students' home languages to promote and encourage students to learn more descriptors (*I, a, the*) in English.
2. Include Juan's grandma in his assessments.
3. Ask the parents and grandma about common routines done within the household, and give suggestions as to what type of structures we have at school. Continuity is important.
4. Share positive things Juan has done at school with his family.
5. Ask Juan some questions. For example: "Who do you play with at home?"

These suggestions were made after we used the *peeling the onion* protocol to explore this question: How do we make Japanese more interesting to our school-age kids?

1. Clarify the vision for the school. Is it a dual language program or is it an enrichment program?
2. Use activities that stem from the children's interests (possible ones: make videos, interviews, games, manga, magazines, power point presentations on the children's interests and passions)
3. Bring in Japanese-speaking "cool people" and experts to be interviewed and to teach something to the children (for instance: flower arrangements, cooking, sports). Work with the

children in advance to give them vocabulary and to help them prepare themselves linguistically for the experience.

4. Elicit help from the children who are fluent.

5. Use media (movies, pop songs) to make Japanese the language of communication. (Some people were cautious about this idea due to the violent nature of some movies).

6. Support bilingual teachers so they *stay* in Japanese and incorporate gestures, visuals and body language and avoid code switching

7. Create times and routines where Japanese is the language of communication (Fridays—Japanese only)

8. Play games in Japanese, so the children who are not very fluent can learn some repetitive phrases and be part of the group even if they don't understand everything (Jorge had some examples).

9. Conduct "experiments" and projects in Japanese and do some of the "frontloading" of the vocabulary so children can participate in Japanese.

10. Stay consistent and persist on the message that Japanese is important!

11. Include as much of the community as possible.

12. Include the families in making language plans and goals with and for their children.

13. Have the families share their language goals with the children.

14. Be explicit about the benefits of bilingualism and share these benefits with the children.

15. Have explicit vocabulary goals for the week, and use this vocabulary consistently with the children.

16. Expose the children to lots of print in Japanese, and read to them in Japanese (include visuals, realia, and gestures, to make books come alive and increase understanding).

17. Sing lots of songs and include visuals and gestures.

18. Prepare engaging activities with the children.

19. Discuss this dilemma with the children and elicit their responses and suggestions.

20. Send home a simple survey to help families understand their own priorities for the after-school program.

21. A simple question could be:
Please rank your priorities for your child's experiences at NLF after-school program from 1 (most important) to 10 (least important) so that we can plan our time accordingly.

- Finish homework
- Play with friends
- Relax after school
- Learn Japanese
- Be creative and engage in the arts
- Participate in physical activities
- Be exposed to a homelike environment with lots of activities to choose from
- Have a safe place to be after school
- Explore his/her own interests after a long day at school
- Engage in projects with other children

APPENDIX C   Sample Planning Forms

Because of the requirement many programs have to submit or post curriculum planning forms in advance, Appendix C offers examples of forms that reflect an integrated approach to planning curriculum using the *Learning Together with Young Children* framework.

Planned Possibilities

BURLINGTON LITTLE SCHOOL PRESCHOOL CURRICULUM, BURLINGTON, WASHINGTON

Week of _____

Important Events—What is happening this week? (School events, family activities, parent nights)

Morning work tables—Self-directed, focused tasks to introduce children to new materials and concepts

Table 1	Table 2	Table 3

Process time activities—Teacher-led activities for coaching and teaching skills

Monday	Tuesday	Wednesday	Thursday	Friday

Focused interests and coexplorations: What observations do we have that show us the children's interests? What are the children excited about? What are we excited about?

Next step for focus: What next steps can we offer children to pursue their interests? What are the underlying values and lessons we would like the children to learn? What new materials, process time activities, or books and games for circle can we offer to extend their interests? What questions will guide our documentation?

Educational display: What documentation displays will help the children continue to investigate and pursue their interests?

Documentation display: What can we display to showcase our recent activities to families and visitors?

Materials needed: What do we need to gather and prepare for our focus of study? Who will do what?

Toddler Play School
Planned Possibilities

(from last week's notes)

Week of _____

Notes: What did we observe today? How does what we observed relate to the ongoing work of the children? What other meaning might we make of what we are seeing?

Sensory/Art	**Monday notes**
Dramatic Play	**Tuesday notes**
Construction/Problem Solving	**Wednesday notes**
Music/Movement	**Thursday notes**
Books/Rhymes	**Friday notes**
Relationships/Identity Development	**Continuing focus**—What next steps do we want to plan for individuals and the group based on this week's observations and notes?

Planning for Possibilities
Puget Sound ESD Head Start, Burien, Washington

Week of _____

Reflections/summary from last week:

Intent/hopes for children's learning this week:

Materials and environmental aspects to support children's learning (social-emotional, language/literacy, cognitive, physical, creative)

Planned activities to support children's learning

Monday	Tuesday	Wednesday	Thursday	Friday

Transition ideas/changes to routine or schedule to support children's learning:

Color code planned health and nutrition experiences. Indicate "Talking About Touching" and lesson number.

Note ILP goals using children's initials.

Planning for Possibilities
Puget Sound ESD Head Start, Burien, Washington

Week of _____

Reflections/summary from last week:

Where did children spend time? What were children interested in? What was the underlying meaning or developmental theme of the play? How can I learn more about the reason/needs behind the children's interest?

Intent/hopes for children's learning this week:

What is the group goal for the upcoming week? i.e., establishing routines, building community, working on cooperation, further explore or extend interest in _____.

Materials and environmental aspects to support children's learning (social-emotional, language/literacy, cognitive, physical, creative)

How can I set the stage for children? How can the environment support/promote each developmental area? How can the available materials and environment support/extend the reflections noted from last week?

How can the available materials and environment support the intent/hopes for this week? How can individual children's ILP goals be supported through available materials and the environment? (Indicate goals using children's initials.)

Planned activities to support children's learning

	Planned activities to support children's learning			
Monday	Tuesday	Wednesday	Thursday	Friday
ie: large group activities, small group activities, cook-ing projects, large motor, songs/stories, health activi-ties, nutrition activities, TAT lessons, etc…	How can the planned activities support/extend the reflections noted from last week? How can the planned activities support this week's intent/hopes? How can individual children's ILP goals be supported through planned activities (Note ILP goals using children's initials).			

Transition ideas/changes to routine or schedule to support children's learning:

Describe plans for transitions and changes to the routine or daily schedule.

How can the whole day, including transitions and routines, be utilized as learning opportunities? How can transitions, routines and the schedule support/extend reflections notes from last week? How can transitions, routines, and the schedule support this week's intent/hopes? How can individual children's ILP goals be supported through transitions, routines, and schedule? (Note ILP goals using children's initials).

Color code planned health and nutrition experiences. Indicate "Talking About Touching" and lesson number.

Planning for Future Possibilities
Puget Sound ESD Head Start, Burien, Washington

Children excited about/interested in:

New challenges to support:

Ideas from parents/families:

Ideas to revisit:

Ideas for parents/families:

Ideas for volunteers:

Each child is capable, intelligent, resourceful, experienced, and a learner.

Planning for Future Possibilities
Puget Sound ESD Head Start, Burien, Washington

Children excited about/interested in: Note what you observe children doing. It may be individuals, small groups of children, or the whole group. Consider what might be behind the interest.	**New challenges to support:** From your observations, note what children may need more practice with or need more opportunities to experience.
Ideas from parents/families: Note ideas you have gathered from families? Consent agenda & minutes. Opportunities to learn this include talking with family support staff, attending parent gatherings, listening for more clues in conversations with parents, and posing questions and providing input opportunities for parents.	**Ideas to revisit:** From your observations, note experiences, skills, or concepts it may be appropriate or interesting to revisit to reinforce, expand, or extend.
Ideas for parents/families: What are ways to involve families? How can connections/communication between home and the center be promoted? How can I acknowledge what parents are doing? How can I invite parents to be part of the plans?	**Ideas for volunteers:** How can I utilize volunteers? Are there specific times volunteers will be available? How can I help "unexpected" volunteers feel welcome and helpful? How can I help volunteers feel appreciated?

Each child is capable, intelligent, resourceful, experienced, and a learner.

Planning Form

Harvest Resources, Seattle, Washington

Observation summaries/Teacher reflections				
Brainstorm possibilities; then choose one or two to pursue	Ideas and hypotheses about children's perspectives to explore	Planned activities	Learning domains	Prep/materials needed
Individualized Plans				

Learning Together with Young Children
Reflecting, Planning, and Taking Action

As you develop plans for children's learning, reflect on one or more of the questions below.

- What details stand out that I can make visible for further consideration?

- What in my background and values is influencing my response to this situation and why?

- How might issues of culture, family background, or popular media be influencing this situation?

- Where do I see examples of children's strengths and competency?

- How do I understand the children's point of view in this situation?

- How are the environment and materials impacting what's unfolding and what changes could be made?

- How are teacher actions impacting this situation?

- What learning domains are being addressed here and what other domains could be addressed?

- What theoretical perspectives and child development principles could inform my understandings and actions?

- What values, philosophy, and goals do I want to influence my response?

Summary of curriculum goals from reflections on questions considered:

Drawing on the principles of the core practices in *Learning Together with Young Children*, explore the possibilities related to your curriculum goals and then choose one or two actions to focus your planning. As you take actions, return to observing and reflecting so your next steps will be relevant and take learning deeper.

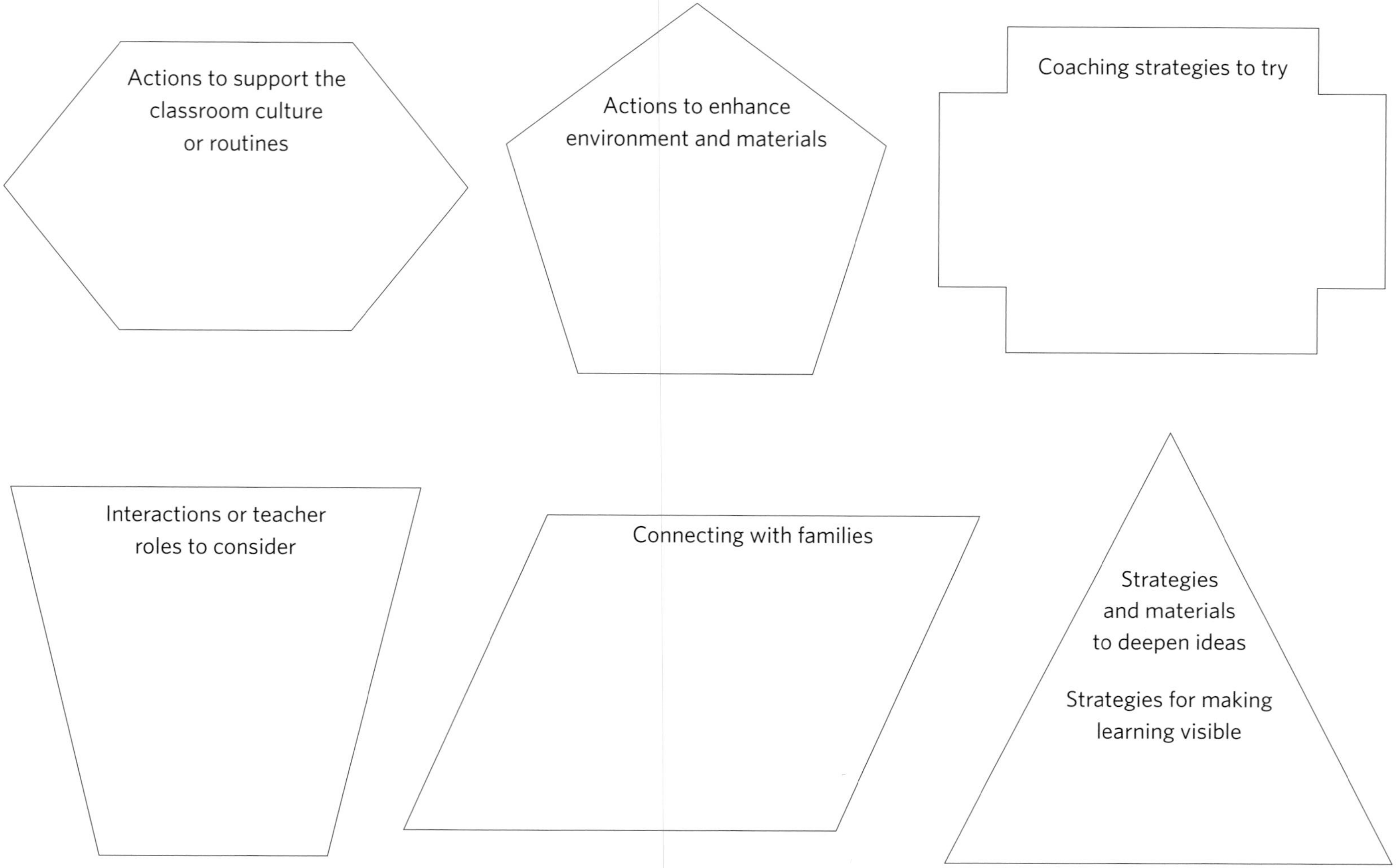

Actions to support the
classroom culture
or routines

Interactions or teacher
roles to consider

Actions to enhance
environment and materials

Connecting with families

Coaching strategies to try

Strategies
and materials
to deepen ideas

Strategies for making
learning visible

Experimental Curriculum Planning Form

New Hampshire Technical Institute Child and Family Development Center, Concord, New Hampshire

Zone (area of room) _____   Week of _____

	Monday	Tuesday	Wednesday	Thursday	Friday
Observation					
Teacher thinking					
Activity/ Scaffolding for tomorrow					

References

Ayres, A. Jean. 2005. *Sensory Integration and the Child: Understanding Hidden Sensory Challenges.* 25th anniversary Ed. Los Angeles: Western Psychological Services.

Berk, Laura, and Adam Winsler. 1995. *Scaffolding Children's Learning: Vygotsky and Early Education.* Washington, DC: National Association for the Education of Young Children (NAEYC).

Bodrova, Elena, and Deborah J. Leong. 2004. "Chopsticks and Counting Chips: Do Play and Foundational Skills Need to Compete for the Teacher's Attention in an Early Childhood Classroom?" *Young Children* 58 (3): 10–17.

Bredekamp, Sue, and Carol Copple, eds. 2009. *Developmentally Appropriate Practice in Early Childhood Programs Serving Children from Birth through Age 8.* 3rd ed. Washington, DC: NAEYC.

Bredekamp, Sue, and Teresa Rosegrant, eds. 1995. *Reaching Potentials through Transforming Curriculum, Assessment, and Teaching.* Vol. 2. Washington, DC: NAEYC.

Brofenbrenner, Urie. 2006. *The Ecology of Human Development: Experiments by Nature and Design.* Cambridge, MA: Harvard University Press.

Brookes, Mona. 1996. *Drawing with Children: A Creative Method for Adult Beginners, Too.* 10th anniversary ed. New York: Penguin Putnam.

Brosterman, Norman. 2014. *Inventing Kindergarten.* New York: Harry N. Abrams.

Carr, Margaret. 2001. *Assessment in Early Childhood Settings: Learning Stories.* Thousand Oaks, CA: Sage.

Carr, Margaret, and Wendy Lee. 2012. *Learning Stories: Constructing Learner Identities in Early Education.* London: Sage.

Carter, Margie, and Deb Curtis. 2009. *The Visionary Director: A Handbook for Dreaming, Organizing, and Improvising in Your Center.* 2nd ed. St. Paul, MN: Redleaf Press.

Clements, Douglas H., and Julie Sarama. 2005. "Math Play: How Young Children Approach Math." *Early Childhood Today* 19:50–57.

Cronin, Sharon, and Elizabeth Jones. 1999. "Play and Cultural Differences. Beginnings Workshop." *Child Care Information Exchange* 125 (Jan–Feb 1999): 45–60.

Cronin, Sharon, and Carmen Sosa Masso. 2003. *Soy Bilingue: Language, Culture, and Young Latino Children.* Seattle, WA: Center for Cultural and Linguistic Democracy.

Curtis, Deb, and Margie Carter. 2011. *Reflecting Children's Lives: A Handbook for Planning Your Child-Centered Curriculum.* 2nd ed. St. Paul, MN: Redleaf Press.

———. 2013. *The Art of Awareness: How Observation Can Transform Your Teaching.* 2nd ed. St. Paul, MN: Redleaf Press.

———. 2015. *Designs for Living and Learning: Transforming Early Childhood Environments.* 2nd ed. St. Paul, MN: Redleaf Press.

Curtis, Deb, Debbie Lebo, Wendy C.M. Cividanes, and Margie Carter. 2013. *Reflecting in Communities of Practice: A Workbook for Early Childhood Educators.* St. Paul, MN: Redleaf Press.

Dahlberg, Gunilla, and Peter Moss. 2005. *Ethics and Politics in Early Childhood Education.* London: Routledge.

Dahlberg, Gunilla, Peter Moss, and Alan Pence. 1999. *Beyond Quality in Early Childhood Education and Care: Postmodern Perspectives.* London: Routledge.

Day, Carol Brunson. 2006. Personal communication reflecting on "Reconsidering Early Childhood

Education in the United States: Reflections from Our Encounters with Reggio Emilia" by Carol Brunson Phillips and Sue Bredekamp. In *The Hundred Languages of Children*, 2nd ed. 1998, 439–56. Edited by Carolyn Edwards, Lella Gandini, and George Forman. Greenwich, CT: Ablex Publishing.

Delpit, Lisa. 2006. *Other People's Children: Cultural Conflict in the Classroom.* New York: The New Press.

Derman-Sparks, Louise, and Julie Olsen Edwards. 2010. *Anti-Bias Education for Young Children and Ourselves.* Washington, DC: NAEYC.

Dillard, Annie. 2013. *An American Childhood.* New York: Harper Perennial.

Dodge, Diane Trister, Laura J. Colker, and Cate Heroman. 2002. *The Creative Curriculum.* 4th ed. Washington, DC: Teaching Strategies.

Duckworth, Eleanor. 2006. *The Having of Wonderful Ideas and Other Essays on Teaching and Learning.* 3rd ed. New York: Teachers College Press.

Edwards, Betty. 2012. *Drawing on the Right Side of the Brain.* 4th edition. New York: Jeremy P Tarcher/Penguin.

Edwards, Carolyn, Lella Gandini, and George Forman, eds. 2012. *The Hundred Languages of Children: The Reggio Emilia Experience in Transformation.* 3rd ed. Santa Barbara, CA: Praeger.

Elkonin, D. [1971] 1977. "Toward the Problem of Stages in the Mental Development of the Child." Translated by Nikolai Veresov. *Soviet Developmental Psychology,* No. 4, 6–20.

Epstein, Ann S., and Mary Hohmann. 2012. *The High-Scope Preschool Curriculum Manual.* Ypsilanti, MI: HighScope Press.

Forman, George. 1996. "Negotiating with Art Media to Deepen Learning. Beginnings Workshop." *Child Care Information Exchange,* 108 (March 1996): 56–58.

Fraser, Susan, and Carol Gestwicki. 2002. *Authentic Childhood: Experiencing Reggio Emilia in the Classroom.* Albany, NY: Delmar.

Freire, Paulo. 1970. *Pedagogy of the Oppressed.* New York: Herder and Herder.

Gallas, Karen. 1994. *The Languages of Learning: How Children Talk, Write, Dance, Draw and Sing Their Understanding of the World.* New York: Teachers College Press.

Gandini, Lella, and Carolyn Edwards. 2001. *Bambini: The Italian Approach to Infant/Toddler Care.* New York: Teachers College Press.

Gardner, Howard. 1999. *Intelligences Reframed: Multiple Intelligences for the 21st Century.* New York: Basic Books.

———. 2011. *Frames of Mind: The Theory of Multiple Intelligence.* New York: Basic Books.

Gatto, John. 2002. *Dumbing Us Down: The Hidden Curriculum of Compulsory Schooling.* Gabriola Island, BC, Canada: New Society Publishers.

Gibbs, Jeanne. 2000. *Tribes: A New Way of Learning and Being Together.* Windsor, CA: CenterSource Systems.

Goleman, Daniel. 1995. *Emotional Intelligence: Why It Can Matter More Than IQ.* New York: Bantam.

———. 2006. *Social Intelligence: The New Science of Human Relationships.* New York: Bantam.

González, Norma, Luis C. Moll, and Cathy Amanti, eds. 2005. *Funds of Knowledge: Theorizing Practices in Households, Communities, and Classrooms.* New York: Routledge.

Gopnik, Alison. 2009. *The Philosophical Baby: What Children's Minds Tell Us about Truth, Love, and the Meaning of Life.* New York: Farrar, Straus, and Giroux.

Gramling, Michael. 2015. *The Great Disconnect in Early Childhood Education: What We Know vs. What We Do.* St. Paul, MN: Redleaf Press.

Greenman, Jim. 2006. *Caring Spaces, Learning Places: Children's Environments that Work.* Redmond, WA: Exchange Press.

Gronlund, Gaye. 2003. *Focused Early Learning: A Planning Framework for Teaching Young Children.* St. Paul, MN: Redleaf Press.

———. 2014. *Make Early Learning Standards Come Alive: Connecting Your Practice and Curriculum to State Guidelines.* 2nd ed. St. Paul, MN: Redleaf Press.

Gullo, Dominic. 2004. *Understanding Assessment and Evaluation in Early Childhood Education.* New York: Teachers College Press.

Hammond, Zaretta. 2015. *Culturally Responsive Teaching and the Brain: Promoting Authentic Engagement and Rigor Among Culturally and Linguistically Diverse Students.* Thousand Oaks, CA: Corwin.

Hanscom, Angela J. 2016. *Balanced and Barefoot: How Unrestricted Outdoor Play Makes for Strong, Confident, and Capable Children.* Oakland, CA: New Harbinger.

———. 2015. "The Decline of Play in Preschoolers—and the Rise in Sensory Issues." *Washington Post*, edited by Valerie Strauss, September 1. https://www.washingtonpost.com/news/answer-sheet/wp/2015/09/01/the-decline-of-play-in-preschoolers-and-the-rise-in-sensory-issues.

Head Start Body Start: National Center for Physical Development and Outdoor Play, and Jeffrey Trawick-Smith. 2010. *From Playpen to Playground—The Importance of Physical Play for the Motor Development of Young Children.* Willimantic, CT: Center for Early Childhood Education at Eastern Connecticut State University.

Hoffman, Eric. 2004. *Magic Capes, Amazing Powers: Transforming Super Hero Play in the Classroom.* St. Paul, MN: Redleaf Press.

Hohmann, Mary, Bernard Banet, and David Weikart. 1979. *Young Children in Action.* Ypsilanti, MI: High-Scope Press.

Horm-Wingerd, Diane. 2002. "The Reggio Emilia Approach and Accountability Assessment in the United States." In *Teaching and Learning: Collaborative Exploration of the Reggio Emilia Approach*, edited by Victoria Fu, Andrew Stremmel, and Lynn Hill, 51–65. Upper Saddle River, NJ: Pearson.

Hunter, Tom. 2004. *Still Growing.* Bellingham, WA: Song Growing Company (compact disc). www.tomhunter.com.

Intrator, Sam, and Megan Scribner. 2003. *Teaching with Fire: Poetry that Sustains the Courage to Teach.* San Francisco, CA: Jossey Bass.

Johnson, James E., James F. Christie, and Thomas D. Yawkey. 1999. *Play and Early Childhood Development.* 2nd ed. Columbus, OH: Allyn & Bacon.

Johnston, James Scott. 2006. *Inquiry and Education: John Dewey and the Quest for Democracy.* Albany, NY: SUNY Press.

Jones, Elizabeth. 2004. "Playing to Get Smart." In *Spotlight on Young Children and Play,* edited by Derry Koralek, 24–27. Washington, DC: NAEYC.

Jones, Elizabeth, and Gretchen Reynolds. 2011. *The Play's the Thing: Teacher's Role in Children's Play.* 2nd ed. New York: Teachers College Press.

Jordan, Ijumaa. 2016. "Ijumaa, Why Is Play an Equity Issue?" Diversity & Equity Education for Adults: NAEYC Interest Forum. https://earlychildhoodequity.wordpress.com/2016/02/10/ijumaa-why-is-play-an-equity-issue.

Juster, Norton. 1988. *The Phantom Tollbooth.* Illustrated by Jules Feiffer. New York: Random House Children's Books.

Katz, Lilian. 1993. *Dispositions: Definitions and Implications for Early Childhood Practices.* Urbana, IL: ERIC Clearinghouse on Elementary and Early Childhood Education.

———. 1998. "What Can We Learn from Reggio Emilia." In *The Hundred Languages of Children: The Reggio Emilia Approach,* 2nd ed., edited by Carolyn. Edwards, Lella. Gandini, and George Forman, 27–48. Greenwich, CT: Ablex Publishing.

———. 2015. *Lively Minds: Distinctions between Academic versus Intellectual Goals for Young Children.* Jamaica Plain, MA: Defending the Early Years.

Kolbe, Ursula. 2005. *It's Not a Bird Yet: The Drama of Drawing.* Byron Bay, NSW, Australia: Peppinot Press.

Kozol, Jonathan. 2012. *Ordinary Resurrections: Children in the Years of Hope.* New York: Crown.

Lee, Wendy, Margaret Carr, Brenda Soutar, and Linda Mitchell. 2013. *Understanding the Te Whāriki Approach: Early Years Education in Practice.* London: David Fulton Publishers.

Louv, Richard. 2005. *Last Child in the Woods: Saving Our Children from Nature Deficit Disorder.* Chapel Hill, NC: Algonquin Books.

MacNaughton, Glenda, and Gillian Williams. 2009. *Techniques for Teaching Young Children: Choices for Theory and Practice.* 3rd ed. Melbourne, Victoria, Australia: Pearson Australia Group.

Malaguzzi, Loris. 1998. "History, Ideas, and Basic Philosophy: An Interview with Lella Gandini." In *The Hundred Languages of Children: The Reggio Emilia Approach,* 2nd ed, edited by Carolyn Edwards, Lella Gandini, and George Forman, 49–98. Greenwich, CT: Ablex Publishing.

Malaguzzi, Loris, ed. 1996. *The Hundred Languages of Children: Narrative of the Possible.* Reggio Emilia, Italy: Reggio Children.

McGhee, Paul. 2003. *Understanding and Promoting the Development of Children's Humor: A Guide for Parents and Teachers.* Dubuque, IA: Kendall/Hunt Publishers.

Meier, Daniel, and Barbara Henderson. 2007. *Learning from Young Children in the Classroom: The Art and Science of Teacher Research.* New York: Teachers College Press.

Meisels, Samuel J., Judy R. Jablon, Dorothea B. Marsden, Margo L. Dichtelmiller, and Aviva B. Dorfman. 1994. *The Work Sampling System.* Ann Arbor, MI: Rebus.

Menzel, Peter, and Faith D'Aluisio. 2007. *Hungry Planet: What the World Eats.* Napa, CA: Material World Books.

Meriwether, Linda. 1997. "Math at the Snack Table." *Young Children* 52 (5): 69–73.

Momaday, N. Scott. February 7, 2007. Weekday radio broadcast. Seattle, WA: KUOW, National Public Radio.

Mooney, Carol Garhart. 2013. *Theories of Childhood: An Introduction to Dewey, Montessori, Erikson, Piaget, and Vygotsky.* 2nd ed. St. Paul, MN: Redleaf Press.

NAEYC. 2007. Beyond the Journal: *Voices of Practitioners.* www.naeyc.org/publications/vop.

Neugebauer, Bonnie, ed. 1999. "Play and Culture: Beginnings Workshop." *Child Care Information Exchange,* 127 (1).

New, Rebecca. 1997. "Next Steps in Teaching 'the Reggio Way:' Advocating for a New Image of Children." In *First Steps toward Teaching the Reggio Way,* edited by Joanne Hendrick, 224–233. Upper Saddle River, NJ: Merrill/Prentice Hall.

Paley, Vivian Gussin. 1990. *The Boy Who Would Be a Helicopter: The Uses of Storytelling in the Classroom.* Cambridge, MA: Harvard University Press.

Palmer, Parker J. 2007. *The Courage to Teach: Exploring the Inner Landscape of a Teacher's Life.* 10th anniversary ed. San Francisco, CA: Jossey-Bass.

Patterson, Catherine, Alma Fleet, and Janice Duffie. 1995. *Learning from Stories: Early Childhood Professional Experiences.* Sydney, NSW, Australia: Institute of Early Childhood, Macquarie University.

Pelo, Ann. 2017. *The Language of Art: Inquiry-Based Studio Practices in Early Childhood Settings.* 2nd ed. St. Paul, MN: Redleaf Press.

———, ed. 2008. *Rethinking Early Childhood Education.* Milwaukee, WI: Rethinking Schools Publications.

Phillips, Carol Brunson, and Sue Bredekamp. 1998. "Reconsidering Early Childhood Education in the United States: Reflections from Our Encounters with Reggio Emilia." In *The Hundred Languages of Children,* edited by Carolyn Edwards, Lella Gandini, and George Forman, 439–456. Greenwich, CT: Ablex Publishing.

Piaget, Jean. 2001. *Language and Thought of the Child.* New York: Routledge Classics.

Piaget, Jean, and Bärbel Inhelder. (1969) 2000. *The Psychology of the Child.* New York: Basic Books.

Project Zero and Reggio Children. 2001. *Making Learning Visible: Children as Individual and Group Learners.* Reggio Emilia, Italy: Reggio Children.

Rinaldi, Carlina. 1998. "Projected Curriculum Constructed through Documentation—*Progettazione*: An Interview with Lella Gandini." In *The Hundred Languages of Children,* edited by Carolyn Edwards, Lella Gandini, and George Forman, 113–26. Greenwich, CT: Ablex Publishing.

———. 2001. "Reggio Emilia: The Image of the Child and the Child's Environment as a Fundamental Priciple." In *Bambini: The Italian Approach to Infant/Toddler Care,* edited by Lella Gandini and Carolyn Edwards, 49–54. New York: Teachers College Press.

Rogoff, Barbara. 2003. *The Cultural Nature of Human Development.* New York: Oxford University Press.

Ruef, Kerry. 2005. *The Private Eye: Looking and Thinking by Analogy.* Lyle, WA: The Private Eye Project.

Schore, Allan N. 2000. "Attachment and the Regulation of the Right Brain." *Attachment and Human Development* 2 (1):23–47.

Seager, Walter and Kurtis Toppert. 2013. *Promoting Grit, Tenacity, and Perseverance: Critical Factors for Success in the 21st Century.* Washington, DC: US Department of Education.

Seefeldt, Carol. 2005. *How to Work with Standards in the Early Childhood Classroom.* New York: Teachers College Press.

Senge, Peter. 2000. *Schools That Learn: A Fifth Discipline Book for Educators, Parents, and Everyone Who Cares about Education.* New York: Doubleday.

Shonkoff, Jack P., Deborah A. Phillips, and the Committee on Integrating the Science of Early Childhood Development. 2000. *From Neurons to Neighborhoods: The Science of Early Childhood Development.* Washington, DC: National Research Council, Academy of Science.

Shore, Rima. 1997. *Rethinking the Brain: New Insights into Early Development.* New York: Families and Work Institute.

Skinner, B.F. 1965. *Science and Human Behavior.* New York: Free Press.

Small, Meredith F. 1999. *Our Babies, Ourselves: How Biology and Culture Shape the Way We Parent.* New York: Anchor Books.

Van Wijk, Nikolien. 2008. *Getting Started with Schemas, Revealing the Wonderful World of Children's Play.* New Lynn, Witakere, Aukland: The New Zealand Playcentre Federation.

Vygotsky, Lev S. 1978. *Mind in Society: The Development of Higher Psychological Processes.* Cambridge, MA: Harvard University.

Wagner, Tony. 2002. *Making the Grade: Reinventing America's Schools.* New York: Routledge Falmer.

Wheatley, Margaret J. 2007. *Finding Our Way: Leadership for an Uncertain Time.* San Francisco: Berrett-Koehler.

Whitney, Trisha. 1999. *Kids Like Us: Using Persona Dolls in the Classroom.* St. Paul, MN: Redleaf Press.

Wien, Carol Anne. 1995. *Developmentally Appropriate Practice in "Real Life:" Stories of Teacher Practical Knowledge.* New York: Teachers College Press.

———. 2004. *Negotiating Standards in the Primary Classroom: The Teacher's Dilemma.* New York: Teachers College Press.

———. 2014. *The Power of Emergent Curriculum: Stories from Early Childhood Settings.* Washington, DC: NAEYC.

Wien, Carol Anne, and B. L. Keating. *The Sculpture Project.* (unpublished manuscript).

Williams, Leslie, and Yvonne De Gaetano. 1985. *Alerta: A Multicultural, Bilingual Approach to Teaching Young Children.* New York: Addison-Wesley.

Wood, Chip. 1999. *Time to Teach, Time to Learn: Changing the Pace of School.* Turner Falls, MA: Northeast Foundation for Children.

Index

academic goals versus intellectual goals, 194

accomplishments, celebrating real, 62–65

accountability systems
effect of, 1
outcomes and, 12

achievement gap, children of color and income, 11

active play
children as sensory/motor beings and, 19–20
choosing materials, 69–70, 73, 74–75, 76–78
offering complexity by layering materials, 90–92
effects on focus and concentration, 108
factors reducing opportunities for, 103
importance of, 103
principles for
continually seeking of proprioceptive and vestibular input, 106–108
creating guidelines to help children take on challenges, 118–122
observing children during, for better understanding and support, 108–111
observing children negotiating during, 126–128
observing children's competence in physical challenges, 116–118
providing indoor space for spreading out and movement, 103, 104, 112–115
providing open-ended equipment, 128–131

advocacy groups, 286

aesthetic sense, cultivating, 73–75

Alerta curriculum, 10

Amanti, Cathy, 37

animals, in learning environment, 42–43

anti-bias education
incorporating into classroom culture, 55–60
self-study guide for reflecting on, 295
using lens of, 275–277

apologies, 261–262

art, children's relationship with, 220

assessment approaches, 16–17
families' ability to understand documentation, 252–254
helping children assess own learning, 164–166
learning stories as, 251–258
narrative, 287–288
relevant and meaningful, 248–258
tool for self, 291–292
transcending scores, 270

attachment theory, 38, 39–40

Ayers, Bill, 1, 273

babies with babies play, 87, 152–154

balancing balls, 116

Bayes, Chris, 219

belief system, teachers need for, 5

Berger, Iris, 154

Bergman, Ingmar, 73

beyond paper and sounds project, 217–219

binkie love, 155

bird-watching park project, 201–202

blocks and bridges coaching lesson, 170–171

Bodrova, Elena, 6

books
displaying visual representations alongside actual materials, 99
making

to celebrate real accomplishments, 62–65
reference, 249
of silly songs, 199–200
to welcome new children and families, 21
using reference, 173–176

boss of the paints coaching lesson, 171–172

bracelet collections, 144–145

brain development
active play and, 103
during early childhood years, 143
impact of learning environment on, 29
in-depth study and, 194
open-ended materials and, 70
school readiness taking precedence over, 8

Bredekamp, Sue, 7

Broader Bolder Approach (BBA), 286

Brookes, Mona, 178

bubble experts, 151–152

Burlington Little School, 308–309

cameras, using, 176–177

Carr, Margaret, 251, 293

Carter, Margie, 275

Center for the Study of Child Care Employment, 287, 288

checklists, 248, 252–254

child-initiated play, value of, 159

children
absence of racial bias, 56
conflicts between, 261–262
as doers and not reflective thinkers, 148–150
giving ownership to, for routines and schedules, 46–48
learning and
coaching, to use tools and strategies, 166–169